Y0-IWC-180

Romancing the Grail

ALSO BY ARTHUR GROOS

Giacomo Puccini: "La bohème" (with Roger Parker)

Magister Regis: Studies in Honor of Robert Earl Kaske (editor)

Medieval Christian Literary Imagery: A Guide to Interpretation (with R. E. Kaske and Michael Twomey)

Reading Opera (co-editor with Roger Parker)

Romancing the Grail

Genre, Science, and Quest in Wolfram's *Parzival*

ARTHUR GROOS

Cornell University Press

ITHACA AND LONDON

THIS BOOK HAS BEEN PUBLISHED WITH THE AID OF A GRANT FROM THE HULL MEMORIAL PUBLICATION FUND OF CORNELL UNIVERSITY.

Copyright © 1995 by Cornell University

All rights reserved. Except for brief quotations in a review, this book, or parts thereof, must not be reproduced in any form without permission in writing from the publisher. For information, address Cornell University Press, Sage House, 512 East State Street, Ithaca, New York 14850.

First published 1995 by Cornell University Press.

Printed in the United States of America

♾ The paper in this book meets the minimum requirements of the American National Standard for Information Sciences—Permanence of Paper for Printed Library Materials ANSI Z39.48–1984.

Library of Congress Cataloging-in-Publication Data

Groos, Arthur.
Romancing the grail: genre, science, and quest in Wolfram's Parzival /Arthur Groos.
p. cm.
Includes bibliographical references and index.
ISBN 0-8014-3068-2 (alk. paper)
1. Wolfram, von Eschenbach, 12th cent. Parzival. 2. Grail—Romances—History and criticism. 3. Perceval (Legendary character)—Romances—History and criticism. 4. Arthurian romances—History and criticism. I. Title.
PT1688.G75 1995
831'.21—dc20

94-39908

For Bonnie Buettner

Contents

Preface

Years ago, when I was incautious enough to announce that a book on Wolfram von Eschenbach was "in progress," I had no idea that its gestation—or the memories of my readers—would be so elephantine. In retrospect, the length of the enterprise stems only partly from the fact that *Parzival*, as the major representation of the Grail myth and the central text in the Middle High German canon, has a complexity unsurpassed in medieval literature and a correspondingly unmanageable, still expanding body of scholarship. More than anything else, I was lured in unexpected directions by changing interests and radical shifts in literary theory. Individual sections may reveal the archaeology of those changes and shifts; the book as a whole is predicated on their diversity.

Originally conceived as a study of the liturgical and astronomical background of *Parzival*, the research soon expanded to include science in general and the attempts to heal the Fisher King in particular. At the same time, involvement with narratological issues led me to broaden the conceptual framework to include author/narrator roles, the interplay of genre expectations, intertextuality, and transgression. Not surprisingly, the problems arising from such a variety eventually begged for resolution on a more theoretical level. As the extent of Wolfram's scientific and medical knowledge became clearer, I found it increasingly difficult to consider these additions part of a "translation" in even the loosest terms. And although Wolfram's treatment of Chrétien de Troyes's *Li Contes del Graal* suggested that differences in social status (clerical versus knightly) and culture (French versus German) were fundamental to the process, the multiplicity of discourses involved had little in common with the New Critical ideal of a unified authorial style.

One possible way of dealing with these problems emerged from conversations with Caryl Emerson on the writings of the Russian theorist Mikhail Bakhtin. In particular, Bakhtin's emphasis on the heteroglot potential of prenovelistic discourse provided a model for dealing with a narrative that seemed less a translation than a transposition and less a self-contained authorial text than a plurality of discourses in dialogue with each other and other narratives. As it turned out, several concepts that Bakhtin developed—not always consistently—over a lifetime of writing on the novel seemed particularly relevant to my concerns. Admittedly, these concepts needed to be read with a corrective lens, since some of the data was outdated and some of the theory dubious. Nonetheless, Bakhtinian theory was heuristically invaluable in reformulating my problems with *Parzival,* and I hope that my discussion will help in turn to clarify Bakhtin's comments on medieval romance.

The book opens with two chapters on the nature and extent of novelistic discourse in *Parzival.* The Introduction begins with a reading of the prologue and epilogue, suggesting how Wolfram equips his narrative with defamiliarizing tactics that range from decentering authority to pluralizing sources, ultimately engaging in a dialogue with the concept of genre itself. It ends with a discussion of the Bakhtinian concepts most conducive to dealing with such a narrative. Chapter 1 posits three criteria for measuring the tendency of *Parzival* in general toward novelistic discourse: the polyglossia of foreign languages and oral-versus-written language registers; the genre pluralism reflected in apparently contradictory statements about winning the Grail (which allude to romance, saint's life, and family chronicle); and the authorial and narratorial roles inscribed in the text.

Chapters 2 to 4 follow the initial stages of Parzival's quest from his discovery of knighthood to his first chivalric adventure, examining basic issues in the representation of aristocratic culture: socialization versus innate predisposition, constructions of King Arthur's court, the entrance into knighthood, and the winning of a wife and a kingdom. Although the foolish hero's acculturation is inherently carnivalistic, a comparison of the Old French and Middle High German texts reveals that Wolfram either subverts or pluralizes Chrétien's representation of this process. The discussion of the Belrepaire episode in Chapter 4 suggests how Wolfram even increases heteroglossia vis-à-vis Chrétien by coordinating references to time and space, narrative strands, and intertextuality to form a dialogic narrative approaching true novelistic discourse.

The second half of the book turns from the Arthurian world to the Grail world and to the different but equally pluralizing variety of discourses, scientific as well as religious, that make that world so resistant to analysis. Chapter 5 begins with the Grail and the elusive redeeming question; it then suggests the unique narrative position of Munsalvaesche by contextualizing Parzival's first visit in a contemporary astronomical and liturgical background for the years 1203–1208. Chapter 6 opens with an examination of Trevrizent's warning history of Anfortas's suffering, comments on the Grail society's attempts to heal his wound, and then proceeds to an interpretation of the entire process and the role of medicine in complicating the narrative's general dialectic between saint's life and romance. In Chapter 7 an analysis of Cundrie's announcement of Parzival's redemption begins with its astronomical content and implications for the hero's world-dominion; it then turns to the setting at Pentecost and connections with twelfth-century debates on imperial power and cultural renovation. Chapter 8 returns to the Grail castle, where a new medical crisis reaches its peak as Parzival arrives to ask a redeeming question that is situated in an elusive gap between competing genre expectations. The final chapter deals with the reunion of Parzival and the hermit Trevrizent and the latter's notorious "Retraction." Rather than resolve the contradictions of the retraction, the discussion posits Trevrizent as a fallible narrator in a decentered narrative universe, who exemplifies the inscrutability of divine providence as well as the unfinalizability of the narrative itself.

❦

A number of colleagues now or formerly at Cornell have been helpful in advising me on the seemingly endless variety of problems that arose in the process of writing this book: Caryl Emerson on M. M. Bakhtin and Russian theory, Danuta Shanzer on medieval Latin and paleography, Robert E. Kaske on exegesis, Carol Kaske on astrology, Alice Colby-Hall on Old French, Winthrop Wetherbee on Neoplatonism, Paul Hyams on history, James John on manuscript libraries, David Powers on Arabic, Thomas D. Hill on Old English analogues, and Bonnie Buettner on Wolfram in general and Gawanology in particular.

Colleagues at other universities have generously offered hospitality, issued invitations to try out drafts of chapters, and provided helpful information and criticism in discussions. They include Ingrid Kasten, Volker Mertens, and Ursula Hennig in Berlin; Peter Kern, Trude Ehlert, Christoph Cormeau, and Gerhard Meissburger in Bonn; Alfred Karnein, Ernst Metzner, Gerd Wolfgang Weber, and Helmut Brackert in Frankfurt; Hartmut and Wiebke Freytag, Jan-Dirk Müller, and Heimo Reinitzer in Hamburg; Silvia Ranawake, Adrian Stevens, Roy Wisbey, Marianne Wynn, and Timothy McFarland in London; Klaus Speckenbach, Klaus Grubmüller, Friedrich Ohly, and Ruth Schmidt-Wiegand in Münster; Hans-Hugo Steinhoff, Hartmut Steinecke, and Ulrich Profitlich in Paderborn; Eckehard Simon at Harvard, Michael Curschmann at Princeton, Ingeborg Glier at Yale, Hubert Heinen at the University of Texas, Mary

Wack, Theodore Andersson, and George Brown at Stanford, and Stephen Jaeger during his Bryn Mawr incarnation. I have also benefited from conversations with Joachim Bumke, Eberhard Nellmann, Walter Haug, Edith Wenzel and Horst Wenzel, L. P. Johnson, Dennis Green, Carl Lofmark, Sidney Johnson, Bill Leckie, Theodore Andersson, James Marchand, James Schultz, Susan Crane, and Marsh Leicester.

Historians of science and medicine have also been generous with their advice: Charles Burnett, William Crossgrove, Bernhard D. Haage, Paul Kunitzsch, John Riddle, Mary Wack, Melitta Weiss-Amer, and especially Gundolf Keil and the staff at the Institut für Geschichte der Medizin in Würzburg. Writing and researching the sections on science and medicine have also been greatly facilitated by the staffs at the Herzog August Bibliothek, the Preussische Staatsbibliothek, the Wellcome Institute and the British Library, the National Library of Medicine, and by the Reference, Interlibrary Loan, and Rare Book and History of Science departments at Cornell's Olin Library.

Many of the friends mentioned have commented on portions of the book, either as lectures or written chapters, invariably to the benefit of the final version (so that I am tempted to say that any remaining errors are entirely theirs). Four colleagues slogged through the entire manuscript: Sidney Johnson and Andrew Galloway as volunteers, Adrian Stevens and Michael Curschmann as readers for Cornell University Press. Their corrections and advice have been very helpful. Final thanks go to Emily Cooney Redinbo, who helped prepare the bibliography, and Jane Dieckmann, who prepared the index.

Portions of this book were written with the assistance of generous support from the John Simon Guggenheim Foundation and a Fulbright Commission Senior Research Fellowship in 1979–80, a short-term Deutscher Akademischer Austauschdienst Research Fellowship in 1984, and a much-appreciated administrative leave from Cornell University in 1989–90.

Chapters 2 to 9 contain previously published material reprinted here with permission. Chapter 2 is a revision of "Perceval and Parzival Discover Knighthood," reprinted by permission of the publisher from *Magister Regis: Studies in Honor of Robert Earl Kaske*, ed. Arthur Groos (New York: Fordham University Press, 1986), copyright 1986 by Fordham University Press, 117–37. Part of Chapter 3 is an abridged version of "Parzival's *swertleite*," *Germanic Review* 50 (1975), 245–59. Chapter 4 is a shortened version of "Dialogic Transformations: The Grail Hero Wins a Wife," *Chrétien de Troyes and the German Middle Ages*, ed. Roy Wisbey and Martin Jones (Cambridge and London: D. S. Brewer and the Institute of Germanic Studies, 1993), 257–76. Part of Chapter 5 is a revision of "Time Reference and the Liturgical Calendar in Wolfram's *Parzival*," *Deutsche Viertel-*

jahrsschrift 49 (1975), 43–65. Chapter 6 appears as "Treating the Fisher-King (Wolfram's *Parzival*, Book IX)," in *German Narrative Literature in the Twelfth and Thirteenth Centuries: Studies Presented to Roy Wisbey on His Sixty-fifth Birthday*, ed. Volker Honemann, Martin Jones, Adrian Stevens, David Wells (Tübingen: Max Niemeyer, 1994), 275–304. Chapter 7 is a slightly shortened version of "Cundrie's Announcement (*Parzival* 782)," *Beiträge zur Geschichte der deutschen Sprache und Literatur* 113 (1991), 384–414. Part of Chapter 8 appeared in more extensive form as "Astronomy and Medicine in Book XVI of Wolfram's *Parzival*," in *Sudhoffs Archiv für Geschichte der Medizin und der Naturwissenschaften* 76 (1992), 74–86. Reprinted by permission of Franz Steiner Verlag Wiesbaden, Stuttgart, Germany. Part of Chapter 9 is a revised and abridged version of "Trevrizent's Retraction: Interpolation or Narrative Strategy?" *Deutsche Vierteljahrsschrift* 55 (1981), 44–63.

Quotations from Wolfram are taken from *Wolfram von Eschenbach*, ed. Karl Lachmann, 6th rev. ed. Eduard Hartl (1926: rpt. Berlin, 1965); those from Chrétien are from *Christian von Troyes sämtliche erhaltene Werke*, ed. Wendelin Förster and Alfons Hilka, 5 vols. (Halle, 1884–1932). Unless otherwise indicated, all translations are my own. Those wishing to read Wolfram in English can choose between the translations of A. T. Hatto or Helen M. Mustard and Charles E. Passage.

ARTHUR GROOS

Ithaca, New York

Abbreviations

ABäG	*Amsterdamer Beiträge zur älteren Germanistik*
AHDLMA	*Archives d'histoire doctrinale et littéraire du Moyen Age*
AKG	*Archiv für Kulturgeschichte*
ATB	Altdeutsche Textbibliothek
Bartsch/Marti	*Wolframs "Parzival" und "Titurel,"* ed. Karl Bartsch. 4th ed., rev. Marta Marti
BLVS	Bibliothek des Literarischen Vereins in Stuttgart
Bumke, *Forschung*	Joachim Bumke. *Die Wolfram von Eschenbach Forschung seit 1945: Bericht und Bibliographie*
Bumke, *Wolfram*	Joachim Bumke. *Wolfram von Eschenbach.* 6th ed.
CC:CM	Corpus christianorum: Continuatio medievalis
CCSL	Corpus christianorum: Series latina
CSEL	Corpus scriptorum ecclesiasticorum latinorum
DTM	Deutsche Texte des Mittelalters
DVJS	*Deutsche Vierteljahrsschrift für Literaturwissenschaft und Geistesgeschichte*
EG	*Etudes Germaniques*
FMS	*Frühmittelalterliche Studien*
GAG	Göppinger Arbeiten zur Germanistik
GLL	*German Life and Letters*
GQ	*German Quarterly*
GR	*Germanic Review*
GRM	*Germanisch-romanische Monatsschrift*
JEGP	*Journal of English and Germanic Philology*
Martin	Ernst Martin. *Wolframs von Eschenbach "Parzival" und "Titurel" II: Kommentar*
MGH	Monumenta Germaniae Historica
MGH:AA	Monumenta Germaniae Historica: Auctores antiquissimi
MGH:SS	Monumenta Germaniae Historica: Scriptores

MH	*Medievalia et Humanistica*
MLN	*Modern Language Notes*
MLR	*Modern Language Review*
MMS	Münstersche Mittelalter-Schriften
MP	*Modern Philology*
MTU	Münchener Texte und Untersuchungen zur deutschen Literatur des Mittelalters
NF	Neue Folge
Pauly-Wissowa	August Friedrich von Pauly and Georg Wissowa. *Paulys Realencyclopädie der classischen Altertumswissenschaft*
PBB	*Beiträge zur Geschichte der deutschen Sprache und Literatur*
PL	*Patrologia Latina*
PMLA	*Publications of the Modern Language Association*
PSQ	Philologische Studien und Quellen
QF	Quellen und Forschungen zur Sprach- und Kulturgeschichte der germanischen Völker
RPh	*Romance Philology*
RR	*Romanic Review*
SM	Sammlung Metzler
Sudhoffs Archiv	*Sudhoffs Archiv für Geschichte der Medizin und der Naturwissenschaften*
Verfasserlexikon	*Die deutsche Literatur des Mittelalters: Verfasserlexikon.* 2d ed., ed. Kurt Ruh et al.
WdF	Wege der Forschung
WMF	Würzburger medizinhistorische Forschungen
WMM	*Würzburger medizinhistorische Mitteilungen*
WW	*Wirkendes Wort*
ZfdA	*Zeitschrift für deutsches Altertum*
ZfdPh	*Zeitschrift für deutsche Philologie*
ZfdS	*Zeitschrift für deutsche Sprache*
ZfrPh	*Zeitschrift für romanische Philologie*

Romancing the Grail

Endings and Beginnings: Wolfram's *Parzival* and Romance Narrative

Interpretations of literary texts frequently privilege beginnings and endings as a means of establishing or confirming assumptions about a narrative. This strategy also constitutes a traditional approach to medieval romances, the prologues and epilogues to which usually provide an *accessus* to the text and negotiate relationships between the author/narrator and the audience.[1] But scholars have also begun to shift their emphasis from rhetorical structures in prologues and epilogues to the cultural and political agenda inscribed within them. The prologues of Chrétien de Troyes (fl. ca. 1160–ca. 1190), for example, which determined the basic genre expectations for his adapters in Germany,[2] can be seen as examining themes ranging from the transition from orality to writing (a fundamental move in establishing the genre of romance itself) to the relationship between *chevalrie* and *clergie* (an issue of fundamental interest to the clerical author and his aristocratic audience).[3]

Wolfram von Eschenbach's *Parzival* (ca. 1210) seems at first glance to raise similar expectations.[4] The introductory 116 lines suggest the out-

[1] On the general tactics of the prologue, see especially Hennig Brinkmann, "Der Prolog im Mittelalter als literarische Erscheinung" (1964). For bibliography on prologues and epilogues, see Olive Sayce, "Prolog, Epilog und das Problem des Erzählers" (1972), esp. 65, nn. 8–9.

[2] For a recent survey, see Martin H. Jones and Roy Wisbey, eds., *Chrétien de Troyes and the German Middle Ages* (1993).

[3] See Walter Haug, *Literaturtheorie im deutschen Mittelalter* (1985), esp. 91–106 (*Erec*), 107–17 (*Lancelot* and *Cligès*); Donald Maddox, *The Arthurian Romances of Chrétien de Troyes: Once and Future Fictions* (1991).

[4] For two interpretations with which the following is largely in agreement, see Helmut Brall, "'diz vliegende bîspel': Zu Programmatik und kommunikativer Funktion des *Parzival*prologes" (1983), and Haug, *Literaturtheorie*, 151–73. On older literature, see the references in Brall, nn. 4–6, and the references under "Prolog" in Bumke, *Forschung*, 433.

lines of a conventional prologue, with sections that first generate audience attention and then introduce the story proper.[5] The first section or *prologus praeter rem* (1.1–3.27) begins with tropes frequently recommended by rhetorical handbooks, a proverb and an exemplum:

> Ist zwîvel herzen nâchgebûr,
> daz muoz der sêle werden sûr.
> gesmæhet unde gezieret
> ist, swâ sich parrieret
> unverzaget mannes muot,
> als agelstern varwe tuot.
> der mac dennoch wesen geil:
> wand an im sint beidiu teil,
> des himels und der helle.
> (1.1–9)

> If inconstancy is the heart's neighbor, that will be bitter for the soul. Blame as well as praise exist wherever an intrepid man's spirit is as motley as the magpie's plumage. But he may yet be blessed, for both heaven and hell have a share in him.

But in spite of their apparent adherence to rhetorical theory, these opening moves have produced more confusion than clarity among modern critics. The proverb introduces a theological term of indeterminate scope and relevance, whereas the ensuing exemplum of the dappled magpie seems to map uncertain psychological assumptions onto inconsistent eschatological consequences. Moreover, these lines appear to take a stance vis-à-vis the treatment of *zwîvel* in Hartmann von Aue's *Gregorius*, replacing that text's black-and-white clerical opening with the gray complexities of a worldly point of view, a paradigmatic tactic in a text that frequently appropriates, secularizes, and problematizes hitherto learned or clerical subjects.

After extending this flying exemplum, or "vliegendez bîspel" (1.15), the narrator seems to hijack the narrative, delighting in obscure allusions and puns as well as the inability of dullards and even the wise to follow his erratic flight plan:[6]

[5] See Brinkmann, "Prolog," 90–94; Arthur Groos, "Wolfram von Eschenbach's 'Bow Metaphor' and the Narrative Technique of *Parzival*" (1972), 402–4.

[6] On the constitution of Wolfram's audience, see Eberhard Nellmann, *Wolframs Erzähltechnik* (1973), 8–11.

ouch erkante ich nie sô wîsen man,
ern möhte gerne künde hân,
welher stiure disiu mære gernt
und waz si guoter lêre wernt.
dar an si nimmer des verzagent,
beidiu si vliehent unde jagent,
si entwîchent unde kêrent,
si lasternt unde êrent.

(2.5–12)

I never knew a man so wise who didn't want to know what sort of guide these stories need and what moral instruction they provide. They never fail both to flee and pursue; they retreat and charge; they praise and blame.

The narrator presents us with a radically altered conception of literature and the contract with his audience. To be sure, there is the traditional rhetorical goal of providing instruction ("guote lêre") by assigning *laudatio* and *vituperatio*, praise as well as blame.[7] But this guide is no longer static or inherent in the narrative. Rather, it has to be pursued in a quest forced on the audience by that narrative's multiplicity—as the plural "mære" (stories) suggests.[8] The text offers no unifying principle, but coexists with all the contradictions of secular existence, as the opposing pairs of verbs suggest. *Parzival* will immerse us in a discourse that is not so much authorial or monologic as fundamentally decentered and pluralistic.

The second part of the prologue devoted to the story proper, the *prologus ante rem* (3.28–4.26), compounds this already substantial ambiguity by shifting to a generality so broad that it could apply to any narrative: the story is about joy and sorrow ("von liebe und von leide"), womanly women ("wîplîchez wîbes reht"), and manly manhood ("mannes manheit"). Moreover, it is so unwieldy that the narrator, whose intimidating presence dominates this section,[9] insists that even if he were three different persons, they would have difficulty accomplishing what he alone intends to do:

nu lât mîn eines wesen drî,
der ieslîcher sunder phlege

[7] See Günther Schweikle, "*stiure* und *lêre*. Zum *Parzival* Wolframs von Eschenbach" (1977), for a different assessment of these lines.

[8] See Stephen C. Harroff, *Wolfram and His Audience* (1974).

[9] See the large number of first-person pronouns: 3.25, 3.26, 4.2, 4.4, 4.7, 4.9, 4.19, 4.23.

daz mîner künste widerwege:
dar zuo gehôrte wilder funt,
op si iu gerne tæten kunt
daz ich iu eine künden wil.
(4.2–7)

Assume that I were three persons, each attempting to equal my artistry: it would take incredible luck if they wanted to tell you what I alone intend to divulge.

The hero finally seems to take on substance in the modified *sapientia et fortitudo* topos with which the narrator greets him as a brave man, slowly wise ("er küene, træclîche wîs" [4.18]), apparently suggesting constant as well as dynamic aspects to his character. But after the parallel evocation of his beauty, "er wîbes ougen süeze" (4.20), the expectation of a defining catalogue of epithets terminates with the sudden reminder that the hero conceived by the narrator is not yet born to the narrative, "den ich hie zuo hân erkorn, / er ist mæreshalp noch ungeborn" (4.23f.), which requires beginning instead with the story of his parents. The "supernarrator," so intimidating in his initial relations with the audience, suddenly lacks control over his narrative, which seems, rather, to have a telos of its own—initiating a self-conscious dialectic between the two that recurs throughout the text.[10]

It is not surprising that the extensive secondary literature on the beginning of Wolfram's *Parzival,* while illuminating details of nearly every word (often with mutually exclusive references to rhetoric, theology, sapiential or encyclopedic lore, literary polemics, and putative stages of the text's genesis), has provided neither clarification of, nor consensus on, the prologue as a whole. We seem constrained to accept the defamiliarizing tactics of Wolfram's opening lines, which replace the static rhetoric of earlier prologues by a fragmented dynamic and theological certainty by the contradictions of a secular perspective, whose import remains to be determined by an audience forced to engage in its own quest for understanding. But if the prologue's wild flight has left us uncertain about the implications of all this, we might turn to the epilogue, the other section of the narrative that traditionally provides information similar to the prologue. Indeed, the extended series of closing tactics in *Parzival* reveals considerably more about this unusual text and its place in Middle High German literature around 1200.

[10] See especially the beginning of Book IX (433.1ff.), the statement that Kyot asked Wolfram to conceal information until adventure brought it to the point where it had to be mentioned (453.1–10), and the beginning of Book XV (734.1–16).

I

A conventional romance epilogue can consist of little more than an announcement that the story has reached its end.[11] More frequently, it rounds off the narrative with a double statement that mirrors the prologue's two parts (the address to the audience and introduction to the story proper), first confirming that the hero and heroine lived happily ever after, then praying for the narrator/author and his listeners/readers. The concluding lines of Hartmann von Aue's *Erec* (ca. 1180), the first major Arthurian romance in Middle High German and the narrative that most often serves as the intertextual backboard for Wolfram's games with genre expectations, provides a concise example:

> [Erec] nâch êren lebete
> und sô daz im got gebete
> mit veterlîchem lône
> nâch der werlde krône,
> im und sînem wîbe,
> mit dem êwigen lîbe.
> durch got des bitet alle
> daz uns der lôn gevalle
> der uns gote gehulde
> (deist goldes übergulde)
> nâch disem ellende.
> hie hât diz liet ein ende.
> (10124–35)[12]

> [Erec] lived so honorably that God, with fatherly reward, granted him and his wife eternal life after their earthly dominion. Pray all of you, for God's sake, that we receive that reward—worth more than gold—that makes us God's vassals after this life of exile. Here this story ends.

Hartmann elegantly compresses three elements of closure into as many sentences: an exit from the episodic sequence of romance time to considerations *sub specie aeternitatis*, a parallel shift from performance to prayer, and a formulaic termination of the narrative as well as its narration with the word "ende."[13]

Wolfram, not surprisingly, makes the closure of *Parzival* a far more

[11] For a representative collection of material, see Käthe Iwand, *Die Schlüsse der mittelhochdeutschen Epen* (1922).

[12] Hartmann von Aue, *Erec* (1963), 262.

[13] See Iwand, *Schlüsse*, 15–37, esp. 23–24 and 33 ("Schlußgebet") and 66–73 ("formelhafte Schlußerklärung").

complex and belabored enterprise.[14] We recall that he emphasizes at the start of the romance that three other narrators would have difficulty keeping up with what he alone intends to undertake. The same holds true for the conclusion. Indeed, three narrative strands slouch toward their separate conclusions, only one of which lends itself to a clear-cut ending. This is the Arthurian narrative, which finishes resoundingly in true romance fashion with marriages of two generations of Arthurian relatives to figures associated with Schastel Marveile and its surroundings: Gawan—Arthur's nephew and the surrogate hero for a third of the romance—to Orgeluse; Itonje and Cundrie—Gawan's sisters—to Gramoflanz and Lischoys; and Sangive—Arthur's sister and Gawan's mother—to Florant. This fourfold union between Brittany, the land that provides the questing heroes of Arthurian romance, and Terre Marveile, the land that consists entirely of adventure (548.10), imparts a pervasive sense of resolution and concluding joy, "endehafte freude" (733.18), to the festivities in Book XIV.[15]

The other two narrative strands, dealing with the Orient and the Grail, function rather differently, not concluding with the happy-end marriage or reunion characteristic of romance and the static nature of much Arthurian romance in particular. Rather, they continue of their own accord through the basic organizational principle of medieval dynastic history—hereditary succession. The Oriental episodes, begun by Gahmuret's adventures in Book I and reintroduced by the arrival of Feirefiz in Book XV, extend beyond the latter's marriage to Repanse de Schoye to continue with the couple's voyage to India, their son and his descendants, all named Prester John (820.5–823.10)—a suggestive allusion with far-reaching implications.[16] The Grail episodes also exert a momentum of their own that does not end with Parzival's accession to dominion at Munsalvaesche and reunion with his family. Wolfram makes a move toward closure with a reference to the "rehte mære" or true stories (we note the plural again) that have told the audience about the five children of Parzival's grandfather Frimutel, four of whom he names and provides with epigrammatic lives:[17]

[14] See Joachim Bumke, "Parzival und Feirefiz—Priester Johannes—Loherangrin: Der offene Schluß des *Parzival* von Wolfram von Eschenbach" (1991); Horst Brunner, "'Von Munsalvaesche wart gesant / der den der swane brahte': Überlegungen zur Gestaltung des Schlusses von Wolframs *Parzival*" (1991).

[15] On the function of courtly festivities, see, for example, Kurt Ruh, *Höfische Epik I* (1967), 11–15.

[16] See Friedrich Zarncke, *Der Priester Johannes* (1879 and 1883), for the basic texts, and Bumke, "Parzival und Feirefiz," 242–55.

[17] The fifth, Repanse, has just been "retired" in the preceding description of her marriage to Feirefiz and voyage to India.

diu rehten mære iu komen sint
umb diu fünf Frimutelles kint,
daz diu mit güeten wurben,
und wie ir zwei ersturben.
daz ein was Schoysîâne,
vor gote diu valsches âne:
diu ander Herzeloyde hiez,
diu valscheit ûz ir herzen stiez.
sîn swert und rîterlîchez lebn
hete Trevrizent ergebn
an die süezen gotes minne
und nâch endelôsme gewinne.
der werde clâre Anfortas
manlîch bî kiuschem herzen was.
ordenlîche er manege tjoste reit,
durch den grâl, niht durch diu wîp er streit.
(823.11–26)

The true stories have come to you concerning Frimutel's five children, that they acted with goodness and how two of them died. The first was Schoysiane, without falsity before God; the second was called Herzeloyde, who cast falsity out of her heart. His sword and knightly existence Trevrizent offered up to God's sweet love for the sake of eternal reward. Noble, handsome Anfortas was manly with purity of heart. In accordance with the rule he rode many jousts, fighting for the Grail, not for women.

But instead of ending with the hero, the narrative assumes the broader focus of a family chronicle, skipping a generation to Lohengrin and, after inquiring rhetorically whether the audience wants to hear more,

Loherangrîn wuohs manlîch starc:
diu zageheit sich an im barc.
dô er sich rîterschaft versan,
ins grâles dienste er prîs gewan.
Welt ir nu hœren fürbaz?
(823.27–824.1)

Lohengrin grew to manly strength, and cowardice hid from him. When he reached the age of knighthood, he won fame in the service of the Grail. Do you want to hear more?

proceeds to relate the history of the Swan-Knight in an addendum that terminates abruptly with a sideswipe at Erec, the first major hero of Arthurian romance (826.29–30).[18]

If Wolfram does not impose clear-cut romance endings on the non-Arthurian portions of his narrative, adding "historical" or chronicle-like continuations for the descendants of principal figures (as well as intertextual polemics), he does not provide us with an easy exit from the act of narration either. The final thirty-line section of the romance, which follows the extension of Feirefiz's and Parzival's histories to Prester John and Lohengrin, immediately involves us in a controversial statement on "sources":

> Ob von Troys meister Cristjân
> disem mære hât unreht getân,
> daz mac wol zürnen Kyôt,
> der uns diu rehten mære enbôt.
> endehaft giht der Provenzâl,
> wie Herzeloyden kint den grâl
> erwarp.
>
> (827.1–7)

> If Master Chrétien de Troyes has not done justice to this story, that may well anger Kyot, who offered us the authentic narratives. The Provençal relates to the end how Herzeloyde's child won the Grail.

Wolfram acknowledges two previous tellers of his tale. Chrétien de Troyes, a cleric and the learned founder of French Arthurian romance, whose last work, *Li Contes del Graal* (ca. 1190), remained a fragment and was continued almost immediately by several adapters, in fact provides the only written source for Wolfram that we know.[19] "Kyot of Provence," an otherwise unknown author from an area known almost exclusively for its lyrics, seems—in spite of more than a century of perspicacious searching by learned positivists—never to have existed at all.[20]

Indeed, scholars are now nearly unanimous in assessing the Kyot refer-

[18] See Ulrich Wyss, "Parzivals Sohn: Zur strukturalen Lektüre des Lohengrin-Mythos" (1979).

[19] The principal study is Jean Fourquet, *Wolfram d'Eschenbach et le "Conte del Graal"* (1966). For a revision of some of Fourquet's conclusions, see Bonnie Buettner, *Gawan in Wolfram's "Parzival"* (1984), 260, 288, 294f.

[20] Kyot is also learned, a "meister wol bekant" (453.11) and a "meister wîs" (455.2). His name is northern French, but his nickname, "la schantiure" (416.21), agrees more with the dominance of lyric in Old Provençal. See Carl Lofmark, "Wolfram's Source References in *Parzival*" (1972).

ences as an example of the fictitious source attributions that characterize romance narratives, ranging from the "liber vetustissimus" ostensibly given to Geoffrey of Monmouth by Walter, Archdeacon of Oxford (*Historia regum Britanniae* I.1), to the translation of an Arabic document that Cervantes claims to have found in Toledo (*Don Quixote* I.9). But given the fact that Wolfram also refers to and describes Kyot's text extensively, we should resist the temptation to dismiss the passage as a meaningless play with conventions. Because the first source reference emphasizes that Kyot translated the story of Parzival from "heidensch" (Arabic) to "franzoys" and that the narrator now merely retells it in German (416.20–30), we might consider reading "Kyot" seriously as the imaginary source that Wolfram projects retroactively from his own narrative in order to justify it. We can, in other words, use the implied differences between Chrétien and Kyot to tell us something about Wolfram. Unlike Chrétien's fragment, which breaks off at line 9234 with the arrival of Gauvain's messenger at Arthur's court, Kyot's version is complete and definitive, "endehaft." And unlike Chrétien's story, which may not do the subject justice, Kyot's narrative is not only right ("reht"), but—as the unusual plural "mære" suggests[21]—invests the "source" with the decentered and pluralistic discourse that we have already seen in the prologue and Wolfram's attempts at closure.

The extended description of Kyot's sources in Book IX amply confirms this impression. In fact, Wolfram explicitly cites a variety of sources, "secret stories about the Grail" (452.30), placing the Grail narrative in a more variegated context than a straightforward Arthurian romance, and anticipating the encyclopedic discussion that follows. The "sources" for Wolfram's "source"—we might call them *Kyots gesammelte Werke*—consist of two representative types of nonliterary discourse, astronomical and historical, both characterized by the dynamic multiplicity we find at the beginning and end of Wolfram's narrative. The first source description (453.11–455.1) relates how Kyot discovered a written Arabic text in Toledo, the contemporary center for the recovery of Greek science from Arabic translations, a center of crucial importance for the science of *Parzival*, as we will see. This first source describes the genealogy as well as the astronomical investigations of its heathen author, Flegetanis, and ends by citing his hesitant "reading" of celestial revelations about the Grail and its guardians. The second source description (455.2–22) summarizes Kyot's

[21] Closing references to the work quoted in Iwand, *Schlüsse*, 66–79 and 120–34, are usually singular, with the sole exception before Wolfram of Veldeke's *Eneit*. Later references, such as Rudolf von Ems's *Willehalm von Orlens* (15601f.) or Pleier's *Tandareis* (18304f.), are clearly derived from Wolfram. Another exception in *Diu Klage* (Iwand, *Schlüsse*, 127) may derive from the pluralistic source conception of Latin history.

quest to locate the Grail family alluded to by Flegetanis. Seeking historical chronicles in Latin (455.4/9), Kyot proceeds through Britain, Ireland, and France—the countries of Arthurian and Tristan romances as well as chansons de geste, respectively—before finally finding "diu mære" in Anjou, a country without a traditional literary genre in the conventional sense. But Anjou, the country ruled by Gahmuret's family, was the early center of a new genre reflecting the feudal aristocracy's preoccupation with titles and patrimony—genealogical literature.[22] We might therefore pause to note the repeated emphasis on plural sources, explicitly derived from the tradition of Latin historiography. Kyot's chronicles, like Wolfram's summary of his own narrative (823.11ff.), consist of the lives of rulers and their immediate families from the founder to the present day. Spanning five generations, the Grail *mære* are highly suggestive, connecting the shadowy patriarch Mazadan (the name etymology *mâc Adam*, son of Adam,[23] relates him to primal man) to the present hero Parzival, subject of these stories, "des disiu mære sint" (455.23). As is often the case with medieval historiography, the particular history of the Grail family is ultimately linked to the general course of salvation history, recapitulating in Parzival the original order and subsequent disorder in the family of man.[24]

We should also note—returning to the epilogue—that the ensuing lines provide us with a brief epitome of these stories which is all the more important because Wolfram claims to be merely translating,

> wie Herzeloyden kint den grâl
> erwarp, als im daz gordent was,
> dô in verworhte Anfortas.
> (827.6–8)

> how Herzeloyde's child won the Grail, as was ordained for him, after Anfortas forfeited it.

This statement places Parzival's career in a nexus of dynastic concerns, revealing that he is a potential inheritor of the Grail kingship not only through his mother, one of the five children of the Grail king Frimutel (823.12ff.), but also through the failure of Anfortas, the senior member

[22] See Georges Duby, "French Genealogical Literature: The Eleventh and Twelfth Centuries," in *The Chivalrous Society* (1977), 149–57. For a more recent discussion of the implications of this pattern of thought, see Gabrielle Spiegel, "Genealogy: Form and Function in Medieval Historical Narrative" (1983).

[23] Martin, *Kommentar*, 64 (on 56.17).

[24] See Spiegel, "Genealogy," 51–52.

of those siblings. Equally important, Parzival's career is described in terms of winning and being foreordained, human striving and divine predisposition—variants of that major paradox of the Christian tradition, merit and grace. The relationship between the two is not specified, and in fact the various genres that articulate them (principally the romance and saint's life) constitute basic elements of Wolfram's narrative, giving it a generic multiplicity, what musicologists might call bitonality. Parzival's career reflects the discursive plurality contained in "Kyot."

The epilogue continues by shifting from the text's source to its narrator, reminding us of Wolfram's role as the recipient of, and mouthpiece for, the "right stories" of Kyot:

von Provenz in tiuschiu lant
diu rehten mære uns sint gesant,
und dirre âventiur endes zil.
niht mêr dâ von nu sprechen wil
ich Wolfram von Eschenbach,
wan als dort der meister sprach.
sîniu kint, sîn hôch geslehte
hân ich iu benennet rehte,
Parzivâls, den ich hân brâht
dar sîn doch sælde het erdâht.
(827.9–18)

The right stories and the conclusion to this adventure have been sent from Provence to us in German lands. I, Wolfram von Eschenbach, do not intend to speak any more of this now than what the master said there. I have correctly named to you the children and the high lineage of Parzival, whom I have brought to the place which, nonetheless, providence had intended for him.

This assertion mirrors Wolfram's first reference to his activity as merely translating his source (416.20–30), now adding, to emphasize the move toward closure, that his ending is also coterminous with Kyot's. Nonetheless, the broader medieval conception of "translation" enables the insinuation of two important refinements.[25] The first is to have named Parzival's family and genealogy "correctly," a particular fetish of Wolfram's (cf. 143.6–14). Naming and genealogy are not essential in Chrétien's romance, as structurally important figures can function anonymously (the Grail king and the hero's mother, for example, have no names); even

[25] See Carl Lofmark, "Der höfische Dichter als Übersetzer" (1972).

Arthur's lineage has no diachronic significance—it perishes with him.[26] But because names and genealogy are the vehicles of historical record, they are central to any genre or text expressing a history or teleology and hence loom large in *Parzival*, transposing Chrétien's adventure romance into a family romance.

Wolfram's second innovation is the inscription of this teleological dynamic, particularly the coordination of God and world, into the act of narration. At the beginning of Book XV, the "supernarrator" asserts control of the narrative after the conclusion of the Arthurian plot,

ich sorge des den ich hân brâht,
wan daz ich trôstes hân gedâht.
(737.25f.)

I would be concerned for the one I have brought here, except that I have thought of a resolution.

But the persistent intrusion of divine providence into the action of the final books—the breaking of Parzival's sword, the announcement of his redemption and call to the Grail castle, the curing of Anfortas—compels a more humble insight in the epilogue, expressed with nearly identical words and the identical rhyme:

Parzivâls, den ich hân brâht
dar sîn doch sælde het erdâht.
(827.17f.)

Parzival, whom I have brought to the place which, nonetheless, providence had destined for him.

The narrator now acknowledges the universal workings of providence, subordinating his text to the larger text of salvation history. We will return to the implications of this tactic in Chapter 9.

The final twelve lines of Wolfram's romance bring us—finally—to the closure of the narrative and its narration that provided our initial point of comparison with Hartmann's *Erec.* Avoiding a simple exit from a series of

[26] The lack of genealogical succession comprises one of the principal tragic elements in the *matière de Bretagne.* Wace's *Roman de Brut* (9641–58) makes the motif explicit in describing Arthur's marriage to Guenevere. It is implicit in Wolfram's version as well: Arthur's son Ilinot has already died in the service of Florie of Kanadic (383.1–10, 585.29–586.11). None of the children of Arthur's immediate relatives seem to have children, with the result that the Arthurian family tree is drastically stunted in comparison with that of Parzival.

episodes by stating that the hero and heroine lived happily ever after, he transposes the travail of romance adventure to the larger arena of life, including fictional characters, narrator, and audience in the all-embracing generality of a proverb, one that might have been more helpful at the beginning of the text:

swes lebn sich sô verendet,
daz got niht wirt gepfendet
der sêle durch des lîbes schulde,
und der doch der werlde hulde
behalten kan mit werdekeit,
daz ist ein nützíu arbeit.
(827.19–24)

Whoever concludes his life in such a way that God is not deprived of the soul through the fault of the body and who nonetheless is able to retain the favor of the world with dignity—that is a worthy endeavor.

This "proverb," commonly assumed to express the basic "idea" of *Parzival*,[27] is a variant of a fundamental theme of Middle High German literature, pleasing God and the world, "got unde der werlt gevallen," a theme that reflects the concerns of an emerging humanism in twelfth-century Germany, a country with secular politics constantly at odds with the church. More than a topical citation, this particular version recapitulates in the course of one extended sentence a quest that ends—but does not promise a resolution—only at the conclusion of a lifelong struggle. Syntax approaches metaphor in expressing the narrative's dynamic: two fundamental concerns, God and the world, receive their due in two sets of three lines; restrictive clauses remind us of the difficulties of each: "not deprived through the fault of," "retain with dignity." But these competing and even antithetical forces might nonetheless ("und doch") be related in the larger dialogic process of attempting to satisfy the demands of God "and yet" those of the world as well. As we will see, Parzival's quest to accommodate these forces in the course of a properly conducted life has a narrative counterpart in Wolfram's appropriation of a variety of genres and genre expectations in a dialogue whose resolution remains uncertain, even at the climactic moment of the text—the redeeming question.

Having generalized the closure of the narrative, Wolfram particularizes his closure of its narration, addressing the final comments to an audience comprised entirely of women:

[27] See Benedikt Mockenhaupt, *Die Frömmigkeit im "Parzival" Wolframs von Eschenbach* (1942; rpt. 1968), 25–42.

guotiu wîp, hânt die sin,
deste werder ich in bin,
op mir decheiniu guotes gan,
sît ich diz mær volsprochen hân.
ist daz durh ein wîp geschehn,
diu muoz mir süezer worte jehn.
(827.25–30)

Good women, if they are sensible, hold me in higher esteem—especially if one of them wishes me well—now that I have finished telling this story. And since it was done for a woman, she should speak [or: concede] sweet words to me.

On its most immediate level, this conclusion reflects the special emphasis Wolfram places on women and female members of his audience in the prologue (2.25–3.24) as well as in frequent asides to "guotiu wîp."[28] But these lines also contribute to the self-conscious complexity of the narrative by addressing a particular woman in that audience, evoking the ambiguous performance situation of a love lyric, particularly the wooing of the beloved in Minnesang.[29] This lyricization of the narrative again places the text in the larger context of another kind of discourse, which Wolfram explicitly raised in the "Self-defense" preceding Parzival's initial adventures (114.5–116.4) as well as in the epilogue that follows them (337.1–30),[30] thus closing a running battle with conventions of the courtly love lyric. Having defined his narrative as better love service than song, he now offers his 24,812-line text as a massive knightly alternative to the slight ephemera of singers, anticipating the synecdochic "sweet words" of reward denied him earlier for his lyrics. The outcome remains ambiguous, because the final word, "jehen," can imply not only a response to his wooing, but also agreement with his text, which continually editorializes against love service. Moreover, the latter meaning also closes the narrative with a simultaneous opening gesture: the act of finishing the recitation, *volsprechen*, anticipates a positive response, *jehen*, thus integrating the text into the reception history of its ensuing performances.

[28] I cannot follow the logic in Hans Bayer's association of Wolfram with Waldensian lay piety and Sophie of Bavaria as the patroness invoked in lines 827.27ff., "'guotiu wîp, hânt die sin' (*Parz.* 827.25): Wolfram von Eschenbach und der thüringische Landgrafenhof" (1980).

[29] See esp. Wolfgang Mohr, "Die *vrouwe* Walthers von der Vogelweide" (1967).

[30] See Michael Curschmann, "Das Abenteuer des Erzählens" (1971), esp. 648–62.

II

If the preceding observations suggest that the conclusion to *Parzival* is substantially different and more complex than in contemporary narratives, this does not make it unique. There is an earlier Middle High German narrative with a "difficult" ending that undoubtedly served as Wolfram's model: Heinrich von Veldeke's *Eneit*. The *Eneit* also avoids a romance ending after the marriage of Eneas and Lavinia in favor of more complicated "historical" closing strategies. Veldeke compares the wedding to Friedrich Barbarossa's festivities for the dubbing of his sons in Mainz in 1184 (13222–52), returns to the narrative, and continues with the story of Eneas's sons (13307ff.), which merges eventually with the transition from the Roman imperium to Christianity (13397ff.) before concluding with an "Amen" (13428). There follow several epilogues, the authorship but not the contemporaneity of which has been challenged (13429–90; 13491–528).[31] The first informs us that the text was finished under the aegis of Hermann of Thuringia, Wolfram's patron. The second commences with an assertion of responsibility that Wolfram's lines, "sîniu kint, sîn hôch geslehte / hân ich iu benennet rehte, / Parzivâls" (827.15–17), appear to have appropriated, even with the same rhyme:

> Ich hab gesaget rechte
> Hern Eneas geslechte
> Und das kunne das von ime quam.
> (13491–93)[32]

I have correctly named Eneas's race and the descendants that came from him.

The emphasis in the *Eneit* on naming and genealogy also integrates the narrative with the course of imperial Roman history and ultimately with salvation history.[33] And Veldeke, alone of the writers of Middle High German narrative before Wolfram, employs the plural conception of sources traditional in Latin historiography in referring to his epic.[34] Wolfram's

[31] See Gabriele Schieb, *Henric van Veldeken (Heinrich von Veldeke)* (1965), 2–3.

[32] The quote, from the edition of Gabriele Schieb and Theodor Frings, *Henric van Veldeken: "Eneide"* (Berlin, 1964), is from the Gotha manuscript rather than Schieb's and Frings's hypothetical reconstruction.

[33] The typological implications of the epilogue have been suggested by Friedrich Ohly, "Ein Admonter Liebesgruß" (1956/57), 22.

[34] Manuscripts have "diu buoch" or "die buch" (13510: MSS H, M). The edition of Ludwig Ettmüller, *Heinrich von Veldeke* (Leipzig, 1852), which follows the oldest transmis-

achievement in pluralizing romance narrative is clearly indebted to Veldeke, whom he later acknowledges as "mînen meister."[35]

The epilogue to *Parzival* is also not without parallel in later thirteenth-century romances, which it profoundly influenced. Individual elements of the conclusion, such as the restriction of the audience to women,[36] appear frequently in formulations that reveal their origin. But the most far-reaching and general effect of Wolfram's narrative beyond the impact of his style seems to be the grafting of a polygeneric consciousness on to Middle High German romance. Even in the majority of romances remaining within the fictional parameters of Arthurian narrative, there is an attempt to integrate geography, individual figures, and even genealogies into the world of Wolfram's *Parzival* and *Titurel*—and not only in such obvious continuations as *Lohengrin* and *Der jüngere Titurel*.[37] Moreover, the epilogues to other narratives, such as Konrad Fleck's *Flore und Blanscheflur* or Rudolf von Ems's *Willehalm von Orlens*, clearly reveal Wolfram's influence. Indeed, Rudolf's turn to history, to take the distinguishing characteristic of the major postclassical romance author, is no sudden innovation, but more properly belongs to a tradition initiated by Veldeke and Wolfram.

Nonetheless, Wolfram's pluralization of romance differs fundamentally in its self-conscious complexity from Veldeke's model as well as from his thirteenth-century imitators. To be sure, all share a common tendency to appropriate other types of "true" narrative, principally history and—to a lesser degree—epic. This tendency reflects a characteristic tension between history and romance inherent in the *matière de Bretagne* from the very beginning of its written tradition, owing to the embedding of Arthur's fabled reign within the larger history of the kings of Britain.[38] Wolfram's narrative, however, constitutes a substantial shift beyond this ge-

---

sion, has "diu buoch" (354.21). According to Helmut Brackert, *Rudolf von Ems: Dichtung und Geschichte* (1968), 151–54, the tradition derives from Latin biblical exegesis and historiography.

[35] Wolfram von Eschenbach, *Willehalm* 76.24. This should explain at least partially why Wolfram praises Veldeke's epic technique, although his references in *Parzival* (292.18, 404.29) are ironical or critical, aimed against conventions of Minnesang and the portrayal of love. See James F. Poag, "Heinrich von Veldeke's *minne;* Wolfram von Eschenbach's *liebe* and *triuwe*" (1962).

[36] See Iwand, *Schlüsse*, 93–95.

[37] Peter Kern, *Die Artusromane des Pleier* (1981), esp. 100–48.

[38] The events of Arthurian romance take place in a twelve-year peace or pause in the epic chronology of rulers and battles described in Geoffrey of Monmouth, *Historia regum Britanniae* (XI.10–11), and even more clearly in Wace, *Le Roman de Brut* (9732ff.). On the hybrid nature of Geoffrey's history, see Robert W. Hanning, *The Vision of History in Early Britain* (1966), 173–76, and Antonia Gransden, *Historical Writing in England* (1974), 186–87, 201–3.

neric tension. As its closing tactics reveal, *Parzival* interweaves three different worlds, Oriental, Arthurian, and Grail, which are unified by their portrayal of a universal chivalric society that enables various characters to move from one to another. These worlds in turn have distinct discourses with different constituent features, ranging from the emplotting of time and space to genre expectations. Moreover, the narrator not only plays these narratives off against each other but also, as the epilogue suggests, plays narrative itself off against the conventions of the lyric, and ultimately human discourse against the dictates of salvation history. The self-conscious manipulation of narrative as well as narration creates a dialogic structure resisting ideological closure that many scholars consider to be a distinguishing feature of novelistic discourse.

III

In fact, Wolfram's text seems to challenge the inclination of some theorists to privilege the modern novel as the origin and fulfillment of such a dynamic. In opposition to this inclination, the ensuing chapters use, with varying degrees of emphasis, three principal and often overlapping concepts that Mikhail Bakhtin employs for analyzing prenovelistic as well as novelistic discourse: *heteroglossia*, the *chronotope*, and *carnival*. Although each already has its own theoretical history, a brief working paraphrase will suffice here; readers wishing more can easily consult Bakhtin's writings as well as the relevant secondary literature.[39]

1. *Heteroglossia*, the broadest of Bakhtin's terms, characterizes the multiplicity of speech registers, languages, and voices that enters novelistic discourse by means of "authorial speech, the speeches of narrators, inserted genres, the speech of characters."[40] Bakhtin organizes novelistic discourse in terms of two opposing tendencies, monologic and dialogic, which tend respectively either to suppress or encourage heteroglossia, and thus acquire a less or more positive valence. This binarism also characterizes medieval romance. Whereas courtly romance in general, including Chrétien's text, tends toward monologic discourse through its unifying rhetorical style and courtly language, I will suggest—following Bakhtin's own assessment of *Parzival*—that Wolfram creates a dialogic narrative with a heteroglot counterstyle and a tendency toward a decentered pluralism of

[39] The most important of Mikhail Bakhtin's works for our purposes are *The Dialogic Imagination: Four Essays* (1981) and *Speech Genres and Other Late Essays* (1986). For the basic study of Bakhtin's writings, see Gary Saul Morson and Caryl Emerson, *Mikhail Bakhtin: The Creation of a Prosaics* (1990).

[40] Mikhail Bakhtin, "Discourse in the Novel," in *The Dialogic Imagination*, 262–63.

speech types, genres, and nonliterary discourses that is already apparent in the prologue and epilogue.

2. Bakhtin's *chronotope* ("timespace") is a neologism invented to recategorize the conception of space and time and their interrelationship in literary discourse. For our purposes its basic element involves the supposition that genres are unique, reflecting distinct ways of representing time and space:

> In the literary artistic chronotope spatial and temporal indicators are fused into one carefully thought-out concrete whole. Time, as it were, thickens, takes on flesh, becomes artistically visible; likewise, space becomes charged and responsive to the movements of time, plot, and history. This intersection of axes and fusion of indicators characterizes the artistic chronotope.[41]

A heteroglot text such as *Parzival* is not informed by a single chronotope, but a variety of chronotopes, making different portions of the narrative both heterochronic and heterotopic. Distinct articulations of time and space will be important in characterizing the pastoral retreat at Soltane, for example, or differentiating the dynamic Grail realm (with its connections to the motions of the planets and the liturgical calendar) from the static Arthurian world (with its traditional setting in a pleasance landscape in May).

3. *Carnival* has several dimensions. Its best-known formulation is Bakhtin's somewhat dated reading of Rabelais's novels as embodying the license of medieval feasts and fairs, thereby subverting societal norms and fixed ideological structures.[42] More important for our purposes is the extension of carnival from a ritual practice to a symbolic one, in particular the conception of the novel as a "carnivalizing" form through the interaction of fixed or authoritative and destabilizing discourses. I use "carnivalizing" in two ways: one refers to a common feature of Chrétien's and Wolfram's narratives, the manner in which the foolish hero's incomprehension defamiliarizes the habitual discourses of chivalric culture; the other characterizes Wolfram's further use of this subversive treatment vis-à-vis his source.

What follows is a heteroglot approach to Wolfram's text, conceived as a study of the variety and interplay of discourses in *Parzival.* To a lesser

[41] Mikhail Bakhtin, "Forms of Time and of the Chronotope in the Novel," in *The Dialogic Imagination,* 84.

[42] Mikhail Bakhtin, *Rabelais and His World* (1968). For a critique and revision of the carnivalesque, see Peter Stallybrass and Allon White, "From Carnival to Transgression," in *The Politics and Poetics of Transgression* (1986).

extent it also involves a dialogue between philology and theory, between close analysis of central episodes in Parzival's quest and issues of novelness raised by Bakhtin. This dialogue is also of Bakhtinian origin. In one of his late essays, a "Response to a Question from *Novy Mir*," Bakhtin argues for a "creative understanding" that would involve both philology and theory, historical analysis of texts and the modern perspective brought to them by the interpreter:

> There exists a very strong, but one-sided and thus untrustworthy, idea that in order better to understand a foreign culture, one must enter into it, forgetting one's own, and view the world through the eyes of this foreign culture. . . . But if this were the only aspect of this understanding, it would merely be duplication and would not entail anything new or enriching. In order to understand it is immensely important for the person who understands to be *located outside* the object of his or her creative understanding—in time, in space, in culture. . . . It is only in the eyes of *another* culture that foreign culture reveals itself fully and profoundly (but not maximally fully, because there will be cultures that see and understand even more). A meaning only reveals its depths once it has encountered and come into contact with another, foreign meaning: they engage in a kind of dialogue, which surmounts the closedness and one-sidedness of these particular meanings, these cultures. . . . Such a dialogic encounter of cultures does not result in merging or mixing. Each retains its own unity and *open* totality, but they are mutually enriched.[43]

The approach attempts to avoid reducing a text to its "original meaning" (which is impossible) or reading it only through a modernizing lens (which distorts). Creative understanding in this sense involves an activity that is both double and dialogic:

> In contrast to relativism and modernizations, it presumes that the text is truly *other* and contains semantic depths otherwise unavailable; in contrast to enclosure within the epoch, it demands what Bakhtin calls the interpreter's own "outsideness," which includes the resources of his or her own culture's experience. The interpreter is not satisfied with recreating the text's original context, he also takes advantage of his own.[44]

Although the dialogue between philology and theory has considerable heuristic value in interpreting medieval texts, it may have implications for

[43] Mikhail Bakhtin, "Response to a Question from *Novy Mir*," in *Speech Genres and Other Late Essays*, 6–7.

[44] Morson and Emerson, *Mikhail Bakhtin*, 289.

modern theory as well. In part, this consists of resisting the often unspoken theoretical master-narratives that privilege modernity to the exclusion of premodern culture, and it thereby contributes to a long-term project (to modify Lee Patterson's phrase) of renegotiating the past.[45] One means of renegotiation, represented by the New Philology and the New Historicism, extends postmodern theory into the premodern period, a retrenchment that increases, so to speak, our knowledge of the modern bases of medieval vernacular and secular culture.[46] Another means of renegotiation, represented by Bakhtinian theory, questions the neo-positivistic division of history into premodern, modern, and postmodern. Bakhtin's theory embraces the entire history of novelistic discourse, positing that many literary texts from classical antiquity to the Renaissance exhibit heteroglossic "potential." This potential is inherent in the nature of novelistic discourse itself, not the result of historical evolution, and thus can emerge at various times in various cultures that are open for whatever reasons to decentering or heteroglot discourses.[47] Of course, Bakhtin's general comments on prenovelistic discourse and romance in particular, now more than a half-century old, need to be tested against textual evidence, to which the discussion now turns.

[45] Lee Patterson, *Negotiating the Past: The Historical Understanding of Medieval Literature* (1987).

[46] I am not always comfortable with the presentism of New Historicism, especially its tendency to measure the past by a stern tribunal of what seems ethically relevant today. See, for example, Gary Saul Morson, "For the Time Being," in *After Poststructuralism: Interdisciplinarity and Literary Theory* (1993), 203–31.

[47] See Morson and Emerson, *Mikhail Bakhtin*, 284–90.

CHAPTER ONE

Between Poetics and Prosaics: *Parzival* and Prenovelistic Discourse

Although the statements on medieval romance by Mikhail Bakhtin seem sketchy in comparison with his discussions of classical, Renaissance, and modern narratives, his few comments on Wolfram's *Parzival* reveal a high evaluation of this text in the history of prenovelistic discourse. Indeed, *The Dialogic Imagination,* Bakhtin's work on general novel theory best known in the English-speaking world, refers with unexpected frequency to Wolfram while ignoring other writers of Arthurian romance such as Chrétien de Troyes and Thomas Malory.[1] This might be explained biographically in terms of Bakhtin's bilingual upbringing and the German orientation of his professors at St. Petersburg, creating a linguistic facility and interest reflected especially in his study of the *Bildungsroman.*[2] But Bakhtin does not refer to other works of Middle High German literature, leaving us with the puzzle of Wolfram's apparently unique place in what specialists now call "the imagined private library of Mikhail Mikhailovich Bakhtin."[3]

The principal reason appears to be his placement of *Parzival* in the second and—for Bakhtin—more protean of two developmental lines leading to the modern novel. Discussing chivalric romances in the essay "Discourse in the Novel," he observes:

[1] Mikhail Bakhtin, *The Dialogic Imagination: Four Essays* (1981).

[2] See the summary comments by Nina Perlina, "Funny Things Are Happening on the Way to the Bakhtin Forum" (1989), 7–9.

[3] Ibid., 8. It is possible to conjecture in what form he read Wolfram's text: two references to the Grail castle as Montsalvat in *The Dialogic Imagination* (155 and 244) suggest nineteenth-century translations. San-Marte (Albert Schulz) translated the name as "Mont Salvage" (251.2, etc.) in his *Parcival: Rittergedicht von Wolfram von Eschenbach* (Leipzig, 1858). The apparent connection is made tenuous by the fact that Bakhtin's name may also have been influenced by Wagner's *Parsifal,* which—following San-Marte—similarly calls the Grail castle "Monsalvat."

> The most profound and perfected novels of this genre, such as Wolfram von Eschenbach's *Parzival*, are already authentic novels. Eschenbach's *Parzival* can no longer be considered a pure example of the First Line of novelistic development. It is the first German novel to be profoundly and fundamentally double-voiced, capable of coordinating the unconditional quality of its intentions with a subtle and considered observing of distances vis-à-vis language, all of which takes into account language that has been somewhat reified and relativized, removing it ever so slightly from the author's lips by means of a faint smile.[4]

The implications of this claim for Wolfram's "novelness" are far-reaching. Bakhtin differentiates the First and Second Lines of development by their resistance and openness, respectively, to what he calls "double-voicedness" or "heteroglossia"—a spectrum ranging from the variety of registers in everyday speech to the multiplicity of genres and their interplay in literary discourse.[5] The First Line is characterized by the tendency toward a single unified language, presenting what appears to be authorial, and hence monoglossic, discourse. The Second Line is characterized by a tendency in the opposite direction, namely toward a decentered or pluralistic narrative style, "incorporat[ing] heteroglossia into a novel's composition, exploiting it to orchestrate its own meaning and frequently resisting altogether any unmediated and pure authorial discourse."[6] Because the Second Line anticipates, and contributes to, the novel, its comparatively few early examples, such as *Parzival*, acquire special significance for Bakhtin, realizing a genre potential that is not so much a development of modern narrative as inherent in the nature of novelistic discourse itself.

In spite of the attractiveness of genre potential as a means of theorizing about premodern literature, medievalists such as Cesare Segre have raised objections to Bakhtin's treatment of medieval romance, drawing attention to his preference for Second Line texts over those of the First and his failure to treat adequately the historical development of the genre, a treatment that would necessarily require a substantially greater emphasis on Old French texts.[7] This criticism is certainly justified, although one might in turn fault Segre's reluctance to admit to his own canon narratives outside the Romance literatures, transpositions into different cultural and linguistic contexts that thereby have inherently greater Second Line potential. Indeed, German romance, with its multilingual discursive

[4] Bakhtin, *Dialogic Imagination*, 377.
[5] On the following, see Gary Saul Morson and Caryl Emerson, *Mikhail Bakhtin: Creation of a Prosaics* (1990), 344–48.
[6] Bakhtin, *Dialogic Imagination*, 375.
[7] See Cesare Segre, "What Bakhtin Left Unsaid" (1985).

consciousness of French and Latin as well as its own literary culture, is situated amid precisely the polyglossic exchange of social and language registers conducive to heteroglot literary discourse.[8]

Segre also criticizes Bakhtin's emphasis on linguistic manifestations of decentered authorial discourse, asserting that this imposes an anachronistic norm on romance, which usually creates structural heterogeneity in linguistically unmarked ways. In a comparative European context, however, this is not at all a modern construct imposed retroactively on the genre.[9] In our particular context it is very much a part of the debate surrounding Middle High German romance early in the thirteenth century, as the literary excursus in Gottfried von Straßburg's *Tristan und Isolde* demonstrates.

Most verse romances of the twelfth and thirteenth centuries could be subsumed under a uniform and impersonal ideal of rhetorical elegance, language, to quote Gottfried's praise of Hartmann von Aue, that is plain and smooth, "ebene unde sleht" (*Tristan*, 4661),[10] and generally restricted to the elevated linguistic register striven for in courtly society. But a second style, characterized in particular by Wolfram's "crooked" German,[11] represents more of a counterstyle, using language that eschews the leveling elegance of rhetoric in favor of a variety of registers. According to Gottfried, the language is high-leaping and far-browsing, with "hochsprünge und witweide" (4641) among linguistic extremes[12] that range from gambling slang, or "bickelworte" (4642), and con-artistry (4665–70) to passages so difficult that they need to be accompanied by commentators, "tiutære" (4684), even requiring searches for explanatory "glosses" in ostensibly necromantic texts (4689f.).[13]

[8] See Bakhtin's "From the Prehistory of Novelistic Discourse" and "Discourse in the Novel," in *Dialogic Imagination*, esp. 61–68 and 366–70 and 378f., respectively, and Morson and Emerson, *Mikhail Bakhtin*, 310–11.

[9] For insular romance, see esp. Susan Crane, *Insular Romance: Politics, Faith, and Culture in Anglo-Norman and Middle English Literature* (1986).

[10] The terms of Gottfried's excursus themselves derive from the language of Latin rhetoric. See Peter Ganz's commentary to lines 4621ff. in Gottfried von Straßburg, *Tristan* (1978), 346–48.

[11] See Wolfram von Eschenbach, *Willehalm* 237.11: "mîn tiutsch ist etswâ doch sô krump."

[12] The size and variety of Wolfram's vocabulary has yet to be thoroughly evaluated. See the overview by Edmund Wiessner and Harald Burger, "Die höfische Blütezeit" (1974), 224–26, and Bumke, *Wolfram*, 21–23 and 35–36. Another indication of Wolfram's eclectic vocabulary is the high incidence of loan words; see Jürgen Vorderstemann, *Die Fremdwörter im "Willehalm" Wolframs von Eschenbach* (1974). Wolfram's use of dialect remains nearly unstudied; see Wolfgang Kleiber, "Dialektale Bestandteile in Wolframs Wortschatz" (1989).

[13] See, most recently, Eberhard Nellmann, "Wolfram und Kyot als *vindære wilder mære*" (1988).

Gottfried's subsequent refusal to insult noble ears by detailing the treatment of Tristan's festering wound, clearly aimed at the extensive attempts to cure Anfortas, also makes explicit a basic social difference: courtly versus uncourtly language, "rede, diu niht des hoves si" (7954). The courtly-uncourtly antithesis that Gottfried posits between himself and Wolfram represents in Bakhtinian terms a larger polarity between exclusive and inclusive tendencies inherent in novelistic discourse itself.[14] The unified courtly language of Gottfried's *Tristan,* Hartmann's narratives, and most First Line verse romances is defined and contained by the leveling norms of traditional poetics, but the variety of registers and discourses in a rare Second Line romance such as Wolfram's celebrates the transgression of these limits and might be more appropriately described by what Bakhtin and others have called "prosaics."[15]

Of course, *Parzival* is still a verse narrative, not a prose novel, and verse inevitably exerts a leveling effect on language through the constraints of rhyme and meter.[16] Bakhtin's estimation of this text as "already an authentic novel" thus seems exaggerated by modern scholarly standards and clearly needs to be scaled down. Two reservations come to mind. Wolfram's world exhibits (it seems to me) a disproportion between the wide variety of imagined social roles and their comparatively limited differentiation by linguistic registers. To be sure, an analysis of Kay's and Gawan's relationship in Chapter 3 will suggest that their language is differentiated and polarized, part of a tendency to carnivalize the court as the center of social interaction. But Wolfram's narrative, although it defamiliarizes both the unified rhetorical ideal of romance verse and the unifying language of the court, is not yet entirely "prosaic," does not yet articulate a universe of individual registers and idiolects.

The second, related limitation concerns the interplay of genres. In most cases the polygeneric tendency of the narrative is intermittent, usually involving bitonality or the opposition of romance with other genres (lyric, saint's life, epic), whereby nonliterary materials such as history, liturgy, and science and medicine help to construct the distinctive discourse of the Grail realm.[17] As we will see, there may be a good reason for the general tendency to dualistic genre voicing, because Wolfram situates his text in a world with clerical and secular, Latin and vernacular cultures, each with competing visions of human existence. This is not always

[14] The differences have too often been merely personalized. See Gerhild Geil, *Gottfried und Wolfram als literarische Antipoden* (1973).

[15] See especially Morson and Emerson, *Mikhail Bakhtin,* and for medieval French literature Wlad Godzich and Jeffrey Kittay, *The Emergence of Prose: An Essay in Prosaics* (1987).

[16] On the problem of verse in romance, Bakhtin is rather oblique. See "Discourse in the Novel," in *Dialogic Imagination,* 378 and n. 47.

[17] See Morson and Emerson, *Mikhail Bakhtin,* 293–300.

the case, of course, as the world of the heathen Orient amply suggests; and the other discourses absorbed into the text, especially science and medicine, often help to destabilize binarisms. The resulting heterogenic pluralism is highly unusual for a medieval narrative around 1200, but *Parzival* is still far from the truly polyphonic use of registers and genres in a Dostoyevsky novel.

Nonetheless, the tendency toward double-voicedness is clearly present and needs to be examined before we turn to an analysis of major stages in Parzival's career. Having already suggested the heteroglot nature of Wolfram's epilogue, I would now like to examine several aspects of his narrative in general that contribute to its decentered and pluralistic discourse: (1) the polyglossia of foreign-language registers, and the distinction between oral and written discourse; (2) the unresolved interplay of genres, as exemplified by the variety of statements on the conditions for winning the Grail; and (3) the authorial role(s) inscribed in the text.

I

Most romances of the twelfth and early thirteenth centuries would be classified among Bakhtin's First Line of novelistic development because of their comparatively uniform style, fashioned under the normative restraints of courtly language and rhetoric. Another constraint is that they are monolingual, that is, composed in a single authorial language that is also the imagined language of their characters. In fact, Middle High German translations usually transpose the monoglossia from the source to the target language.[18] They contain obvious strata of loan words from other languages, but do not often use this variety self-consciously to construct foreign language as a distinct linguistic register and thus destabilize the authority of the text or pluralize its discourse.

Hartmann von Aue's narratives, for example, rarely admit foreign languages: only *Gregorius* draws attention even to the fact that it is a "tiutsche getihte" (172). The legendary texts understandably allude to the clerical world of Latin, such as the verses attributed to Notker Balbulus, "mêdiâ vîtâ / in morte sûmus," in *Der arme Heinrich* (92f.) or the reference to God as "cordis speculâtor" (1357). In *Gregorius*, the abbot's occasional latinisms in expressions such as "crêde mich" (1025, 1628) also illustrate the antithesis between clerical and chivalric linguistic registers—the hero's "tiutsch wort" (1626) about knighthood being as intelligible to the abbot as "kriechisch" (1630). But Latin is never explicitly mentioned, even though a formal education in it forms the basis of Gregorius's re-

[18] See Carl Lofmark, "Der höfische Dichter als Übersetzer" (1972).

markable progress from a "grammaticus" at eleven to an expert in "dîvînitas" three years later and thence to a reader "von lêgibus" and a "lêgiste" (1181–97).

Hartmann's Arthurian narratives understandably reflect the impact of French aristocratic culture rather than clerical Latin. Here, too, French colors the style through the use of loan words, reaching special prominence in listing the Round Table and guests at Erec's wedding (1629–98, 1902–77); but it intrudes only twice as a foreign language distinct from the German of the narrative. In *Erec*, the translation of "Joie de la curt" as "des hoves vreude" states that the former term is unknown among Germans, "daz selbe wort ist unerkant under tiutschen liuten" (8003f.), perhaps implying—in addition to the fact that it is not a German term—that Hartmann's audience was not generally conversant with French. At the Castle of Bad Adventure in *Iwein*, the hero encounters a maiden reading in *wälhisch*, "diu vil wol, ist mir gesaget, / wälhisch lesen kunde" (6456f.), a linguistic other explained by displacement to the source.

Wolfram's imagined linguistic world, in contrast, presents a much greater plurality, not only of the transgressive linguistic registers and "crooked" nonrhetoric mentioned, but also of foreign-language speakers and languages. Indeed, the narrator actively decenters the primacy of his own language by keeping his audience aware that the discourse he presents to them in German is at one or even two removes from the original (187.23, 314.21, 416.30, 827.9). As we have seen in the Introduction, Wolfram denies authority to "von Troys meister Cristjân" (827.1), claiming instead to have derived his multiple narratives from sources in three *different* foreign languages. In order of origin these are the Arabic of Flegetanis's astronomical treatise found in Toledo, the Latin chronicles about the Grail family, and Kyot's synthesizing French narrative that the narrator in turn transmits in German: "swaz [Kyot] en franzoys dâ von gesprach, / daz sage ich tiutschen fürbaz" (416.28f.).

It is thus no accident that Wolfram imagines a more thoroughly plurilinguistic world than what is conventionally assumed for courtly society or represented in earlier Middle High German romances.[19] This polyglossia is neither leveled out by translation nor limited to the hero, presenting a situation that may be closer to the contemporary reality of a major court such as that of Landgrave Hermann of Thuringia—and not unlike the simultaneous presence of the vernacular, French, and Latin documented for England at a comparable period.[20] Moreover, the variety

[19] See Joachim Bumke, *Courtly Culture: Literature and Society in the High Middle Ages* (1991), 82–88.

[20] See M. T. Clanchy, "Languages of Record," in *From Memory to Written Record* (1993), 197–220. For a European perspective, see Bernhard Bischoff, "The Study of Foreign

is accompanied by another major linguistic difference, the broad spectrum between oral and written discourse, a spectrum barely acknowledged by early romance.

Wolfram occasionally constructs French for his German audience as a linguistic other through the designation *welsch* (4.28, 85.18, 357.7), but he also particularizes it by differentiating speakers of French according to discrete geographical regions, "Anschevîn" (62.5f.) and "Franzois od Brâbant" (85.19). More frequently, French comprises, so to speak, the lingua franca of international chivalric society. The Grail messenger Cundrie speaks it (312.20f.), as does another heathen member of the Grail society, the Queen of Janfûse (329.13). Parzival's heathen relatives, Belakane and Feirefiz, are also fluent in "franzois" (55.19f., 744.27). And throughout the entire romance we are distanced from the German of the narrative by reminders that the discussion is originally conducted in French—for example, when Queen Ampflise's chaplain greets Gahmuret, "bien sei venûz, bêâs sir / mîner frouwen unde mir" (76.11f.), or when the narrator reminds us that the epithet *bêâ curs* means "fair body": "der name ist tiuschen schœner lîp" (187.22f.).[21] Moreover, three important moments are specified as being "en franzois"—Cundrie's announcements of Parzival's condemnation and salvation at the ends of Books VI and XV (314.20 and 779.11), and the hero's own valedictory address to Arthurian society (786.3).[22]

Latin is no longer the undifferentiated discourse of a monastic elite.[23] As a representative of religious culture, it is restricted to the sacramental realm of the church in lay aristocratic society, especially in the mass, whose tag word is the concluding "beneditz" (94.1, 196.19, 705.9, 802.27). As the language of the schools and twelfth-century secular clerics, Latin is far more prominent, comprising one of the languages spoken by Cundrie (312.21) and the principal source for *meister* Kyot's chronicles (455.4). More specifically, as the language of scientific discourse, it becomes especially prominent in the extensive discussions of astronomy and medicine in Book IX and again, toward the end of the romance, in the astronomy of Gramoflanz's love letter (715.16f.) and

---

Languages in the Middle Ages" (1961); expanded version in his *Mittelalterliche Studien*, II (1967), 227–45.

[21] In contrast to Tristan's greeting of Marke in Gottfried's narrative, which is translated, "deu sal le roi et sa mehnie: / künec und sine massenie / die gehalte got der guote!" (3259–61), the chaplain's salutation is not translated; and unlike Hartmann's gloss on *joie de la curt* cited above, the narrative aside draws attention to the difference between the implied language of the narrative and German.

[22] The process continues in Wolfram's *Willehalm*; cf. 163.16f., 420.2f., 449.9f., and the aside in 237.3ff.

[23] Clanchy, *Memory*, 214–15.

Cundrie's announcement (782.1–16), or in the medicinal lists of precious stones derived from Marbode of Rennes's *Liber lapidum* (791.1–30) and the *arômatâ* used to reduce the danger of plague at Munsalvaesche (789.21–790.8).

Not surprisingly, *heidensch* is usually associated with Cundrie (312.21), who even intersperses her announcement of Parzival's redemption in Book XV with the names of the planets in a latinized but recognizable Arabic that forcefully documents the impact of Gerard of Cremona's translation project in Toledo (782.1–12).[24] And although heathens understandably speak French in sections of the narrative localized in Europe, the bilingualism also goes in the other direction, a rarity in medieval literature: Orgeluse conveys a series of orders to her squire Malcreature in *heidensch* (529.20).[25] The term *heathenish* seems to be an orientalizing designation for a religious and linguistic other, but it is also generalized because the sphere of reference cannot be limited to Arabic alone. Feirefiz, for example, commands twenty-five armies, not one of which understands the language of the other—an indication of the vast power that attracts knights of totally disparate origins (736.28–737.4).[26]

Other languages also figure in the narrative. The Hebrew *bâruc*, used to designate the caliph of Baghdad, is of uncertain origin. Greek makes its appearance in the snakes listed as possible sources for the poison in Anfortas's wound (481.8–10). A more self-conscious use of Greek elaborates on the precious stone in Feirefiz's helmet, called *anthrax* there and carbuncle here, "antrax dort genennet, / karfunkel hie bekennet" (741.13f.). It is of course unlikely that Wolfram knew Greek—the comment is taken from Isidore of Seville's *Etymologiae* (XVI.xiv.1).[27] But his imagined world clearly includes that language "there" as something linguistically different from what is spoken "here." The same is true of the Babel spoken at the tournaments in Books II and VII, which includes the tongues spoken by the "Bertûn" and "Irschman" as well as "Franzois od Brâbant" (85.16–19), or even shouts in "schottesch" (357.7). These are imagined individual foreign languages, a far cry from the unintelligible linguistic other suggested by the abbot's response to Gregorius's chivalric vocabulary as "Greek," that is, foreign (1630).

To this variegated group of languages and language speakers in Wolf-

[24] See Paul Kunitzsch, "Die Arabica im *Parzival* Wolframs von Eschenbach" (1974), 34, and "Die Planetennamen im *Parzival*" (1969).

[25] Another exception is of course Willehalm (*Willehalm*, 83.19, 105.27), who learned both *heidensch* and *caldeis* in captivity (192.6–22).

[26] See Wolfram's *Willehalm* 73.7–12, which specifies the number of languages as seventy-two, sixty of which are non-Christian.

[27] See Herbert Kolb, "Isidorische 'Etymologien' im *Parzival*" (1970), esp. 125–27.

ram's imagined world, we should add a further category that is attaining increasing prominence in vernacular culture during the late twelfth and thirteenth centuries, namely, the interaction between oral and written discourse.[28] That Wolfram presupposes for chivalric culture a spectrum of possibilities is suggested by Kaylet's attempt in Book II to convince Gahmuret that he has won the tournament, adducing two parallel types of evidence to support his claim ("des"): the oral agreement of every participant, "des jehent hie gar die zungen" (85.16), and the written confirmation of an imagined letter, "des les ich hie den wâren brief" (85.23)—a parallelism reflecting the use of both oral testimony and written documents in judicial argument.[29] A similar parallelism links written and oral discourse in the statement that no one ever read or told about a woman more beautiful and better than Condwiramurs: "daz munt von wîbe nie gelas / noch sus gesagte mære, / diu schœnr und bezzer wære" (224.12–14).

Indeed, the lay illiteracy insisted on by earlier scholars as the historical background of Wolfram's narrative is at odds with the diversity emerging from contemporary studies of courtly culture.[30] To put the similar diversity of Wolfram's imagined world into perspective, it may again be helpful to sketch the comparatively limited extent to which reading and writing are part of the imagined world of Hartmann von Aue, who explicitly constructs an authorial identity as an educated ("gelêret") knight in *Der arme Heinrich* (1) and *Iwein* (21). Most such references occur in the self-consciously learned comments by the narrator in prologues and asides.[31] Within the narratives themselves few characters read: the maiden in *Iwein*

[28] See Clanchy, *Memory*; Joachim Bumke, "Höfische Kultur: Versuch einer kritischen Bestandsaufnahme" (1992), 477ff.

[29] See Clanchy, *Memory*, 260–66. Similarly, Gramoflanz recognizes Itonje as his beloved through a "letter" he read in the field, namely, the fact that he has seen her brother (724.19–21).

[30] See Herbert Grundmann, "Dichtete Wolfram von Eschenbach am Schreibtisch?" (1967), and the response by Dennis H. Green, "Dichtete Wolfram von Eschenbach am Schreibtisch?" (1978). Recent scholarship has traced a much more literate and diverse image of courtly life. See Michael Curschmann, "Hören—Lesen—Sehen: Buch und Schriftlichkeit im Selbstverständnis der volkssprachlichen literarischen Kultur Deutschlands um 1200" (1984); Bumke, *Courtly Culture*, 425–58; Josef Fleckenstein, *Curialitas: Studien zu Grundfragen der höfisch-ritterlichen Kultur* (1990), esp. the chapters by Fleckenstein, "Miles und clericus am Königs- und Fürstenhof," 302–25, and Sabine Krüger, "'Verhöflichter Krieger' und *miles illitteratus*," 326–49.

[31] On reading, see Hartmann von Aue, *Erec*, 7305, 7493, 9019, 9723; *Gregorius*, 722, 3143; *Der arme Heinrich*, 2, 29; *Iwein*, 22. It also extends to the prayers in *Der arme Heinrich* (23) and *Gregorius* (3995) that those who hear or read the tale pray for the author/narrator—a topos of didactic literature. The narrator mentions books and written texts in *Der arme Heinrich* (2f., 7, 17), *Erec* (7491, 8698), and *Iwein* (22).

whose reading in "wälhisch" is explicitly displaced to the source (6456f.), and the three principals of *Gregorius,* who must read the incest story inscribed on the ivory tablet for the plot to advance.[32] Of these, only Gregorius, with his extensive clerical training, is portrayed as a reader of books.[33] Writing, often considered a separate skill because of the difficulty of working with parchment, occurs less frequently:[34] Gregorius's mother engraves the history of her son on the ivory tablet (726, 740),[35] a message designated as a "brief" (767). And only one figure employs real missives: King Arthur sends letters close, writs with seals or evidence of their authenticity, "brieve und wortzeichen" (1895).[36]

Wolfram's references to the elements of literate culture surpass Hartmann's to an almost exponential extent. Inasmuch as *none* of them derives from Chrétien's *Conte del Graal,* we are confronted by the paradox of a self-styled knightly *illitteratus* foregrounding in his narrative the very elements he claims ignorance of. To begin with, elements of writing appear in a variety of forms. Although asserting that he does not know a single letter himself (115.27), the narrator nonetheless states that Kyot had to learn the "karakter a b c" (453.15) to master Arabic. Individual "buochstabe" are inscribed on Gahmuret's tomb (108.2), and "karakten" (470.24) appear in the divine script on the edge of the Grail. Both forms of inscription on stony surfaces are also designated as an "epitafium" (107.30, 470.24, 781.15). The more permanent form of inscription that is engraved or "ergraben" on Gahmuret's tomb also characterizes engraving on metals, such as the owner's name on the spear tip that wounds Anfortas or Trebuchet's work on Frimutel's sword (479.20, 643.19).

There is a surprising diversity of two basic types of documents, manuscripts and letters. This also includes the writing materials of literate culture in allusions to parchment and ink as Gawan and Feirefiz prepare to write missives with their own hands (625.13, 785.28) or the comparison of Feirefiz's complexion with written parchment (747.26), to which one should add the contested reference to a wax tablet for counting the hea-

[32] There is frequent mention of what is found *geschriben* on the tablet (733, 1784, 2389, 2465, 2469, 2601). The abbot reads it when the foundling is brought to him (1041); Gregorius reads it continually after it is revealed to him (1745, 1758, 2282, 2319, 2390) in accordance with its injunction (750); and his wife and mother ultimately reads it, precipitating the second catastrophe (2481).

[33] See lines 746, 1163, 1465, 1579, 1583, 1585, 2685, and 3475.

[34] Indeed, *schrift* still means religious texts rather than handwriting: *Gregorius* 748, *Armer Heinrich* 90. On the separation of the two, see Clanchy, *Memory,* 88–97, 226–29.

[35] Another form of inscription is the description in *Erec* of the various stories engraved, or *ergraben* (7545, 7552, 7564), on Enite's riding gear.

[36] On *Wortzeichen,* see the Grimms' *Deutsches Wörterbuch,* 27 (Leipzig, 1922), 1650, and the discussion of *wârzeichen* in n. 45 below.

then forces in *Willehalm* (16.14f.), which might confirm Wolfram's literacy.[37] References to manuscript books involve common types of writings in aristocratic lay culture. The most prominent religious texts are the psalters read by Sigune, Trevrizent, and Guenevere (438.1, 460.25, 644.24), reflecting the rise of private devotion among an increasingly literate aristocracy, a rise corroborated by psalters in the circle of Landgrave Hermann of Thuringia.[38] As a well-established hermit, Trevrizent also seems to have a small library of other writings, for although his assurance of reading "der wâren buoche mære" (462.12) might be interpreted as referring to the books of the Bible, there appear to be more than that in the books, "sîniu buoch" (459.22), located inside his cell.[39] Secular writings range from texts on history and genealogy to science and medicine. Kyot's search among the appropriate "latînschen . . . chrônicâ" (455.4/9) turns up the history of the Grail family, a type of genealogical literature favored in the twelfth century as a means of legitimizing dynastic aspirations.[40] Scientific writings are represented by the Arabic manuscript found by Kyot in Toledo (453.13), including the astronomical text of Flegetanis (453.20), and by the various "arztbuoche" (481.6) consulted in the attempt to heal Anfortas. Finally, there are the unconventional writings of aberrant religious circles, such as the "deceptive books" consulted by Nabuchodonosor (102.4) or Clinschor's necromantic texts (66.4).

Five letters are written during the narrative. Three are quoted in full, as befits their derivation from the literary mini-genre of rhymed love letters:[41] Gahmuret's to Belakane, more a declaration of divorce than of love (55.21–56.26), Ampflise's to Gahmuret (76.23–77.18), and Gramoflanz's to Itonje (715.1–30). Inasmuch as the only earlier example of a love letter in Middle High German, Lavinia's missive to the hero of Heinrich von Veldeke's *Eneit* (286.20–35), lacks the usual love greeting, Wolfram's familiarity with the genre probably derives from other sources as well, which range potentially from Latin *artes dictaminis* or collections of letters to *Saluts d'amour* in Old Provençal or Old French. In Wolfram's

[37] 16.14f. See Dieter Kartschoke, *Wolfram von Eschenbach: "Willehalm"* (1968), 274–75, and the different resolution by Joachim Heinzle, "Stein und Banner. Zu Wolframs *Willehalm* 16.10–19" (1987).

[38] The "Landgrafenpsalter" and the "St. Elizabeth's Psalter." See Arthur Haseloff, *Eine thüringisch-sächsische Malerschule des dreizehnten Jahrhunderts* (1897).

[39] On the small size of personal libraries, see Clanchy, *Memory*, 104–05.

[40] See Georges Duby, "French Genealogical Literature," in *The Chivalrous Society* (1977), 149–57.

[41] For a survey with emphasis on Latin and French, see Ernstpeter Ruhe, *De amasio ad amasiam: Zur Gattungsgeschichte des mittelalterlichen Liebesbriefes* (1975).

Titurel, Schionatulander states that he knows letter-books in French, "brievebuoch en franzoys weiz ich wol" (164.2).[42] Indeed, the missives of both Gramoflanz and Ampflise suggest familiarity with rhetoric (especially repetition and *annominatio*), and even an understanding of the structure of Latin and Romance love epistles.[43] This gesture toward rhetoric is significant: Wolfram is not ignorant of its stylistic devices and forms but concentrates their use in an intercalated and written mini-genre.

The other two letters are true correspondence (as opposed to a literary genre) and are merely mentioned: Gawan's message to Arthur and Guenevere and Feirefiz's instructions to his waiting army (785.27–30). Although it is not quoted, Gawan's missive represents a special case involving public and private discourse, delivered not only in written form in the hand of its author but also as an oral message conveyed by the squire who delivers it—a presumably not uncommon combination in diplomatic missions.[44] Feirefiz's missive is a letter close entrusted to messengers and commanding the transport of riches to be distributed as tokens of his largess.

Letters are usually accompanied by signs confirming the author's identity. Because Gahmuret leaves a farewell in his own hand in Belakane's purse (55.17f.), there is no question of its authorship. But messages, both oral and written, often have some attached proof, or *wârgeleite* (76.18), signifying their veracity. In oral messages, this is usually a ring (51.23, 607.15, 608.2, 633.20/29, 634.9), recognizable by its unique construction or its owner's sign or seal. Rings exchanged as love tokens also accompany love letters, such as Ampflise's to Gahmuret or Gramoflanz's to Itonje (76.17, 710.6, 713.13, 714.12f.), especially when the recipient can recognize his or her own token (76.19f., 634.9f.). In contrast, letters concerning affairs of state, such as Feirefiz's writ to his army, require validating signs, or *wârzeichen* (626.11, 785.29).[45] Because both are autographs,

[42] Martin, *Kommentar*, 563, associates this passage with Latin sources. Joachim Heinzle, *Stellenkommentar zu Wolframs "Titurel"* (1972), 211, notes that the separation in MS G could mean "Briefe, Bücher."

[43] On structure, divided into a *salutatio, exordium* or *captatio benevolentiae, narratio, petitio*, and *conclusio*, see Ruhe, *Amasio*, 110. It is observed as well as transgressed in the two letters closest to the genre. Gramoflanz's letter could be viewed as following this order in 715.1–2 (*invocatio*), 2–4 (*captatio*), 5–20 (*narratio*), 21–27 (*petitio*), 28–30 (*conclusio*). After emphasizing the genre in the first line, "dir enbiutet minne unde gruoz," Ampflise's proceeds in a similar manner in 76.23f. (*invocatio*), 24f. (*captatio*), 26–30 (*narratio*), 77.1–10 (*petitio*), only to lapse into an imperious outburst in 77.11–15 before returning to the *conclusio* in 77.16–18.

[44] The messenger sent to King Arthur at the very end of Chrétien's fragment is given a purely oral message (9077–9154). On the combination of oral and written messages, see Clanchy, *Memory*, 263–64.

[45] See the entry *Wahrzeichen* in Grimms' *Wörterbuch* (1922). The term seems to enter courtly literature through two works well-known to Wolfram, Veldeke's *Eneit* (95.25) and Eilhart von Oberge's *Tristrant* (6357).

it is not clear whether the necessity to authenticate messages with other semiotic systems reflects distrust of the disembodied word or the fact that letters, like other forms of writing, were usually dictated to scribes and thus not recognizable as authorial discourse.

In this context, Gawan's letter to Arthur is particularly interesting, especially as it is—again—entirely Wolfram's invention.[46] Written elegantly in Gawan's own hand, "gefuoge mit der hant" (625.15), it does not need a confirming seal, being recognizable as authentic:

der brief niht insigels truoc:
er schreib in sus erkant genuoc
mit wârzeichen ungelogen.
(626.9–11)

The letter bore no seal: he wrote it very recognizably, with undisguised signs of its authenticity.

In contrast to the *wârgeleite* (76.18) of a ring accompanying Ampflise's letter to Gahmuret, the authenticating *wârzeichen* here seem to inhere in the writing. One possibility, the crosses frequently added to documents by the author as a pledge of their veracity before Christ (the most common type of *signum* before the general spread of individual signatures),[47] does not clarify what makes the letter valid or recognizable. The more likely explanation is that an elegant script directly reflects a figure noted for his refinement, which also implies that Arthur and Guenevere can recognize the characteristic *ductus* of their nephew's court hand.

In any event, the recipient of the letter treats the document as an extension of its author, conflating the script and the hand that wrote it:

diu künegîn zem brieve sprach
"ôwol der hant diu dich schreip!
âne sorge ich nie beleip
sît des tages daz ich sach
die hant von der diu schrift geschach."
(645.2–6)

The Queen spoke to the letter: "Blessed be the hand that wrote you! I have never been free of care since the day I last saw the hand that caused this writing."

[46] In Chrétien's text, the message is oral (9097–9137).
[47] Clanchy, *Memory*, 232–33, 254–60, 304–08.

The same is true of Ampflise's letter to Gahmuret, to which he bows on recognizing her handwriting, an extension of the royal presence: "er neic, dô er die schrift ersach" (76.21).[48] Gramoflanz's letter to Itonje is similarly perceived as direct authorial speech, because Arthur reads what the author spoke with his own mouth, "ûz sîn selbes munde" (714.24).

In Wolfram's linguistic world, then, writing—and reading—are still undifferentiated extensions of speaking, whence statements that a letter or written language "speaks" (55.20, 76.21f., 108.2, 483.29, 714.24f.). This is not uncommon during the transition from oral to written culture, in which "reading" could designate reading in private or reading aloud for others to hear, and "writing" could refer to dictation as well as actually placing a stylus to parchment. John of Salisbury states in the *Metalogicon* (I.13) that letters are shapes indicating voices, frequently speaking voicelessly the utterances of those who are absent: "Litterae autem, id est figure, primo vocum indices sunt . . . et frequenter absentium dicta sine voce loquuntur."[49] We should thus be wary about forcing a distinction between illiteracy and literacy onto the narrator's apparent opposition of speaking and reading in statements such as "ich sage iu als Kyot las" (431.2).

It is with some regret that I must also mention a third type of writing in addition to books and letters: the beginnings of administrative lists and recordkeeping. Where there is wealth and power, there is bureaucracy as well. Indeed, the gold table service at the Grail castle is so extensive that four carts bring it in for four knights to place on tables, each shadowed by a clerk, "ieslîchem gieng ein schrîber nâch" (237.28), detailed to collect it afterward. Of course, it is uncertain whether this whimsical illustration of the Grail's wealth reflects the activities of a court chancellery or the beginnings of inventories, but the presence of four scribes may imply knowledge of scriptoria at larger courts.

Given such a variegated approach to language and writing, it is not surprising to find a corresponding variety of literate persons in the narrative. Three are especially learned. The heathen Cundrie wins the prize for scholarly diversity, having explicit command of "alle sprâche," that is, "latîn, heidensch, franzoys," as well as an education in the seven liberal arts, represented by "dîaletike," "jêometrî," and "astronomîe" (312.20–25). In addition, she is also an expert in medicine, "swaz von erzenîe mac geschehn, / des tuot si gewaltec wol" (579.26f.). Kyot the clerical "meister" (453.11, 455.2, 827.14) is scarcely less impressive as a research scholar, having learned his Arabic "abc's" (453.15) to read manuscripts

[48] I am indebted to Horst Wenzel for this observation.

[49] See Clanchy, *Memory*, 253–93, who begins his discussion with this quote.

in Toledo and scoured Latin texts in Britain, France, and Ireland before finding the Grail family chronicle "ze Anschouwe" (455.2–12). Trevrizent explicitly claims the ability to read and write about biblical texts, "der wâren buoche mære / kunde ich lesen unde schrîben" (462.12f.), an ability supported by his psalter (460.25) and what appears to be a small library (459.22). As we will see in the final chapter, his notorious "Retraction" is prefaced by a biblical paraphrase that also reveals a precise knowledge of standard twelfth-century exegesis. Unless one interprets Trevrizent's statement in 462.11 as describing his having taken holy orders, none of these figures is a priest or monk, the transmitters of learning in earlier centuries, an indication of the secular appropriation of cultural leadership that will emerge as a major element of the narrative. In fact, there is one problematic reference to priestly learning: Clinschor is a practitioner of magic, "ein phaffe der wol zouber las" (66.4), making him a member of what has been called "the clerical underworld."[50]

Even if we discount these unusually learned figures, the incidence of reading and writing among others contrasts with older preconceptions about lay illiteracy, suggesting a broader diversity of cultural activity that breaks down the antithesis of *clericus* and *litteratus* versus *laicus* and *illitteratus*.[51] Certainly what we know about the broad cultural interests of the Thuringian court suggests that Wolfram's imagined world is not drastically in advance of the facts.[52] Whatever the case, most of Parzival's relatives in addition to Trevrizent are portrayed in acts of literacy—except for Herzeloyde, whose flight from court to a preliterate pastoral existence at Soltane robs her son of the chance for literary acculturation. In contrast, as we have seen, Gahmuret, Gawan, and Feirefiz write letters with their own hands (55.18, 625.15, 785.27–29). This is surprising for a culture in which letters were likely to be dictated, given the difficulty of writing on parchment, an act usually reserved for professional scribes. Belakane receives and reads a letter (in French) from Gahmuret (55.19f.), as do Gahmuret from Queen Ampflise (76.21), Arthur and Guenevere from Gawan (644.29, 649.7, 650.11/25), and Itonje from Gramoflanz, the last of which Arthur reads in public (714.21f.). Sigune and Guenevere read

[50] See Richard Kieckhefer, *Magic in the Middle Ages* (1989), 151–75. On Clinschor, see Walter Blank, "Der Zauberer Clinschor in Wolframs *Parzival*" (1989), and Timothy McFarland, "Clinschor. Wolfram's Adaptation of the *Conte du Graal*: The Schastel Marveile Episode" (1993).

[51] See Clanchy, *Memory*, 224–52; Fleckenstein, "Miles und clericus," 302–49.

[52] On the special interest in education among the landgraves of Thuringia, see Bumke, *Courtly Culture*, 432, and *Mäzene im Mittelalter* (1979), 159–68 and 378–83. See also Ursula Peters, *Fürstenhof und höfische Dichtung: Der Hof Hermanns von Thüringen als literarisches Zentrum* (1981).

their psalters at private devotions (438.1, 644.24), an activity that reflects the well-documented latinity of aristocratic women.[53] There is even one allusion to the education of a child, Obilot, whose tutor seems well versed in contemporary linguistic debates on *integumentum*:

> wan mir mîn meisterin verjach,
> diu rede wære des sinnes dach.
> (369.9f.)

For my tutor told me: "speech is the cover of meaning."

Finally, there is what might be called the group reading of the mysterious inscriptions that appear on the Grail (483.20, 484.9), forming an elite interpretive community. As we will see in Chapter 8, this "divine" narrative, inscribed by a divine author through a supernatural narrator for only a brief time on the edge of the Grail, but apparently legible to everyone in its presence, will prove to be an elusive text indeed—a supreme mystery in an age of transition from oral to written lay culture.

II

The analysis of the epilogue in the Introduction implied that although Wolfram's *Parzival* is conventionally designated as a romance, it is, contrary to the assumptions of many philologists and New Critics, not a self-contained authorial narrative in a unified genre. Its interacting narratives create a decentered and polygeneric discourse, open to dialogue with other texts as well as with the concept of genre itself. Because the identification of Wolfram's allusions to other texts and authors has largely been accomplished by earlier scholars,[54] a brief overview will suffice before turning to the problem of genre and an illustrative example of the narrative's generic openness, the bewildering diversity of statements about attaining the Grail.

Wolfram's references to other literary texts are so numerous that most of the corpus of Middle High German literature around 1200 is dated with reference to *Parzival*.[55] The explicit mention of authors, works, and literary characters includes, first and foremost, Hartmann von Aue's *Erec*, followed by Heinrich von Veldeke's *Eneit*, *Tristan* (probably in Eilhart von Oberge's version), Hartmann's *Iwein*, the *Nibelungenlied*, as well as other

[53] Bumke, *Courtly Culture*, 340–42.

[54] See the overview in Bernd Schirok, *Parzivalrezeption im Mittelalter* (1982), 18–27.

[55] See Werner Schröder, "Zur Chronologie der drei großen mittelhochdeutschen Epiker" (1957).

heroic epics, and Walther von der Vogelweide. Many allusions can be explained in context as illustrative comments on particular figures or their actions. For example, the pervasive references in Book VIII to Veldeke's *Eneit* and Germanic epics draw attention to the mock-epic nature of the episode, in which the relationship between Gawan and Antikonie or the conflict of Vergulaht and Kingrimursel have different outcomes from their literary referents, the encounter of Dido and Aeneas or the antagonisms of Germanic saga respectively. Other allusions, particularly to Hartmann's romances, seem more self-consciously intertextual. Whereas the remarks on Lunete's advice in *Iwein* occur in the Sigune scenes, creating a competing study of *triuwe*,[56] references to *Erec* escalate the competition to an extended genre battle over Arthurian narrative itself, to which we return in Chapters 3 and 4.

Beyond allusions to specific works and figures, the narrative often draws attention to its own heteroglossia by referring to or incorporating features of other genres. The lyric features most prominently in the narrator's participation in the Walther-Reinmar feud in the "Self-defense" between Books II and III, as well as in references to the narrative as better love service than song there, at the end of Book VI, and in the epilogue (114.5–116.4, 337.1–6, 827.25–30). The explicit reference to Walther von der Vogelweide opens a dialogue modeled on *Spruchdichtung* in the defense of Kay (297.24ff.). The epic appears on the margins of the narrative, first with the chanson de geste beginning of Gahmuret's disinheritance and the Aeneas-like stay with Belakane that also begins his part in the foundation of a dynasty, the typology between father and son being replicated in the move from epic to romance modes from Books I–II to III.[57] Chanson de geste elements return with the reminiscences of the *Rolandslied* that accompany Feirefiz and his massive heathen armies in the background of the final episodes.

The most important genre dialogue is that between the romance and the saint's life, two homologous forms of prenovelistic discourse representing competing approaches to secular existence.[58] The transformation of Trevrizent from knight to hermit follows a common legendary development from lay existence in the world to religious retreat from it, a pattern also traced earlier by Condwiramurs's uncles. The stages of Sigune's passion

[56] See my "'Sigune auf der Linde' and the Turtledove in *Parzival*" (1968).

[57] See, for example, Herbert Kolb, "Chanson-de-geste-Stil im *Parzival*" (1975); Petrus W. Tax, "Gahmuret zwischen Äneas und Parzival: Zur Struktur der Vorgeschichte von Wolframs *Parzival*" (1973).

[58] On the relation between saint's life and romance, see Max Wehrli, "Roman und Legende im deutschen Hochmittelalter," in his *Formen mittelalterlicher Erzählung* (1969), 155–76; Alison Goddard Elliott, *Roads to Paradise: Reading the Lives of the Early Saints* (1987).

and transfiguration seem to provide a secular alternative to this pattern, the vita of this *Minneheilige* suggesting how human love can also become a way to salvation. The beginning and especially the concluding events of Parzival's career also engage in the interplay between hagiographic and chivalric genre expectations. As we will see in later chapters, Herzeloyde's flight from the world, presented as anti-worldly asceticism, burdens her son with a consequential ignorance of knightly society, and Parzival's healing of the Fisher King competes with saintly miracles in the *Kaiserchronik.*

This polygeneric conception of Wolfram's narrative differs from the syncretic model usually suggested for romance. Its relationships with other genres involve more than mere "borrowing," because they are not synthesized into a single unifying discourse, but coexist and even compete—hence the metaphor of bitonality used earlier. We might illustrate this conception of *Parzival* as a heteroglot romance by interpreting a notorious textual problem in terms of its genre pluralism: the multiplicity of statements about winning the Grail. Indeed, the usual approach to the so-called *Gralprämissen* involves a reductiveness that the narrative does not allow, because it seems deliberately open to a variety of ways for resolving the hero's quest.

First, the requirement that the Grail hero be a knight (483.21) involves a chivalric quest. Given the fact that Wolfram's narrator defines himself in terms of knightly class, "schildes ambet ist mîn art" (115.11), and sends Parzival on a quest defined in knightly terms, "schildes ambet umben grâl" (333.27), it is not surprising to find at least one explicit reference to winning the Grail by fighting:

> wan swers grâles gerte,
> der muose mit dem swerte
> sich dem prîse nâhen.
> sus sol man prîses gâhen.
> (503.27–30)

For whoever desired the Grail had to make his way to the prize with the sword. Thus should one strive for fame.

Second, the narrative is replete with very different motifs emphasizing providence and grace. From his hermit uncle, Parzival learns that the Grail community in general consists only of those called by God (471.21ff.) and that the Grail in particular can only be won by divine dispensation:

jane mac den grâl nieman bejagn,
wan der ze himel ist sô bekant
daz er zem grâle ist benant.
(468.12–14)

Indeed, no one can win the Grail except that person who is acknowledged in heaven as being called to it.

Third, Wolfram also insists on the importance of *sippe*, relating the principal figures over several generations that ultimately go back to an "Adamic" ancestor, Mazadan; indeed, his narrative at times seems less the biography of the hero than the history of the Grail family, "the true stories about Frimutel's five children" (823.11f.). Accordingly, Parzival also wins the Grail by virtue of the fact that he is the sole viable co-heir to Frimutel's patrimony, "er was ouch ganerbe dar" (333.30).[59]

There thus seem to be three potential ways of attaining the Grail, fighting, being called, and inheriting, each of which reflects three major genres: romance narrative, saint's life or *legende*, and dynastic chronicle. These generically different approaches are not only valid on their own but also enter dialogically into combinations and permutations with one another. Given the emphasis on reconciling *got unde werlt* throughout *Parzival*, it is not surprising that the hero himself combines the first and second, fighting and being called, quoting Trevrizent to the effect that

den grâl ze keinen zîten
niemen möht erstrîten,
wan der von gote ist dar benant.
(786.5–7)

no one could ever win the Grail by fighting, except the person called to it by God.

The second and third ways to win the Grail, divine dispensation and inheritance, figure in the hero's differentiation of his father's worldly lands from the Grail kingdom:

Gahmuret mîn vater hiez,
der mirz mit rehtem erbe liez:
mit sælde ich gerbet hân den grâl.
(803.11–13)

[59] See Walter Delabar, *"Erkantiu sippe unt hoch gesellschaft": Studien zur Funktion des Verwandschaftsverbandes in Wolframs von Eschenbach "Parzival"* (1990), 200–20.

My father was Gahmuret, and he left me [Waleis and Norgals, etc.] as my lawful inheritance; with God's favor I have inherited the Grail.

The first and third, fighting and inheritance, predominate in the hero's problematic departure at the end of Book VI:

schildes ambet umben grâl
wirt nu vil güebet sunder twâl
von im den Herzeloyde bar.
er was ouch ganerbe dar.
(333.27–30)

He whom Herzeloyde bore will now engage in much knight-errantry in pursuit of the Grail. He was also co-heir to it.

And all three possibilities cadence, not surprisingly, in the summarizing statement in the epilogue, where the narrator combines family, striving, and predestination in concluding that the narrative has ultimately revealed

wie Herzeloyden kint den grâl
erwarp, als im daz gordent was
dô in verworhte Anfortas.
(827.6–8)

how Herzeloyde's child won the Grail, as was ordained for him after Anfortas had forfeited it.

One implication of this polyphonic treatment of the central theme of the Grail quest is that Wolfram's narrative may have exerted the profound influence suggested by its broad manuscript transmission not because of its message but, rather, because of its messages. As decentered, nonauthorial discourse, the text places a variety of narrative worlds in relation to each other, but does not fully privilege any of them. In acknowledging the plurality of existence through the interplay of genres and characters, the narrative validates many ways of negotiating quests through life. This multiplicity of possibilities and the avoidance of ideological closure, unlike the reductiveness of clerical strictures, makes understandable Wolfram's later reputation as the epitome of secular wisdom: "leien munt nie baz gesprach."[60]

[60] Wirnt von Grafenberg, *Wigalois der Ritter mit dem Rade* (1926), 6346.

III

A similar multiplicity surrounds the roles Wolfram constructs for himself and his protean narrator. The two are difficult to separate and often merge, like the analogous roles of lover and poet-performer in Minnesang.[61] However, they are inscribed in a more clearly delineated context demarcated on the one hand by the "source" attributed to Kyot and on the other by the reception posited for the text. We therefore begin with this larger context before focusing on "Wolfram."

As noted, Kyot's sources consist of two representative types of nonliterary discourse, scientific and historical. Both are repeatedly characterized as written, the former in heathen, or "heidenischer," script (453.13), the latter in Latin books, "latînschen buochen" (455.4). Flegetanis wrote about the Grail, "schreip" (453.30, 455.1), speaking (again we note the tendency to consider writing as speech) both its name and history (454.18/21). Kyot read—"las" (455.9/13)—his chronicles, finding the dynastic history of Mazadan written correctly, "geschriben rehte" (455.16), in Anjou. Both texts constitute Wolfram's source, what we earlier called *Kyots gesammelte Werke*. It might be most appropriate, therefore, to designate Kyot's imagined authorial role as that of a *scholarly compiler*, a role already assumed by twelfth-century historiographers, and one that later becomes increasingly important in exegetical and encyclopedic texts.[62]

Wolfram's narrative and its reception are also imagined as written. The famous comment at the end of Book VI asks the woman who sees this story written, "diu diz mære geschriben siht" (337.3), to avow that the author/narrator speaks better of women than he sang about one of them (337.5f.). It clearly presupposes a literate female audience capable of reading a written text, a reflection of the generally higher educational level of aristocratic women than men. And, in contrast to the topos of religious literature requesting readers and hearers to pray for the author, as in Hartmann's *Der arme Heinrich* (23) and *Gregorius* (3995), this is imagined as a purely secular activity. Moreover, on two occasions the narrator makes cross-references that can only be to a manuscript text. At the end of Book XV, Parzival leaves the Arthurian court, giving his version of the

[61] For recent examples, see Dietmar Peschel-Rentsch, "Wolframs Autor: Beobachtungen zur Entstehung der Autor-Figur an drei beispielhaften Szenen aus Wolframs *Parzival*" (1990), and, closer to the following, Adrian Stevens, "Heteroglossia and Clerical Narrative: On Wolfram's Adaptation of Chrétien" (1993), esp. 241–46.

[62] See A. J. Minnis, *Medieval Theory of Authorship* (1988). Minnis places the principal development of authorial roles in the thirteenth century; a study of twelfth-century histories and romances would suggest significant earlier developments.

conditions for attaining the Grail as stated by Trevrizent in Book IX, "als Trevrizent dort vorne jach" (786.4); at the beginning of Book XVI the narrator relates how the Grail inhabitants are awaiting the hero and the resolution of the crisis "als Trevrizent dort vorne jach" (788.15). In both cases, the deictic reference "dort vorne" directs readers literally and spatially "back there" to a previous section of the written manuscript.

Of course, this does not preclude the inscription of references to oral performance by the narrator.[63] His is a protean role, ranging from collusion with the audience, following "our hero"[64] or reminding us of something related before, to the aggressive bully of the prologue and the puzzle poser of the bow metaphor, or the shrinking authority at the beginning of Book XV, who asserts control of the narrative, only to become a cheering bystander in the battle between Parzival and Feirefiz, and then a passive witness to divine intervention. This narrator's allusions to his text as speech do not imply a transcription of an illiterate author's recitation, but represent a performance role, based on the idea that a written text is re-created in the act of reading aloud.[65]

Given such references to the written nature both of Wolfram's sources and the reception of his text, not to mention the extensive references to literary culture throughout *Parzival* (*none* of them in Chrétien's text), the fact that the main illiterate in the narrative seems to be the author-narrator himself should give us pause, and an appreciation of this irony finally seems to be taking hold.[66] The claim to illiteracy occurs only as a parenthetical statement in the larger context of the "Self-defense," namely, that the narrative should not be considered a book:

> swer des von mir geruoche,
> dern zels ze keinem buoche.
> ine kan decheinen buochstap.
> dâ nement genuoge ir urhap:
> disiu âventiure
> vert âne der buoche stiure.
> (115.25–30)

[63] For a listing of the now extensive literature, see Bumke, *Wolfram*, 193–94, especially Michael Curschmann, "Das Abenteuer des Erzählens: Über den Erzähler in Wolframs *Parzival*" (1971); Eberhard Nellmann, *Wolframs Erzähltechnik* (1973); Dennis H. Green, *The Art of Recognition in Wolfram's "Parzival"* (1982).

[64] Nellmann, *Wolframs Erzähltechnik*, 47–50, perceptively draws attention to the use of this technique in novels.

[65] See the topos "munde nie gelas" (224.14, 315.14, 326.24).

[66] See, for example, the revised standard introduction by Bumke, *Wolfram*, 7–8.

> Anyone who wants that of me should not count it as a book. I don't know a single letter of the alphabet. Enough books have their origin there: this narrative goes without the guidance of books.

As the narrator knows at least the letters "a b c" (453.15), this protestation cannot be taken literally. Indeed, as Hans Eggers and Friedrich Ohly suggested decades ago,[67] its basis is an exegetical topos based on Psalm 70.15, possibly suggesting the very opposite of what it seems to assert. Certainly it is hard to overlook the irony involved in a performance situation, in which the narrator claims illiteracy while reading *Parzival* to a courtly audience.[68]

Indeed, it seems increasingly likely that Wolfram was a latinized layman, which would account not only for the diversity of his imagined world but also for the borrowings from learned Latin culture that pervade his narratives. Nonetheless, the controversy over whether Wolfram obtained this wide knowledge through his own reading or through intermediaries still remains heated.[69] In support of the former possibility, I would like to present in abbreviated form the clearest example of Wolfram's connection to the written culture of the Latin Middle Ages:[70] his list of Greek snake names in 481.8–10, the context of which refers to handbooks of medicine, specifically to the use of herbs (481.6/15).

It should therefore not be surprising that the entire list can be found in some manuscripts of Pseudo-Apuleius's *Herbarius*, specifically in glosses to illustrations of snakes indicating various plants as antidotes to snakebite. Of particular interest is the fact that the first two snakes in Wolfram's list, "aspîs" and "ecidemon," originally comprised the gloss on an illustration of the battle between the asp and the snake-killing ichneumon. A German subbranch of the transmission corrupts *ichneumon* to *ecidemon*,[71] the exact form Wolfram uses for the snake list and the animal

[67] Hans Eggers, "*Non cognovi litteraturam* (zu *Parzival* 115.27)" (1963); Friedrich Ohly, "Wolframs Gebet an den heiligen Geist im Eingang des *Willehalm*" (1961/62).

[68] On this and the following, see Curschmann, "Hören—Lesen—Sehen," esp. 231–36.

[69] See Bumke, *Wolfram*, 7–10.

[70] For a more detailed discussion, see my "Wolframs Schlangenliste (*Parzival* 481) und Pseudo-Apuleius" (1994).

[71] This branch (a3) has German glosses as well as a similar iconographical and textual pattern. See Heide Grape-Albers, *Spätantike Bilder aus der Welt des Arztes* (1977), 2–4, 15–18, and 164–65. The gloss transmission is as follows in the two main Pseudo-Apuleius manuscripts, Leiden Cod. Voss. Lat. Q 40 (saec. xii) and Österreichische National-

on Feirefiz's heraldic emblem.[72] More interesting is the fact that Wolfram's doubling of the ecidemon as both snake and animal also seems traceable to this precise manuscript group, where the gloss becomes detached from the illustration, making it unclear whether "aspis ecidemon" refers to the snake and animal in that illustration or are serpents explaining the rubric indication that the herb cures snakebite. Although one could avoid the problem of Wolfram's literacy by insisting again that he had a clerical "assistant," it seems to me far more likely that the double reading of the *ecidemon* as both snake and animal will only have occurred to an imaginative reader-author who had to puzzle out for himself the ambiguous relationship between the snake gloss, indication, and illustration in a manuscript page of the *Herbarius.*

But how do we reconcile this evidence of Wolfram as a reader as well as his familiarity with foreign languages and written culture—none of it derived from Chrétien de Troyes—with the fact, emphasized by advocates of his illiteracy, that he nowhere admits to reading his source or writing his narrative, and explicitly claims an ignorance of letters? One should not exclude the possibility that Wolfram was only partly literate, his impressive learning an example of the still incompletely understood centrality of memorial techniques in the transition from oral to written culture. One might even suggest traces of that technique in Kyot's command that the narrator retain the story in his mind until it had to be told (453.5–10) or in the tendency of *Parzival* to be written in thirty-line segments—a possible reflex of the prevalence of numerical memory structures in twelfth-century education.[73]

However, it seems more plausible to me that Wolfram's claim is a carefully considered pose. Inasmuch as he emphasizes that the narrative is only a transposition of Kyot's, we might consider the dyad *litteratus*-Kyot/

---

bibliothek Cod. 187 (saec. xiii), and in the *Parzival* manuscripts D (St. Gallen 857) and G (Cgm 19):

Voss. 40	*Vienna 187*	*D*	G
aspis	aspis	aspis	aspis
ecidemon	ecidimon	ecidemon	ecidemon
acontios	acontios	ehcuntius	ehcontinus
lisis	lisis	lysis	lisis
iecis	jecis	jecis	Iecis
miatros	miatros	meatris	meatrys

[72] See 736.10, 739.16, 741.16, 756.24, 768.24. Wolfram also imagines a country called Ecidemonis (683.20).

[73] See Mary Carruthers, *The Book of Memory: A Study of Memory in Medieval Culture* (1990), esp. 29, 63, 80–107, and 124 on numerical memory grids, and the treatise "De tribus maximis circumstantiis gestorum" by Hugh of St. Victor on pp. 261–66.

illitteratus-Wolfram as symbolically representing the entire spectrum of authorial roles. Having constructed a fictitious source for the learned compiler Kyot, capable of synthesizing sources in Arabic and Latin into Old French, Wolfram fabricates a role for himself that is the opposite of a learned *meister*—the secular analphabetic. The construction of both roles may have more to do with the mixed clerical and knightly composition of his audience, their backgrounds and their prejudices, than with Wolfram himself. Moreover, the fiction of transposing the narrative of the learned cleric Kyot into that of the unlearned knight Wolfram recapitulates a process informing the narrative itself, namely, the appropriation of materials from Latin clerical culture into vernacular fiction.

Whatever the ultimate historical truth or fiction of Wolfram's role may be, his pose also serves ultimately to differentiate his narrative from existing Middle High German tradition. It is possible that it rejects what Russian formalists would call the antecedent "literary series" of his narrative, and this has usually been taken as a rejection of the "learned" Hartmann von Aue's romances. But the passage seems less specific than this, rejecting the bookishness of the existing First Line romance tradition in general, suggesting a conception of his narrative as a counterromance belonging "ze keinem buoche," and his "krumbes tiutsch" (*Willehalm*, 237.11) as a counterstyle. Both moves support Bakhtin's placement of his text in the Second Line anticipating the decentered discourse of the modern novel.

CHAPTER TWO

From Pastoral to Romance: The Grail Hero Discovers Knighthood

Salimbene of Parma, one of the most interesting commentators on the career of Emperor Friedrich II, relates with obvious disapprobation a variety of *superstitiones* tested on human subjects by that ruler, including several experiments in the behavioral sciences. On one occasion, the emperor wished to discover what language and mode of speech children would have if they grew up without hearing or speaking to anyone: "cuiusmodi linguam et loquelam haberent pueri, cum adolevissent, si cum nemine loquerentur."[1] He commanded the guardians of an unspecified test group to suckle and bathe their charges, but not to caress or speak to them, hoping thereby to ascertain whether they would speak Hebrew, Greek, Latin, Arabic, or the language of their natural parents. Unfortunately, the experiment failed, for the children were unable to live without the clapping of hands, the gestures, the silly faces, and the endearments of their wetnurses: "Non enim vivere possent sine aplausu et gestu et letitia faciei et blanditiis baiularum et nutricum suarum." Commentators cite an experiment of Pharaoh Psamtik referred to by Herodotus (II.2) or a later attempt attributed to James IV, and one could also add the extensive discussion from classical antiquity to the present about natural language and "wild" children.

But it might be more interesting to repress such diachronic urges and consider a medieval analogue to Friedrich's experiment. Indeed, the question whether "nurture" or "nature" is more important, particularly whether acquired learning or innate ability predominates in child development, becomes an issue in twelfth-century literature as the communal

[1] Salimbene of Parma, *Cronica Fratris Salimbene de Adam Ordinis Minorum* (1905–13), 350. For a survey of the larger context of Friedrich's experiments, see Thomas Curtis Van Cleve, *The Emperor Frederick II of Hohenstaufen* (1972), 317.

and defensive focus of the heroic epic is challenged by an interest in the individual and his development in romance.[2] Arthurian narratives in particular seem to have been fascinated by a fictional experiment similar to Friedrich's, but less extreme in conception and outcome: a noble youth is raised by a mother or mother-surrogate in isolation from society, where he is denied the education appropriate to his gender, station, and heritage.

The situation raises a variety of questions in the nurture/nature controversy, questions of no little concern for an aristocracy avidly engaged in legitimizing itself dynastically through a politics of marriage. What will happen when the youth comes in contact with knightly society? How far can he develop on his own? Put less circumspectly: does nobility always manifest itself? The literary "experiment," commissioned by members of this same aristocracy for an aristocratic audience, raises the satisfying prospect of asking what will happen in the apparent absence of the benefits of genealogy and consanguinity, and then confirms their powerful influence as the narrative moves toward its happy end, often concluding in a marriage that reaffirms the hero's heritage and points to its dynastic continuation.

Romance lends itself to representing a hero's search for identity and a place in the chivalric world, particularly through the knightly quest,[3] which is often played out between different worlds with potentially heterogeneous genre expectations and chronotopes. Usually the narrative shifts from otherworldly to chivalric realms, with an implicit progression from fairy tale to romance. The most prevalent version seems to be that of The Fair Unknown (*Le Bel Inconnu*), the son of a fairy mother and a knight-errant, often Gawan (the playboy of the Arthurian world), who leaves the maternal Otherworld in order to discover his identity and paternal heritage in chivalric society. The "sources" of the story and the relationships between texts are still debated.[4] Other Arthurian heroes also experience an isolated childhood, for example in Ulrich von Zatzikhoven's *Lanzelet* (ca. 1210) or the Old French and Middle High German

[2] See R. W. Southern, "From Epic to Romance," in his *The Making of the Middle Ages* (1953), 219–57; R. W. Hanning, *The Individual in Twelfth-Century Romance* (1977).

[3] See Friedrich Ohly, "Die Suche in Dichtungen des Mittelalters" (1965); Anthony van der Lee, *Zum literarischen Motiv der Vatersuche* (1957).

[4] See the still basic studies of Albert Mennung, *Der "Bel Inconnu" des Renaut de Beaujeu in seinem Verhältnis zum "Lybeaus Disconus," "Carduino" und "Wigalois"* (1890), and William Henry Schofield, *Studies on the "Libeaus Desconus"* (1895). The attempt of D. D. R. Owen, "The Development of the Perceval Story" (1959), to derive the Fair Unknown stories from a Celtic source and *Perceval* from it is unconvincing. For a more reasoned analysis, see Christoph Cormeau, *"Wigalois" und "Diu Crône": Zwei Kapitel zur Gattungsgeschichte des nachklassischen Aventiureromans* (1977), 68–103.

prose *Lancelot* (ca. 1230). Moreover, the "experiment" can also be conducted in romances with a different genre heteroglossia—between chivalric and religious socio-literary expectations, as in Hartmann von Aue's *Gregorius,* or between chivalric and mercantile ones, as in *Guillaume d'Angleterre.* By the late thirteenth century, the conventions were familiar enough for Heldris de Cornuälle's *Roman de Silence* to present a radical twist based on the construction of gender rather than class: the orphaned hero is actually a heroine, whose proposed education as a boy engenders a protracted debate between Natura and Noreture (Nurture).[5]

The most famous—and possibly earliest—version of this theme seems to be that of the Grail hero, whose mother retires from courtly society after her husband dies in knightly combat, hoping thereby to prevent her infant son from suffering the identical fate. Withdrawing to an isolated forest, she establishes a noncourtly community based on farming and hunting, and forbids her vassals to mention knighthood to her son, lest he be tempted to follow in his father's spursteps. This shift to an "alternative" existence also has narratological implications, suggesting a regression from romance to pastoral modes. When the inevitable happens and the hero accidentally encounters a group of knights, the meeting triggers an irresistible desire to realize his innate potential and sets him on a quest that ultimately integrates him into the chivalric world.

Although the basic story apparently derives from widespread types of the folk tale,[6] both Chrétien de Troyes and Wolfram von Eschenbach present the episode in remarkably different ways.[7] Both recognize the necessary interaction of personality and social context in the development of their heroes. They differ radically, however, in the introductory focus and the genre structures in which it is inscribed. Chrétien seems to render the hero's discovery of knighthood as a paradigmatic treatment of "nurture" or socialization, only to reveal later in a reversal typical of his rhetorical style that the hero's rapid progress from pastoral to chivalric existence is actually made possible by his inborn nature (1480–84). Wolfram reads Chrétien's story against the grain, beginning with the "nature" or innate ability of his hero, only to subordinate this reversal to a more fundamental binarism informing Parzival's career and the genre expectations in which it is emplotted: the dialogue between salvation history and individual development, God and the world, religious narrative and chivalric romance.

[5] Heldris de Cornuälle (1972), 2257–2688.

[6] See Wolfgang Mohr, "Parzival und die Ritter" (1958); Dennis Green, "Parzival's Departure—Folktale and Romance" (1980).

[7] In addition to the works cited above, see Karl Bertau, "Versuch über den späten Chrestien und die Anfänge Wolframs" (1972); rpt. in his *Wolfram von Eschenbach: Neun Versuche* (1983), esp. 40–47.

I

Chrétien's romance begins with an introductory scene in which the unnamed "son of the widow lady of the lonely wild forest" (74f.) leaves his mother's manor one morning to visit her harrowers, whom he eventually encounters laboring in the woods of Valdone (295ff.). But a posse of five knights interrupts the hero's journey, and his responses to their questions interrupt in turn their hot pursuit of several fugitives.[8] The scene consists of three distinct sections: (1) the hero's departure and reaction to the approach of the knights (69–158); (2) the moment of the encounter (159–81); and (3) a lengthy mutual interrogation that concludes with the continuation of their respective journeys (182–361/64).

Chrétien commences the action of his story with a *Natureingang*, or nature-introduction, describing the joys of a spring morning,

> Ce fu au tans qu'arbre florissent,
> Fuellent boschage, pré verdissent
> Et cil oisel an lor latin
> Doucemant chantent au matin
> Et tote riens de joie anflame
> (69–73)

It was the season when trees bloom, bushes put forth leaves, meadows turn green, birds in their language sweetly sing at dawn, and all things are aflame with joy

to which the youth responds spontaneously:

> Et maintenant li cuers del vantre
> Por le douz tans li resjoï,
> Et por le chant que il oï
> Des oisiaus qui joie feisoient:
> Totes cez choses li pleisoient.
> (86–90)

And at once the heart in his chest rejoiced at the sweet season and the song that he heard of rejoicing birds: all these things pleased him.

The parallels between the objective natural setting and a subjective reaction to it, between external and internal pleasure in the season, imply a

[8] See Peter Haidu, *Aesthetic Distance in Chrétien de Troyes* (1968), 113–26; Rupert T. Pickens, *The Welsh Knight: Paradoxicality in Chrétien's "Conte del Graal"* (1977), 71–88.

preconscious state of wholeness in which the nameless hero is a still undifferentiated member of the natural world. At the same time, the similarity of this *Natureingang* to common motifs of the courtly love lyric, such as the expansive heart, draws attention to the larger range of social expectations as well as to corresponding literary ones that will be raised during the course of this scene. The pastoral world is contiguous with the world of courtly romance into which Perceval will soon be assimilated.[9]

The simpler harmony of that pastoral world is immediately disturbed by a "mout grant noise" (103), a cacophony of unfamiliar artifacts intruding on the joyful sounds of spring. Knightly society impinges on the natural scene in two parallel and increasingly detailed stages. Each proceeds from the external action to Perceval's responses, emphasizing the interruption of his forest journey and focusing our attention on his reaction, first to hearing and then to seeing armed knights on horseback for the first time. The whole is a masterpiece of rhetorical brilliance that reflects Chrétien's clerical delight in manipulating his material.[10]

The first of these two stages begins by identifying the source of the intrusion, five armed knights, and the hero's aural perception, "il oï" (100). In accordance with the rapid approach of the intruders and its vivid impression on the youth, the ensuing lines dilate on this description by means of progressive amplification. The narrator explains the noise in general terms as emanating from the arms of the approaching figures: "Et mout grant noise demenoient / Les armes de çaus qui venoient" (103–4). He then becomes more precise, specifying the branches of oaks and hornbeams against which those arms resound, "Car sovant hurtoient as armes / Li rain des chasnes et des charmes" (105–6), before identifying the particular components of knightly equipment—lances, shields, and hauberks (leitmotifs of the entire scene, as we will see)—and the noises particular to them:

> Les lances as escuz hurtoient,
> Et tuit li hauberc fremilloient;
> Sonoit li fuz, sonoit li fers
> Et des escuz et des haubers.
> (107–10)

[9] Two further motifs underscore the prefigurative nature of Perceval's childhood, his already extensive practice at kissing (albeit with the bitter-tasting mouths of his mother's handmaidens, 725–28) and self-defense (with pillows and shields, 1531–35). By means of such ironic revelations what seems at first glance to be socialization is revealed as equally due to Perceval's inborn aristocratic nature.

[10] See Bertau, "Versuch," 40–42, 48–49.

> The lances knocked against the shields, and all the hauberks clinked; the wood and the iron of the shields and hauberks resounded.

A further reference to the fact that the hero can hear but not see, "li vaslez ot et ne voit pas" (111), introduces his inaccurate subjective response in an interior monologue, which proceeds deductively from his mother's instructions to associate these sounds with devils.

When the knights finally come into view, the narrator repeats the entire process of progressive amplification and subjective response, which is now based on sight. This second stage begins again with a general reference to the intruders and the hero's perception, "il les veïst" (126). It also becomes more specific as he sees them emerge from the forest, "il les vit an apert / Que del bois furent descovert" (127f.), proceeding to catalogue precisely what the hero perceives ("et . . . et")—the lances, shields, and hauberks he has just heard, as well as their colors:

> Et vit les haubers fremianz
> Et les hiaumes clers et luisanz
> Et les lances et les escuz
> Que onques mes n'avoit veüz,
> Et vit le vert et le vermoil
> (129–35)

> And he saw the jingling hauberks, and the bright, gleaming helmets, and the lances and the shields—which he had never seen before—and he saw the green and the vermilion.

The description of Perceval's response again introduces an interior monologue that deductively associates his sensory perceptions with the instruction of his mother. In accordance with the rhetorical drama of this scene as well as with the narrative's emphasis on the hero's ignorance of external reality, the monologue expands through two deliberations, the first identifying what he now sees as angels, the opposite of what he heard,[11] "Ce sont ange que je voi ci" (138), the second escalating this assessment to include the supreme being: "Ci voi je Damedeu" (146). Both provide a further example of Perceval's inability to associate unfamiliar things or forms of behavior with their meaning.

The actual meeting between Perceval and the knights—a "close encounter of the third kind" between pastoral and chivalric worlds—nar-

[11] The opposite associations via sound and sight are not gratuitous: the devil is often associated with noise, angels with luminescence.

rows the focus on the hero's foolishness and prepares for the carnivalizing social comedy of their mutual interrogation. Having misassociated unfamiliar *signantia* with unknown *signata*, sounds and sights with the extremes of creation, devils and angels as well as God, the youth proceeds to misapply his conclusion to a received form of behavior, throwing himself to the ground and reciting *all* the creed and prayers he knows (156–58). This extreme response in turn causes the knights to assume that the youth might die of fright. Their first exchange initiates a process of mutual correction in which the assumptions of the one are negated by the other: the knights' assumption of Perceval's fear by his "'Non ai je [peor]'" (172), his "'Estes vos Deus?'" by their emphatic denial (174). The open-ended reformulation and positive response in one lapidary line, "'Qui estes dons?'—'Chevaliers sui'" ("Who are you then?"—"I am a knight" [175]), narrows the cosmic confusion to a courtly comedy of errors.

The narrator provides us first with a preliminary understanding of Perceval's misconception of the approaching knights (132), which the hero soon confirms: he has neither seen nor heard of them before: "'ne nul n'an vi / N'onques mes parler n'an oï'" (177f.). We now understand the constant emphasis on the hero's sensory perceptions. According to a widespread concept known as intromission (the psychological counterpart of nurture), perception depends primarily on the action of external sensory impressions on the mind, which stimulate it to match them with images stored in the memory.[12] Having no courtly *imaginatio*, no already acquired store of images of aristocratic life to match with what he perceives, the hero can only engage in free association. Perceval's socialization therefore begins by establishing a repository of images for functioning in knightly society—hence the importance of things and their names, such as the lances, shields, and hauberks already introduced as leitmotifs of the encounter.

The final segment of the encounter between Perceval and the knights, a delightful mutual interrogation, exemplifies Henri Bergson's category of comedy designated as the "interférence des séries," and has a variety of analogues in medieval *Schwank* literature and folk tales.[13] In this version of that pattern, Perceval frustrates the knight's requests for information by

[12] The basic classical and patristic sources for this idea are Boethius, *De consolatio Philosophiae* (V. Met. iv.33–40), CCSL 94.98–99, and St. Augustine, *De Trinitate* (Book XI), CCSL 50, 332–55. For a survey, see E. Ruth Harvey, *The Inward Wits: Psychological Theory in the Middle Ages and the Renaissance* (1975).

[13] On the comedy, see Haidu, *Aesthetic Distance*, 120–26; on Schwank motifs, see Mohr, "Parzival und die Ritter," 203–4.

responding with questions of his own instead. In spite of the knight's repetition of his question in four increasingly insistent attempts to force Perceval's attention back to his request, the hero does not desist from his own questions until his own curiosity is satisfied.

The broad humor of this exchange of non sequiturs proves to be subversive, revealing the inherently carnivalizing nature of the encounter between pastoral and chivalric worlds, which is emphasized by the foolish hero's incomprehension of the habitual discourses of the knights.[14] Although the knight and Perceval assume a relationship of authority and subservience that is maintained in their forms of address, "vaslez" or "tu" and "sir" or "vos," respectively, the conversation actually questions this relationship, destabilizing the superior power and authority assumed by the chivalric world. Whereas the *vaslet*'s incongruous questions seem ignorant or foolish (200, 245–48), they gradually reveal a wily self-interest, eliciting information about knightly weapons that enables him to judge their effectiveness and potential threat to his pastoral existence (202–7, 273–76). At the same time, the knight's condescending responses to Perceval's questions gradually reveal a touch of foolishness in his pompous restating of the obvious (195–97, 236–41).

This exchange stereotypes the hero as literal-minded and the knight as metaphorically inclined. Perceval conflates the relationship between things and names, which leads to the assumption that his interlocutor's name is "Knight" (190) and that one can be "made" (181, 333) or transformed (285) into a knight like some artifact. It also reveals that the relationship between signifiers and things signified in any society is arbitrary and based on conventions that are not free of incongruity. The fact that the knights are also uncertain about this relationship reveals in turn the uncertain ontological grounding of courtly society and its tenuous authority vis-à-vis the narrator's implicitly clerical stance.

Chrétien illustrates the point three times with the now familiar three pieces of knightly equipment, beginning with the lance. Because Perceval is an expert at throwing, "lancier" (95), a javelot, which the narrator emphasizes at the outset of his journey by throwing, "lançant" (97), a series of warm-up tosses in rhetorically complete but impractical directions (ahead and behind, up and down [98–99]), he is surprised to discover that a lance is not thrown but used to strike a blow. The knight, who has never thought about the meaning of his weapon, is equally surprised to discover that anyone would assume a lance is *lancee*, a discrepancy that

[14] See Mikhail Bakhtin, "Discourse in the Novel," in *The Dialogic Imagination* (1981), 402, and the discussion of Gary Saul Morson and Caryl Emerson, *Mikhail Bakhtin: The Creation of a Prosaics* (1990), 360–61.

Chrétien emphasizes by means of *annominatio*, revealing his clerical perspective (in which etymology is a dominant pattern of thought),[15]

> "Jel te dirai: ce est ma *lance.*"
> "Dites vos" fet il, "qu'an la *lance*
> Si con je faz mes javeloz?"
> "Nenil, vaslez, tu es toz soz,
> Einz an fiert an tot demanois."
> (197–201)

> "I'll tell you: it is my lance." "Tell me," he said, "does one throw it as I do my javelins?" "Not at all, young sir, you are very foolish; one strikes a blow with it."

Similarly, the fact that what a knight carries in his hand "is called" a shield, "'Escuz a non ce que je port,'" causes Perceval to question the separation of the name from the thing, "'Escuz a non?'" (224f.), and the knight to dissociate the significance from the thing, embarking on a flight of feudal allegory that attributes to the shield the "bone foi" and "servises" of a trusty vassal (227–30). Finally, the knight transfers his metaphorical inclinations from the feudal to the futile, bathetically asserting that a hauberk is as heavy as iron because it is made of iron: "'S'est aussi pesanz come fers, / Qu'il est de fer'" (263–65).[16]

This carnivalizing exchange frames the beginning of Perceval's career, illustrating the gap between the hero's uncultured ignorance, which makes him appear less than human, even beastlike, to condescending courtly observers (244–48), and the knight's naive familiarity with the arbitrary *lois* that govern all societal activity from the names of things to the manners of human interaction. The chivalric socialization of Perceval will soon bridge this gap, and in fact it has already begun. Perceval's first three questions—not surprisingly—concern the lance, shield, and hauberk, the three pieces of knightly equipment whose unfamiliar sight and sound initially led to his misidentification of knights. Now that his hereditary sphere of interest has been revealed and stimulated, these same pieces of equipment illustrate his progress in learning about the realia of knightly society. The hero first inquires only what the lance is, "'Que est ice que vos tenez?'" (191), then asks about the shield as well as its use,

[15] See Ernst Robert Curtius, "Etymology as a Category of Thought," in his *European Literature and the Latin Middle Ages* (1963), 495–500.

[16] The majority of manuscripts have this reading, rather than the reductive variant "de fer est il?" chosen by Hilka.

"'Ce que est et de quoi vos sert?'" (214), and finally demands to know what the hauberk is, what the knight does with it, and what use it has: "'Qu'est ce que vos avez vestu? / . . . Qu'an feites vos et que vos vaut?'" (261–68).

Furthermore, the knight's responses to these progressively more complicated and inclusive questions elicit comments from Perceval in turn that compare his presocial natural world with the chivalric world and reveal his growing interest in the latter. Perceval's first response rejects the lance in favor of a javelin because the latter can be thrown to kill animals at a greater distance (202–8). The next response again ignores the chivalric use of armor in order to apply it to the hunting situation with which he is familiar, but indirectly acknowledges the superiority of the strange weapon (273–76). The hero's third response, a series of questions rather than a defensive value judgment, probes the basic difference between his natural state and the social state of the knights. Knights are not born, but made:

> Li dist: "Fustes vos einsi nez?"
> "Nenil, vaslez, ce ne puet estre
> Que nule riens puisse einsi nestre."
> "Qui vos atorna donc einsi?"
> (282–85)

He said: "were you born this way?" "Not at all, young sir, no one can be born like this." "Then who dressed you this way?"

By the conclusion of the encounter, the apparent difference between the knowledgeable *chevaliers* and the ignorant *vaslet* has narrowed appreciably. We see this particularly in the changing relationship between the two, in the increasing affinity of the knight for the youth to whom he initially condescends, "biaus douz amis" (194), but whom he quickly comes to like (223) and is loath to leave (250–52), and whom he finally calls "biaus frere" (299). The two are indeed related. The *seignor* of the knights is not that different from the *seignor* of the manor. The young knight, who was dubbed only five days previously and fills his new role somewhat awkwardly, is but a slightly older version of Perceval, whom Gornemant will knight in turn a few days hence. Chrétien's representation of chivalric society is not radically disparate from the presocial pastoral world. Implicit socialization begun by the chance encounter now becomes the explicit goal of a quest, and the pastoral hero enters the world of romance.

II

The encounter between the hero and knights in Wolfram von Eschenbach's *Parzival* is considerably shorter than in his source. The difference is substantial: Chrétien's scene extends for 292 lines (69–361), Wolfram's for only 169 (120.11–125.30). This is a surprising anomaly, given the general tendency of medieval adaptations—including Wolfram's romance as a whole—to be longer than their sources. Earlier scholarship explained this tendency either by the loss of Gallic charm or by the infusion of German profundity, depending on which side of the Rhine it originated on. Recent work suggests that medieval "translation" required fidelity to the sense (i.e., content and actions), but allowed greater freedom of character and motivation as well as style and expression.[17] In most instances, there resulted what we might call a commenting translation.

But Wolfram explicitly suggests that his predecessor may not have done justice to the story (827.1–2), and he seems to engage in a subversive rereading of Chrétien's introductory scene, decentering its authoritative rhetorical stance and easy genre transition from pastoral to romance and foregrounding the scene's implicitly heteroglossic conflict between two diverse worlds. The reduction and rearrangement of the hero's encounter with knights presents a more complicated and disjunctive relationship between narrative expectations such as heredity and socialization, knightly adventure and religious norms. Wolfram creates a pattern of conflict and interference whose resolution—clerical hierarchy and secular appropriation seem to be implicit options—becomes the goal of Parzival's career.

The most immediate and obvious difference between the two romances stems from their differing points of departure.[18] Since Chrétien's narrative begins with this scene, the audience shares Perceval's ignorance of his heritage while it observes his responses to hearing, seeing, and talking to armed knights for the first time, and it must gradually be informed by the development of the story as well as by narrative asides. In Wolfram's narrative, however, the audience already knows the background of Parzival's parents from Books I and II, and it has already learned from the first 125 lines of Book III much of what must be intimated or revealed during the course of Chrétien's scene.

The most consequential result of placing Parzival's encounter with the knights in this larger context is that the beginning of Book III can suggest Parzival's development *before* he has any contact with the outside chivalric world. Although he is not yet mature, "versunnen" (117.19, 161.7), and

[17] See Carl Lofmark, "Der höfische Dichter als Übersetzer" (1972).

[18] See Green, "Parzival's Departure," 379–80.

is deprived of his kingly heritage (118.2) and contact with knighthood (117.20–29), Parzival develops nonetheless. And he develops not through any process of socialization, as does Chrétien's hero, but through the emergence of characteristics and interests inherited from his parents. In terms of the modern slogan: innate nature,[19] not external nurture, seems to predominate at the beginning of Parzival's development. In terms of audience expectations, Wolfram appears to undermine the suspense of the "experiment" by confirming the importance of aristocratic heritage at the beginning of the hero's career rather than having it emerge gradually.

As always with Wolfram, however, there are complications. Parzival's parents, like those of his Old French counterpart, are members of the knightly aristocracy, but they are descended from two different societies within that aristocracy: Gahmuret from the Arthurian world, in which Parzival begins his knightly career; Herzeloyde from the Grail world, of which he will ultimately be regent. Both worlds, represented by heterogeneous chronotopes with divergent conceptions of time and space, also involve the hero in different types of adventures, inscribing his career in a nexus of multiple genre expectations.

The paternal influence emerges first, which the narrator emphasizes in an introductory reference to the hero as "Gahmuretes kint" (117.15). Gahmuret's epitaph celebrates him as unmatched in any land by any man yet born (108.13–16), and it quickly becomes clear that the strapping son born to Herzeloyde after his death will be that man. We first see Parzival learning to fashion a bow and arrow for shooting birds; he soon progresses to larger game with a javelin, a more lethal but still unknightly weapon, bringing home stags on his shoulders, as—unlike Chrétien's *vaslet*—he does not even seem to have been taught to ride a horse. In addition to such prowess, a second characteristic emerges as he listens to birdsong while hunting:

> die süeze in sîn herze dranc:
> daz erstracte im sîniu brüstelîn.
> (118.16f.)

The sweetness pierced his heart; it made his little bosom swell.

When the watchful Herzeloyde notices the emotional impact on Parzival, she immediately associates it with his heritage:

[19] See Julius Schwietering, "Natur und *art*" (1961/62).

si wart wol innen daz zeswal
von der stimme ir kindes brust.
des twanc in art und sîn gelust.
(118.26–28)

She noticed that the birdsong swelled her child's breast. His inborn nature and desire so compelled him.

She is entirely correct, as a similar expansion of the breast—also described with *swillen* and the rhyme *brust/gelust*—characterizes Gahmuret's definition of his own indeterminate striving in the opening scene of Book I:

"mîn herze iedoch nâch hœhe strebet:
ine weiz war umbez alsus lebet,
daz mir swillet sus mîn winster brust.
ôwê war jaget mich mîn gelust?"
(9.23–26)

"But my heart strives towards the heights: I do not know why it beats so that my left breast swells so. O where does my desire drive me?"

These two characteristics, prowess and emotional sensitivity, clearly reveal that in spite of his social deprivation, Parzival is very much the son of his father, already evincing the innate natural capacity for knightly deeds and love that traditionally identify the hero of chivalric romance.

The emergence of Herzeloyde's heritage in the young Parzival is less easy to document, partly because that influence at first seems negative. In contrast to Chrétien's pastoral beginning, her retreat to the wasteland after Gahmuret's death evokes genre expectations of the saint's life.[20] The opening prologue of Book III draws attention to her eremitical existence with a commentary on womanly fidelity and vows of poverty, singling out Herzeloyde as a woman who gives up "the world's riches" for "the glory of heaven" (116.23f.)—all topoi of the hagiographic romance.[21] Even the emphasis on the *herzen jâmer* (117.6 and 11) that plays with the etymology

[20] The saint's life and the romance are closely related. See Max Wehrli, *Formen mittelalterlicher Erzählung* (1969), 155–76; Charles Altman, "Two Types of Opposition and the Structure of Latin Saints' Lives" (1975); Alison Goddard Elliott, *Roads to Paradise: Reading the Lives of the Early Saints* (1987), 42–102; and Bakhtin's comments on the "novel of ordeal" in "The *Bildungsroman* and Its Significance in the History of Realism," in *Speech Genres and Other Late Essays* (1986), 11–13.

[21] See Sidney M. Johnson, "Herzeloyde and the Grail" (1968), esp. 155; Alois Wolf, "*Ein mære wil ich niuwen, daz saget von grôzen triuwen*: Vom höfischen Roman Chrétiens zum Meditationsgeflecht der Dichtung Wolframs" (1985), esp. 10–17.

of her name reminds us of the penitential focus of this new life. Herzeloyde's retreat pointedly negates the chronotopic parameters of courtly existence—the homology of sunshine and activity, the setting in a pleasance landscape, and the emphasis on joy represented by the summer dance with garlands:

> ein nebel was ir diu sunne:
> si vlôch der werlde wunne.
> ir was gelîch naht unt der tac:
> ir herze niht wan jâmers phlac.
> Sich zôch diu frouwe jâmers balt
> ûz ir lande in einen walt,
> zer waste in Soltâne;
> niht durch bluomen ûf die plâne.
> ir herzen jâmer was sô ganz,
> sine kêrte sich an keinen kranz
> (117.3–12)

> The sun was as a fog to her: she fled the joys of the world. Night and day were the same to her: her heart found nothing but grief. Thus the grief-stricken lady moved from her kingdom to a forest, to the wasteland of Soltane, not for the sake of flowers on the meadow. Her heart's grief was so total that she paid no attention to any garland.

But although Herzeloyde's eremitical retreat deprives her son of a worldly education, she does not concern herself with his spiritual training either. Unlike Perceval, who already knows the creed and a series of prayers by heart (156–58), receiving detailed instructions about behavior in churches and minsters, Parzival is disadvantaged even in this respect, and will not learn socially acceptable norms of religious behavior until Gurnemanz takes him into his care. Fortunately, the hero is not a tabula rasa religiously, because the *imago Dei* assumed to be in every human being enables him to respond instinctively to the word *God.* In accordance with Wolfram's reversal of emphasis from nurture to nature, this response is extramissive rather than intromissive.[22] Parzival intuitively yearns to understand an innate idea before he begins to experience the world.[23] Proceeding from a question about Herzeloyde's slaughter of the

[22] See David C. Lindberg, "Alhazen's Theory of Vision and Its Reception in the West" (1967), esp. 321–22.

[23] On the relationship between naming and experience, see Irene Hänsch, "*Parzivâl. der nam ist rehte enmitten durch*: Zum Problem von Namen und Identität in Wolframs *Parzival*" (1982).

birds to one about God, he establishes a larger concern about the creator and his creatures that hovers over his entire knightly career and will be raised again after his failure at the Grail castle, "wê waz ist got?" (332.1).

Herzeloyde's answer characteristically has little to do with socialization and social forms:

> "ôwê muoter, waz ist got?"
> "sun, ich sage dirz âne spot.
> er ist noch liehter denne der tac,
> der antlitzes sich bewac
> nâch menschen antlitze.
> sun, merke eine witze,
> und flêhe in umbe dîne nôt:
> sîn triwe der werlde ie helfe bôt.
> sô heizet einr der helle wirt:
> der ist swarz, untriwe in niht verbirt.
> von dem kêr dîne gedanke,
> und och von zwîvels wanke."
> (119.17–28)

> "O mother, what is God?" "Son, I tell you without jest. He is brighter than the day, who took upon himself the countenance of a man. Son, note this wisdom and pray to him in need: His fidelity always offered the world help. But there is one called the Lord of hell: he is black, and faithlessness does not avoid him. Turn your thoughts from him, and also from inconstant wavering."

This instruction is neither heretical nor misleading, as scholars have occasionally claimed;[24] rather, it reduces religion to basic elements:[25] the antithesis between light and dark as well as God and the devil, the incarnation of the word, and the right and wrong relationships, respectively, between man and God, man and the devil. In keeping with her ascetic withdrawal from the chivalric world to the pastoral world, in which the queen and her son the squire live in apparently unmediated harmony with her peasants and farmhands, Herzeloyde practices a faith indepen-

[24] See Walter Johannes Schröder, *Die Soltane-Erzählung in Wolframs "Parzival"* (1963); Alois Haas, *Parzivals "tumpheit" bei Wolfram von Eschenbach* (1964), 56–71; and Gertrud Jaron Lewis, "Die unheilige Herzeloyde" (1975).

[25] On this passage as a "winziges Religionskompendium" in accord with biblical imagery and dogma, see Benedikt Mockenhaupt, *Die Frömmigkeit im "Parzival" Wolframs von Eschenbach* (1942; rpt. 1968), 63.

dently of any social situation or social forms.[26] This extreme solution seems satisfactory for her (as it was for St. Francis and popular religious movements): the narrator's lament over her death is hagiographical in tone, emphasizing that her virtues spared her the pains of purgatory.[27] It remains to be seen, however, whether Parzival's career can accommodate his dual heritage from Herzeloyde and Gahmuret, the pluralistic role models of isolation from and involvement in society, pastoral/religious narrative and chivalric romance.

The encounter with the knights illustrates the difficulty of this resolution in paradigmatic fashion. In accordance with the apparent reversal of emphasis from "nurture" to "nature," Wolfram reduces the beginning of the encounter, eliminating Chrétien's rhetorical amplification of Perceval's sensory perceptions in order to reduce the emphasis on intromission and socialization. Thus, when Parzival embarks on his hunt, he is not already attuned to the joyful sounds of the world around him, but intently produces his own music, breaking off a branch to make a whistle from a leaf. And when the knights interrupt him a few moments later, there is no increasingly precise description of the weapons he hears, but merely the observation that he hears hoofbeats before associating this noise with the devil (120.15–23). Furthermore, there is no corresponding repetition to describe how Parzival sees the approaching knights. What comprises the first eighty-nine lines of Chrétien's scene takes only twelve in Wolfram's.

The reduction of the conclusion to this episode is even more drastic. Wolfram's inquisitive knight, Karnahkarnanz, requests information from the hero about the fugitives only once, eliminating Chrétien's humorous series of five questions and non sequitur responses. And whereas Perceval responds with a series of progressively more complicated questions about knightly equipment and makes a progressively more positive comparison of the chivalric world with his own, Parzival seems to regress instead. After asking first about knights and knighting (123.4/6), he gradually disappoints Karnahkarnanz's assumption that he may be of knightly lineage by simpering over the chain-mail skin of his interlocutor,

> "waz mahtu sîn?
> du hâst sus manec vingerlîn
> an dînen lîp gebunden"
> (123.21–23)

[26] One could even see resemblances to the "religion reduced to an essential core," in opposition to the "learned subtleties" of high culture, that social historians find in early popular culture. See Carlo Ginzburg, *The Cheese and the Worms: The Cosmos of a Sixteenth-Century Miller* (1982), 25.

[27] See my "Wolfram's Lament for Herzeloyde (*Parzival* 128.23ff.)" (1974).

"What might you be? You have so many little rings bound to your body."

The knight's reply describes the use of sword and chain mail as weapons in the give-and-take of combat, which Parzival, still thinking of chain mail as skin, uncomprehendingly reduces to the hunting situation familiar to him:

"ob die hirze trüegen sus ir vel,
so verwunt ir niht mîn gabylôt.
der vellet manger vor mir tôt."
(124.12–14)

"If the stags wore their skin this way, my javelot would not wound them—
It fells many of them dead in front of me."

This exchange does not reveal progressive adaptation to knightly society, but persistent foolishness. It is not surprising that the narrator calls Parzival *tump* for the first time at this juncture (124.16) or that the knights depart, admiring his beauty but lamenting his witlessness:

"ôwî wan wær dîn schœne mîn!
dir hete got den wunsch gegebn,
ob du mit witzen soldest lebn."
(124.18–20)

"O if only your beauty were mine! God would have given you perfection,
if you could live sensibly."

At this juncture, the narrative is clearly complicated by an unexpected contradiction. Wolfram's placement of this scene in a larger context appears first to emphasize Parzival's natural progress independently of any socialization. Now, however, he seems to reverse direction, emphasizing Parzival's foolishness after he comes into contact with the outside world. Why should he first reveal the hero's innate ability, and then deny it? The answer seems to lie in the intervening moment: Parzival's confusion of knights with God.

The first indication of Wolfram's interest in this moment, which is not part of the scene's folkloric archetype,[28] is his restructuring of the narrative. In Chrétien's version, the confusion of knights with God takes up only twenty-two lines (159–81); Wolfram's revision more than triples its

[28] This scene comprises the bulk of the passages without folklore parallels listed by Green, "Parzival's Departure," 384; on its centrality see Mohr, "Ritter," 208–10.

length (120.24–123.2), making it the central event of the encounter. Whereas Chrétien presents the moment as a transition between two longer passages extended by amplification and repetition, respectively, Wolfram inverts this structure, creating an expanded central section with doubling and amplification that is flanked by a brief introduction and conclusion. By separating the knights from their leader, he lets us observe Parzival confuse knights with God in two successive and increasingly detailed encounters. The first of these, involving three unnamed knights, proceeds rapidly from Parzival's confusion, in which he imagines that each is a god, "der knappe wânde sunder spot, / daz ieslîcher wære ein got" (120.27f.), to a prayer for help invoking their collective help in the second person singular like a Trinity:[29]

> lûte rief der knappe sân
> "hilf, got: du maht wol helfe hân."
> (121.1f.)

Then the youth cried loudly, "Help, God! You can surely help."

The second encounter unfolds in a parallel but more detailed manner. Whereas the three knights merely come galloping along (120.24), the narrator describes Karnahkarnanz's arrival and explains the reasons for his haste (121.12–27). And whereas the knights are armed "from the feet up" (120.5), the narrator itemizes Karnahkarnanz's dandyish equipment in lavish detail, beginning with the hem of his surcoat and proceeding upward (122.1–12). In accordance with its importance and the emphasis on perception, Parzival's confusion of Karnahkarnanz with God is described several times.[30] The introductory reference merely summarizes his reaction, citing the unfamiliar radiance as an explanation (121.30f.). The second reference emphasizes Parzival's mistake by using the same key words and even the same rhyme ("got"/"spot") as his initial response to the three knights:

> der knappe wânde, swaz [Karnahkarnanz] sprach,
> ez wære got, als im verjach
> frou Herzeloyd diu künegîn,
> do sim underschiet den liehten schîn.

[29] The model is Abraham's address of the three angels as God in the second person singular (Genesis 18.2–3). With Augustine's *De Trinitate* II.x–xi, the Trinitarian interpretation becomes standard (CCSL 50, 105–7).

[30] On the perceptual levels, see D. H. Green, *The Art of Recognition in Wolfram's "Parzival"* (1982), 62–65.

dô rief er lûte sunder spot
"nû hilf mir, hilferîcher got."
(122.21–26)

The youth imagined, no matter what [Karnahkarnanz] said, that he was God, as Lady Herzeloyde, the queen, told him when she explained his bright radiance. So he cried out loudly without jest, "now help me, God of help!"

As the narrator makes clear, Parzival's confusion ultimately derives from the misapplication of his mother's instruction, which he follows point for point in associating God with light and human form and in beseeching help. Even the rhyme at the transition from indirect to direct discourse, "got"/"spot," is identical with that introducing her comments (119.17f.).

Wolfram's other examples of such confusion in the narrative,[31] usually characterizing heathen attitudes, suggest that the association of knights with God is indeed consequential, introducing a religious complication to the rapid emergence of Parzival's chivalric potential. The first instance—using the "got"/"spot" rhyme—points out that Nabuchodonosor, who imagined himself to be a god ("ein got"), would now be an object of ridicule, "der liute spot" (102.7f.). Flegetanis succumbs to the devil's temptation to elevate creatures above their creator, praying to a calf

als ob ez wær sîn got.
wie mac der tievel selhen spot
gefüegen an sô wîser diet . . . ?
(454.3–5)

as if it were his god. How can the devil inflict such mockery on so wise a people?

Even Parzival's dead father becomes the object of religious veneration in the Near East, with heathens praying to him as a god: "ez betent heiden sunder spot / an in als an ir werden got" (107.19f.).

From this perspective, Parzival's confusion ceases to be the humorous compliment to chivalry that observers have traditionally seen in it. Karnahkarnanz's response to his adoration provides a different perspective, denying the implication of the prayer and asserting his own subservience

[31] Several passages in Acts (10.25, 14.11–18, and 28.6) describe idolatry in New Testament times. See Gerd Wolfgang Weber, "Irreligiosität und Heldenzeitalter" (1981), esp. 489 n. 42.

to the commandments of God, "'ich pin niht got, / ich leiste ab gerne sîn gebot'" (122.29f.). Nonetheless, the hero's subsequent insistence that his knights are brighter than God, "noch liehter danne got getân" (126.10), seems to imply a lingering "heathen" or "idolatrous" attitude toward chivalry. It is thus not surprising that Ither's armor, which becomes the hero's identifying feature during his single-minded pursuit of knighthood, is of heathen provenance (679.8), or that Parzival's advice to Gawan at the end of Book VI resembles the credo of heathen *Minneritter*.[32] Similar motifs pervade the Good Friday scene, beginning with Kahenis's request that the armed hero be mindful of the Peace of God—if he is not a heathen (448.19f.).

The reference to Flegetanis derives heathen idolatry from the devil's temptation of man, and it is not surprising to find reminiscences of this archetypal pattern in our scene as well. Indeed, Parzival eagerly hopes to encounter the devil when he hears the riders approaching (120.17–20),[33] only to find knights whom he confuses with gods. Even after being informed to the contrary by his "knight-god," or "ritter got" (123.21),[34] he still insists that he has seen "knights brighter than God." This lingering confusion of creatures with their creator humorously but insistently recalls the temptation of Adam by Lucifer, "Ye shall be as gods" (Genesis 3.5). The narrator even observes rather pointedly during this scene, crediting his source with something it does not contain, that Parzival is the handsomest man since the time of Adam:[35]

> von der âventiure ich daz nim,
> diu mich mit wârheit des beschiet.
> nie mannes varwe baz geriet
> vor im sît Adâmes zît.
> (123.14–17)

These allusions explain why the hero is not called foolish or stupid for the first time until this particular moment, by the knights as well as by the narrator (121.5, 124.16). This may seem rather late, given Parzival's per-

[32] See the attitude expressed by Feirefiz (768.26–30) and *Willehalm* 338.13–14; and the comments by Joachim Bumke, *Wolframs "Willehalm"* (1959), 169–75, esp. 173–74.

[33] On the importance of *strîten*, see Martin H. Jones, "Parzival's Fighting and His Election to the Grail" (1975).

[34] "ritter-got" is the reading in a majority of manuscripts (Ddgg), although Lachmann took "ritter guot" or "good knight" (MSS Ggg). The more difficult reading is also more appropriate: "ritter-got" precisely expresses Parzival's confusion and reversal of priorities.

[35] See L. P. Johnson, "Parzival's Beauty" (1978); Ingrid Hahn, "Parzivals Schönheit: Zum Problem des Erkennens und Verkennens im *Parzival*" (1978).

vasive ignorance of society at the beginning of Book III; but the conjuncture of secular and religious discourses requires us to differentiate several types of ignorance in a hero who is brave but only slowly wise (4.18).[36] Indeed, Parzival's gradual acquisition of secular and religious experience, formalized by the instruction of Gurnemanz in Book III and Trevrizent in Book IX, respectively, must be coordinated during the narrative, correcting two different types of ignorance and two corresponding types of transgression that reflect his dual heritage.

Parzival's ignorance of society might best be characterized by isolation and lack of experience, considering that he is deprived of his aristocratic heritage, "an künecl̂icher fuore betrogn" (118.2). This deficiency manifests itself in comic behavior, a carnivalizing misreading of unfamiliar cultural contexts, as Parzival introduces heteroglossia into episodes by reading one kind of discourse into another, using his mother's simplistic maxims in courtly society, for example. This behavior creates serious difficulties for others (endangering Jeschute and prompting Kay's beating of Cunneware and Antenor); however, these difficulties are rectified by the knightly adventures that lead him back to court and his election to the Round Table in Book VI.

But Wolfram also suggests a more consequential type of ignorance in our particular scene: the moral deficiency attributed to every human being as a result of the Fall. This type of ignorance, paradigmatically revealed at the moment of Parzival's confusion of knights with God, leads the hero in his inordinate pursuit of knighthood, involving him in three irremedial sins against kin (the death of his mother, the murder of Ither, and the failure to redeem Anfortas), the consequences of which, as we learn in Book IX, can only be accommodated within the context of salvation history.

That Parzival's confusion of knights with God involves this second, Adamic type of ignorance is suggested by further parallels to the patristic and poetic tradition of the Fall.[37] Because of Lucifer's name etymology ("light bearer"), this moment is frequently characterized metaphorically as the confusion of a lesser radiance with the divine light. According to Boethius's *De consolatione Philosophiae* (V. Pr. 2.10), for example, man's choice of vice turns his eyes from the sovereign light to inferior obscurities, blinding him with ignorance:

[36] Alois Haas's fourfold *stultitia* leads rather far astray, although the analysis of the present scene emphasizes Parzival's Adamic nature (*Parzivals "tumpheit,"* 64, 67). The more text-oriented study of Heinz Rupp, "Die Funktion des Wortes *tump* im *Parzival* Wolframs von Eschenbach" (1957), delineates a differentiation between worldly and religious ignorance, especially in Books III and IX.

[37] On the light imagery, see also Wolf, "*Ein mære wil ich niuwen,*" 17–24.

> Nam ubi oculos a summae luce ueritatis ad inferiora et tenebrosa deiecerint, mox inscitiae nube caligant, perniciosis turbantur affectibus, quibus accedendo consentiendoque quam inuexere sibi adiuuant seruitutem et sunt quodam modo propria libertate captiuae. (CCSL 94.90)

This choice causes a sudden "darkening" or "clouding" of man's spiritual sight or original mental capacities.[38] The *Vorauer Genesis* states that the devil cast man into the prison of "ignorantia," and in this benighted state,[39]

> do wurden in dev ougen
> des neist nechein lovgen
> zallen sunden ů̊f getan.
> dev inneren ûz getan.
> ir uirnunft wart plint.
> same wurden ellev ir kint.

> then their physical eyes were—there is no doubt of this—opened to all sins and their spiritual eyes closed. Their reason became blind. All their children became like them.

In terms of the psychological model handed down to the Middle Ages by St. Augustine's *De Trinitate*, the *imago Dei* in man, a reflection—among other attributes—of the Trinity's wisdom, becomes perverted by Adam's turn toward himself. Ignorance is thus a primary result of the Fall ("primus homo propter peccatum in ignorantiam ceciderat"), and it is recapitulated by subsequent acts such as the adoration of human beings as gods.[40]

This is not to suggest that Parzival is reducible to an allegory of Adam. Quite the contrary: Parzival is Parzival, the son of Gahmuret and Herzeloyde, and has a precise fictional genealogy extending over five generations. But he is also, as are all men, a descendant of Adam, a fact that Wolfram emphasizes by giving the name Mazadan, "relative of Adam," to Parzival's great-great-great-grandfather. As a result, the biblical archetype

[38] St. Augustine provides the basis for this tradition. See Joseph Mausbach, *Die Ethik des heiligen Augustinus* (1909), II, 226–40.

[39] Ed. Josef Diemer, *Deutsche Gedichte des elften und zwölften Jahrhunderts* (1849; rpt. 1968), 8. See also Brian Murdoch, *The Fall of Man in the Early Middle High German Biblical Epic* (1972), 96–105.

[40] On ignorance as a result of the Fall, see St. Thomas Aquinas, *Summa theologiae* I.–II.85.3, and the discussion of his predecessors in Odon Lottin, *Psychologie et morale aux XIIe et XIIIe siècles* (1949), III, 12–18. On ignorance as a perversion of the Trinitarian *imago Dei*, see Robert Javelet, *Image et resemblance au douzième siècle* (1967) I, 251, 314; II, 215 n. 65, 224–25 n. 178, 226 n. 181, 227–28 n. 207, 234 n. 290, 235 n. 308, 240 n. 374. On idolatry as a continuation of this pattern, see I, 261–62, and II, 222.

and the romance hero remain potentially homologous throughout the romance—another example of discursive pluralism or bitonality, here used to give depth to the characterization of the hero. Just as Adam's fall plunges the first man into ignorance, Parzival's confusion of knights with God makes the hero *unversunnen*, unable to act according to his senses, "mit witzen leben" (124.20). And just as Adam is exiled from paradise to a state of mortality subject to time, Parzival leaves a pastoral idyll marked only by the seasons (120.5), beginning a quest delineated by the episodic daily pattern of romance time (120.11).[41] The Adamic homology will reappear, as a parallel or contrast, in ensuing books of the narrative because Parzival, like all men, is burdened by "der sünde wagen" (465.5), the "wagon-load of sin" bequeathed to ensuing generations by the first man. The ontogeny of sin recapitulates the phylogeny of sin.

III

Like all men, however, the Grail hero is also capable of redemption, and the treatment of his ultimate success reveals the significance of Perceval's and Parzival's differing introductions to knighthood. For Chrétien, the confusion of knights with God is a humorous but not otherwise consequential example of worldly inexperience, even if the carnivalizing exchange gently questions the authority of knightly culture. In accordance with a mechanical conception of guilt, or *Schuldautomatismus*,[42] Perceval's heartless departure from his mother initiates a concatenation of sin leading to his failure at the Grail castle. He cannot remedy the consequences of his transgressions by himself—the solution must be provided by the appropriate religious instance. What Chrétien's hero has committed in the pursuit of his legitimate role in chivalric society can be remedied only by adherence to the proper forms of religious life in the Good Friday scene. But after suddenly experiencing the pangs of contrition, Perceval is confessed by the hermit in accordance with twelfth-century practice and given a penance of fasting and daily attendance at mass.[43] And there the matter ends, so far as we can tell: knightly socialization coexists easily with religious socialization, not a surprising development in a narrative by a cleric writing for a secular court.

Wolfram's romance poses the problem differently. Parzival's confusion

[41] On pastoral time and pastoral time versus novel time, see Bakhtin's "Forms of Time and of the Chronotope in the Novel," in *Dialogic Imagination*, 103 and 128.

[42] See Wilhelm Kellermann, *Aufbaustil und Weltbild Chrestiens von Troyes im Percevalroman* (1936), 109 and 120–21.

[43] See Bonnie Buettner, "The Good Friday Scene in Chrétien de Troyes' *Perceval*" (1980).

of knights with God is consequential: it marks the beginning of his unconscious *superbia,* reversing the relative priorities between God and world. This reversal underlies a pursuit of knighthood above all else, which leads to the deaths of Herzeloyde and Ither as well as the failure at the Grail castle, and it is not surprising that the portrayal of the hero in Books III through VI frequently emphasizes the epistemological confusion underlying his adventures. As a result, the goal of Wolfram's Good Friday scene is not ritual socialization by penance but a confessional dialogue devoted to rectifying Parzival's moral ignorance and its consequences, beginning with a conversion, a "turning around" of his subconsciously "heathen" attitude. Indeed, Parzival programmatically places knightly renown in this life ahead of paradise for the soul, even coordinating his inverted hierarchy of values in a manner similar to the epilogue (cf. 827.22):

> "Mac rîterschaft des lîbes prîs
> unt doch der sêle pardîs
> bejagen mit schilt und ouch mit sper,
> sô was ie rîterschaft mîn ger."
> (472.1–4)

"If knighthood can win earthly fame and yet paradise for the soul as well with shield and spear, then knighthood was always my desire."

Trevrizent's instruction appears to reverse these priorities, so that he can absolve the hero of his sins and yet encourage his knightly quest: "wand in der wirt von sünden schiet / unt im doch rîterlîchen riet" (501.17–18). As clear as this reconciliation of revelation and socialization, God and world, appears to be in the religious context of the Good Friday colloquy, the actual resolution brought about by the redeeming question at Munsalvaesche is considerably more ambiguous, as we will see in Chapter 8.

CHAPTER THREE

Carnivalizing the Court: Parzival's Knighting Ceremony

As Parzival approaches King Arthur's court for the first time, Wolfram interrupts the narrative and issues an abrupt warning to Hartmann von Aue, the founding father of the Arthurian tradition in Middle High German:

mîn hêr Hartmann von Ouwe,
frou Ginovêr iwer frouwe
und iwer hêrre der künc Artûs,
den kumt ein mîn gast ze hûs.
bitet hüeten sîn vor spotte.
ern ist gîge noch diu rotte:
si sulen ein ander gampel nemn:
des lâzen sich durch zuht gezemn.
anders iwer frouwe Enîde
unt ir muoter Karsnafîde
werdent durch die mül gezücket
unde ir lop <gebruchet>.[1]
sol ich den munt mit spotte zern,
ich wil mînen friunt mit spotte wern.
(143.21–144.4)

Sir Hartmann von Aue! One of my guests is coming to the palace of Lady Guenevere your lady, and your lord King Arthur. Please keep him from mockery: he is neither a fiddle nor a rote. They should find another

[1] Lachmann's emendation to *gebrücket* makes little sense. L. P. Johnson draws my attention to the reading in Gg, *gebruchet*, from *brücken* ("zerbröckeln"), which continues the metaphor of the mill.

> plaything—let them do that for the sake of good breeding. Otherwise your lady Enite and her mother Karsnafide will be dragged through the mill, and their reputation ground to bits. If I have to twist my mouth in mockery, I will defend my friend with mockery.

It has long been recognized that this aggressive challenge is one of an extended series of references to Hartmann's narratives in Wolfram's text.[2] This particular invocation explicitly expands the practice of heteroglossia to intertextuality, to a contest between the two authors, contrasted by the emphatic use of "my" and "your": Wolfram's "guest" and "friend" comes to Hartmann's court, presided over by the latter's "lord" and "lady," Arthur and Guenevere. *Parzival*'s novelistic interplay of discourses is thus enriched by an intertextual battle not found in Chrétien's text: taking place in a post-*Erec*ian world, it appropriates the figures and events of Hartmann's romances into the pre-history of Wolfram's narrative.[3]

In addition to self-consciously inscribing a competition between authorial discourses into the narrative, this moment also presents an encounter between conflicting genre expectations, bringing Wolfram's *bel inconnu*, unsocialized and lacking in knightly training and manners, to Hartmann's well-established Arthurian court, an ostensibly ideal society and traditional point of departure for chivalric adventure.[4] Wolfram's *gast* is thus a stranger in the sense that ignorance makes his behavior uncertain, whereas that of Hartmann's Arthur's court is predictable. In this instance, the warning about protecting Parzival from mockery anticipates the traditional behavior of Kay, who bluntly advises Arthur to rid himself of two evils by setting Parzival against Ither like the whip that spins a top (150.16f.). Moreover, Wolfram's threat to avenge any misbehavior of Hartmann's Arthur's court by ruining Enite's and her mother's reputations has already been put into action: Chrétien's nameless Tent Maiden has become Jeschute, Erec's sister and thus Enite's sister-in-law, who has debased the family's reputation herself through her misalliance with Duke Orilus. In turn, Orilus's mistreatment of Jeschute is reminiscent of Erec's

[2] See Rüdiger Schnell, "Literarische Beziehungen zwischen Hartmanns *Erec* und Wolframs *Parzival*" (1973); Kathryn Smits, "Einige Beobachtungen zu gemeinsamen Motiven in Hartmanns *Erec* und Wolframs *Parzival*" (1980); Peter Wapnewski, "Gregorius und Parzival, Hartmann und Wolfram," in his *Wolframs "Parzival": Studien zur Religiosität und Form* (1955), 15–27.

[3] Gary Saul Morson and Caryl Emerson speak of "'other-author zones,' in which the values and beliefs of those authors become part of the dialogue of the novel." *Mikhail Bakhtin: Creation of a Prosaics* (1990), 337.

[4] See in general Kurt Ruh, "Artus-Idealität," in his *Höfische Epik des deutschen Mittelalters I* (1967), 11–15, and especially Walter Haug, "Die Symbolstruktur des höfischen Epos und ihre Auflösung bei Wolfram von Eschenbach" (1971).

abuse of Enite, recapitulating in another couple from the same family the dysfunctional relationship between Hartmann's hero and heroine.

This first encounter between Parzival and the Arthurian world also diversifies Chrétien's carnivalizing contrast between foolish and refined behavior by making it part of a larger discourse on social discipline. I say larger discourse because this involves not only the absence of courtliness in a narrow sense that Parzival first manifests at Arthur's court but also the lack of general good conduct that Gurnemanz, the captain of true behavior, "houbetman der wâren zuht" (162.23), then corrects. The latter involves disciplining the body (in particular, mastering the hunger or tiredness that rule Parzival's actions), learning to control speech, internalizing rules of behavior, and refining innate knightly skills. But this general chivalric education is not necessarily identical with courtliness, as we will shortly see.[5]

A general antithesis between the hero and the Arthurian world is suggested by the portrait of Parzival as he approaches the court across a meadow strewn with flowers, a pleasance landscape that Arthur's Nantes shares with Gurnemanz's Graharz. The narrator first draws attention to the hero's lack of education, fine manners, and courtly experience:

> in zôch *nehein* Curvenâl:
> er kunde kurtôsîe *niht,*
> als *un*gevarnem man geschiht.
> (144.20–22; my emphasis)

> *No* Curvenal [Tristan's tutor] had educated him. He did *not* know anything about *courtoisie,* as happens to a man who has *not* traveled.

The hero's appearance is equally deficient, judging from the length of its description (144.23–145.2). Clothing, as the *Schneiderstrophen* in the *Nibelungenlied* and similar scenes remind us, indicates status in courtly society, reflecting the importance of the visual.[6] Parzival looks inelegant—his feeble pony stumbles along; its reins are of bast, and the saddle is not covered with new leather; his outfit lacks samite or ermine, a cord to tie his cloak, or a jacket and surcoat. His only equipment consists of a javelot, a hunting weapon that will soon figure prominently in the action.

Everything that Parzival lacks the Red Knight he encounters seems to

[5] See Helmut Brall, "Familie und Hofgesellschaft in Wolframs *Parzival*" (1986), 541–45.

[6] On the visual importance of clothes, see Joachim Bumke, *Courtly Culture: Literature and Society in the High Middle Ages* (1991), 128–55; Gerhard Jaritz, "Zur materiellen Kultur des Hofes um 1200" (1986), 31–32.

have in abundance (145.7–146.3). Indeed, the portraits of the two men invite comparison. Called simply The Red Knight in Chrétien's narrative, Ither von Gaheviez is another refugee from the imagined world of Hartmann's *Erec*, where he is listed among the members of the Round Table (1658f.).[7] Here he appears as the epitome of Arthurian knighthood, destined to bear the highest fame of the Round Table, "der ob der tavelrunder / den hœhsten prîs solde tragn" (160.6f.). Ither's courtliness emerges immediately from his polite treatment of the hero and the carefully formulated messages to Arthur and Guenevere, messages that Parzival delivers with inelegant brevity. Unlike Parzival, Ither has enjoyed a proper upbringing by no less a personage than Arthur's father (145.12). Above all, the Red Knight is modishly resplendent in uniformly red equipment, the description of which uses the word "rôt" thirteen times in seventeen lines (145.17ff.).

In spite of the fact that Parzival and Ither are contrasted at length in terms of the absence and presence of training, speech, and equipment, the foolish hero soon kills Ither with his javelot and appropriates his armor, thereby becoming the Red Knight himself. The metonymical association of two such disparate figures through their shared armor has several dimensions. Most obviously, the demise of the best Arthurian knight at the hands of an apparent fool relativizes the putative ideality of Arthur's court. This is underscored by a fairy-tale motif, the enchantment that keeps Cunneware from laughing until she sees the person who will win the highest fame, "den hôhsten prîs" (151.14f.). Her laughter magically singles out the "fool" Parzival from all the "worthy men" at court, reversing the apparent disparity between Ither (who would have won the highest fame at the Round Table) and the hero, who will win the highest fame of all (221.25). At the same time, the ensuing murder and corpse robbing of Ither has negative consequences as well, the implications of which emerge only gradually during the narrative. The following chapter will discuss the ways in which Wolfram uses Parzival's encounter with the court and with Ither to subvert traditional romance genre expectations, by (1) destabilizing the authority of the Arthurian world as an idealized, unified society; and (2) carnivalizing the hero's acquisition of knighthood. The chaotic world order of post-Hartmannian romance thereby becomes a fitting context for the unchivalric beginnings of Parzival's knightly career.[8]

[7] See Werner Schröder, *Die Namen im "Parzival" und im "Titurel" Wolframs von Eschenbach* (1982), 57.

[8] On older and newer levels of knighthood in general, see Horst Brunner, "*Artus der wise höfsche man*: Zur immanenten Historizität der Ritterwelt im *Parzival* Wolframs von Eschenbach" (1983).

I

One of the most intriguing changes in the first appearance of Arthur's court involves a shift of location.[9] In Chrétien's narrative, Perceval seeks out King Arthur at Carduel (Carlisle), a castle situated on the coast, "un chastel sor mer assis" (843), whereas Wolfram moves the king to the geographically more apropos French city of Nantes. The shift is puzzling, given the rarity of this locale in twelfth-century narratives.[10] Wolfram's alteration seems to derive from the conclusion of Chrétien's *Erec*, where the hero asks Arthur to crown him at his court, "Qu'il le coronast a sa cort" (6547), whereupon the king has the ceremony performed "a Nantes an Bretaingne" (6553). Wolfram's reading of the ambiguous pronoun antecedent "his" as "Arthur's" thus seems to be another intertextual connection to the story of Erec, taking from Hartmann's source the name of a city not specified by Hartmann himself.

A second change involves the promotion of Arthur's *chastel* to a capital city, or "houptstat" (144.7).[11] Unlike subsequent episodes with itinerant celebrations of courtly love at the Round Table—more precisely, the Round Tablecloth (309.11–25), and later the ersatz Round Tablecloth (775.6–11)—this shift introduces us to the court as the fixed center of the king's political and judicial power. As a result, the population density of the two narratives is substantially different: Chrétien's hero encounters only a rural charcoal burner from whom he obtains directions; Wolfram's youth rides on a well-traveled, broad road, greeting both knights and merchants in his simplistic way. The equal treatment of socially disparate groups prepares the subversive differentiation that follows, beginning with a fisherman/innkeeper.[12]

The creation and addition of this episode to Chrétien's story introduces the hero to nonaristocratic society, using Parzival's ignorance as a carnivalizing foil to reveal the underside of the innkeeper's existence, a

[9] For a general comparison, see Wolfgang Mohr, "König Artus und die Tafelrunde: Politische Hintergründe in Chrétiens *Perceval* und Wolframs *Parzival*" (1979).

[10] Schröder, *Namen*, 148, declines to suggest a source for Nantes. The only early entry cited by G. D. West, *An Index of Proper Names in French Arthurian Verse Romances*, 1150–1300 (1969), 121, is Chrétien's *Erec*. Nantes also serves as the location of Marie de France's *Chaitivel*; the place name "Nauns" in *Equitan* (12) is contested.

[11] It may be a reflection of the gradual shift from itinerant lordship (*Reiseherrschaft*) to settled lordship (*Residenzherrschaft*) during the High and Late Middle Ages, a shift already begun below the imperial level by the landgraves of Thuringia in the twelfth century. See Hans Patze, "Die Bildung der landesherrlichen Residenzen im Reich während des 14. Jahrhunderts" (1972), 7–9.

[12] Eduard Schröder attempts to derive the episode from Hartmann's *Gregorius*, "Parzival und Gregorius" (1912).

function it will repeat immediately thereafter at the court. The innkeeper is a *vilân* (143.3/11) because of the lack of aristocratic birth, or *ungeslähte,* that manifests itself in a lack of virtue (142.15–18). His response to Parzival's hunger illustrates the deficiency:

der sprach "in gæbe ein halbez brôt
iu niht ze drîzec jâren.
swer mîner milte vâren
vergebene wil, der sûmet sich.
ine sorge umb niemen danne um mich,
dar nâch um mîniu kindelîn.
iren komt tâlanc dâ her în.
het ir phenninge oder phant,
ich behielt iuch al zehant."
(142.22–30)

He said: "I wouldn't give you half a loaf of bread in thirty years. Anyone who expects my largess for nothing is wasting his time. I don't care about anyone but myself, and then for my children. You won't come in here today. But if you had pennies or valuables, I'd take you in immediately."

The innkeeper rejects the gift economy of chivalric society, with its reciprocal nexus of feudal obligations and hospitality, in favor of a mercantile economy devoted to his immediate family. The ignoble desire for material gain, expressed by reference to coins or barter, disparages noble largess as giving away something for nothing.

But Wolfram's churl represents more than an aristocratic stereotype: he needs to be viewed together with the Arthurian court as a representation of social groups in the capital city. In fact, the *vilân*'s extreme greed has an aristocratic counterpart in King Arthur's extreme generosity. The king responds to the hero's greeting with a polite benevolence that Parzival takes literally, turning a formulaic expression into a Rash Boon:

"junchêrre, got vergelt iu gruoz,
den ich vil gerne dienen muoz
mit dem lîbe und mit dem guote.
des ist mir wol ze muote."
"wolt et got, wan wær daz wâr!
der wîle dunket mich ein jâr,
daz ich niht ritter wesen sol."
(149.7–13)

"Young Sir, may God repay your greeting. I would gladly deserve it with my person and my wealth; I am indeed of a mind to do so." "If only God wanted that to be true! All this time that I am not a knight seems to me a year."

Arthur's attempt to temporize only digs him in deeper, as Parzival places a claim on Ither's knightly armor and Kay turns his anticipated mockery on the king, daring him to refuse and risk being considered ungenerous. The centrality of largess in chivalric culture thus enables Wolfram to define two socially opposite and heteroglot economic discourses at Nantes: the innkeeper is not "milte" for nothing (142.24), while Arthur is driven to concessions to avoid a reputation for being "unmilte" (150.11).

A comparison with Wolfram's source suggests yet another intertextual basis to this social polarization. Chrétien's charcoal burner not only knows the way to Carduel but also explains that the hero will find Arthur both happy and sad following the victory over King Rion and the departure of his nobles for their own castles, implying some communication between socially diverse classes throughout the kingdom. While Parzival's innkeeper even guides his guest to Nantes the next morning, he refuses to approach the court because of the impropriety of such a presumption:

"wie wol mîn lîp daz bewart!
diu mässenîe ist sölher art,
genæht ir immer vilân,
daz wær vil sêre missetân."
(144.13–16)

"I certainly won't! The court is of such birth that if a peasant were ever to approach them it would be very wrong."

This radical separation of the noncourtly from the courtly paraphrases Hartmann's definition of Arthurian society as an exclusive institution:

deiswâr dâ was ein bœser man
in vil swachem werde:
wan sich gesament ûf erde
bî niemens zîten anderswâ
sô manec guot ritter alsô dâ.
(*Iwein*, 38–42)

Truly an ignoble man was held there in very low esteem: for nowhere else at any time on earth were there gathered so many good knights as at that place.

Taking Hartmann's social model to the extreme, Wolfram imagines the capital city as polarized into mutually exclusive mercantile and courtly interests. No citizenry appears in this *houptstat*: except for the encounter with Ither, the hero meets only children between leaving the innkeeper and arriving at court. By constructing Nantes in terms of social antitheses, Wolfram indirectly subjects Hartmann's Arthurian exclusivity to a comparison with the next city in Parzival's quest, Pelrapeire, which the hero rescues and rules a few weeks later in Book IV. This may be the reason why he transforms Chrétien's Belrepaire, which contains ruined minsters with timorous monks and nuns and a tiny group of defenders, with no merchants to provide food or drink (1752–73), into a populous secular community. Parzival enters a city crowded with defenders, proceeding from foot soldiers, archers, and men-at-arms to armed merchants organized by their guilds and then to a well-defended court with numerous knights (183.3–30). As we will see in the next chapter, the hero's managing of supplies for this large populace—extending the control of his body learned at Gurnemanz's to control of the body politic—presages the ability to integrate disparate social groups and rule a kingdom.[13]

Even without the comparison implied by the situations at Nantes and Pelrapeire, Wolfram subverts the idealizing reputation of Hartmann's Arthur's court from the outset. The court at Nantes is in chaos, in contrast to the typical celebration of regal wealth and power with which, for example, Hartmann's *Iwein* begins and the Arthurian books of *Parzival* will end. To be sure, much of this is—again—already in Chrétien's narrative. But the confusion is heightened not only by the intertextual dialogue with Hartmann but also because the threat is now an internal one, revealing the fragile basis of the dominion inherited by Arthur from Utependragon. Unlike Chrétien's nameless Red Knight, Wolfram's Ither is the son of Utependragon's sister, was raised by his uncle, is a king in his own right, and has been a member of Arthur's own household (145.11f., 145.28, 160.11).[14] Fastidiously overturning a goblet for the public assertion of his claim rather than the more traditional straw torch,[15] which might dirty his elegant outfit (146.19–30), Ither has just spilled wine in

[13] The contrast in rulership and control is illustrated by the motif of overfeeding: Parzival distributes food carefully in order to prevent *überkrüpfe* (191.13, 201.14); Arthur's falcon escapes because of *überkrüphe* (281.29).

[14] See Leslie Seiffert, "The Terms of Kindred, or Kindred on Good and Bad Terms: Parzival's Vulgar Slaying of His Father's *neve* Ither" (1990); and Walter Delabar, "*Erkantiu sippe unt hoch geselleschaft*" (1990), 75–132.

[15] See Ruth Schmidt-Wiegand, *Studien zur historischen Rechtswortgeographie. Der Strohwisch als Bann- und Verbotszeichen* (1978), 127–28; and Walter Mersmann, *Der Besitzwechsel und seine Bedeutung in den Dichtungen Wolframs von Eschenbach und Gottfrieds von Straßburg* (1971), 105, on the legal implications of *underwinden* (146.21/25).

Guenevere's lap, a blunder that heightens the chaos as well as draws attention to her, though whether to allude to adultery or the absence of a legitimate heir is unclear. Because the queen's lament later asserts that Ither died seeking his inheritance, "sîns erbeteils er gerte, / dâ man in sterbens werte" (160.9f.), it appears that his claim is not groundless. In any case, the familial conflict between Arthur and Ither as children of siblings threatens the integrity of the entire kingdom, whose power base of vassals and fiefs is not large, at least according to Kingrun's estimate (221.13–18).[16]

The confusion caused by this internal challenge to Arthur's rule in his own capital city is heightened by the king's lack of authority. Parzival is unable to identify the regal person not once—as in Chrétien's scene—but twice, first assuming that all knights in the courtyard are "Arthurs" (147.22f.), then not recognizing the lord of the noisy palace:

> sus vil kund er in schalle,
> er sprach "got halde iuch hêrren alle,
> benamn den künec und des wîp.
> mir gebôt mîn muoter an den lîp,
> daz ich die gruozte sunder . . .
> dar an ein kunst mich verbirt,
> ine weiz niht welher hinne ist wirt."
> (147.28–148.8)

> In the midst of the noise he was able to say: "May God keep all you lords, especially the king and his wife. My mother commanded me on my life to greet them separately. . . . But one thing I lack—I don't know which of you in here is the lord."

The first association of "knights" as "Arthurs" continues his difficulty in distinguishing names and proper names, but the subsequent inability to locate the sovereign in the chaos also implies the lack of an authoritative regal presence. As Walter Map's famous definition states, the court should be oriented around the regent as its focal point, the multitude striving to please that person alone:[17] "dicam eam [curiam] multitudinem quodammodo se habentem ad unum principium. Multitudo certe sumus infinita, uni soli placere contendens." Here, however, the crowd ignores

[16] Brall, "Familie und Hofgesellschaft," 565–66. It may not be entirely coincidental that Landgrave Hermann I negotiated a plan with Henry VI in 1196 to bequeath his fiefs to his daughter Hedwig. See Hans Patze, *Die Entstehung der Landesherrschaft in Thüringen* (1962), I, 251.

[17] Walter Map, *De nugis curialium* (Dist. i, c. 1) (1983), 2.

the king, adding to the confusion by pressing in on Parzival in the courtyard and palace as well as when he exits. The terms used to characterize the crush of people, various forms of *dringen* (147.15, 148.20, 150.30, 153.19), frequently designate unruly crowds in court criticism.[18]

Given this situation, it is highly ironic that Arthur has only Kay, the seneschal whose presence traditionally generates disharmony, to maintain order. To be sure, Wolfram's excursus in Book VI absolves Kay of the moral deficiencies traditionally imputed to him "in many lands," denying that he was a *ribbalt* (296.13–22). But contravening Chrétien's and Hartmann's genre conventions only underscores the disorder by making the seneschal a bouncer:

Artûses hof was ein zil,
dar kom vremder liute vil,
die werden unt die smæhen.
(296.25–27)

Arthur's court was a goal to which many strangers came, worthy as well as unworthy.

What Wolfram says about these crowds and their motley social and moral composition is again reminiscent of conventional court criticism in the High Middle Ages[19] and further undercuts the court's putative ideality. Moreover, Wolfram's address to his patron, Landgrave Hermann I of Thuringia, noting that some people who were "in" at court should be "out," and that he therefore has "need of a Kay," adds a further dimension:

dir wære och eines Keien nôt,
sît wâriu milte dir gebôt
sô manecvalten anehanc,
etswâ smæhlîch gedranc
unt etswâ werdez dringen.
des muoz hêr Walther singen
"guoten tac, bœs unde guot."
(297.19–25)

[18] See Bumke, *Courtly Culture*, 415–23; Peter Ganz, "*curialis / hövesch*" (1986), 47–48; Klaus Schreiner, "'Hof' (*curia*) und 'höfische Lebensführung' (*vita curialis*) als Herausforderung an die christliche Theologie und Frömmigkeit" (1986), 93. The fact that the court crowds around Parzival also anticipates his future role as regent.

[19] See Claus Uhlig, *Hofkritik im England des Mittelalters und der Renaissance* (1973); Rolf Köhn, "'Militia curialis.' Die Kritik am geistlichen Hofdienst bei Peter von Blois" (1979); and the articles listed in the preceding footnote.

> You also could use a Kay, since true largess got you such a motley following, sometimes a contemptible crowd, and sometimes a noble throng. That is why Sir Walther [von der Vogelweide] had to sing "Good day, bad and good."

Although the comparison with a chaotic court offers a backhanded compliment to Hermann's regal generosity, the analogy to a landgrave does King Arthur no service either, demoting him and equating his retinue with the infamous group around Hermann. No such poem by Walther von der Vogelweide survives, but Wolfram seems to be alluding to his criticism of Hermann's court in the *Sprüche* known as the *1. Philippston* (20.4–15):[20]

> Der in den ôren siech von ungesühte sî,
> daz ist mîn rât, der lâz den hof ze Dürengen frî:
> wan kumet er dar, dêswâr er wirt ertœret.
> ich hân gedrungen unz ich niht mê dringen mac.
> ein schar vert ûz, diu ander in, naht unde tac.
> grôz wunder ist daz iemen dâ gehœret.
>
> (20.4–9)

> If anyone has problems with his ears, my advice is for him to avoid the court at Thuringia. For if he goes there, he'll go deaf. I've crowded in until I can't crowd in any more. One mob comes in, the other out, day and night. It's amazing that anyone there can hear.

These excurses and asides subvert the idealizing unity Hartmann ascribes to Arthur's court. Whereas for Hartmann—as we have seen—the large assembly of knights around King Arthur creates a putatively cohesive society (*Iwein*, 38–42), for Wolfram the presence of a court attracts diverse, even conflicting social groups in which "knightly" and "courtly" are no longer identical. Social heterogeneity and linguistic diversity expose the court as an exclusionary institution to a carnivalizing interplay of discourses that decenters its authority, anticipating the similar function Bakhtin postulates in late medieval and Renaissance culture for the public square.[21]

This diversification, articulated by linguistic registers as well as by social differences, emerges especially in the relationship between the seneschal

[20] Walter von der Vogelweide, *Gedichte* (1965); Bumke, *Courtly Culture*, 421.

[21] See Emerson and Morson, *Mikhail Bakhtin*, 445–48.

Kay and Arthur's nephew Gawan,[22] and merits a brief excursus. In Hartmann's *Erec*, their friendship is—in spite of the seneschal's problematic moral character—so close that the two knights walk hand in hand together (1154–57). Although Wolfram's Kay and Gawan are also friends, the relationship is marked by a series of sociolinguistic distinctions. Kay addresses Gawan with *hêrre* and *ir* (298.13, 298.15–17, etc.), but Gawan calls Kay a *friunt* (298.10) and addresses him with *du* (299.25f.), an expression of social standings so disparate that the seneschal can assert that King Arthur's sister's son is too highborn to risk avenging him, "ir sît mir râch ze wol geborn" (298.25).[23]

This social disparity also introduces heteroglossia into the traditionally unified language of the court. Kay speaks a surprisingly colloquial idiolect, marked by proverbial turns of phrase derived from the hunt or rural life and the kitchen (150.22, 152.4–6, 294.4f., 296.18–20, 207.1f.), even accosting Parzival familiarly in the gruff manner of a peasant, "ein gebûr spræche sân" (294.23). Gawan, as a well-bred person (299.16), speaks so elegantly, "wol" (303.11), that Parzival rejects his courtesy as a meaningless gesture extended indiscriminately to all:

> Dô sprach er "bistuz Gâwân?
> wie kranken prîs ich des hân,
> op du mirz wol erbiutes hie!
> ich hôrte von dir sprechen ie,
> du erbütesz allen liuten wol."
> (304.1–5)

> Then Parzival said, "Is it you, Gawan? What small honor I have from your receiving me well here! I always heard it said of you that you treat everyone well."

The verbal spectrum is extreme, ranging from Kay's direct sarcasm to Gawan's dissembling flattery, a more problematic aspect of his courtliness than the elegant handwriting discussed in Chapter 1. These diverse languages are reminiscent of an anecdote from Walter Daniel's life of Ailred of Rievaulx, in which the rough, aggressive anger of a soldier contrasts

[22] On Kay in general, see Jürgen Haupt, *Der Truchseß Keie im Artusroman* (1971), esp. 47ff.; Albrecht Classen, "Keie in Wolframs von Eschenbach *Parzival*: 'Agent provocateur' oder Angeber?" (1988). On Gawan, see Keith Busby, *Gauvain in Old French Literature* (1980), and the works listed by Bumke, *Wolfram*, 189–91. My analysis of Gawan follows Bonnie Buettner, "Gawan in Wolfram's *Parzival*" (1984), 14–41.

[23] See Gustav Ehrismann, "Duzen und Ihrzen im Mittelalter" (1903/04), esp. 150.

with the benevolent affability and patience of the bishop courtier.[24] But the vita's difference between a knight and a cleric is located here between lower and upper nobility, knightly court official and princely courtier.

As his language suggests, Kay has many attributes of a parvenu, and Wolfram uncharacteristically gives him no family history. Called a knight (158.24) and consistently praised for his bravery (290.3, 293.19, 296.13–15, 296.22), the seneschal is defined—and defines himself—through his office rather than lineage.[25] The position is far from the honorific one often held by powerful lords at royal courts and closer to the familial service traditionally posited for *ministeriales*:[26] Kay jokes with Kingrun about being lords of their respective kitchens as well as winning Cunneware's forgiveness with doughnuts (206.29ff.), later begging his colleague to stand in for him in serving Cunneware's brother Orilus (278.28–279.10). Above all, he characterizes his actions as duty to the king and court, beating Cunneware for laughing at the unknightly Parzival rather than the many "worthy men" who have ridden into Arthur's presence (152.7–12) or threatening to resign his position if not allowed to avenge the Red Knight's insult to the Round Table (290.14–18).

In spite of identifying with his office, Kay never masters the demands it places on him. Wolfram suggests that the seneschal knew how to honor and serve those who had "kurtôsie" and "werde cumpânie" rather than sycophants (296.29–297.4), implying an ability to differentiate between extremes of form and substance in the social practice of courtliness. But he does not seem to have internalized the discourse whose boundaries he so militantly patrols. Far from exhibiting a courtier's equanimity and self-control, Kay aggressively vents his anger on those around him (152.13, 221.20, 298.12, 651.7), beginning with the beating of Cunneware that marks him as unwise (152.1). Although he later claims to have done this for the sake of "courtly manners" and to "improve" her (218.25f.), the transgression—more reminiscent of a Germanic *recke* such as Siegfried or Wate—suggests that the seneschal's "courtliness" is gender specific, limited to males.

Indeed, Kay seems especially uncomfortable in dealing with the new

[24] It is discussed by C. Stephen Jaeger, *The Origins of Courtliness* (1985), 38–40.

[25] See 151.21, 153.1, 290.23, 295.17, 296.17, 304.17.

[26] The spectrum emerges as early as Eilhart von Oberge's representation of King Marke's seneschal Tinas, who is highborn, "ein forste hôch geborn," courtly and powerful, "hobisch unde rîche," only serving at major representative festivities of the king, "der scuzzele he doch niht en trûg, / wan in grôzer hôchzît" (318–31). At the other extreme is the nameless seneschal at the Irish court, a common "dish-carrier," or "schuzzeltreger" (1949). Cited from Franz Lichtenstein, ed., *Eilhart von Oberge* (Straßburg, 1877), 39–40 and 104.

idealizing roles of women in courtly society, and Arthur's court in particular. Its most obvious manifestation is a hostility to the discourse of courtly love and its practice at the Round Tablecloth, from which he is notably absent—a hostility partially shared by the narrator (216.26–217.6). The reputation as a *merkære* (297.6), with which Wolfram admits that Kay reaped slander from the hypocrites and tricksters he turned away, usually characterizes those who interfere with lovers in Minnesang.[27] Moreover, there is a strong streak of misogyny in the seneschal, who labels Gawan's lament the reaction of an "old woman" (298.14), accuses him of being unduly influenced by women (299.3–12), and ridicules the "mass of ladies" he accumulates in his adventures (675.14).

Characteristically for Wolfram's carnivalizing representation of Arthur's court, the hardened warrior's accusations of the courtier prince are not without a grain of truth. Gawan's status as a courtier seems beyond question: he is called *kurtois* and *höfisch* more than any other figure.[28] However, he enters the narrative as a small boy with different aspirations, yearning only to break lances in combat (66.15–22). When he reappears with the "highest fame" at the Round Table (301.7), replacing Ither in this role, there have been no intervening adventures to explain this reputation. But Guenevere's lament for Ither, emphasizing his importance to the women of the court, suggests that fame may be based on the practice of courtly love rather than knightly prowess (160.3–30). Kay's resentful attack similarly implies that Gawan's position at court has feminized him and reduced his effectiveness as a knight: a single strand of woman's hair, no matter what color, would suffice to turn him from battle (299.3–6). Moreover Kay's "lord's sister's son" (298.15) owes his position at court to maternal affiliation, a dependence implying cowardice (299.10–12). The narrator appears to support Gawan,

> sus was der wol gelobte man
> gerant zer blôzen sîten an
> mit rede: er kunde ir gelten niht,
> als wol gezogenem man geschiht,
> dem scham versliuzet sînen munt,
> daz dem verschamten ist unkunt.
> (299.13–18)

[27] See Haupt, *Keie,* 73–78.

[28] 380.28, 619.25, 672.25 and 430.20, 677.24, 756.22, respectively. David Blamires, *Characterization and Individuality in Wolfram's "Parzival"* (1966), 366–67. Arthur becomes "der wîse höfsche man" only through his resolution of Gawan's conflicts in Book XIV (699.22, 717.1, 728.9).

> Thus, the well-praised man was attacked on his undefended side with speech. He didn't know how to repay it, as often happens to a well-bred man whose mouth is closed by shame, which is unknown to the shameless.

But he also raises the question whether this "high praise" is justified and Gawan's knightly prowess, or "undefended side," vulnerable to the attack.

In keeping with the dialogic portrayal of the two men and the conflicting discourses of arms and love associated with them, the episode prepares one further ironic reversal. Gawan—as in *Erec*—does not need knightly combat to bring the hero into court. Riding out without sword and spurs (299.29) to deal with what appears to be a knightly challenge, and thereby apparently confirming Kay's accusation of cowardice, he finds Parzival in a love trance instead, about whose nature the "tavelrunder hôhster prîs" is "al wîs" (301.7f.), which the narrator unexpectedly grounds in an imagined adventure involving Gawan's defeat by Lehelin and a love trance over Inguse de Bahtarliez (301.9–20). In contrast, Parzival's defeat of Kay punishes the seneschal for his knightly intrusion into Lady Love's domain by breaking his left foot and right hand, which prevents him from either mounting a horse or wielding a sword. The seneschal's injuries do not heal until much later (675.4), by which time Gawan has redeemed himself and broken the adventure of Schastel Marveile in a highly appropriate fashion—undergoing the ordeal of the Magic Bed.

II

In accordance with the frequent linking of society and individual in romance narratives, Wolfram's carnivalizing treatment of Arthur's court has a counterpart in Parzival's murder and corpse robbing of Ither, with which the hero begins his knightly career. The episode has been a frequent subject of scholarly analyses in recent decades,[29] most of which agree on a basic difference between *Li Contes del Graal* and *Parzival*. Chrétien neither views the murder of the Red Knight as a reprehensible act nor associates it with the hero's guilt. Indeed, it is lauded by King Arthur as a great service that has eliminated a dangerous challenge to his author-

[29] See especially Wolfgang Mohr, "Parzivals ritterliche Schuld" (1951/52); Wolfgang Harms, *Der Kampf mit dem Freund oder Verwandten in der deutschen Literatur bis um 1300* (1963), 150–52; Dennis H. Green, "Homicide and *Parzival*" (1978); Leslie P. Johnson, "Dramatische Ironie in Wolframs *Parzival*" (1972). Rudolf Rosskopf, *Der Traum Herzeloydes und der Rote Ritter* (1972), is extremist.

ity. Rather, Perceval's unfeeling departure from his mother and her ensuing death occasion a sin that explicitly causes his subsequent failure at the Grail castle (6399ff.). Wolfram views the problem of Parzival's guilt in a different light, adding the murder of Ither to the death of his mother and his failure at Munsalvaesche. This not only decenters Chrétien's mechanical concatenation of sin but also places a new emphasis on knightly guilt, a guilt that is all the more profound not only because Parzival is related to Ither and in killing his "own flesh" (475.21) has incurred a blood guilt that can never be expiated, but also because it makes him a participant in the self-perpetuating "wagon-load of sin" that began with Cain's slaying of Abel:

> "Kâins vater was Adâm:
> der sluoc Abeln umb krankez guot. . . .
> dô huop sich êrst der menschen nît:
> alsô wert er immer sît."
>
> (464.16ff.)

> "Adam was the father of Cain, who slew Abel for the sake of paltry possessions. . . . Only then did human enmity arise, and it has lasted ever since."

Wolfram's transposition of Chrétien's clerical guilt mechanism into a more problematic knightly discourse raises a puzzling institutional and social problem as well. Chrétien's Gornemant subsequently trains the hero in the proper use of knightly weapons, then formally inducts him into "l'ordre de chevalerie" (1637). Wolfram's Gurnemanz also instructs Parzival but does not perform a dubbing at the end of his training. It has been suggested that this surprising omission reflects Wolfram's unfamiliarity with knighting ceremonies,[30] as the *swertleite* in twelfth-century Germany appears to have been restricted even within the upper nobility and became more widespread only after 1200.[31]

Statistically plausible though this explanation may be,[32] it overlooks the

[30] Joachim Bumke, "Parzivals 'Schwertleite'" (1964). Earlier discussions of this scene are cited on 236 n. 4.

[31] In *Parzival,* Wolfram employs circumlocutions with *schilt,* "schildes ambet," "schilt gewinnen," etc., whereas in *Willehalm* he uses the normal terminology with circumlocutions of *swert,* "swert geben," "swert umbe gurten," etc. (Bumke, 243–45). Bumke's admission that the events surrounding Parzival's acquisition of armor almost attain the significance of a knighting (239–40) has in fact given the impetus for my interpretation.

[32] See Joachim Bumke, *Studien zum Ritterbegriff im 12. und 13. Jahrhundert* (1964), 101–18, and *Courtly Culture,* 231–47.

fact that Wolfram knew twelfth-century German texts that refer to or describe knightings—the *Kaiserchronik*, the *Nibelungenlied*, Hartmann von Aue's *Erec*, and Heinrich von Veldeke's *Eneit*. More important, this explanation ignores Wolfram's source: because *Li Contes del Graal* contains a very explicit description of a *swertleite*, it is illogical to assert that he deleted Chrétien's knighting ceremony because he had insufficient knowledge of what it entailed. It seems to me, rather, that Wolfram eliminated the dubbing at Gornemant's castle because he preferred to illustrate his hero's entrance into knighthood in a less exculpatory manner, suggesting that Parzival becomes a knight not through any public ceremony conferring and confirming his status, but by appropriating the murdered Ither's armor. Indeed, the brief scene outside Nantes in which Iwanet dresses the ignorant hero in the dead knight's equipment is a carnivalized *swertleite* that emphatically links his knightly guilt and knightly career, ironically drawing attention to their relationship through Ither's stolen armor.

The major differences between the Old French and Middle High German corpse-robbing scenes seem straightforward. Chrétien devotes a total of fifty-five lines to stripping the Chevalier Vermeil and Perceval's insistence on taking only the armor (1120–75), but only fifteen lines to a description of arming the hero (1176–91). Wolfram completely reverses this emphasis, deleting details of the hero's attempts to remove the dead knight's armor (1121f., 1126–29) and expunging or greatly reducing the broad comedy of his responses (1133–42, 1153–73). At the same time, he elaborates the investiture of Parzival, expanding the few lines of his source to some three times their original length. One might say that Chrétien describes how the dead knight is stripped down to the toes, "Tantost Yonez le desvest / Et jusqu'an l'artoil le deschauce" (1148f.), whereas Wolfram describes how the eager youth is armed from the feet up, "von fuoze ûf gewâpent wol / wart Parzivâl mit gernder dol" (157.15f.).

The additions to Chrétien's text draw attention to Parzival's acquisition of knightly equipment. The narrator's laconic observation emphasizes the brutally direct and abrupt transfer of armor:

> entwâpent wart der tôte man
> aldâ vor Nantes ûf dem plân,
> und an den lebenden geleget,
> den dannoch grôziu tumpheit reget.
> (156.21–24)

The armor was removed from the dead man right there on the meadow before Nantes, and placed on the living one, who was still urged on by great simplicity.

The most immediate result is the hero's helplessness. To a greater extent than Chrétien, Wolfram provides Parzival with on-the-spot training, a further reflection of his continuing foolishness. Iwanet instructs him (*lêren*) in removing and putting on the armor, "'daz kan ich wol gelêren dich'" (156.18), drawing a sword, "daz lêrt ern ûz ziehen" (157.23), and guiding a horse while wielding a shield and spear:

> Ywâneten niht bevilte,
> ern lêrte in underm schilte
> künstleclîch gebâren
> und der vînde schaden vâren.
> er bôt im in die hant ein sper:
> daz was gar âne sîne ger.
> (158.1–6)

> It wasn't too much for Ywanet to teach him to maneuver behind a shield and inflict damage on the enemy. He placed a spear in his hand, though he had certainly not asked for it.

The result, as the narrator assures us by spuriously invoking the authority of the "source," makes a better picture of the "compleat knight" than any artist from Cologne or Maastricht could paint (158.13–16).[33]

The investiture on the meadow outside Nantes thereby attains a significance in Wolfram's text that it does not have in his French source: Parzival's acquisition of knightly armor, his transgressive realization of Arthur's Rash Boon, involves a change of status. The change is made most explicit by Iwanet's insistent objections to Parzival's former attire and weapons, stressing that he should no longer wear his rough brogues,

> Iwânet sprach "diu ribbalîn
> sulen niht underem îsern sîn:
> du solt nu tragen ritters kleit."
> (156.25–27)

> Iwanet said: "The brogues shouldn't be under the armor: you should now wear knightly attire."

or use a javelot,

[33] Cologne, because of its association with the cult of the Three Kings, is known for its portraits of horsemen, Maastricht for the excellence of its artwork. See Wolfram's similar comment on the exemplary knighthood of Heimrich der Schetis, Willehalm's younger brother (*Willehalm* 241.25–30).

"ich enreiche dir kein gabylôt:
diu ritterschaft dir daz verbôt"
(157.19f.)

"I will not hand you any javelot: knighthood forbids you that."

because he is from this moment on a *knight* and must deport himself according to his new station. Significantly, these objections and their emphasis on "knightly attire" and "knighthood" are not in Chrétien's narrative. The change is also suggested by the fact that references to Parzival as a squire cease and he is called a man for the first time, implicitly at the moment that the armor is transferred from the "dead man" to the "living one" (156.21ff.), then explicitly as the foolish "man" (161.17, 162.1) rides away on Ither's charger, recalling the tradition that the age of maturity commences with induction into knighthood.[34]

These allusions support Parzival's assertion when he arrives at Gurnemanz's castle that Arthur has already made him a knight, "mich hiez ein künec ritter sîn" (163.22). In fact, Wolfram's elaboration of several motifs commonly associated with dubbings conveys the impression that the ingenuous actions of the two eager youths beside the murdered Ither's corpse represent a transgressive knighting ceremony. The first motif is that of Parzival's new spurs. Chrétien places no great emphasis on his hero's spurs except to illustrate ignorance of their use, "Ne d'esperon rien ne savoit" (1188f.). Wolfram expunges the reference and instead presents the buckling on of Parzival's spurs with several striking details:

zwuo liehte hosen îserîn
schuohterm über diu ribbalîn.
sunder leder mit zwein porten
zwêne sporen dar zuo gehôrten:
er spien im an daz goldes werc.
(157.7–11)

He shod him with two shiny iron hose over the boots. Two spurs worked in gold went along with them, and he fastened them on not with leather straps, but with ribbon.

There are two possibilities for the initial lines of this passage. Lachmann's reading, which associates the straps with the spurs, is unusual but possi-

[34] See the references in Bumke, *Ritterbegriff*, 107–09, and Robert W. Ackerman, "The Knighting Ceremonies in the Middle English Romances" (1944), 285. That Wolfram was familiar with this tradition is suggested by the fact that Vivianz associates his *swertleite* with his entrance into manhood (*Willehalm* 66.7–9).

ble.[35] Leitzmann places a comma after "ribbalîn" and a period after "porten," which would associate the straps with the shoelike iron hose. In either case, by emphasizing that the straps are not leather, the most commonly used material, but woven or embroidered cloth, Wolfram implies that their specification refers to a context other than everyday usage, such as the formal occasion of a *swertleite.*

The same is true of the spurs themselves. Chrétien does not indicate their composition in the corresponding scene of his romance, later alluding to the fact that they are made of steel (1428), whereas Wolfram explicitly states at the outset that they are gilded, "goldes werc." During the twelfth and thirteenth centuries, gilded spurs came to be associated with the prerogatives of the knightly class.[36] Moreover, they are the only type specified in descriptions of dubbings, on some occasions comprising the most salient feature of the ceremony.[37] The *Vita Heinrici IV. imperatoris* indicates that gilded spurs were desired knightly equipment in Germany as early as the beginning of the twelfth century,[38] and at least one student of medieval institutions concludes that "one frequently put spurs, most often gilded, on a new knight from the twelfth century on."[39]

The second motif, the hero's investiture with the Red Knight's sword, acquires a similar significance. In Chrétien's text, the buckling on of Perceval's sword is only one of a paratactic series of actions in arming the hero (1176–85). Wolfram focuses his attention on Ither's sword only after this process has been completed:

> [Iwanet] gurte im umbe ein scharpfez swert:
> daz lêrt ern ûz ziehen
> und widerriet im fliehen.
>
> (157.22–24)

[35] The standard works on the history of the spur, listed by Lynn White, *Medieval Technology and Social Change* (1964), 1, assume that straps are normally made of leather. The Middle High German dictionaries of Lexer and Benecke-Müller-Zarncke do not cite spur straps as a use for *borten,* but Alwin Schultz, *Das höfische Leben zur Zeit der Minnesinger* (1889), II, 83, provides two later examples.

[36] See Karl Treis, *Die Formalitäten des Ritterschlags in der altfranzösischen Epik* (1887), 76–78; Ernst Heinrich Massmann, *Schwertleite und Ritterschlag* (1932), 156–60; and Fritz Pietzner, *Schwertleite und Ritterschlag* (1934), 110–11.

[37] See Ackerman, "Knighting Ceremonies," 298–300, and the tables in Treis, *Formalitäten,* 117, and Pietzner, *Schwertleite,* 110. The significance of spurs in Perceval's dubbing ceremony is illustrated by the fact that Gornemant asks the hero to refer to him as the man "qui vostre esperon vos chauça" (1687).

[38] "Gaudebat aurum non se iam in luto calcari, dum ferreis calcaribus inopia cogeret uti." Cited from the edition of Georg Heinrich Pertz (1855), 19.

[39] François L. Ganshof, "Qu'est-ce que la chevalerie?" *Revue générale belge* (1947), 79. See also Lynn White's criticism of Massmann's undervaluation of German evidence in *Medieval Technology,* 150.

Iwanet girded a sharp sword around him: he taught him to draw it, and counseled him not to flee.

Two modifications are particularly striking. Whereas Yonez merely shows his friend how to buckle on the sword himself so that it hangs loosely (1183f.), Iwanet explicitly girds it around Parzival's waist. The gesture is certainly more formal; in fact, the term *swert umbe gurten* is a technical term employed by Middle High German writers—including Wolfram—to describe knighting ceremonies.[40] Moreover, the admonition not to flee, which would be gratuitous in Chrétien's scene, is entirely appropriate here: the investiture of a new knight often concluded with an exhortation to observe the obligations of his new station. In knighting ceremonies and handbooks on knighthood, the admonition to be brave is frequent, and its obverse, the admonition not to flee, not uncommon.[41]

In spite of the paucity of historical evidence, then, it seems that Wolfram models the scene outside Nantes on knighting ceremonies. Indeed, we need look no further than Chrétien's narrative for a source that provides these details.[42] In the scene at Gornemant's castle that Wolfram "deletes," Chrétien calls special attention to spurs and sword in a parallel manner ("Et li prodon"), states that it was the custom for him who made a knight to attach the spurs and that girding on the sword confirmed the bestowal of knighthood, then concludes with an exhortation:

Et li prodon s'est abeissiez,
Si li chauça l'esperon destre:

[40] Sources are listed in Massmann, *Schwertleite,* 39. Willehalm uses the expression to refer to Vivianz's *swertleite,* "was wold ich swerts umb dich gegurt?" (67.10). In accordance with his interpretation, Bumke argues that the reference in *Parzival* 157.22 is to be taken "only in the literal sense, without connection to a knighting" ("Parzivals 'Schwertleite'," 243 n. 20).

[41] On the general topic of "Ritterpflichten," see Massmann, *Schwertleite,* 175–79; Pietzner, *Schwertleite,* 107–11; Treis, *Formalitäten,* 87–95. For admonitions not to be cowardly or flee: "Rittersitte" (20–26), ed. Hermann Menhardt, *ZfdA* 68 (1931), 153–63; Thomasin von Zirclaria, *Der wälsche gast,* "du solt den strit nimmer gevliehen" (7490) (1852; rpt. 1965); Heinrich Wittenweiler, *Der Ring,* "du scholt nit fliehen" (4795), ed. Edmund Wiessner (Leipzig, 1931); Johannes Rothe, "Ritterspiegel," "und niht flihin noch abegehin" (3363), in *Mitteldeutsche Gedichte,* ed. Karl Bartsch, BLVS 53 (Stuttgart, 1860); *Valentin und Namelos,* "dar scoltu nimmer avegân" (873), ed. Wilhelm Seelmann, Niederdeutsche Denkmäler, 4 (Norden, 1884). Vivianz makes a vow not to flee at his *swertleite* (*Willehalm* 41.12 and 66.25ff.).

[42] See the large number of sources listed in Treis, *Formalitäten,* 117, and Pietzner, *Schwertleite,* 110, in which the sword and spurs are the only weapons mentioned. On dubbing in Chrétien, see Jean Flori, "Pour une histoire de la chevalerie: L'adoubement dans les romans de Chrétien de Troyes" (1979), and Barbara Nelson Sargent-Baur, "Promotion to Knighthood in the Romances of Chrétien de Troyes" (1983/84).

La costume soloit teus estre
Que cil qui feisoit chevalier
Li devoit l'esperon chaucier. . . .
Et li prodon l'espee a prise,
Si li çainst et si le beisa
Et dit que donee li a
La plus haute ordre avuec l'espee
Que Deus et feite et comandee:
C'est l'ordre de chevalerie,
Qui doit estre sanz vilenie.
(1624–38)

And the worthy man bent down and fastened on his right spur for him. It was the custom at that time that whoever dubbed someone a knight should fasten on his spur for him. And the worthy man took the sword and girded it on him and kissed him and said that with the sword he had given him the highest order God had created and ordained: The order of chivalry, which must be without baseness.

III

This interpretation of Parzival's investment with Ither's armor as a transgressive *swertleite,* based on the Old French source but displaced from Chrétien's Goort to Wolfram's Nantes, has a variety of implications. It would make unnecessary the "uncomfortable thought that the most knightly of the courtly poets seems to be so unfamiliar with the most important chivalric institution."[43] In fact, the discomfort is unnecessary: whereas Chrétien legitimizes his hero's actions by separating the murder of the Red Knight from the knighting ceremony at Goort, Wolfram combines these two events outside the walls of Arthur's capital, emphasizing that Parzival becomes a knight *and* commits a serious sin by means of one and the same act. The knighting ceremony, apparently absent at Graharz, is proleptically present in carnivalized form at Nantes.

Moreover, Wolfram imbues this scene with extensive reminiscences of a *swertleite,* even though he does not explicitly designate it as such, implying that the hero's entrance into knighthood is unwarranted and even travesties that ceremony. Iwanet is a squire, not a knight, ingenuously initiating the hero into the profession to which he himself does not yet belong.[44] Nor does Parzival have any clear idea of knighthood, except that a knight

[43] Bumke, "Parzivals 'Schwertleite'," 243.
[44] On the following, see Treis, *Formalitäten,* 26–29, 74, 82, 100–08; Massmann, *Schwertleite,* 95–104; and Pietzner, *Schwertleite,* 77–83.

wears armor and that it is in *Ither's* armor that he is supposed to become a knight (154.7). Because the *swertleite* consisted principally of two closely related features, the investiture of a candidate with his equipment, which was often passed on from one member of a family to another, and the implied or demonstrated facility in using that equipment, Parzival's appropriation of his relative's armor and his ignorance of its use constitute a highly problematic entry into knighthood.

And because the most visible characteristic of a knight is his armor, Ither's equipment becomes a constant reminder of Parzival's acquisition of knighthood and his knightly guilt. This relationship is intimated at the beginning of his visit with Gurnemanz by the wound incurred in the fight with Ither. Whereas the Red Knight strikes Perceval on the shoulder, Ither's warning blow hits Parzival on the head (155.3), leaving a puzzling mark whose significance will be revealed by the discussion of Cain's fratricide in Book IX:

"sîn zimierde ist rîche:
dez harnasch stuont rîterlîche
ê ez kœm von dem gehiuren.
von einer quaschiuren
bluotige amesiere
kôs ich an im schiere."
(164.21–26)

"His outfit is splendid and his armor fit him like knight before it was removed from the handsome fellow. But I immediately noticed the bloodstains of a bruise on him."

Shortly thereafter the metonymy of the "knight" and his "armor" is formalized by Gurnemanz's transfer of the sobriquet "The Red Knight" from Ither to Parzival in the form of a chiasmus ("der ritter rôt"—"der rôte ritter"), which separates the two individuals but unites their knightly careers in the armor they share:

der wirt erkante den ritter rôt:
er dersiufte, in derbarmt sîn nôt.
sînen gast des namn er niht erliez,
den rôten ritter er in hiez.
(170.3–6)

The host recognized the Red Knight, and sighed in compassion. His name he transferred to his guest, and called him the Red Knight.

A comparison with *Li Contes del Graal* reveals, not surprisingly, that Wolfram emphasizes this epithet and imbues it with connotations that his source does not have. As we have seen, Chrétien attaches no particular significance to Perceval's murder of the Red Knight and the theft of his armor, and he therefore refers only twice to his hero as "le chevalier vermoil."[45] Wolfram refers to his hero with vastly greater frequency as "der rôte ritter" or "der ritter rôt" and avoids other variations almost without exception.[46] This epithet could have been suggested to Wolfram by his knowledge that red is a traditional color of Cain's clothing[47] or by familiarity with an earlier Red Knight, the homicidal Mabonagrin in Hartmann's *Erec*, another motif that would locate the hero in the chaotic post-*Erec*ian world characteristic of Books III–IV:

sîn ros was grôz unde hô,
starc rôt zundervar.
der varwe was sîn schilt gar:
sîn wâpenroc alsam was,
er selbe rôt, als ich ez las,
gewâfent nâch sînem muote.
ich wæne sîn herze bluote
swenne er niht ze vehtenne vant:
sô mordic was sîn hant.
(*Erec*, 9015–23)

His horse was tall and large, strong and fire-red. His shield was the same color, as was his surcoat. As I read, he himself was red, armed according to his mood. I imagine his heart bled whenever he found nothing to fight about, so murderous was his hand.

Whatever its origins, the motif of the Red Knight occurs principally from Books III to IX, from the beginnings of Parzival's knightly career to his absolution by Trevrizent, and it therefore appears to function as a reminiscence of his knightly guilt.

This does not necessarily imply that Parzival's knightly career is entirely

[45] In addition to "le chevalier vermoil" (2596 and 3961), Chrétien uses nonrecurring variations such as "armez d'unes armes vermoilles" (2387), "li vaslez as armes vermoilles" (2768), "ses armes vermoilles sont" (2848), "li vaslez qui vos demanda armes vermoilles" (4016f.), "armes totes dorees" (4106).

[46] See 170.6, 176.20, 202.21, 206.16, 218.4, 221.6, 276.4/21, 278.25, 280.9, 305.11, 307.18, 309.16, 315.11, 383.24, 388.8, 389.4/29, and 392.20.

[47] On Cain's clothing, see *Le Mystère d'Adam*, ed. Paul Studer (1962), 29: "chaym sit indutus rubeis vestibus."

sinful or contributes nothing to his development.[48] Such allusions and their frequent reminiscences of Parzival's *swertleite* do, however, emphasize that the hero's knighthood and knightly guilt begin simultaneously and remain linked until Trevrizent reorders his priorities, absolving him of sin and yet advising him how to live as a knight (501.17f.). The epithets employed to describe Parzival after this turning point reflect the changed situation, with references to "der rôte ritter" being notably infrequent. Nonetheless, as Parzival discovers during his battle with Gawan, which begins ominously with the motif of his red armor (679.8–11), the emblem obtained in his *swertleite*, "'diu alten wâpen mîn'" (689.1), remains with him, symbolically drawing attention to a fundamental problem of knighthood, namely, that the feats of arms that determine chivalric success are never free of the danger of homicide, of recapitulating the archetypal deed of Cain.

Wolfram reminds his hero of this inescapable fact of knightly existence in the battle with Feirefiz, bringing Parzival's career full circle from the murder of a distant relative in his first encounter to the threat of actual fratricide in his last one.[49] Yet Ither's sword, with which Iwanet concluded Parzival's *swertleite*, breaks at the decisive blow,

got des niht langer ruochte
daz Parzivâl daz rê nemen
in sîner hende solde zemen:
daz swert er Ithêre nam
als sîner tumpheit dô wol zam.
(744.14–18)

God no longer wished for corpse-robbing to be apparent in Parzival's hand: the sword he took from Ither, as befitted his simplicity then.

suddenly relativizing the hero's knightly endeavors by means of different genre discourses that compete with his romance quest, the miracle and the saint's life, whose intrusion into the narrative we examine in later chapters.

[48] The latter position has been taken by Herta Zutt, "Parzivals Kämpfe" (1968).

[49] According to Carl Wesle, "Zu Wolframs *Parzival*" (1950), Parzival's duel with Feirefiz is partially modeled on that between Mabonagrin and Erec, which would also implicitly terminate the connections between the hero and the world of *Erec*.

CHAPTER FOUR

Dialogic Transpositions: The Grail Hero Wins a Wife

Although comparisons still form a basic ingredient of studies on Chrétien's *Li Contes del Graal* and Wolfram's *Parzival*, the results frequently resemble the undifferentiated hunter-gathering of so much nineteenth-century scholarship. Admittedly, it is not easy to theorize a relationship between these two texts that can accommodate the way in which Wolfram decenters and pluralizes his "source." Indeed, neither classical theories of translation nor the freedom of medieval practice seems adequate for dealing with Wolfram's treatment of Chrétien's narrative,[1] because—as Karl Bertau observed several decades ago[2]—the process also involves transpositions from a clerical to a knightly perspective, and from a French to a German horizon of expectations. As the preceding two chapters suggest, the latter shift spans a broad range from cultural institutions to intertextuality, whereas the former replaces the nameless structure and episode-generating figures (Mother, Tent Maiden, Cousin, Red Knight, etc.) by named characters with a detailed genealogy, shifting the narrative from adventure romance to family romance.[3]

The importance of this transposition of social, cultural, and genre determinants should not, however, preclude an even more general consideration. The process also reflects a basic shift in the nature of novelistic discourse itself, from monologic to dialogic narrative, and more particularly from First to Second Line romance. For heuristic purposes, the

[1] See George Steiner, *After Babel: Aspects of Language and Translation* (1975), 254–56; Carl Lofmark, "Der höfische Dichter als Übersetzer" (1972).

[2] See Karl Bertau, "Versuch über den späten Chrestien und die Anfänge Wolframs" (1972).

[3] These are subgenres within one narrative tradition. See Mikhail Bakhtin, *Problems of Dostoevsky's Poetics* (1984), 101–06.

distinction might be characterized by extreme types: monologic narratives present a unified and controlled authorial world; dialogic narratives juxtapose, play with, and incorporate a universe of competing viewpoints—those of the author, a narrator, any number of characters—and inscribe them in a variety of discourses ranging from differing linguistic registers to distinct genre styles. In reality, however, the extreme antithesis has to be modified, since Wolfram has transposed a comparatively homogeneous narrative to a more heterogeneous one, transposed, in Bakhtinian terms, a still monologic romance to a more nearly dialogic one. Chrétien's clerical rhetoric provides an apparently unifying principle that already exploits small-scale possibilities for dialogic discourse. Wolfram's decentered chivalric narrative, with its more highly differentiated role for the narrator, delights not only in dialogic structures within and between episodes, but also relates Parzival's adventures to those of other figures in the text, and ultimately engages in dialogue, even genre battles, with other texts.

I

In this chapter I will attempt to exemplify this thesis by discussing a central episode in the Grail story, Perceval's winning of Blancheflor and Parzival's of Condwiramurs. There is a relative paucity of scholarship on this episode, except for treatments of the love relationship,[4] possibly because Chrétien and Wolfram appear to present essentially the same event, and an archetypal one at that: the hero's rescue of a damsel in distress. Chrétien's version presents a series of events during the course of a week, first at Blancheflor's and then at Arthur's castle:

> Day 1. The "new knight" arrives at the besieged city of Belrepeire, which he finds bereft of food and comfort. A series of receptions leads him to the lady of the castle, whose description—and the reaction of bystanders—makes them seem destined for each other. After a meager meal, the hero retires to his empty chamber. During the night, the scantily-clad lady comes to arouse . . . his interest in her plight, first threatening suicide and then enticing him with her kisses.
>
> Day 2. After stating that he will fight for her love, Perceval breaks the year-long siege of the castle by defeating Anguingueron in single combat, forcing the seneschal to withdraw his troops and agree to captivity at the appropriate prison, which—on the third attempt—devolves on Arthur's

[4] On Chrétien, see François Suard, "Place et signification de l'épisode Blanchefleur dans le *Conte du graal* de Chrétien de Troyes" (1973); on Wolfram, see Bumke, *Wolfram,* 180.

court. The townspeople are relieved (but annoyed at his escape), and Perceval and the lady withdraw to the pleasures of each other's company.

In the meantime, Clamadeu arrives with his army and—after consulting advisors—launches a full-scale assault in waves of first twenty knights, then 500 knights and 1000 foot soldiers, which Perceval and the townspeople repel. A barge laden with supplies arrives at the castle, thereby effectively rendering a siege by Clamadeu impossible. The inhabitants of the castle celebrate by feasting, and the hero and lady of the castle disport themselves in private.

Day 3. Heedless of the entreaties of his mistress and her people, Perceval engages Clamadeu in a now anticlimactic single combat, which the hero wins, offering him the same choices as Anguingueron. While the townspeople rejoice, Clamadeu frees his prisoners and follows his seneschal on the road to Arthur's court.

Day 4 onward. The ensuing days are telescoped into a description of Clamadeu's journey: following Anguingueron's path, he stays three nights in the same lodging as the seneschal before him, arriving one day later at Dinasdaron, where King Arthur is celebrating Pentecost. While Kay supervises the festivities, Clamadeu arrives to deliver his message to Arthur, punctuated by the repeated prophecy of the fool, and then to the maiden whom Kay struck. The narrative then returns to Belrepeire, where the restive hero, in spite of the entreaties of his mistress and her people, departs to find his mother, promising to return.

Chrétien presents his version of this episode with the elegant structure and sophisticated elaboration of themes characteristic of his learned rhetorical style. The events of the first two days at the castle of Belrepeire suggest a pattern of anticipation and fulfillment, first through a reception on the first day that culminates in the presentation of Perceval and Blancheflor as a potentially ideal couple, then through the hero's winning of her favor on the second day in a series of encounters that culminates in his victory in a pitched battle. The narrator elaborates this pattern, among other things, by intimating a metonymic relationship between public and private behavior, board and room, or—more bluntly—food and sex. On the first evening, both are inadequate: the inhabitants of the castle dine on meager provisions (1910–17), after which Perceval retires alone to a bed that promises every comfort one could imagine—except, the narrator assures us, female companionship:

> Trestot l'eise et tot le delit
> Qu'an seüst deviser an lit,
> Ot li chevaliers cele nuit

Fors que solemant le deduit
De pucele, se lui pleüst,
Ou de dame, se lui leüst;
Mes il n'an savoit nule rien.
(1935–41)

> That night the knight had all the comfort and pleasure one can imagine in bed, except the company of a maiden, if it had pleased him, or of a lady, if it had been allowed him—but of that he knew nothing.

On the second evening, absence becomes presence: the arrival of a barge loaded with supplies provides the opportunity for a lively feast (2578–81), and Perceval and Blancheflor disport themselves freely:

Or se puet li vaslez deduire
Delez s'amie tot a eise:
Cele l'acole, et il la beise,
Si fet li uns de l'autre joie.
(2574–77)

> Now the youth may disport himself with his love; she embraces him, and he kisses her, and each gives pleasure to the other.

Although the plot thus suggests a self-contained structure of anticipation and fulfillment, both the heroine's and hero's actions complicate this expectation. Blancheflor's nocturnal visit at the end of the first evening creates an ironic discrepancy between the narrator's assurance of propriety and the ambiguity of her actual behavior—scanty attire, symptoms that resemble Ovidian love sickness (sweating, sleeplessness, etc.),[5] and patently manipulative actions. This discrepancy introduces a competition for control of the story between the narrator and a figure within the story, which subverts the narrator's authority, and even reverses sex roles, allowing Blancheflor to play the predator while Perceval becomes her innocent prey. Moreover, Blancheflor's sudden shift to hypercorrect behavior the next morning, which begins with an apology for the "inadequate lodging" of the previous night, appropriates the narrator's metonymic play with public and private metaphors of food and sex, transforming it into a synecdochic one, part of a sophisticated ploy to induce the hero to reject her public suggestions and thus to undertake what her private visit has aroused him to do.

[5] See Adrian Stevens, "Heteroglossia and Clerical Narrative: On Wolfram's Adaptation of Chrétien" (1993).

The narrator's presentation of Perceval's actions does not proceed any more smoothly. Here, too, ironic discrepancies between the hero's actions and the expectations of socioliterary conventions also open possibilities for the interplay of discourses. On two occasions, Perceval applies the rules of behavior impressed on him by Gornemant, remembering not to talk too much (1857–61) and never willingly to slay a vanquished opponent (2238–42). Both occasions seem to represent an advance over his foolish attempts to apply his mother's advice, because the new strictures are passive, helping him avoid inappropriate action.[6] Nonetheless, the immediate contexts—significant for their relationship to the dominant concerns of love and prowess in courtly romance—suggest that the hero's application of Gornemant's advice remains mechanical and inappropriate. On the first occasion, the narrator marks Blancheflor's importance by introducing her with the catalogue description of feminine beauty typically reserved for heroines in Chrétien's romances.[7] Perceval's silence immediately creates an ironic disjunction between Gornemant's instructions and romance genre expectations, a disjunction emphasized by the bystanders, who wonder whether the strange knight is dumb while also observing that he and their lady seem made for each other:

> "Deus!" fet chascuns, "mout me mervoil
> Se cist chevaliers est muiaus.
> Granz diaus seroit; qu'onques si biaus
> Chevaliers ne fu nez de fame:
> Mout avient bien delez ma dame,
> Et ma dame aussi delez lui,
> S'il ne fussent muël andui;
> Tant est cil biaus et cele bele
> Qu'onques chevaliers ne pucele
> Si bien n'avindrent mes ansanble;
> Que de l'un et de l'autre sanble
> Que Deus l'un por l'autre feïst
> Por ce qu'ansanble les meïst."
>
> (1862–74)

"By God," said each, "I wonder if this knight is dumb. It would be a great pity, for never was so handsome a knight born of woman. He looks very well next to my lady, and she next to him; if only both were not silent. He is so handsome and she so beautiful that never knight nor lady

[6] See Peter Haidu, *Aesthetic Distance in Chrétien de Troyes* (1968), 156.
[7] See Alice Colby, *The Portrait in Twelfth-Century French Literature* (1965).

looked so well together. It seems that God has created one for the other in order that he might bring them together."

On the second occasion, Perceval remembers Gornemant's admonition to spare a vanquished opponent while Anguingueron is hastily enumerating the unstrained qualities of mercy. The discrepancy between an abstract rule and the actual context in which he applies it again draws attention to the gap between the foolish hero and sophisticated courtly society.

But the hero also makes choices pertaining to love and chivalry that can only be attributed to an emerging heritage that is helping him to bridge that gap. Prior to Blancheflor's nocturnal visit the narrator emphasizes that the hero knew and thought nothing of the pleasures of a lady's company in bed (1941f.). The action that night does not progress beyond lying "boche a boche" (2065, 2068) and exchanging kisses, a relatively innocent natural activity that he practiced on his mother's handmaids (725–28) even before his mother's advice permitted him to apply it to the Tent Maiden (546–49, 693–95). But when, on the ensuing morning, Perceval explicitly demands concubinage, "druërie" (2104), as his reward for breaking the siege, he suddenly progresses to a socially complex form of love relationship, mentioned here for the first time in the romance, that he cannot have known previously. There is a similar leap in chivalric behavior immediately after Perceval's mechanical offer of mercy to Anguingueron: the victorious hero returns to the castle, countering the townspeople's annoyance over his failure to kill the seneschal with an eloquent defense of his moral integrity (2348ff.).

As these examples suggest, the momentum of Chrétien's narrative often derives from rhetorical opposition, such as natural or ignorant versus sophisticated chivalric behavior, and progresses by alternating between them. Indeed, this principle of rhetorical dialectic extends to the third day at Belrepeire, creating new variations that frustrate the closure implied by the previous pattern of anticipation and fulfillment. Whereas the hero's recourse to Gornemant's precepts seemed to provoke their dialectical opposite, leading from preconditioned to instinctual aristocratic behavior, the narrator now begins to negate the role of advice itself by shifting attention to the hero's antagonist. Rejecting the sound advice of a squire (2390–92) and accepting that of a misguided "mestre" (2395), who misinterprets every important motif introduced by the narrator during the previous day, Clamadeu intensifies the hostilities, and thereby hastens his own army's defeat. Nonetheless, he denies the closure implied by this defeat as well as by the providential arrival of supplies in the beleaguered city, and, in an inversion of the motif of advice, challenges the hero to single combat without listening to anyone's counsel, a challenge that the hero accepts, also without listening to the advice of his mistress and the townspeople. Although Perceval thereby regains control of his destiny in a way that stands in pointed contrast to Blancheflor's initial manipulation of his actions, he causes an extension of the combat so anticlimactic that the narrator refuses to elaborate on the final duel (2678–81).

This generation of events out of a spirit of rhetorical dialectic seems to represent a major organizing principle of Chrétien's narrative. The most common forms of discursive dialogue, such as between the narrator and characters, are local, deriving from individual moments or from the elaboration of themes and their reversal from one character or episode to another. The main dialogic potential of this rhetorical dominant lies in repeating the hero's role as fool and in the carnivalizing conflict between his simplistic actions and sophisticated social or literary conventions as he proceeds from episode to episode. But herein lies a problem: repetition of such moments generates a series of episodes and a thematic dialectic but does not create any concomitant impression of their larger unity. Perceval's treatment of the defeated Anguingueron and Clamadeu provides a good example.

The hero offers both men the choice of presenting themselves to Blancheflor, then Gornemant, then Arthur, a choice that surveys his adventures in reverse order and anticipates his eventual return to the latter's court. The arrival of the seneschal and his lord there three days after their defeat allows the fool to repeat his prophecy about Kay's punishment (2866–71) and thus to anticipate once more Perceval's eventual return. The process will subsequently be repeated after the defeat of Li Orguelleus, whom the hero also orders to Arthur's court as a condition of his mercy (3950–80) and whose arrival again triggers the fool's prophecy (4074–76). But there is no immediate indication of the relative importance or interrelationship of these two parallel events, except for the fact that Li Orguelleus is given only one choice, which could reflect either distance from Blancheflor and Gornemant or proximity to Arthur. The extent and structure of the series remains uncertain.

A principal reason for this uncertainty seems to be that Chrétien's emphasis on exploiting the local rhetorical possibilities of individual episodes or themes avoids the organization and orchestration of larger interrelationships that characterizes more overtly dialogic forms of narrative. Again, another of Bakhtin's concepts provides a point of departure:[8] the chronotope, or differentiation of discourse through the articulation of time and space. In *Li Contes del Graal* chronotopic markers usually denote

[8] See, for example, his "Forms of Time and of the Chronotope in the Novel," *Dialogic Imagination*, esp. 151–55.

a change from one episode to another, rather than distinguish or create relationships between them. Chronological references to the events before and after Perceval's sojourn at Belrepeire clearly delineate one-day time periods: the first day in the woods, the progression from abusing the Tent Maiden the following morning to his knighting by Gornemant on the morning after that (635/1597). His subsequent visit to the Grail castle, the encounters with the cousin and the Tent Maiden, Li Orguelleus's arrival at court, and the episode with the drops of blood in the snow also encompass a day each or have a clear reference to morning or night (2976, 3356f., 3998, 4160–64), while the festivities that celebrate his integration into the Arthurian world last two days, emphasizing the conclusion of his first series of adventures. Large-scale chronological references, however, remain confusing. The adventures between Perceval's first and second Arthurian visits last a few weeks at most, although it is difficult to reconcile ambiguous and conflicting evidence.[9] The time period mentioned by the fool's prophecy (1264), which links the initial and concluding Arthurian episodes, varies in the manuscripts from forty days (the most common number) to a fortnight and even a week, not one of which accords entirely with the cumulative time elapsed in individual episodes and with other points of reference, the celebration of Pentecost at court (2785) and the snowfall after Perceval's departure from the Grail castle (4162).

References to space also serve primarily to delineate individual episodes. Geographical change from one place to another is indicated by a path or road (861, 3422, 3644) or by the transition from forest to meadow or plain (630–40, 1306f., 1703f.). The fact that Perceval's journey after leaving the Tent Maiden proceeds along the coast to the castles at Carduel, Goort, and Belrepeire, each located above or facing the sea—"sor mer" (843/863); "vers mer" and "vers le gort" (1322, 1332); "fors des murs n'avoit neant / fors mer et eve et terre gaste" (1708f.)—gives some coherence to these episodes. But it is uncertain whether the wild landscape at Belrepeire reflects the local effects of the siege or marks a climax to the series. The ensuing episode at the Grail castle breaks the pattern, as Perceval's journey shifts inland to a river valley—a puzzling direction, since he intends to return to his mother. The articulation of space after this becomes less precise: Perceval leaves the Grail castle on a path leading into the forest (3422f.), where he meets his cousin, who

[9] See Hermann J. Weigand, "Die epischen Zeitverhältnisse in den Graldichtungen Chrestiens und Wolframs" (1938), rpt. in English in his *Wolfram's "Parzival"* (1969), esp. 21–33. The most recent study by Margret Sauer, *Parzival auf der Suche nach der verlorenen Zeit* (1981), presents further considerations on 153–66 and some results (whose basis is not entirely clear) in tables after 362.

then directs him to a paved road (3644) in the woods (3832), where he encounters the Tent Maiden and Li Orguelleus.

Chrétien thus seems to employ changes of time and space primarily to differentiate episodes from each other, only hinting at interrelationships between them, such as the importance of events at Belrepeire, the only prolonged episode in the hero's first series of adventures (it lasts a month, if we subtract the surrounding one-day episodes from the 40 days prophesied by the fool), or the Grail castle's apparently unique location. The vagueness accords with the treatment of other potential structuring principles, such as genealogy and kinship,[10] implying the absence of large-scale relationships. Inasmuch as Chrétien's highly controlled rhetorical style seems to raise expectations of just such an organization, it is not suprising to find that Wolfram does not hesitate to fill in his absences with a wide variety of modifications.

II

Wolfram transposes Chrétien's episode at Belrepeire into a narrative that subverts the social basis of the hero's relationship to the heroine, altering the thematic elaboration of events and substantially increasing their dialogic potential. The modest expansion of Chrétien's 1274 lines (1699–2973) to 1318 lines (179.13–223.30) still retains the clear-cut pattern of anticipation and fulfillment for events of the first and second day at Pelrapeire. This pattern is further emphasized by one of Wolfram's most obtrusive additions, a first-person narrator, who comments at length on the lack and then on the abundance of provisions in the beleaguered city. These two commentaries are clearly interrelated. Surveying the initial deprivation of the inhabitants, the narrator observes that his lord would not have liked to be a soldier there, "wær ungern soldier dâ gewesn" (184.4f.), and that the inhabitants are starving without anything to drip into their coals, "in trouf vil wênic in die kolen" (184.18). The arrival of provisions the following day reverses this condition and the narrator's opinion:

> den burgærn in die kolen trouf.
> ich wær dâ nu wol soldier.
> (201.4–5)

Fat dripped into the castle-dwellers' coals. I'd be glad to be a soldier there now.

[10] See Elisabeth Schmid, *Familiengeschichten und Heilsmythologie* (1986), 35–71.

This first-person kitchen humor fulfills a subversive intertextual function, uncoupling, so to speak, the metonymy between food and sex in Chrétien's narrative, and directing our attention to the public consumption of food.

The reason for this change is that Parzival's adventures do not culminate in concubinage but in marriage and kingship. As a result of this shift, perhaps the most important and far-reaching in the entire romance, the narrator does not lead us immediately from the public dining-hall to the privacy of the bedchamber, but pauses to emphasize Parzival's ability to distribute and manage provisions, dealing with scarcity on the first day, then with abundance on the second. The divergences from Chrétien are instructive: on the first night, Blancheflor commands the table to be set, and all sit down to eat briefly but eagerly (1921f.); Condwiramurs apportions the meager supplies to her people on the advice of Parzival, with the result that they have scarcely anything to themselves (191.1–5). On the second day, the arrival of a barge with provisions creates a great commotion among Chrétien's townspeople and merchants, who rush to purchase all the supplies and prepare a feast, freeing the hero to disport himself in private with his *amie* (2574f.). Wolfram's hero, who has just received the townspeople's fealty as their *hêrre*, immediately exercises his rule through the queen's marshal, who imposes order and brings the merchants to the new regent for public negotiations (200.24–201.1). Moreover, Parzival then serves his people with his own hands, beginning with small portions in order to observe moderation and not overstuff their shrunken stomachs, a procedure the narrator emphasizes (201.8–18).

Parzival thus demonstrates a new and sovereign control over the appetite that ruled his own behavior as recently as his sojourn at Graharz, confirming Gurnemanz's assessment that he is destined to be a ruler, "volkes hêrre" (170.22). This shift in focus, already apparent in the change from *Ritterlehre* to *Fürstenlehre*, from Gornemant's brief chivalric rules delivered at Perceval's dubbing to Gurnemanz's general advice on deportment and future kingship, is a consequential one. The narrative conventions for knights-errant are not identical with those for kings and rulers. The christological overtones of Parzival's feeding of the multitude and serving of his people, for example, together with references to divine providence (185.18, 200.16), appropriate the discourse of medieval political theology on the ideal ruler as an *imago Christi* or *christomimetes*,[11] presaging a unique reign for Parzival, "der reine" (the flawless) and "der unlôse niht ze hêr" (the moderate man without arrogance [201.9/18]).

[11] See Ernst Kantorowicz, *The King's Two Bodies: A Study in Medieval Political Theology* (1957), 42–86.

Given this radical alteration of the hero's and heroine's relationship from private concubinage to public rule and marriage, it is not surprising that the bedroom scenes following the first and second day's distribution of food also have a different focus. There is still a pattern of anticipation and fulfillment in the portrayal of the hero's and heroine's adventures at night, but it is sexless—a dry run with a different agenda. Wolfram's narrator immediately asserts the authority to guarantee the maidenly propriety of Condwiramur's visit to the hero's chamber:

Daz kom als ich iu sagen wil.
ez prach niht wîplîchiu zil.
(192.1–2)

That came about as I intend to tell you. It did not break the bounds of womanly modesty.

Rejecting the private sexual motivation of Chrétien's *pucele*, he attributes the queen's nocturnal visit to a public feudal obligation, the search for *auxilium* and *concilium*:

dô gienc diu küneginne
niht nâch sölher minne
diu sölhen namen reizet
der meide wîp heizet,
si suochte helfe unt friundes rât.
(192.9–13)

The queen did not go in search of such love as evokes the name that has maidens called women; she sought help and the counsel of a friend.

A brief comparison of the two heroines' actions confirms this shift in motivation. Blancheflor, sweating with Ovidian anticipation of her "avanture" (1954), dresses in a *short* coat of *scarlet* silk, "un mantel cort de soie an grainne" (1952), before proceeding to wake the hero with teary embraces, then disclaims any ulterior motive before drawing attention to the fact that she is nearly nude, "je sui pres que nue" (1986). Condwiramurs, driven, "twanc" (192.5/20), by anguish over the death of friends and vassals, dresses in a *long* silk coat, "von samît einen mantel lanc" (192.19), over a *white* shift (192.15), and stops in supplication before the hero's bed. The narrator intrudes with an editorial comment to emphasize that neither the hero nor the heroine are capable of doing what their counterparts do in Chrétien's narrative:

> si heten beidiu kranken sin,
> er unt diu küneginne,
> an bî ligender minne.
> (193.2–4)

They both had no idea, he and the queen, of lovemaking.

There is irony in this nocturnal encounter, but it differs from Chrétien's.[12] Having emphasized the innocence of the approaching queen, the narrator also alerts his audience to the erotic potential of the meeting with metaphors of the *Minnekrieg* and a rhetorical question:

> an ir was werlîchiu wât,
> ein hemde wîz sîdîn:
> waz möhte kampflîcher sîn,
> dan gein dem man sus komende ein wîp?
> (192.14–17)

She was dressed for combat in a white satin shift: what could be more battlelike than a woman coming thus to a man?

But the actions of the principals and the suspicions of the audience will remain distinct, as Condwiramurs agrees to "lie together" (*bîligen*) without "wrestling" (194.1–2). In contrast to Chrétien's narrative, where the lovers spend the night kissing until dawn, Parzival and Condwiramurs continue their discussion, the hero's earnest promise of aid coinciding with the narrator's ironic marking of the transition from night to day with a dawn song motif, "diu naht het ende und kom der tac" (196.2).[13] The following night will confirm the lack of physical love intimated by the hero's and heroine's ignorance, not the innuendos shared by the narrator and audience.

The second night in Wolfram's narrative accordingly alters the retreat to private joy in the midst of general feasting that Chrétien describes. It is a formal wedding night: Parzival and Condwiramurs have been publicly asked about consummating their relationship, and have assented.[14] In the bedroom, the narrator intrudes with a lengthy excursus, first on the be-

[12] See Stevens, "Heteroglossia" (1993).

[13] Wolfgang Mohr, "Spiegelungen des Tagelieds" (1971). John Greenfield, "The 'Tageliet' in Wolfram's *Parzival*" (1987), discusses only Parzival's and Condwiramurs's reunion in Book XV.

[14] See Marlis Schumacher, *Die Auffassung der Ehe in den Dichtungen Wolframs von Eschenbach* (1967), 37–47.

havior of women, then of men in a particular type of relationship. Parzival's *mâze* resembles that of a faithful, constant man:

er denket, als ez lîht ist wâr,
"ich hân gedienet mîniu jâr
nâch lône disem wîbe,
diu hât mîme lîbe
erboten trôst: nu lige ich hie.
des hete mich genüget ie,
ob ich mit mîner blôzen hant
müese rüeren ir gewant.
ob ich nu gîtes gerte,
untriwe es für mich werte." . . .
sus lac der Wâleise.
(202.5–19)

He thinks, as may well be true, "I have served this lady all my years for her reward. Now she has offered me solace, and I am lying here. It would once have satisfied me if I could have brushed her garment with my bare hand. If I desired her too greedily now, I should be disloyal to myself." . . . Thus lay the Waleis.

This moderation of the constant and loyal servant resembles that of a courtly lover, who, after having served in pursuit of his lady's consolation for years, still treats her with solicitude at the moment of reward.[15]

Wolfram's excursus thus suggests that Parzival and Condwiramurs combine the features of two very different kinds of relationship, marriage and courtly love. Parzival accordingly is Condwiramurs's lord (*hêrre*) as well as lover, *âmîs* (200.5–7); she is his lady and wife, "frowe unde wîp" (302.7). This combination of love and marriage is no more unusual in Arthurian romance than is their conflict in the Tristan legend, both types of narrative reflecting a complex interplay in the High Middle Ages between secular and clerical systems of discourse as well as generational conflicts between young bachelors and seniors in aristocratic society.[16] But the complete inactivity of this wedding night also suggests the presence of a third discourse, something about Wolfram's couple that makes them unique.

[15] It is the exact opposite—to cite the scene that may be the target of Wolfram's humor—of the eagerness of Gunther, whose wedding in the *Nibelungenlied* also comprises two evenings and whose lust finds the same metaphorical expression in the desire to rumple his bride's shift.

[16] See Georges Duby, *The Knight, the Lady, and the Priest* (1983).

Parzival and Condwiramurs seem to lack the already existing passion that characterizes most romance heroes and heroines, including their randy counterparts in Chrétien's narrative. As late as their first night together, Parzival remains bothered by "Lîâzen minne" (195.11) and Condwiramurs mourns Liaze's brother Schenteflurs, killed in the siege of her castle (195.1–6). In spite of the opportunity traditionally afforded to romance heroes and heroines by their first meeting (as Gahmuret and Belakane amply demonstrate), Parzival and Condwiramurs have not fallen in love[17] and do not even seem eager to consummate their marriage now.

Condwiramurs does consider herself married and dresses as well as acts accordingly on the following morning, wearing a woman's headdress and ceding her possessions to her husband (202.21–28). In this respect, she shares the attitude of Sigune, who asserts that her love for Schionatulander makes him her husband in the sight of God even though she remains a virgin (440.7f.). The parallel with the "love-saint" Sigune hints at a religious and ascetic component in Parzival and Condwiramurs's marriage that knightly couples in romance narratives usually lack. Unlike Erec and Enite, for example, who can scarcely wait to consummate their marriage with two or three nights of lovemaking,

> "jâ enwirde ich nimmer vrô,
> ich engelige dir noch bî
> zwô naht oder drî."
> (*Erec*, 1873–75)

> "Truly, I shall never be happy unless I lie with you for two nights or three."

Wolfram's hero and heroine remain chaste for two days and three nights:

> si wâren mit ein ander sô,
> daz si durch liebe wâren vrô,
> zwên tage unt die dritten naht.
> (202.29–203.1)

> They remained with each other, happy in their affection, for two days and the third night.

They thus repeat the biblical example of Tobias, who remains continent for three nights, consciously enacting a typology with Adam and Eve that

[17] See, for example, Martin Jones, "Formen der Liebeserklärung im höfischen Roman bis um 1300" (1987).

imitates the prelapsarian ignorance of lust (Tobias 8.1–10).[18] Parzival and Condwiramurs, of course, do not so much imitate the biblical model as accidentally recapitulate it. One is tempted to suggest that they unconsciously retain a modicum of primal innocence, a positive "Adamic" element that shapes their love and forms a counterpart to the negative "Adamic" overtones of Parzival's knighthood (see Chapter 2). Indeed, they experience pleasure in each other's company but do not seem motivated by the lust that characterizes postlapsarian sexual relations.[19] For this reason, the narrator adds a motif to his source, stating that Parzival and Condwiramurs consummate their marriage only after he remembers the advice of his mother and of Gurnemanz:

> von im dicke wart gedâht
> umbevâhens, daz sîn muoter riet:
> Gurnemanz im ouch underschiet,
> man und wîp wærn al ein.
> (203.2–5)

He often thought about embracing her, as his mother had advised; Gurnemanz had also taught him that husband and wife were one.

Sex is for them an act of will rather than a natural inclination and, therefore, a learned activity. Of course, it is licit within matrimony, and Wolfram, who seldom employs the biblical "one flesh" metaphor to describe marriage, invokes it while recalling Gurnemanz's advice (173.1).[20]

In order to suggest the unusual nature of Parzival and Condwiramurs's relationship, then, Wolfram subverts the private concubinage of Chrétien's couple into a public marriage and rulership in which three different types of discourse interact. Most obviously, the hero and heroine combine the roles of husband and wife with that of lover and lady found in romance. At the same time their inaction as husband and wife coexists with more extreme clerical conventions regarding marriage, a discourse increasingly important in the sacralization of this relationship in the twelfth century, and one that is often invented post hoc in ecclesiastical encomia of rulers.[21] The marriage of this hero and heroine not only combines the secular roles of king and queen with those of knight and lady

[18] On the nights of Tobias, see Dyan Elliott, *Spiritual Marriage: Sexual Abstinence in Medieval Wedlock* (1993), 171; Schumacher, *Auffassung der Ehe*, 37–47.

[19] It is described at length in St. Augustine's *De civitate Dei* (Book XIV), the fundamental locus for the Middle Ages.

[20] Schumacher, *Auffassung der Ehe*, 115–18.

[21] On the "Tobiasnächte" as a characteristic of rulers, see Peter Browe, *Beiträge zur Sexualethik des Mittelalters* (1932), 116.

but also satisfies the demands of secular and clerical culture, reconciling chivalric narrative and the religious vita, and thus suggesting its central role in realizing a main theme of Wolfram's heteroglot romance, that of satisfying both God and the world, *got unde der werlt gevallen.*

III

The increased role of the narrator and the intertextual subversion of Chrétien's narrative by the theme of marriage and kingship do not exhaust the ways in which Wolfram pluralizes Parzival's sojourn at Pelrapeire. Bakhtin's concept of the chronotope, the differentiation of discourse through the coding of time and space, a possibility utilized only tentatively in *Li Contes del Graal*, suggests another important point of comparison. Wolfram's transposition introduces several types of chronotopic differentiation that not only organize and orchestrate the episodes in Parzival's first set of adventures but also create dialogic relationships with the adventures of other figures in the narrative as well as with other romances.

One type of chronotopic differentiation involves characters, providing them with a specific name, a place of origin, and a family as well as a genealogy, transforming the largely functional and therefore anonymous figures in Chrétien's adventure romance into particularized characters interacting in a family romance. During the hero's reception at Belrepeire, for example, Blancheflor appears in the company of two lords (*prodome* [1790]); she later mentions an uncle, a holy prior, who has sent six loaves of bread and a bottle of boiled wine (1910–14). Wolfram assumes their identity, making it necessary to double the number of clerics, and proceeds to particularize them. Kyot of Katelangen and Manpfilyot have names, a specific social class, a kinship relationship with Condwiramurs, a personal history that explains their change of estate, and an appearance that indicates they live outside the beleaguered city:

> Von Katelangen Kyôt
> unt der werde Manpfilyôt
> (herzogen beide wâren die),
> ir bruoder kint si brâhten hie,
> des landes küneginne.
> durch die gotes minne
> heten se ûf gegebn ir swert.
> dâ giengen die fürsten wert
> grâ unde wol gevar.
> (186.21–29)

> Kyot of Katelangen and noble Manpfilyot—they were both dukes—brought forth their brother's child, the queen of that land. For the love of God they had renounced their swords. Now these noble princes, gray-haired and handsome, entered.

Both dukes are interesting in their own right as members of a family and dynasty rather than as anonymous agents of a rhetorical narrative principle. Whereas Chrétien states that an uncle provides a meager amount of food—schematically designated as "bread and wine"—for the night's meal, beginning the pattern of deprivation that will characterize the entire evening, Wolfram lets Kyot speak for himself, volunteering twice as many loaves and vessels of wine as Chrétien's nobleman, but extending this schematic doublet to a longer and more nourishing shopping list and invoking sibling rivalry to goad his brother into contributing as well:

> "frouwe, ich sende iu zwelf prôt,
> schultern unde hammen drî:
> dâ ligent ähte kæse bî,
> unt zwei buzzel mit wîn.
> iuch sol ouch der bruoder mîn
> hînte stiuren: deȥ ist nôt."
> dô sprach Manpfiljôt
> "frouwe, ich send iu als vil."
> (190.10–17)

> "Lady, I shall send you twelve loaves of bread, three shoulders and hams; eight cheeses will be included, and two butts of wine. And my brother should also contribute tonight, for you have need of it." Then Manpfilyot said, "Lady, I shall send an equal amount."

Another example, Perceval's sending defeated knights to Arthur's court to lament Kay's beating of the damsel who laughed at him, illustrates how chronotopic elaboration of character also organizes the narrative. Wolfram separates Kingrun's and Clamide's arrival into two distinct episodes, with Orilus's appearance comprising a third. As is typical of the switch from the impersonal rhetoric of adventure romance to the multivoiced dialogism of family romance, the relationships between characters structure Chrétien's uncertainly connected events. Kingrun, Clamide, and Orilus form a series with a principle of intensification, progressing from a seneschal to his king and then to the brother of the injured woman; simultaneously, Kay's responses at court reveal increasing anxiety as he proceeds from jocular shop talk to self-justification and then to judicious absence from dinner. Moreover, Parzival gives the defeated Kingrun a choice of three people to whom he can surrender, Gurnemanz, then Condwiramurs, then Arthur (198.3–199.12); Clamide has a choice of two, Gurnemanz, then Arthur (214.5–215.12); and Orilus only one, Arthur (267.9–268.2)—a clear progression. This is not a mechanical and potentially infinite linear series, but a graduated one that simultaneously builds and narrows to a climax.

A second type of chronotopic differentiation organizes episodes rather than characters, providing them with distinctive chronological and spatial attributes. In contrast to the time references in Chrétien's narrative, which provide a point of transition between episodes but relate them to each other inconsistently and even contradictorily, Wolfram's allusions form a unified pattern. The period that elapses between Parzival's robbery of Jeschute and her reconciliation with Orilus, "more than an entire year" (139.20), accommodates other references to Arthur's celebration of Pentecost (216.14) and the snowfall after Parzival's failure at the Grail castle (281.12). Within this larger time frame, most episodes are clearly delineated by references to morning and evening.[22] Book III encompasses seventeen days, with the sojourn at Gurnemanz's castle lasting a full fourteen days (176.29) rather than the one in Chrétien; the chronology of Books V–VI is equally clear, comprising only three days. As in Chrétien's Perceval-Blancheflor episode, there is a break in the continuity of episodes at the end of Book IV; but the consistency of Wolfram's large-scale chronological organization enables us to estimate its duration and confirm the importance of Parzival's stay with Condwiramurs. If the events of Book III encompass seventeen, those of Books V and VI three days, then the remainder of the time spent in Book IV accounts for most of the "more than an entire year" anticipated by the narrator after the first Jeschute episode—by far the most extensive stay in Parzival's career.

The organization of space also differs substantially from Chrétien's narrative.[23] Whereas Perceval's journey proceeds along the seacoast from

[22] Parzival's first day in the woods, the encounters with Jeschute, Sigune, and the innkeeper, and the first episode at Arthur's court begin in the morning (128.13, 129.15, 143.16), as does the sojourn with Gurnemanz (166.20). Parzival takes leave of Condwiramurs one morning (223.15), riding until he meets the Fisher King in the evening (225.2), sleeps at the Grail castle, where he wakes up early the following day and again at mid-morning (245.2 and 28). During the second day he encounters Sigune, then Jeschute and Orilus, after whose defeat Wolfram—emending the chronotopic vagueness of his source—explicitly raises the issue of where the heroes will find accommodations that night (271.14–22). The third day is devoted to Parzival's love trance and ensuing events.

[23] On the organization of space see Marianne Wynn, "Scenery and Chivalrous Journeys in Wolfram's *Parzival*" (1961); Wolfgang Harms, *Homo viator in bivio: Studien zur Bildlichkeit des Weges* (1970), 221–49.

Arthur's court at Carduel to Belrepeire, then suddenly shifts inland to the Grail castle, Parzival takes an inland route, organized by the direct and gradual upward progression from Arthur's court, now located on the meadow at Nantes, to the mountains of Munsalvaesche. And whereas Chrétien's narrative uses changes in space to delineate episodes without suggesting any clear large-scale pattern, Wolfram's relates them chronotopically through three fantastic journeys that confirm the geographical suggestion of a graduated progression. They proceed from Nantes to Graharz,

> gewâpent reitz der tumbe man
> den tac sô verre, ez het lân
> ein blôz wîser, solt erz hân geriten
> zwêne tage, ez wære vermiten.
> (161.17–20)

The foolish man rode so far in armor that day that a sensible one without armor would have avoided attempting it in two.

Graharz to Brobarz,

> "hetz anders iemen mir gesagt,
> der volge wurde im niht verjehn,
> deiz eines tages wære geschehn:
> wan swelch mîn bote ie baldest reit,
> die reise er zwêne tage vermeit."
> (189.22–26)

"If anyone else had told me that it happened in one day, he wouldn't be believed, for whichever of my messengers rode as fast as possible, he couldn't avoid taking two days."

and Brobarz to Munsalvaesche:

> uns tuot diu âventiure bekant
> daz er bî dem tage reit,
> ein vogel hetes arbeit,
> solt erz allez hân erflogen.
> mich enhab diu âventiure betrogen,
> sîn reise unnâch was sô grôz
> des tages do er Ithêren schôz,
> unt sît dô er von Grâharz
> kom in daz lant ze Brôbarz.
> (224.22–30)

> The narrative informs us that he rode so far that day that a bird would have difficulty flying all that distance. If the narrative has not deceived me, his journey was not nearly so far on the day he shot Ither and later when he traveled from Graharz to Brobarz.

The increasing speed and distance of the hero's superhuman rides, the only such travels in the narrative, also differentiate these stations chronotopically from one another, with the extended sojourns at Graharz and Pelrapeire providing distinct intermediate stages between the Arthurian and Grail worlds.

Those two worlds are also differentiated by a contrasting organization of time and space. Chrétien's narrative intimates a disjuncture between the normal world of Arthurian adventure and the Otherworld of the Grail castle, which does not obey the laws of space and time, appearing suddenly—"parut" (3051)—between a broad, unfordable river and the woods (3034). Wolfram's narrative invests this difference with an extensive chronotopic organization: whereas the Arthurian world is localized in a pleasance or *locus amœnus* landscape at a fixed time of year (May or Pentecost), the Grail world is placed in a rugged and inaccessible landscape and in a dynamic mode of telling time, the liturgical calendar—a contrast of chronotopes that is emphasized in the famous commentary on the incompatibility of Arthur, "the man of May," and the snowfall from the Grail realm at the beginning of Book VI (281.14–22). We will return to the implications of this passage in the next chapter.

Such chronotopic differentiation and orchestration of both figures and episodes contributes to a further large-scale organization of the narrative, the interrelation of the hero's adventures and the adventures of other characters in the romance, as well as between Wolfram's *Parzival* and other Middle High German narratives—dialogism in the traditional sense of intertextuality. One brief example of each will suffice.

The most obvious set of parallel adventures involves those of Gawan, whose lady Orgeluse is explicitly introduced as the most beautiful woman except for Condwiramurs (508.22f.), one of a host of motifs relating Parzival's career and that of his Arthurian counterpart.[24] But the most specific parallel between Parzival's marriage to Condwiramurs and the adventures of another figure involves Gahmuret's winning of Belakane, a diachronic parallel across generations not found in Chrétien's narrative. Gahmuret and Parzival, father and son, win their wives by breaking the

[24] See, for example, Wolfgang Mohr, "Parzival und Gawan" (1958); rpt. in his *Wolfram von Eschenbach: Aufsätze* (1979), 62–93; Marianne Wynn, "Parzival and Gawan: Hero and Counterpart" (1962); and Sidney Johnson, "Parzival and Gawan: Their Conflict of Duties" (1970).

siege of a castle, and Wolfram's episodes are clearly conceived with reference to each other. Belakane and Condwiramurs are described, alone of the women in *Parzival*, in an introductory portrait with the "rose in the dew" topos of Mariological poetry (24.6–10, 188.6–14).[25] The queens have been left defenseless by the deaths of Isenhart and Schenteflurs, respectively; their castles, bordered by land on one side and sea on the other, are beset by two armies. Gahmuret and Parzival enter the besieged cities unopposed, are introduced to the queens in a manner that intimates their predestination as hero and heroine, and after a sleepless night set forth and single-handedly break the siege, whereupon the queens publicly proclaim them as their future lords and husbands.

Indeed, a father-son typology emerges triumphantly in Parzival's knightly activities, as references to him as Gahmuret's progeny during the battles with Kingrun and Clamide attest (197.1, 212.2).[26] However, Gahmuret's sexually prominent nature, which derives from the fairy strain in his genealogy (56.18) and leads him to three different experiments involving chivalry and love (knight-errantry and Belakane; courtly love and Ampflise; tournaments and Herzeloyde), exerts a surprisingly weaker influence. The attraction to Liaze prevents Parzival from falling in love with her relative and look-alike Condwiramurs, a pointed contrast to the rapacious glances exchanged by Gahmuret and Belakane on their first meeting. The absence of Gahmuret's sexual proclivity on Parzival's wedding night has already been explicitly foreshadowed by the narrator's comment on the hero's missed opportunity with Jeschute (139.15–19). And although Parzival has offered service for reward at Pelrapeire, just as his father did at Patelamunt, the anticipated love service will be subsumed by the new pattern of public and private sovereignty, enabling him—unlike Gahmuret—to combine knight-errantry and kingship, love and marriage.

[25] See Anselm Salzer, *Die Bilder und Beiworte Mariens in der deutschen Literatur und lateinischen Hymnenpoesie des Mittelalters* (1967), 183–92.

[26] The challenge posed by Gahmuret's epitaph suggests that we read Parzival's success in terms of his father's. The change from "er ist von muoter ungeborn" (108.14) on the epitaph to the annoucement of the hero's birth "er ist alrêrst geborn" (112.11) implies a relationship that we can track in terms of the motif of fame. Gahmuret's first statements programmatically establish a concern with *prîs* (7.23) that is perpetuated in his epitaph (108.12): he begins by achieving "den prîs in heidenschaft" (15.16), then attains "den hœhsten prîs" in breaking the siege of Patelamunt and at the *vesperîe* at Kanvoleis in Books I and II (97.21, 82.4). Parzival raises the same expectations in breaking Cunneware's enchantment, which prevents her from laughing until she sees him who will win "den hœhsten prîs" (135.18). Parzival's first knightly encounters in Book IV confirm this promise; indeed, Kingrun asserts to his defeated lord Clamide before the entire Arthurian court that the hero is "der âne liegen ist gezelt / mit wârheit für den hôsten prîs" (221.24f.), thus fulfilling the challenge to posterity inscribed in Gahmuret's epitaph.

The conclusion of Book IV, briefly describing Parzival's yearlong sojourn, the most extensive in the romance, therefore shows the hero as both knight and regent, frequently participating in tournaments up to the borders of his kingdom (222.20–28) while rebuilding his ravaged domain and establishing loyalty through regal largess (222.10–19), a pointed contrast to the wanderlust of his father. Moreover, the relationship between the royal couple and lovers is so total that Condwiramurs can be said to have the earthly ideal, "den wunsch ûf der erde" (223.2), a clear expression of the fact that their achievement anticipates the accession to supreme dominion at the Grail, the "wunsch von pardîs" (235.21).

It would in fact be tempting to suggest that the events of Book IV, with their careful structure of anticipation and fulfillment as well as the contrast to the serial relationships of Gahmuret, both raise and resolve the typical romance problem of the hero's relationship to his wife. A characteristic feature of Parzival's adventures, in contrast to those of the other principal male figures in the narrative, is the untroubled nature of his marriage to Condwiramurs, a fact the hero acknowledges and Trevrizent cites as a principal reason to hope for his salvation (733.9–16, 468.1–9). Unlike romance heroes such as Erec and Iwein, Parzival's career does not involve the bipartite pattern of winning both a wife and kingdom, followed by their loss and recovery, and one has the impression that the graduated doublings of Book IV imply a self-contained beginning and completion of Parzival's love relationship.[27] To be sure, the encounter with the Grail in Book V involves him in the traditional pattern of loss and recovery of his principal future kingdom, but this analogue draws attention to a basic change: the attainment of a wife and the Grail kingdom are separate thematic issues.

On an even broader level, Parzival's winning of Condwiramurs differs from Chrétien's treatment of the same episode through its dialogic relationship with another narrative, Hartmann von Aue's *Erec.*[28] We saw in the preceding chapter how Wolfram's invocation of Hartmann von Aue before the first appearance of Arthur's court explicitly imagines *Parzival* as taking place in a post-*Erec*ian world, appropriating the figures and events of Hartmann's romances into the pre-history of Wolfram's narrative. Wolfram also invests the ties of consanguinity between Gurnemanz and

[27] Although it is risky to base an argument on Lachmann's division of the narrative into books, it is interesting to note that the beginning and end of Book IV, which bracket the entire episode at Pelrapeire, complete a circular pattern, beginning with "dannen schiet sus Parzivâl" (179.13) and ending with "schiet er al eine dannen" (223.30).

[28] For a more conventional interpretation of the broader issues of the relationship, see Rüdiger Schnell, "Literarische Beziehungen zwischen Hartmanns *Erec* und Wolframs *Parzival*" (1973).

Condwiramurs with a new significance by involving them in Hartmann's history of Erec's adventures as well as in the current enmity of Erec's extended family, thus amplifying the intertextual genre battle between the romances. As we learn at the end of Book III, Gurnemanz lost two sons in the adventures that Hartmann's hero apparently resolved at the beginning and conclusion of *Erec*, Lascoyt having perished in the Sparrow Hawk contest and Gurzgri in the *joie de la curt* at Brandigan (178.11–26). The third son, Schenteflurs, has recently died defending Condwiramurs against Kingrun and Clamide, who is presented by Wolfram as king of Brandigan (184.20) and a cousin of Mabonagrin (220.9), the warning example of destructive private love in *Erec*.

Wolfram's appropriation of Hartmann's narrative history and the extension of its ruinous consequences into his own narrative suggest that Erec's success did not permanently restore the social order by breaking the adventure at Brandigan. Indeed, the damage described there is officially resolved only in Wolfram's narrative by Clamide's suit for Arthur's forgiveness in an intertextual summit meeting:

> "nu bin ich, künec Artûs,
> her geriten in dîn hûs,
> betwungen von ritters hant.
> du weist wol daz in mîn lant
> dir manec laster ist getân:
> des vergiz nu, werder man,
> die wîle ich hie gevangen sî,
> lâz mich sölhes hazzes vrî."
> (220.12–19)

> "King Arthur, I have now ridden into your castle, compelled by the hand of a knight. You know very well that many offenses have been committed against you in my country. Ignore that now, noble man, and while I am captive here, keep me from such enmity."

Moreover, two of Erec's relatives through marriage, Orilus (husband of Erec's sister Jeschute) and Clamide (cousin of Mabonagrin and husband-to-be of Orilus's sister Cunneware), continue to inflict suffering and disorder in Wolfram's narrative. Parzival's triumph over these representatives of immoderate chivalry thus makes him a perfect match for the chaste Condwiramurs, whose beauty, according to the narrator, not only outshines the two Isoldes, but also that of Jeschute, Enite, and Cunneware—Erec's sister, wife, and sister-in-law (187.14–19). There are, of course, other parallels, which would have to be pursued in another context. Suffice it to say that Wolfram's revised "version" of Hartmann's *Erec* constructs a metanarrative between his text and the principal anterior Arthurian romance in Germany. Its variety suggests that Wolfram's dialogic imagination creates a pervasive intertextual dynamic, which, for lack of a better term, we might provisionally call "Parzivlage." This emphasis on social and literary complexity in the Arthurian world differs from the stress on non-literary discourses—scientific, medical, liturgical—in the Grail world, to which we turn our attention in the ensuing chapters.

CHAPTER FIVE

Parzival and the Grail: Time, Space, and the Liturgical Calendar at Munsalvaesche

I

Given the extensive variety of interpretations surrounding the Grail, many of them mutually exclusive and highly speculative, it might be best to begin our discussion of Parzival's failure at Munsalvaesche with the first appearance of this mysterious object in Book V.[1] During the procession that brings it into and then out of the main hall, the narrator offers two successive "definitions" of what the Grail "was." The first occurs at Repanse de Schoye's entrance:

[si truoc] den wunsch von pardîs,
bêde wurzeln unde rîs.
daz was ein dinc, daz hiez der Grâl,
erden wunsches überwal.
(235.21–24)

[She carried] the perfection of paradise, both root and branch. That was a thing called the Grail, an overflowing of earthly perfection.

The second occurs less than one hundred lines later, in response to an imagined objection that nothing like this has ever existed:

wan der grâl was der sælden fruht,
der werlde süeze ein sölh genuht,

[1] For a summary, see Bumke, *Wolfram*, 141–46 and 182–84; *Forschung*, 259–63 and index. On the implications of the Grail society, see also Bumke, "Die Utopie des Grals: Eine Gesellschaft ohne Liebe?" (1982); and Walter Blank, "Die positive Utopie des Grals" (1989).

er wac vil nâch gelîche
als man saget von himelrîche.
(238.21–24)

For the Grail was the fruit of blessedness, such a satiety of worldly sweetness that it almost equaled what one says of heaven.

The Grail first appears as a vaguely described "thing" with a strange name ("grâl"). The most mysterious object in the narrative, "it" is introduced as a floating signifier, one that will attract a large number of later significations. Indeed, these initial definitions evoke not only the inclusiveness implied by the metaphor "root *and* branch," but also transcendence. As an "overflowing of earthly perfection" in the first statement, the Grail equals the "perfection of paradise"; as a "satiety of earthly sweetness" in the second, it approaches the abundance of "heaven." Both comments progress from an ideal of earthly perfection toward something beyond it, and in tracing a trajectory from paradise to heaven cover the entire course of salvation history. In terms of its chronotopic encoding of space and time, then, the Grail invites utopian significations of both plenitude and transcendence.

Characteristically, the narrator does not allow his construction of the Grail to remain stable, and immediately subverts its transcendent plenitude. The last-cited passage hedges on the Grail's ideality by limiting its copiousness "almost" to equaling heaven, more precisely, almost to equaling what "one says about" heaven, thereby drawing attention to the fact that it is a mediated approximation, the representation of a representation. The narrator even negotiates it with his audience:

man sagte mir, diz sag ouch ich
ûf iwer ieslîches eit,
daz vorem grâle wære bereit
(sol ich des iemen triegen,
sô müezt ir mit mir liegen)
swâ nâch jener bôt die hant,
daz er al bereite vant
spîse warm, spîse kalt,
spîse niwe unt dar zuo alt,
daz zam unt daz wilde.
(238.8–17)

I was told, and I also tell you this on each of your oaths, that in front of the Grail—if I'm deceiving anyone about this, you will have to lie with me—

> was ready whatever anyone extended his hand for, that he found ready warm food, cold food, new food and old, meat both tame and game.

By making explicit the complicity of the audience in constructing this utopian plenitude, the narrator undercuts its ideality, reducing the Grail's abundance to a catalogue of foods with a comic jingle of alimentary opposites (warm-cold, new-old, tame-game).

This characteristic tendency simultaneously to create and subvert meaning while negotiating it with the audience extends to the larger context of the Grail narrative, beginning with the procession in which these representations of the Grail are embedded. Analyses of the scene have suggested that a variety of techniques create a simultaneously vivid and mysterious impression.[2] While evoking the Grail procession in the present tense, commanding the audience to hear or see (*hœrt, seht*), the narrator also distances it from their imaginations by stating that he is only conveying what he was told (*man sagte mir*) that one saw (*man sach*), that is, that he is representing a past event at third hand.[3] The uncertainty caused by shifts between present performance and past event, or their occasional coalescence (235.8), is further heightened by the fact that the narrator belabors the number of participants, playfully foregrounding his ability to add instead of concentrating on the procession itself, the progress of which is merely alluded to by vague intransitive verbs (*komen, gên, nîgen, stên*).

In accordance with the superabundance of the Grail, the narrator also creates an impression of a splendid material culture in the main hall of the castle by an emphasis on light, furniture, clothes, and precious materials, as well as by the profusion of numbers and adjectives describing them. At the same time, the verbs associated with this materiality again remain imprecise, suggesting only that things are worn or carried, or stating identity with *was* and *wâren*,[4] while impersonal constructions imply a group experience without clarifying relationships between individuals.[5] In

[2] See especially James F. Poag, "*Diu verholnen mære umben grâl*" (1974); Kurt Ruh, "Wolfram von Eschenbach heute" (1975), and "Parzival und der Gral," in his *Höfische Epik des deutschen Mittelalters II* (1980), 58–69; Dagmar Hirschberg, *Untersuchungen zur Erzählstruktur von Wolframs "Parzival"* (1976), 105–29; Dennis H. Green, *The Art of Recognition in Wolfram's "Parzival"* (1982), 89–106; and Kenneth J. Northcott, "Seeing and Partly Seeing: Parzival's Encounter with the Grail" (1983).

[3] *hœrt*: 232.12, 234.30, 237.21, and 238.2; *seht*: 233.12; *man sagte mir*: 235.19, 238.8; *man sach*: 234.16, 235.18, 236.30, and 237.27.

[4] The most important of the former are forms of *tragen* (232.19/21/27, 233.3/15/17, 234.10/27, 235.1/13/18/21/26, 236.9/29, and 237.2/19/22) or *bringen* (234.19, 236.14). On forms of *wesen*: 232.10/15/17/20/26/28, 233.10/11/14/19/20, 234.3/14/21/23/26, 235.10/23/27, and 236.2/23/25.

[5] See 232.24, 234.16, 235.8/9/18, 236.19/30, 237.2/3/14/25/27, and 238.3/8/24/25.

short one could say that the representation of the Grail and its surroundings uses nouns to create a sense of splendor and verbs to elicit a feeling of mysteriousness, with the vagueness of the latter subverting the concreteness of the former.

Not surprisingly, Parzival has difficulty coming to terms with a ritual that seems both overdetermined and indeterminate. The narrator reveals the hero's developing reactions through two passages placed strategically after the descriptions of the Grail we have just discussed. At first, he thinks of the queen, whose coat he is wearing, heedless of the implications of the investiture or the procession around him (236.12–15). Then he considers asking about it but is hindered by Gurnemanz's advice:

> wol gemarcte Parzivâl
> die rîchheit unt daz wunder grôz:
> durch zuht in vrâgens doch verdrôz.
> er dâhte "mir riet Gurnamanz
> mit grôzen triwen âne schranz,
> ich solte vil gevrâgen niht.
> waz op mîn wesen hie geschiht
> die mâze als dort pî im?
> âne vrâge ich vernim
> wiez dirre massenîe stêt."
>
> (239.8–17)

> To be sure, Parzival noticed the splendors and the great marvel, but courtliness kept him from asking. He thought: "Gurnemanz advised me with faultless loyalty not to ask too many questions. What if my stay here goes the same way as there with him? Without questioning I will perceive how things stand at this court."

Parzival clearly notices the "splendors and great marvel" displayed for him, and in avoiding a question actually comes close to formulating one, which we might approximate as "hêrre, wie stêt ez dirre massenîe?"—"Lord, how do things stand at this court?" But like his Old French counterpart he refrains from speaking because of the advice "not to ask too many questions," a decision generally interpreted as both too literal and too narrow.[6] Indeed, Sigune even suggests later that the redeeming question is worthy, "werdeclîch" (441.22).[7]

[6] Chrétien presents the deliberations twice, in 3243–53 and 3294–3305, and mentions the lord's advice not to speak too much, "trop parler" (3251, 3296). See Ursula Hennig, "Die Gurnemanzlehren und die unterlassene Frage Parzivals" (1975); Volker Mertens, "Parzivals doppelte Probe" (1979).

[7] The fact that there also exists a positive counterpart to the hero's foolish silence

While Parzival is deliberating, "in dem gedanke" (239.18), his train of thought is derailed, first by a squire bearing a splendid sword and scabbard, then by the Grail king, who presents them to him with the comment that he himself wore them until "God wounded me" (239.26f.). The narrator, unable to alter the course of the action, intrudes:

> ôwê daz er niht vrâgte dô!
> des pin ich für in noch unvrô.
> wan do erz enpfienc in sîne hant,
> dô was er vrâgens mit ermant.
> och riwet mich sîn süezer wirt,
> den ungenande niht verbirt,
> des im von vrâgn nu wære rât.
> (240.3–9)

> Alas that he did not ask then! I am still unhappy for him because of that, for by accepting it he was prompted to ask. I am also sorry for his sweet host, who will not be spared an unspeakable affliction that questioning could have spared him.

Two important issues emerge from this lament. The admission that Parzival is being prompted raises the question whether the Grail inhabitants contribute to his failure by disobeying the prohibition against warning (483.24–30);[8] the concern for Anfortas draws attention to the presence of an *ungenande*, an "unnamed" or "unspeakable" illness whose harm will be resolved only by a countering speech act—the redeeming question.[9]

But what is Parzival supposed to ask, and why does he fail? Chrétien seems to frame these problems within an unambiguous horizon of expectations. In accordance with the otherworldly aura of the Grail realm, Perceval needs to ask a fixed set of questions pertaining to its mysteries, "Why does the lance bleed?" and "Whom does one serve with the Grail?"[10] True to their mythic or fairy-tale origins, these predetermined questions

---

suggests how central control of affect and of the body is in the discourse on courtliness. See Uwe Ruberg, *Beredtes Schweigen in lehrhafter und erzählender deutscher Literatur des Mittelalters* (1978), 223–37.

[8] See Christoph Steppich, "'Hinweise geben wird euch schaden': Zu Wolframs *Parzival* 483.24–30" (1990).

[9] The opposition probably derives from folkloric taboos surrounding illness and the corresponding use of incantation or naming the affliction as part of its cure. See the references in Primus Lessiak, "Gicht. Ein Beitrag zur Kunde deutscher Krankheitsnamen" (1914), 133–34.

[10] On the larger nexus of this problem, see E. Jane Burns, "Quest and Questioning in the *Conte du graal*" (1988).

are repeated throughout the narrative, first by the hero's *cousine germaine* (3552f., 3568f.), then by the Loathly Damsel (4652–61), and again during the Good Friday scene, where Perceval makes them the central element of his confession, closely paraphrasing the Damsel's accusations (6372–80). He fails because of an equally fixed conception of guilt, namely, the fact that his first sin (abandoning his dying mother) occasions a second one (remaining silent at the Grail castle), a mechanical linkage first revealed by his cousin (3593–95) and then explained in greater detail by the hermit (6392–6414).[11]

As is typical of his tendency to decenter monologic or authoritative discourse, Wolfram problematizes Chrétien's fairy-tale adventure and the rigidly clerical conception of sin that prevents the hero from breaking the enchantment. Although Wolfram, too, emphasizes the necessity of asking, the question is not fixed but evolves during the course of the narrative, its precise formulation remaining unclear until Parzival finally utters it in Book XVI. To begin with, the passages corresponding to the expositions of the question by Chrétien's *cousine germaine*, the Loathly Damsel, and the hermit clarify its nature only gradually. Sigune's inquiry whether he has done the question justice, "hâstu vrâge ir reht getân" (254.30), seems to imply that something resembling Chrétien's costumal determinism underlies the adventure,[12] but her condemnation of the hero is less specific:

"ir sâhet doch sölch wunder grôz:
daz iuch vrâgens dô verdrôz!
aldâ ir wârt dem grâle bî;
manege frouwen valsches vrî,
die werden Garschiloyen
und Repans de schoyen,
und snîdnde silbr und bluotec sper. . . .
iuch solt iur wirt erbarmet hân,
an dem got wunder hât getân,
und het gevrâget sîner nôt."

(255.5–19)

"Oh that you could not be bothered to *ask* there, even though you saw great *marvels*! You were in the presence of the Grail, many faultless

[11] See Amelia A. Rutledge, "Perceval's Sin: Critical Perspectives" (1980/81). For an attempt to relate the problem to twelfth-century theology, see David G. Hoggan, "Le Péché de Perceval: Pour l'authenticité de l'épisode de l'ermite dans le *Conte du graal* de Chrétien de Troyes" (1972).

[12] See Erich Köhler, "Die Rolle des 'Rechtsgebrauchs' (costume) in den Romanen des Chrétien de Troyes" (1962); and Donald Maddox, *The Arthurian Romances of Chrétien de Troyes* (1991), 82–118.

women—the worthy Garschiloye and Repanse de Schoye—and the silver knife and bloody lance. . . . You should have had compassion on your host, on whom God has inflicted a *marvel*, and should have *asked* about his distress." (My emphasis)

In fact, as Sigune's repetition of *wunder* and *vrâgen* (255.5–6, 255.18–19) reveals, Chrétien's predetermined double question has been fragmented into two distinct options. The first deforms and demotes the pairing of the Grail and the lance by placing them in a catalogue of events at the Grail castle, dilating that in turn by naming the women in the procession or adding a silver knife to the bleeding lance. The second introduces a moralizing discourse, emphasizing compassion for a divine punishment inflicted on the Fisher King. It is not clear whether both options are valid or are related causally, that is, whether Parzival could have asked either about the procession or Anfortas's suffering, or whether the former was intended to lead to a question about the latter.

Cundrie's public condemnation of the hero in Book VI follows a similar pattern of doubling, but reverses the order, reproaching him first for not having compassion and asking a question that would "redeem" the Fisher King (315.26–316.10), then for remaining silent when receiving the sword and seeing the Grail procession, silver knife, and bleeding spear (316.21ff.). This reversal may point to an evolution of the question, a first approximation of which we get in Book IX from Trevrizent, who reduces the hitherto double option to compassion:

"unprîs der dâ bejagte,
sît er den rehten kumber sach,
daz er niht zuo dem wirte sprach,
'hêrre, wie stêt iwer nôt?' "
(484.24–27)

"He won only shame there, since, seeing true misery, he did not ask the host: 'sire, what is your distress?' "

Indeed, it is to this reproach that Parzival also tailors his confession:

"der ûf Munsalvæsche reit,
unt der den rehten kumber sach,
unt der deheine vrâge sprach,
daz bin ich unsælec barn."
(488.16–19)

> "The person who rode to Munsalvaesche, and saw true misery and uttered no question—I am that unfortunate child."

As we will see in Chapter 8, the question that Parzival ultimately poses does focus on Anfortas's suffering but takes yet another form. Apparently, the redeeming question is not fixed but variable, not objective but subjective, reflecting the hero's changing awareness of himself and his place in the narrative.

Corresponding to this destabilization of the question from a mythic to a novelistic action, that is, from a preordained fairy-tale motif to a speech act expressing the hero's individuality, there is a change in the nature of his failure. Wolfram both expands the number of Perceval's transgressions and disconnects their mechanical relationship. In summarizing the hero's sins, Trevrizent adds the murder of Ither to his complicity in the death of Herzeloyde, forming a group of two great sins, "zwuo grôze sünde" (499.20). But unlike Chrétien's formulation, these transgressions do not cause his third sin at the Grail castle, which is discussed separately and then added to the first two, "die sünde lâ bî dn andern stên" (501.5). Trevrizent only states, before he learns of Parzival's failure, that ignorance or *tumpheit* prevented the unknown knight from asking, "sîn tumpheit daz gebôt / daz er aldâ niht vrâgte" (484.28f.).

We saw in Chapter 2 that Parzival's sinful ignorance begins with his confusion of knights with God, a confusion that recapitulates Adam's fall and is part of the moral deficiency passed down from the first man to the family of man. This displacement of causality from immediate to proximate and even phylogenetic origins complements the technique of deferral in the Grail narrative in general, overdetermining events with a host of details that makes them seem ultimately indeterminate. Although a general study of Book V would continue to uncover other forms of this dialectic, it might be more useful to focus on a particularly important and far-reaching aspect of this process, using the chronotopic background of Parzival's first visit to Munsalvaesche as a means of placing the hero's failure in a contemporary context.

II

Our point of departure is the mysterious snowfall at the beginning of Book VI, which occasions a close encounter of the Arthurian and Grail realms. Parzival has spent the night in the *jeune bois*, whose mixed landscape suggests an intermediate geography between the pleasance of the Arthurian world and the wasteland of the Grail castle. With an ironic aside at the static chronology of Arthurian romance in general and the confusing references of *Li Contes del Graal* in particular, Wolfram transforms his source's inconsistency into a commentary on two chronotopically distinct narrative strands and their weaving into the "double fabric" of his text:

> von snêwe was ein niwe leis
> des nahtes vast ûf in gesnît.
> ez enwas iedoch niht snêwes zît,
> istz als ichz vernomen hân.
> Artûs der meienbære man,
> swaz man ie von dem gesprach,
> zeinen pfinxten daz geschach,
> odr in des meien bluomenzît.
> waz man im süezes luftes gît!
> diz mære ist hie vast undersniten,
> ez parriert sich mit snêwes siten.
> (281.12–22)

During the night new snow had fallen heavily on him. But it wasn't the time for snow, if things are the way I've heard. Whatever was told about Arthur, the man of May, happened at Pentecost or in the blossom-time of May. What sweet breezes they attribute to him! Here this story is cut of a double fabric and slashed with the color of snow.

As Michael Curschmann has observed, this snow marks not only a geographical border between the Arthurian and Grail worlds but also a boundary between two conceptions of time.[13] Wolfram juxtaposes the static spring-time chronotope of Arthurian romance with the dynamic one of the Grail realm (informed, as we will see, by the motions of the planets and the movable cycle of the liturgical calendar). These worlds are both heterochronic and heterotopic, a fundamental indicator of the novelistic pluralism of *Parzival.*

Having outlined the heterotopic nature of the geography covered by Parzival's three fantastic rides to Graharz, Pelrapeire, and Munsalvaesche in the previous chapter, we can focus here on the Grail narrative's unique relationship to time, as reflected in unusually accurate references to an internal chronology.[14] Of particular interest are two calculations made by

[13] Michael Curschmann, "Das Abenteuer des Erzählens: Über den Erzähler in Wolframs *Parzival*" (1971), 642.

[14] The basic information can be consulted in Hermann J. Weigand, "Die epischen Zeitverhältnisse in den Graldichtungen Chrestiens und Wolframs" (1938), rpt. in English in his *Wolfram's "Parzifal"* (1969). Earlier studies include: F. W. Rührmund, "Chro-

Trevrizent and Queen Guenevere, neither of which has any equivalent in Chrétien's text.[15] The first occurs on Good Friday in Book IX. Parzival recognizes that he last visited Trevrizent's cell on the day he departed from the Grail castle, taking a knight's lance with him. In response to a hesitant inquiry about how much time has elapsed, the hermit responds:

> "fünfthalp jâr unt drî tage
> ist daz irz im nâmet hie.
> welt irz hœrn, ich prüeve iu wie."
> ame salter laser im über al
> diu jâr und gar der wochen zal,
> die dâ zwischen wâren hin.
> (460.22–27)

"It's been four and a half years and three days since you took it from him here. If you want to hear, I'll show you." In the psalter he read for him the years and even the number of weeks that had elapsed since then.

Contrary to what commentators assume, Trevrizent does not require the psalter for his calculation.[16] He immediately knows that four and one-half years and three days have elapsed, then refers to his psalter only to demonstrate the calculation to a potentially dubious Parzival.

The second time reference, made by Queen Guenevere in Book XIII, is equally puzzling. Gawan's messenger arrives with his lord's letter at King Arthur's court and finds the queen reading her psalter at chapel: "diu künegîn zer kappeln was, / an ir venje si den salter las" (644.23f.). This introductory allusion to a psalter clearly prepares another time reference. Again, however, critics conclude prematurely that Guenevere arrives at it by "consulting her calendar."[17] She merely exchanges pleasantries with Gawan's messenger, then reminisces for fifty lines before remarking:

---

nologische Bestimmung der Begebenheiten in Wolframs *Parzival*" (1848); Carl Jauker, *Über die chronologische Behandlung des Stoffes in den epischen Gedichten Wolframs von Eschenbach* (1882), 3–14. Recent studies touching on the problem of time are Hans-Hugo Steinhoff, *Die Darstellung gleichzeitiger Geschehnisse im mittelhochdeutschen Epos* (1964), 44–66; Petrus W. Tax, "*Felix culpa* und *lapsit exillis*: Wolframs *Parzival* und die Liturgie" (1965); Margret Sauer, *Parzival auf der Suche nach der verlorenen Zeit* (1981).

[15] Chrétien's *Perceval* 6620–38 states five times in a not entirely consistent manner that five years have elapsed. In the discussion with the hermit, it is Perceval who says he has lived in enmity toward God for "bien a cinc anz" (6364).

[16] Weigand states: "Trevrizent figures out, by reference to his church calendar, that it was exactly four and a half years and three days before," *Wolfram's "Parzival,"* 58. The standard commentaries also assume that the calculation is made on the basis of a calendar. See Bartsch/Marti, 137; Martin, *Kommentar*, 354.

[17] Weigand, *Wolfram's "Parzival,"* 60. The commentaries of Bartsch/Marti and Martin merely refer the reader to the explanation of Trevrizent's reference.

"fünftehalp jâr und sehs wochen
ist daz der werde Parzivâl
von dem Plimizœl nâch dem grâl
reit."
(646.14–17)

"It's been four and a half years and six weeks since the noble Parzival rode from the Plimizoel in search of the Grail."

As does Trevrizent, the Queen immediately knows how much time has elapsed since Parzival's departure.

Both passages thus confront modern readers with two strikingly detailed time references, both indirectly associated with a psalter, but apparently arrived at easily and independently of it. The indirectness of the calculation is supported by the nature of psalters themselves, which are read in their entirety once each week and hence provide no direct means of computing a longer period of time. Although one might assume that the psalters in *Parzival* also contain calendars, these would be based on the Roman system, which does not divide the month into weeks and hence is incompatible with the allusion to weeks in both Trevrizent's and Guenevere's calculations (460.26, 646.14).[18]

The basis of their references must therefore be an implicit chronology obvious to Wolfram's characters, if not to his audience. The system itself can be easily determined by correlating the two statements. Taking into account the fact that Trevrizent refers to events of one day earlier than Guenevere, the only calculation required is to subtract one figure from the other. The Queen's statement occurs four and one-half years and six weeks *minus* four and one-half years and two days, that is, forty days later than the hermit's. Forty days after Good Friday is the Vigil of the Ascension, the third of three Rogation Days that precede Ascension, which accounts for the Queen's presence in church and places both references in the context of the liturgical calendar, the predominant means of chronological orientation during the Middle Ages.[19]

[18] Illustrated thirteenth-century psalters traceable to Thuringia or to the circle of Landgrave Hermann have Roman calendars. See the "Übersicht der Handschriften" in Arthur Haseloff, *Eine thüringisch-sächsische Malerschule des dreizehnten Jahrhunderts* (1897), 9–25 and 353–59.

[19] We should recall that Parzival has remained ignorant of time during his wanderings because, as he admits after hearing Trevrizent's calculation, his alienation from God has kept him from church: "alrêrst ich innen worden bin / wie lange ich var wîselôs / unt daz freuden helfe mich verkôs. . . . / swâ kirchen ode münster stuont, / dâ man gotes êre sprach, / kein ouge mich dâ nie gesach" ("Only now do I realize how long I have traveled aimlessly without the consolation of joy. . . . Wherever churches or minsters stood, and God's praise was celebrated, no one ever saw me there" [460.28ff.]).

At first glance, it seems impossible to correlate Trevrizent's and Guenevere's statements with the events of Books V and VI to which they refer, because the points of departure, Good Friday and the Vigil of the Ascension, are movable feasts that vary as much as five weeks from year to year according to the date of Easter. Inasmuch as no specific year is mentioned, one cannot determine events of almost five years earlier with any precision, because the variation in the liturgical calendar will carry over into any calculation based on it. Working with the earliest and latest possible dates for Good Friday, the day of Trevrizent's calculation, Hermann J. Weigand concludes: "Assuming the earliest possible date for Good Friday, March 20, we would arrive at the eighteenth of September . . . but if Easter was late, it may have been mid-October or even a week later."[20] This still leaves us with a puzzling anomaly. Wolfram, as Weigand observes, "is a stickler for exact dates," yet the five-week latitude of this calculation does not tally with the exactitude—to the day—of Trevrizent's and Guenevere's references.

There is, however, a consideration that could circumvent this problem. Weigand assumes that the variable church year and the fixed secular calendar cannot be correlated over the five-year period of the narrative. An exception to this incompatibility, which would allow the rapid accuracy of Trevrizent's and Guenevere's references, occurs when Easter falls on the same day five years apart, making the liturgical and secular calendars identical in both years, and permitting the calculation of liturgically based references over an interval of more than four and one-half years. Such a coincidence occurred only once in Wolfram's literary lifetime, during the decade generally associated with the composition of *Parzival*: in 1203 and 1208.[21]

Positing an imagined internal chronology of 1203 for Books V to VI and 1208 for Books IX to XIII would account for the facility of Trevrizent's and Guenevere's references as well as for their potential intelligibility to contemporary audiences. These would have been most obvious if performances coincided exactly with the time scheme suggested here, a possibility that admittedly cannot be demonstrated. However, they would also have been clear at other times during both years, requiring a contemporary audience to reckon back, or ahead, to the fifth anniversary of Parzival's departure from the Grail castle or King Arthur's court. Al-

[20] Weigand, *Wolfram's "Parzival,"* 58–59.

[21] See the table of Easter dates in Hans Lietzmann, *Zeitrechnung der römischen Kaiserzeit, des Mittelalters und der Neuzeit* (Berlin, 1956), 50. The time period 1203–08 is compatible with Wolfram's allusions to events of 1203–04: the siege of Erfurt (379.18–20) and (?) the sack of Constantinople (563.8–11). Joachim Bumke, *Wolfram*, 21, supports the usual dating in the first decade of the thirteenth century.

though such a calculation seems a formidable task today, it would have been relatively easy for Wolfram's audience, given the liturgical basis of time reckoning and the prevalence of memory techniques for facilitating just such tasks. The *Cisiojanus* is probably the most familiar aid[22] and could be used in combination with other mnemonic devices to calculate days of the week and even relate movable and fixed calendars.[23]

Even without memory aids the computation for homologous years such as 1203 and 1208 is simple within the framework of the liturgical calendar, requiring only a minimal knowledge of major church feasts. The half-year (twenty-six weeks) after Easter comprises the seven weeks from Easter to Pentecost and the nineteen weeks from Pentecost to the nineteenth Sunday after Pentecost. Adjusting this date to Trevrizent's reference by the two-day difference between Good Friday and Easter and by the three days that have elapsed past the four and one-half year mark, the fifth anniversary of Parzival's visit to the hermit would occur five days earlier, on the Tuesday of the eighteenth week after Pentecost. Applying the same process to Guenevere's reference, one-half year minus six weeks or twenty weeks after the Vigil of the Ascension would be the Wednesday of the eighteenth week after Pentecost, the anniversary of Parzival's departure from Arthur's court.

Modern readers can easily correlate the eighteenth week after Pentecost with the year 1203 by consulting a standard handbook of time reckoning:[24] Parzival would arrive at the Grail castle on Monday, September 29, which is also Michaelmas, established both as a major liturgical feast and a secular holiday by the Synod of Mainz in 813.[25] He would depart on Tuesday, the thirtieth, encounter Sigune, then Orilus and Jeschute, borrow the lance from Trevrizent's cell, and finally spend the night in the snow-covered *jeune bois*. On Wednesday, October 1, he would be received at King Arthur's court, only to be condemned by Cundrie and depart on a wild ride at random until his reappearance four and one-half years and two days later on Good Friday.

[22] Rolf Max Kully, "Cisiojanus. Studien zur mnemonischen Literatur anhand des spätmittelalterlichen Kalendergedichts" (1974), esp. 100–05 on origins and dating; Arne Holtorf, "Cisiojanus" (1978); Heribert A. Hilgers, "Versuch über deutsche Cisiojani" (1979).

[23] Hilgers, "Versuch," 139. An early example of how sophisticated such memorial devices could be is the popular *Massa compoti*, composed by Alexander de Villa Dei in 1200. See Walter Emile van Wijk, *Le Nombre d'or: Etude de chronologie technique suivie du texte de la "Massa Compoti" d'Alexandre de Villedieu* (1936).

[24] See Herbert Grotefend, *Zeitrechnung des deutschen Mittelalters und der Neuzeit* (1891–98), I. 64–65.

[25] Thuringia followed the usage of Mainz. See Hans Patze and Walter Schlesinger, *Geschichte Thüringens II.1: Hohes und spätes Mittelalter* (1974), 208–11; for calendars, see Grotefend, *Zeitrechnung* (1892), II. 1, 38–42 (Erfurt) and 113–118 (Mainz).

Such a chronology, of course, remains only a hypothesis. It provides no certain basis for dating the completion or first performance of different books of *Parzival*, as Wolfram apparently revised and emended his text over a period of years.[26] It could, however, provide an imagined time scheme for one period during the narrative's composition. This scheme can serve a variety of heuristic purposes, ranging from evaluating the verisimilitude of natural phenomena to engaging in a dialogue between Wolfram's text and its contemporary context. We might begin with the former, specifically with the weather, which Weigand's approximation localizes in mid-September to mid-October. Parzival's arrival at the Grail castle on Michaelmas, September 29, and the anticipation of the snow the following night would coincide more precisely with a commonly assumed transition from summer to autumn or winter.[27] This coincidence is not insignificant, inasmuch as medieval conceptions of natural phenomena often associate changes from season to season with sudden meteorological shifts,[28] which are also associated with months of the secular calendar.[29]

The determining factor in the snowfall, of course, is the planet Saturn. Its traditional influences of cold and melancholy, which are heightened in autumn, are obviously present in Book V.[30] But Trevrizent attributes the planet's particularly intense effect to its unique location:

> "dô der sterne Sâturnus
> wider an sîn zil gestuont,

[26] See the works listed in Bumke, *Wolfram*, 203.

[27] Michaelmas is the first day of winter in the division of the year into summer and winter and is frequently considered the first day of autumn in a system of four seasons. See Grotefend, *Zeitrechnung*, I, 89–90.

[28] See, for example, Pliny, *Naturalis historia* II.xli.108 (1967), I, 165; Isidore of Seville, *Etymologiae* V.xxxv.8 (1962); Bede, *De temporibus liber* (1943), 298; Bartholomaeus Anglicus, *De rerum proprietatibus* IX.vii (1601; rpt. 1964), 443–44; Vincent of Beauvais, *Speculum naturale* XV.lxiv (1624; rpt. 1964), col. 1132.

[29] September commences with intense heat but concludes with cooler weather, whereas the first part of October is again warm: "Est autem mensis iste [September] mutabilis & instabilis, cuius calor in principio est intensus, sed in fine remittitur & tepescit, iam frigiditatem sapiens autumnalem. . . . [October] in principio sui adhuc est calidus." Bartholomaeus Anglicus, *De rerum proprietatibus* (IX.xvi–xvii), 449–50. This monthly pattern resembles the climate in *Parzival*: a predominance of summerlike weather, interrupted by cooler weather at the end of September that anticipates a temperature change, "frigiditatem sapiens autumnalem," as does Anfortas's wound, "diu wunde wesse vor, / ê der ander frost kœm her nâch" (493.5f.).

[30] See Wilhelm Deinert, *Ritter und Kosmos im "Parzival"* (1960), 16–18. Deinert's references can be supplemented by Raymond Klibansky, Erwin Panofsky, and Fritz Saxl, *Saturn and Melancholy* (1964), 127–95, and Louise Gnädinger, "Rois Peschiere/Anfortas: Der Fischerkönig in Chrestiens und Wolframs Graldichtung" (1978).

daz wart uns bî der wunden kuont,
unt bî dem sumerlîchen snê.
im getet der frost nie sô wê."
(489.24–28)

"When the planet Saturn stood once again at its '*zil*,' we knew that from the wound and from the summery snow. The cold never caused him so much anguish."

The meaning of this passage remains contested, as *zil* appears to be a term of Wolfram's invention.[31] In terms of our narrative chronology, though, there is a possibility that the reference alludes to Saturn's actual position at the end of September 1203, when the planet was approaching opposition to the sun.[32] Saturn generally functions in astrology as a nocturnal anti-sun;[33] at opposition, the sun's influence would cease at sunset as Saturn commenced its domination of the sky at night—the time of its effects during Books V–VI.[34] As we will see in Chapter 8, the puzzling reference to Mars and Jupiter in Book XVI also has a contemporary counterpart in a conjunction of these planets at the end of September 1208.

More important than such parallels between natural phenomena in *Parzival* and the historical context of 1203–1208 would be the fact that Wolfram's construction of a liturgical as well as an astronomical background also creates a commentary on Parzival's failure at the Grail castle, what in Bakhtinian terms might be called a "dialogizing background."[35] The explicit factor in the decision to refrain from asking the redeeming question is his adherence to the timeless courtly code of Gurnemanz in spite of the obviously different demands of the unique chronological situation at the Grail castle. Parzival is prompted not only by the inhabitants of Munsalvaesche but also by God's direction of the universe, which or-

[31] See Deinert, *Ritter und Kosmos*, 24–28. Deinert's attempt to equate MHG *zil* with Lat. *domicilium* is not convincing because the more appropriate translation for the Latin term, evidenced by later writers, is *hûs*. See Deinert, 26 n. 1, and Georg-Karl Bauer, *Sternkunde und Sterndeutung der Deutschen im 9.–14. Jahrhundert* (1937), 131–32.

[32] See William D. Stahlman and Owen Gingerich, *Solar and Planetary Longitudes for Years − 200 to + 2000 by Ten-Day Intervals* (1963), 453.

[33] Franz Boll, Carl Bezold, and Wilhelm Gundel, *Sternglaube und Sterndeutung* (1966), 59.

[34] As Berthold of Regensburg states in his sermon on the seven planets, Saturn "hât grôze kraft, swenne er ûf gêt." *Predigten*, ed. Franz Pfeiffer (1862; rpt. 1965), I, 63. According to Pliny, the directly opposite force of the sun even appears to drive a planet toward the highest point of its orbit and thus toward an influential stationary position, or *statio* (= "zil"?). *Naturalis historia* (II.xvi.70), 149.

[35] See Gary Saul Morson and Caryl Emerson, *Mikhail Bakhtin: Creation of a Prosaics* (1990), 337.

dains the position of Saturn so that its influence on Anfortas's wound is strongest—and hence his suffering and need of assistance are most obvious at this precise moment.[36]

But Parzival is prompted not only by the influence of the planets, the realization of the divine plan in space, but also by the biblical readings, or pericopes, for the feasts of the liturgical calendar, the manifestation of that same plan in time. Indeed, the lectionary texts and sermons for the eighteenth Sunday after Pentecost and the feast of Michaelmas discuss situations remarkably similar to his. This is not to suggest that Parzival should be familiar with these sermon texts—regular attendance at mass is not part of Gurnemanz's basic religious instruction, which is limited to showing him how to make his offering and cross himself (169.19). These sermons seem instead to provide a background commentary on the narrative, implicitly extending the dialogue between Wolfram and his audience on the events of Book V to the contemporary liturgy.

Of course, these readings and the sermons based on them offer clerical didacticism rather than authorial discourse. And although the parallels between *Parzival* and contemporary sermons invite a relationship of text and commentary, they are actually far more disparate: Wolfram's hero seems deficient when measured against church doctrine, but clerical strictures seem reductive when applied to his situation. This dialogue between secular and clerical, literary and religious discourses constitutes one of the games in which Wolfram engages his readers and listeners. In much the same way, the opposition between Kay and Gawan as members of the lower and upper nobility, parvenu seneschal and princely courtier, both reflects and caters to disparate elements of his secular aristocratic audience.

During the period postulated for Parzival's visit, there are four main pericopes: the Epistle and Gospel readings for the eighteenth Sunday after Pentecost (Ephesians 4.1–6 and Luke 14.1–11), and those for the feast of Michaelmas on September 29 (Revelations 12.7–12 and Matthew 18.1–10).[37] The Gospel reading for the eighteenth Sunday after Pentecost (Luke 14.1–11), the most common text for contemporary sermons,[38] provides a striking parallel to the situation at Munsalvaesche,

[36] See esp. Deinert, *Ritter und Kosmos*, 12–15.

[37] For basic studies on the system of readings, see Ernst Ranke, *Das kirchliche Perikopensystem* (1847); G. Godu, "Epîtres" and "Evangiles," *Dictionnaire d'archéologie chrétienne et de liturgie* (Paris, 1907–53), V.1, 245–344 and 852–923; Walter Howard Frere, *Studies in the Early Roman Liturgy. II: The Roman Gospel Lectionary* (1934) and *III: The Roman Epistle Lectionary* (1935). For discussions of early German pericopes, see Karl Stejskal, "Altdeutsches Epistel- und Evangelienbuch," *ZfdPh* 15 (1883), 10–48, and Paul Pietsch, *Evangely und Epistel Teutsch* (1927).

[38] For sample sermons, see Anton E. Schönbach, *Altdeutsche Predigten* (1886–91; rpt.

dealing with two interrelated subjects, whether one should heal on the Sabbath, and the parable of how a guest should behave at a feast:

> (14.1) And it came to pass, when Jesus went into the house of one of the chiefs of the Pharisees on the sabbath-day to eat bread, that they watched him. (2) And behold, there was a certain man before him that had the dropsy. (3) And Jesus answering, spoke to the lawyers and Pharisees, saying: Is it lawful to heal on the sabbath-day? (4) But they held their peace. But he taking him, healed him, and sent him away. . . . (7) And he spoke a parable also to them that were invited, marking how they chose the first seats at the table, saying to them: (8) When thou art invited to a wedding, sit not down in the first place, lest perhaps one more honorable than thou be invited by him; (9) And he that invited thee and him, come and say to thee, Give this man place: and then thou begin with shame to take the lowest place. (10) But when thou art invited, go sit down in the lowest place; that when he who invited thee cometh, he may say to thee: Friend, go up higher. Then shalt thou have glory before them that sit at table with thee. (11) Because every one that exalteth himself, shall be humbled: and he that humbleth himself, shall be exalted.

Expositions of this text in contemporary sermons make the parallel to Book V of *Parzival* even clearer. Dropsy, like Anfortas's infirmity, is associated with a potentially fatal affliction of the genital area that renders the affected person noxious and obviously in need of medication:

> Die wazzersůcht die wirdit, swenne sich die blase irdenit und brichit und strichit danne die vůchtene inzwischen vel und vleisch und swillit der mensche und stinkit im der adim vil ůbele . . . daz ist ein vil bose sůche, der wirt selden ende wan mit deme tode.

> Dropsy develops when the bladder expands and breaks and spreads the liquid between skin and flesh, swelling a man and making his breath smell horribly. . . . It is a horrible disease that seldom ends except in death.[39]

1964), I, 133–35 and 377–78; II, 164–65; III, 153–56; Anton E. Schönbach, "Weingartner Predigten," *ZfdA* 28 (1884), 4–5. The designation varies from the seventeenth to the eighteenth Sunday, depending on whether the sermons are numbered from the octave of Pentecost or Pentecost itself. For a list of published sermons, see Karin Morvay and Dagmar Grube, *Bibliographie der deutschen Predigt des Mittelalters* (1974), under the various Latin incipits for Luke 14.1, "Cum intraret Iesus in domum" (p. 230); 14.2, "Hydropicus erat ante illum" (p. 248); 14.8, "Cum vocatus fueris ad nuptias" (p. 231); and 14.11, "Omnis qui se exaltat" (p. 260).

[39] Schönbach, *Altdeutsche Predigten*, I, 134.

Moreover, dropsy—like Anfortas's wound—is associated with a punishment for sin, sometimes specified as concupiscence or lust.[40] The remedy in both cases heals a spiritual injury underlying the physical one inflicted by God, and both cures are miraculously effected in instances of physically immedicable injuries by words of compassion that heal where salves, bandages, and all other remedies have failed, "mit sinen worten ane salbin, ane binden, ane aller slachte arcteie."[41]

Failure to respond to such an affliction on the basis of a literal prohibition such as the law of the Pharisees or Gurnemanz's advice, expressed in both cases by silence, is extremely consequential, as the expositions of the Gospel parable and Parzival's fate illustrate. The parable is consistently equated in Middle High German sermons not only with the proper behavior at a real feast but also with the behavior prerequisite to admission to the heavenly feast. Of course, Munsalvaesche is not an allegory of the Heavenly City, but, as we have seen, it *almost* equals the kingdom of heaven (238.21–24). These correspondences between the Gospel text and the Grail society draw our attention to the parallels between the behavior prescribed for admission to that feast and Parzival's actual conduct. The invitation of Luke 14.9–10 has an arresting equivalent in the request that Anfortas makes the moment his guest enters the main hall:[42]

er liez in dâ niht langer stên:
in bat der wirt nâher gên
und sitzen, "zuo mir dâ her an.
sazte i'iuch verre dort hin dan,
daz wære iu alze gastlîch."
(230.25–29)

He let him stand there no longer: the host asked him to come closer and sit "here beside me. If I sat you further away, that would be treating you too much like a stranger."

In a manner similar to the advice of the Gospel text, Parzival complies with the request to take the seat of honor. Why, then, does he fail to ask the redeeming question, the ultimate purpose of this request?

[40] Schönbach, *Altdeutsche Predigten,* II, 164.

[41] Schönbach, *Altdeutsche Predigten,* I, 134.

[42] Schönbach, *Altdeutsche Predigten,* III, 155: "swenne der wirt denne chumt, der sprichet denne zuo dir: 'friunt, sitze du her uf baz al hoher zuo mir'; des hastu denne lob unde ere von allen den die da sint."

III

There is general unanimity that the hero undergoes a test at Munsalvaesche, but the marked divergence of opinions concerning the nature of that test and the reasons for his failure suggests that Wolfram's text provides no single solution, inviting—like the Grail itself—a multitude of explanations.[43] One approach that has provided a common denominator for some interpretations is the assessment of Parzival's failure in general terms as an indication of pride or lack of humility.[44] As an attitude characterized by self-love, pride offers a tempting explanation for Parzival's recourse to Gurnemanz's advice and courtly behavior in order to avoid calling attention to himself with unseemly curiosity, "durch zuht in vrâgens doch verdrôz" (239.10), and hence for his lack of compassion for Anfortas. One must be more hesitant about concluding that the courtly code is therefore a form of pride.[45] *Zuht* is an integral part of the etiquette at Munsalvaesche—the term is mentioned some ten times during the course of the Grail procession.[46] As sermons for the eighteenth Sunday after Pentecost illustrate, living "mit zuht unde mit diemuote" is associated with the proper response at the feast in Luke 14; indeed, the two are virtually identical:[47] "wan nach iwer ladunge, so sult ir ouch leben mit allen zuhten, mit aller diemůte also" (For after your invitation you should live with all good behavior, that is, with all humility).

One must be equally hesitant in emphasizing pride as the sole cause of Parzival's failure. Pride shares with other types of improper behavior a more important common origin: a confusion of priorities that places the individual above his fellow man and worldly above religious concerns. Parzival's elevation of courtly *zuht* over the more appropriate response could accordingly be viewed not so much as the immediate cause of his failure but, rather, as the result of an already established confusion of what the situation demands of him. Gurnemanz places the admonition not to ask too many questions within a larger emphasis that Parzival's speech should be guided by his senses:

[43] The ambiguity is implied in Mertens's title (see n. 6). How far astray the speculations can go is exemplified by Petrus W. Tax, "The Grail Kingdom and Parzival's First Visit" (1978).

[44] See Herbert Kolb, "*Schola humilitatis*: Ein Beitrag zur Interpretation der Gralerzählung Wolframs von Eschenbach" (1956); and Walter Henzen, "Zur Vorprägung der Demut im *Parzival* durch Chrestien" (1958).

[45] See Kolb, "*Schola*," 84–86, and the counterargument by Henzen, "Demut," 430–32, and more recently Kurt Ruh, *Höfische Epik des deutschen Mittelalters, II*, 68.

[46] 232.8, 234.1, 235.4, 236.7/16, 238.5/30, 239.10, and 240.19/22.

[47] Schönbach, *Altdeutsche Predigten*, III, 156 and 153–54.

"ir kunnet hœren unde sehen,
entseben unde dræhen:
daz solt iuch witzen næhen."
(171.22–24)

"You can hear and see, taste and smell—that should bring you sense."

And Trevrizent similarly identifies no particular behavior as the cause of Parzival's failure but blames a more general inability to follow the motivation of his God-given senses, "dô dir got fünf sinne lêch, / die hânt ir rât dir vor bespart" (488.26–27).

In fact, several other behavioral models also seem applicable to Parzival's confusion at the Grail castle. Another factor has long been noticed as an influence on his actions, love:[48] "unsweet discomforts" disturb his perception of space and color as he leaves Graharz (179.13–22), thoughts of love trouble his mind as he approaches the Grail castle (224.10–18), thoughts of Repanse de Schoye draw his attention during the Grail procession (236.10–15), and Love herself emerges to dominate the psychomachia between *minne* and *witze* in the snow-covered landscape of Book VI. But there is also another motivating force in Parzival's confusion of priorities at Munsalvaesche: anger. Anger is diametrically opposed to the Epistle admonition for the eighteenth Sunday after Pentecost to walk "with all humility and mildness" (Ephesians 4.2); it is also inappropriate at the Grail castle, where mildness protects against pride: "ir müest aldâ vor hôchvart / mit senften willen sîn bewart" (472.13f.).

The contribution of anger to Parzival's confusion seems to be the reason for Wolfram's creation of a brief scene that seemed so inappropriate to a G-manuscript scribe that he deleted it entirely.[49] A verbally adroit courtier or "redespæher man" (229.4), acting as if he were angry (229.7), enrages Parzival in turn, who clenches his fist so hard that blood shoots out of his nails, requiring intervention by the Grail retinue:

"nein, hêrre," sprach diu ritterschaft . . .
"dar gêt: ir sît im werder gast:
und schütet ab iu zornes last."
(229.15ff.)

"No, sir," spoke the knights . . . "Please enter—you are his honored guest—and put off the burden of your anger."

[48] See Gerhard Bauer, "Parzival und die Minne" (1963).

[49] See Hermann J. Weigand, "A Jester at the Grail Castle in Wolfram's *Parzival*?", (1952), esp. n. 1.; and Bumke, *Forschung*, 293.

The "burden of anger" in medieval psychology is a consequential one, determining both the immediate and subsequent behavior of an individual. According to the basic clerical definition of Gregory the Great, anger not only disrupts social concord through verbal abuse or bodily injury but can also induce a longer-lasting and nonviolent effect—silence:

> Aliquando ira perturbato animo quasi ex iudicio silentium indicit; et quo se foras per linguam non exprimit, intus deterius ignescit ut iratus quisque collocutionem suam proximo subtrahat.[50]
>
> Sometimes when the mind is disturbed, anger as if in judgment commands silence; and in proportion as it does not vent itself outwardly by the lips, inwardly it burns the worse, so the angry man withholds from converse with his neighbor.

Parzival's behavior during his visit to the Grail castle follows a similar pattern. Angry and confused, he falls silent before the suffering Anfortas, relying on the outward veneer of courtly behavior to save face rather than obeying the promptings to a higher *zuht* that he barely notices in his confusion. Still seething under the influence of his disturbed senses, he spends a restless night with dreams punctuated by sword blows, jousts, and charges (245.9–13). Wolfram emphasizes this traumatic experience by citing its physiological effects, comparing it with Herzeloyde's dream, and interpreting it as the anticipation of future suffering (245.4/7f./19). Indeed, the most popular medieval oneiromantic handbook interprets a dream of armed combat as presaging not only future suffering but also an outburst of public anger, "ira in publico."[51] Parzival awakens the next morning, immediately erupting in fury:

> nieman er hôrte noch ensach:
> ungefüege leit im dran geschach.
> daz het im zorn gereizet. . . .
> al schrînde lief der junge man
> wider zu sîme orse sân.
>
> (247.5ff.)

[50] Gregory the Great, *Moralia in Job* (V.45.79), CCSL 143, 277. The translation is cited from *Morals on the Book of Job by S. Gregory the Great* (Oxford, 1844), I, 305. The popularity—and controversial reception—of the association of anger and silence is suggested by the fact that St. Thomas Aquinas devotes an article to it in the *Summa theologica* (I.–II., Quaes. 48, art. 4).

[51] Cited from *"Somniale Danielis": An Edition of a Medieval Latin Dream Interpretation Handbook* (1981), 105. For a German version, see Paul Graffunder, "Daniels Traumdeutungen: Ein mittelalterliches Traumbuch in deutschen Versen" (1906/07), 77–80 and 281–84.

> He neither heard nor saw anyone, which provoked a furious outburst of anger. . . . Screaming, the young man ran back to his horse.

Perfectly in accordance with this pattern of behavior, Sigune accuses Parzival of *galle*, the physiological cause of anger and the cause of uncharitable conduct in a general sense, which has destroyed his compassion (255.15f.), and Cundrie reproaches King Arthur for accepting the hero to the Round Table because he "galls" its reputation (314.26–28).

The archetypal example of such rancor, as Trevrizent observes in Book IX, is Lucifer's revolt and expulsion from heaven:

> "Irn megt im ab erzürnen niht:
> swer iuch gein im in hazze siht,
> der hât iuch an den witzen kranc.
> nu prüevt wie Lucifern gelanc
> unt sînen nôtgestallen.
> si wârn doch âne gallen:
> ja hêr, wâ nâmen si den nît,
> dâ von ir endelôser strît
> zer helle enpfâhet sûren lôn?"
> (463.1–9)

> "You can force nothing from him with anger. Anyone who sees you angry at him will think you are out of your wits. Now, observe what happened to Lucifer and his companions. They were without gall: indeed, sir, where did they get the envy from which their endless battle in hell receives a bitter reward?"

It thus seems no coincidence that the battle between Lucifer and God's angels described in Revelations 12.7–10 is also the Epistle text and the topic of numerous sermons for Michaelmas, the day postulated for Parzival's visit to the Grail castle.[52] As a contemporary sermon on an antiphon for this feast explains, Michael is not only the guardian of the Heavenly Jerusalem but also the guardian angel of "Christian knights."[53]

The clerical interpretation of Michaelmas in terms of chivalric culture brings the dialogue between Wolfram's narrative and the liturgical back-

[52] For Middle High German sermons on Michaelmas, see Schönbach *Altdeutsche Predigten*, I, 76–78, 177–80, 223–24, 350–51; III, 229–30: Wilhelm Wackernagel, *Altdeutsche Predigten und Gebete aus Handschriften* (1876), 31–32; Johannes Kelle, *Speculum ecclesiae, altdeutsch* (1858), 120–26 and 126–27; Hermann Leyser, *Deutsche Predigten des XIII. und XIV. Jahrhunderts* (1838), 107–10.

[53] Schönbach, *Altdeutsche Predigten*, I, 77.

ground into even closer focus.[54] The Middle High German adaptation of St. Bernard's sermons for Michaelmas, for example, discusses two antithetical types of behavior based on the distinction between the Knights Templar and secular knighthood and invites a comparison between the Grail's *tempeleisen* and Parzival. Like the behavior demanded of St. Bernard's Templars and Wolfram's Grail knights, admission to the Heavenly City requires humility, chastity, voluntary poverty, and above all, peaceful submission to God's ordinances: "swo [die engel] vinden dimůticheit, kůscheit, willicliche armůte und andere gůte werk, da vrowent sie sich. . . . und vor allen dingen minnent sie den vriede und die einmůt, ob die in gote sint."[55] The improper behavior, like that attributed to secular knights by clerics and to Parzival by Cundrie, reflects an ignorance of God's design, the absence of true charity and concord, and results in exclusion from the realm of light.[56]

Their common focus notwithstanding, the relationship between the sermons for Michaelmas and Wolfram's text remains ambiguous. The sermonizing commentary on admission to the heavenly kingdom seems to underscore Parzival's failure, illustrating the extent to which his behavior also fails to meet clerical standards of conduct for secular knights. However, the religious indictment of Parzival by Cundrie and indirectly by the sermons is obviated by the fact that a higher dispensation eventually absolves the hero, granting him a second chance at the end of the romance. Whether Wolfram thereby relativizes the religious discourse associated with Cundrie's message and the sermons, subsuming it into a larger secularizing process (and, as it were, romancing the Grail narrative) remains to be seen.

For the present I want to bring this discussion full circle, if not to a close, by noting that sermons for Michaelmas not only condemn specific sins but also trace them to a common origin, lack of "gotes geist," explaining deeds in terms of the thoughts in which they originate. This strategy, like that of Trevrizent in Book IX, follows standard confessional practice in assuming that actions are the result of an already established and more general pattern of thought.[57] As the sermons for Michaelmas

[54] The thematic and chronological relationship between the two feasts is observed by medieval liturgical handbooks: Honorius of Autun, *Gemma animae* (IV.83), *PL* 172.722; Sicard of Cremona, *Mitrale seu de officiis ecclesiasticis summa* (VIII.17), *PL* 212.399; Guilelmus Durandus, *Rationale divinorum officiorum* (VI.131) (1568), fol. 275^{v}.

[55] Schönbach, *Altdeutsche Predigten*, I, 350.

[56] Ibid.

[57] Trevrizent similarly attempts to learn Parzival's entire history, from the initial anger against God (462.5), to the emergence of "thoughts" in "deeds" (466.29f.), as a prerequisite to exhorting him to "convert" or turn his mind to a proper attitude toward his creator, "nu kêret iwer gemüete" (467.9).

observe, the pattern of sin begins with the devil, who presumed that he was like God and even was a god;[58] it continues in the temptation of Adam and his descendants with false assurances that they would also be as gods.[59] We saw in Chapter 2 that Parzival's encounter with the knights in Book III seems to initiate a similar pattern in the romance. Parzival's confusion of knights with God stands symbolically over his entry into the world, the beginning of a confusion of priorities that seems, ultimately, to underlie his failure at Munsalvaesche.

Of course, the events of Book V also look ahead to the colloquy between Trevrizent and Parzival on Good Friday four and one-half years later. It has been observed that numerous motifs of Book IX, from the snowfall that again dominates the landscape to the lengthy discussions of the Grail society, are designed to remind Parzival and Wolfram's audience of the hero's failure at Munsalvaesche.[60] The liturgical chronology underlying the Grail narrative also underscores this retrospective focus. The main religious examples that Trevrizent employs in his instruction of the hero—the rebellion of Lucifer, the fall of Adam, the murder of Abel—figure prominently in the liturgy and sermons for Michaelmas. But they also prefigure themes of the Easter season and thereby anticipate the discussion in Book IX. As the sermons suggest, the battle between God and the devil results in Adam's fall and initiates the chain of sin that begins with the murder of Abel, but ultimately concludes with Christ's redemption of man on Good Friday.[61] Just as Good Friday represents the turning point of the liturgical calendar, the discussion with Trevrizent is also the turning point of Parzival's career, resolving the results of his confusion of men with God on the day on which God is most manifestly man. With that first hesitant question about time inside the hermit's cell (460.17f.), the hero initiates a process that brings him into harmony with the liturgical calendar and the divine plan of salvation, apparently resolving the conflict between God and world in a manner that preserves each sphere of interest while linking them as well:

> wand in der wirt von sünden schiet
> unt im doch rîterlîchen riet.
>
> (501.17f.)

[58] Schönbach, *Altdeutsche Predigten,* III, 229.
[59] Schönbach, *Altdeutsche Predigten,* I, 76.
[60] See Walter Henzen, "Das IX. Buch des *Parzival*: Überlegungen zum Aufbau" (1951).
[61] Schönbach, *Altdeutsche Predigten,* I, 76–77.

His host absolved him of sin, and yet counseled him as a knight.

This apparently hierarchical resolution is to be expected in a book that, more than any other in *Parzival*, consistently emphasizes religious concerns over chivalric ones. As we see in ensuing chapters, however, the developments that culminate in the redeeming question also suggest a different and more secular alternative.

CHAPTER SIX

The Enchanted Body: Treating the Fisher King

The extensive Good Friday colloquy in Book IX brings a radical change to the narrative, apparently narrowing the heteroglossic interplay of the preceding books to a more unified religious discourse. Most studies of Book IX understandably approach various aspects of this "small *Summa theologiae*" (as it has been called), emphasizing the ultimate congruence of salvation history and individual redemption through the hero's confession and absolution.[1] The course of true redemption, however, never did run true, and this conversation is no exception, digressing to include other histories, especially that of the Grail king and the crisis at Munsalvaesche. Like the misadventures of youthful regents that often furnish brief warning examples within romance narratives, the story of Anfortas is a cautionary tale, one that subsumes his catastrophic past into a larger adventure that will ultimately be "broken" by Parzival. By presenting Anfortas's pursuit of illicit love as an example of pride to counter Parzival's own *hôchvart* (472.13ff.), Trevrizent inadvertently illuminates a primary difference between the two men, motivating and preparing the replacement of the maimed uncle by his chaste nephew at the end of the romance.[2]

[1] See the works listed by Bumke, *Wolfram*, 189, to which should also be added Wolfgang Mohr's "Parzivals ritterliche Schuld" (1952). The confessional nature of Chrétien's scene has been elucidated by Bonnie Buettner, "The Good Friday Scene in Chrétien de Troyes' *Perceval*" (1980).

[2] The preparation for this exchange begins at the end of Book II, when Queen Herzeloyde and her attendants rejoice in the robust male baby with the prominent *visellîn* (112.25), a moment that simultaneously celebrates Parzival's birth and engenders his narrative (112.5–20). At Gurnemanz's castle, lovely maidens enter his bath uninvited, washing and massaging his bruises, and teasingly eager to see if anything has happened to him "down there" (167.28). These allusions draw attention to Parzival's sexual poten-

Unlike Parzival's eventual progression from knight-errant to regent, the story of Anfortas begins with dynastic succession and degenerates into misguided knight-errantry (478.1ff.). Elected king as the eldest son of Frimutel while still a youth, Anfortas's uncontrolled desires spurn the restriction of the Grail king's sexual activity to marriage, urging him to seek the reward of love through *âventiure.* The opposition between adolescent license and adult restraint, knightly dissipation and kingly monogamy, is dramatically underscored by Anfortas's battle cry of "Amor" (478.30), its appropriated Latin word flaunting his rejection of the alliance between the regulatory script that appears on the Grail (478.14) and clerical limitation of sexual activity to marriage. Setting out alone in quest of love, an unkingly escape into the private sphere, Anfortas unexpectedly encounters a heathen opponent who brings his sexual adventures to an abrupt end with a spear thrust through the testicles, "durch die heidruose sîn" (479.12).[3] The exhausted king struggles back to the Grail castle, where a surgeon attends to the wound:[4]

> "in de wunden greif eins arztes hant,
> unz er des spers îsen vant:
> der trunzûn was rœrîn,
> ein teil in den wunden sîn:
> diu gewan der arzet beidiu wider."
> (480.5–9)

"A surgeon probed the wound until he found the iron spearhead; the shaft was of reed, a part of which was also in the wound; the doctor retrieved both."

Such injuries will not have been entirely unknown in medieval medical practice, as discussions for treating them in handbooks attest.[5] But the

tial, a potential that remains unfulfilled until the conclusion of his *trinoctium castitatis* with Condwiramurs in Book IV. The restriction of Parzival's sexual activity to marriage not only fulfills clerical and sacramental ideals but also advances the more pragmatic secular goal of untroubled dynastic continuity. Parzival's biography thus contrasts sharply with that of Anfortas.

[3] Chrétien's text has "parmi les hanches ambedeus," which has a widespread meaning of "genitalia." See Clovis Brunel, "Les Hanches du Roi Pêcheur (Chrétien de Troyes 3513)" (1960).

[4] Two earlier investigations are especially relevant: Waltraut F. Dubé, "Medieval Medicine in Middle High German Epics" (1981), and Bernhard D. Haage, "Prolegomena zu Anfortas' Leiden im *Parzival*" (1985), expanded in his *Studien zur Heilkunde im "Parzival" Wolframs von Eschenbach* (1992), 88–113 and 145–80.

[5] E.g., Constantinus Africanus, "De vulneribus testiculorum," in his *De morborum cogni-*

drama of the scene, related by Trevrizent, the brother of the victim, to Parzival, their unknown nephew and future ruler, is heightened by two facts that make this particular wound unique. First, Anfortas is an unmarried and childless king, whose injury threatens the dynastic succession at Munsalvaesche, plunging the realm into a lengthy and traumatic crisis. Second, the treatment involves far more than removing the spearhead and splinters and then bandaging the incision. The king has to be taken before the Grail, the sight of which keeps its beholder alive, because of an unexpected complication—the wound is discovered to be poisoned: "des küneges wunde geitert was" (481.5).[6]

The ensuing treatment therefore necessitates finding antidotes to a poison from the heathen knight's country of Ethnise,[7] located near the exit of the river Tigris from paradise, an identification made possible by the heathen's overconfident engraving of his name on the spear (479.15–20). The assumption that the poison derives from serpents is logical, given the widespread belief that the deserts beyond paradise were literally crawling with snakes: "post paradysum sunt loca multa deserta et invia, ob diversa serpentium et ferarum animalia."[8] Accordingly, a variety of medical books was consulted in researching snake venoms, all to no avail—a cure was against the divine will:

> "swaz man der arzetbuoche las,
> diene gâben keiner helfe lôn.
> gein aspîs, ecidemon,
> ehcontîus unt lisîs,
> jêcîs unt mêatrîs
> (die argen slangenz eiter heiz
> tragent), swaz iemen dâ für weiz,
> unt für ander würm diez eiter tragent,
> swaz die wîsen arzt dâ für bejagent
> mit fisiken liste an würzen,
> (lâ dir die rede kürzen)
> der keinz gehelfen kunde:
> got selbe uns des verbunde."
> (481.6–18)

---

tione et curatione (VI.7), *Opera omnia* (Basel, 1536), 126; Roger Frugardi of Salerno, *Chirurgia* (1918), 219–20.

[6] Translations usually choose the more modern "infected," a possibility also considered by Dubé, "Medicine," 143. However, Wolfram explicitly states that the spearhead was poisoned (479.8), and the immediately following discussion of snake remedies focuses on poison. See Haage, "Prolegomena," 108–09 and *Heilkunde*, 151–52.

[7] On the derivation of Ethnise from Solinus, see Paul Hagen, "Untersuchungen über Kyot" (1901), 188–89.

[8] Honorius of Autun, *Imago mundi* (1982), 52.

"All the medical books one consulted provided no help at all. Whatever anyone knows as a remedy for the asp, ecidemon, akontias and lysis, echis and miatros—these vicious snakes carry a hot poison—or for other poisonous reptiles, whatever antidotes learned doctors with their medicinal knowledge derive from herbs—to make this story short—none of them could help: God himself prevented us from doing so."

As the presumed origin of the poison on the margins of paradise as well as God's prevention of a cure suggest, Trevrizent's cautionary narrative immediately raises a conflict between supernatural and natural, religious and medicinal discourses that seems to resist resolution.

The initial response to the medical crisis seems entirely professional: a surgeon (480.5/9) probes the wound, recovering the spear tip and fragments of the shaft; a survey of the established medical literature (481.6) considers a variety of snake venoms as well as the repertory of herbal antidotes (481.8–14). It, too, is conducted, if the third-person references, "man las" and "die wîsen arzt" (481.6, 481.14), are any indication, entirely by medical specialists. Indeed, the details of this passage reveal Wolfram's extraordinary familiarity with contemporary medical literature—the Greek snake names (481.8–10) derive from glossed illustrations in twelfth-century manuscripts of Pseudo-Apuleius's *Herbarius*,[9] and the "hot" nature of snake poison (481.11) comes from the Galenic tradition transmitted to medieval Europe by Arabic science.[10] Nonetheless, the treatment fails because, as is revealed immediately thereafter, God himself prevented it, "got selbe uns des verbunde" (481.18). At this point, the medical specialists apparently submit to the divine will and abandon the case; at least, we hear no more about them.

The failure of professional medical practitioners appears to force the members of the Grail community to undertake a second and more extensive series of cures on their own initiative. This group effort emerges in the prominence of "we," "us," and "our" in the ensuing sections of Trevrizent's reminiscence—some nineteen times in sixty lines. Each of the medicines is introduced with "wir gewunnen" or a similar statement recording the obtaining of materia medica (481.19/30, 482.6/19/27/29, 483.6), and each section registers the group's involvement in testing the cure as well as its ensuing disappointment. As we will see, these puzzling antidotes have analogues in medieval medical tradition, but extrapolate from it, creatively and even experimentally, attempting to produce results

[9] See my "Wolframs Schlangenliste (*Parzival* 481) und Pseudo-Apuleius" (1994).

[10] Vincent of Beauvais, *Speculum naturale* (1624; rpt. 1964), col. 1466, refers the concept of "hot" venom to Avicenna, *Liber Canonis* (Bk. IV) and Constantinus Africanus, *Liber Pantegni* (Bk. VIII).

that will counteract the paranormal situation presented by Anfortas's suffering.

That situation resembles the enchantments under which people or places are frequently placed in romance narratives. Usually, the suspension of causality or the intrusion of supernatural forces, whether inherent or caused by magic, is resolved by a predetermined action or by a countermagic that returns things to normal.[11] The most prominent such enchantments in *Parzival* are the adventures to be "broken" at Munsalvaesche and Schastel Marveile, which are ruled by maimed regents, the wounded Anfortas and the castrated Clinschor, respectively. But there is also a hierarchy of enchantments, recapitulating other differences between the Arthurian and Grail worlds. Whereas Clinschor is himself a magician whose sorcery is employed by Orgeluse and designed to be broken only by a knight capable of defeating her enemy Gramoflanz, Anfortas is the victim of a higher dispensation: God's will frustrates any attempt by human medicine or magic to heal his wound, until the divine enchantment is broken by the power of the redeeming question.

The wound thus becomes the contested site of competing but unequal discourses, in which divine intervention partially suspends natural causality, leaving the wound susceptible to the worsening effects of astrological influences and ongoing putrefaction, but making it unresponsive to normal human medication. The remarkable remedies undertaken by the inhabitants of Munsalvaesche accordingly seem directed toward circumventing the divine suspension of causality with extraordinary means, as a list of the materials suggests: (1) herbs from paradise, (2) the Golden Bough, (3) the blood of the pelican, (4) the heart of the unicorn as well as the carbuncle that grows under the unicorn's horn, and (5) the herb dracontea in conjunction with *des trachen umbevart.* I will discuss each in turn before turning to their larger implications.

I

The first cure, an herb from paradise, immediately links two disparate discourses, medical history and salvation history:

"wir gewunnen Gêôn
ze helfe unde Fîsôn,
Eufrâtes unde Tigrîs,
diu vier wazzer ûzem pardîs,
sô nâhn hin zuo ir süezer smac

[11] See Erich Köhler, "Die Rolle des Rechtsgebrauchs (costume) in den Romanen des Chrétien de Troyes" (1962).

dennoch niht sîn verrochen mac,
ob kein wurz dinne quæme,
diu unser trûren næme."
(481.19–26)

"We sought the help of the Gehon, and the Phison, Euphrates, and Tigris, the four rivers flowing out of paradise—so near that its sweet smell is not spent—to see whether any herb might come therein that would relieve our sadness."

The main details of this passage, the intense odor of the Garden of Eden and the medicinal herbs carried by the four rivers emerging from it, derive from the numerous traditions spawned by the description of paradise in Genesis 2.[12] The first detail alludes to the conception of paradise as an aromatic spice garden, a commonplace from the hexaemeral tradition to the twelfth-century Platonists and thirteenth-century encyclopedists,[13] and one that entered the vernacular as early as the *Wiener Genesis.*[14] The second detail appears to have its origins in God's expulsion of Adam and Eve from paradise in order to prevent them from eating of the Tree of Life and thus becoming immortal (Genesis 3.22). This eventually led to the belief that matter carried out of paradise by its four rivers could be life-extending or medicinal, generating apocryphal legends such as Seth's return to paradise in search of remedies for the infirmities of Adam's old age.[15] Indeed, it may not be coincidental that Adam's illness is often specified as podagra, the same affliction bothering Titurel, the senior member of the Grail family and oldest living descendant of the "Adamic" progenitor Mazadan.[16]

[12] See Reinhold Grimm, *Paradisus coelestis, Paradisus terrestris* (1977), 121–28; Martin, *Kommentar,* 367–68. On the lore of paradise, see Arturo Graf, "Natura, condizioni e meraviglie del paradiso terrestre," in his *Miti, leggende e superstizioni del medio evo* (1892), I, 16–43, 136–57 (notes), and appendix 1, 197–217.

[13] See, for example, Alcimus Ecdicius Avitus, *De spiritalis historiae gestis* (I.238–50), in *Opera,* MGH:AA 6.2 (1961), 209–10; Theodulf of Orleans, "De Paradiso," ed. Ernst Dümmler, in MGH: Poetae I (1881), 573; Peter Damian, "De gaudio Paradisi," in *L'opera poetica di S. Pier Damiani,* ed. Margarete Lokrantz (Uppsala, 1964), 80–83. For Chartrian examples, see Bernard Silvestris, *Cosmographia* I.3.317–38 and II.9.3 (1978), 112–13 and 138; Alain de Lille (1955), I.70–71; for encyclopedias, see Thomas of Cantimpré, *Liber de natura rerum* X.2 (1973), 315.

[14] *Die frühmittelhochdeutsche "Wiener Genesis,"* 232–63 (1972), 103–05. On the description of the garden, see Rainer Gruenter, "Der paradisus der *Wiener Genesis*" (1955).

[15] See Graf, *Miti,* 175–76; Franz Kampers, *Mittelalterliche Sagen vom Paradiese* (1897), 94–99; *Evangelium Nicodemi* (chap. 19), ed. Montague Rhodes James, *The Apocryphal New Testament* (Oxford, 1960), 126–27.

[16] Titurel is described in 501.26 as having podagra. Its Adamic component is suggested by the fact that although the Grail is an "approximation" of paradise (238.23f.), it

This idea of obtaining herbs from paradise can be found in Greek and Hebrew sources,[17] as well as in medieval Latin ones, entering vernacular medicine as early as the tenth-century Old English *Leechbook.*[18] Interest in the effluvia of paradise flourished amidst the fascination with the Near East generated by the crusades. In the *Iter ad Paradisum,* Alexander the Great's expedition up the Ganges to paradise finds gigantic leaves and fragrant fruit carried downstream that provide shelter as well as food, an episode also narrated by Pfaffe Lamprecht's *Alexander.*[19] The *Lucidarius* similarly reports that there are people living along the Ganges who "vahent daz obez daz da rinnet uz dem paradiso."[20] Whereas the influential letter of Prester John expatiates on various areas near paradise, where intense fragrances travel a distance of three days and rivers carry precious herbs,[21] the lesser-known Elysaeus is more explicit, describing the four rivers as carrying out odoriferous fruits that cure the sick.[22] The *folium Indicum* even becomes scientific fact in Hermann of Carinthia's *De essentiis.*[23] The entire complex also seems to have been known in courtly culture, for example, in the *Pantheon* of Gottfried of Viterbo, chaplain of Emperor Friedrich I and tutor of Heinrich VI:[24]

> Flumina bis bina Paradisus habere notatur.
> Tigris & Euphrates Phisonque Gehonque vocatur,
>   Aurum cum gemmis fluminis unda vehit.
> Optima per fluvium currentia poma tenentur,
> Infirmis oblata viris medicina videntur,
>   Solus odoratus sanat odore caput.

Paradise is said to have four rivers, called the Tigris, Euphrates, Phison, and Gehon, whose flood waters carry gold and gems. Magnificent fruits are obtained from the current of the rivers; they are seen offered to the sick as medicine—the smell, by its fragrance alone, cures the person.

---

can prevent those viewing it from dying (501.29f.) but cannot prevent signs of aging such as Titurel's podagra and grey hair (469.24). On Adam and podagra, see Johannes Beleth, *Summa de ecclestiasticis officiis* (cap. 151), CC:CM 41A, 290; Honorius, *PL* 172.944c; Herrad of Hohenburg, *Hortus deliciarum* (1979), II, 266.

[17] See Thomas Malvenda, *De Paradiso voluptatis* (1605), 122–23; Louis Ginzberg, *The Legends of the Jews* (1906–38), I, 173–74 and V, 196–97.

[18] *Leechbook,* in Godfrid Storms, ed., *Anglo-Saxon Magic* (1948), 307.

[19] *Alexandri Magni Iter ad Paradisum* (1859), 20; Lamprecht, *Alexander* (1884), 361–62.

[20] *Lucidarius* (1915), 12. The passage derives from Honorius's *Imago mundi* (1982), ed. Flint, 54, which in turn is taken from Solinus, *Collectanea rerum memorabilium* (1864), 208.

[21] Friedrich Zarncke, *Der Priester Johannes* (1879), 912–13.

[22] Friedrich Zarncke, *Der Priester Johannes* (1883), 123.

[23] Hermann of Carinthia, *De essentiis* (1982), 224.

[24] In Johannes Pistorius, ed., *Rerum Germanicarum scriptores* (1726), I, 29.

The second remedy obtained by the Grail retinue is another medicinal herb, "the same branch" given by the Sibyl to protect Aeneas:

> "do gewunne wir daz selbe rîs
> Dar ûf Sibille jach
> Enêas für hellesch ungemach
> und für den Flegetônen rouch,
> für ander flüzze die drin fliezent ouch.
> des nâmen wir uns muoze
> unt gewunn daz rîs ze buoze,
> ob daz sper ungehiure
> in dem helschen fiure
> wær gelüppet ode gelœtet,
> daz uns an freuden tœtet."
> (481.30–482.10)

"Then we obtained the same branch that the Sibyl promised Aeneas as protection against the pains of hell and the smoke of the Phlegeton as well as the other rivers that flow there. We went to great lengths and obtained the branch as a reward, to see if the horrible spear that is killing our joy had been poisoned or tempered in the fire of hell."

The reference derives from the Sibyl's promise of the Golden Bough as a safeguard on Aeneas's journey to the underworld in Virgil's epic (VI.136–41). Although Virgil does not state that it protects against physical dangers, the Sibyl of the *Roman d'Eneas* informs the hero that he needs the "ramet d'or" as a present to Proserpina in order to ensure his return (2310–15), and she gives him a salve or "oignement" to safeguard against the poisonous smoke during the descent (2393–96).[25] Heinrich von Veldeke's Sibyl is even more expansive, requiring the "rîs" as the precondition of the journey (86.31–88.14) and providing the hero with a salve against the fires of hell as well as with an herb ("krût") to eat as protection against its stench (86.15–38).[26] Wolfram's Golden Bough seems to conflate Veldeke's *krût* and *rîs* in the vague manner of medieval "citation,"[27] not bothering to mention an author well-known to his audience and already quoted elsewhere (292.18–23). The bough's defense against the smoke of the Phlegeton, not mentioned in the Old French *Roman*, derives from Veldeke's association of that river with the burning water surrounding the "real hell" (101.12–38).

[25] *Eneas: Roman du XIIe siècle* (1891).
[26] *Heinrich von Veldeke* (1852).
[27] Friedrich Panzer, *Vom mittelalterlichen Zitieren* (1950), 13–14.

The third remedy, pelican blood, proceeds up the great chain of being from plants to animals:

> "ein vogel heizt pellicânus:
> swenne der fruht gewinnet,
> alze sêre er die minnet:
> in twinget sîner triwe gelust
> daz er bîzet durch sîn selbes brust,
> unt lætz bluot den jungen in den munt:
> er stirbet an der selben stunt.
> do gewunnen wir des vogels bluot,
> ob uns sîn triwe wære guot,
> unt strichens an die wunden
> sô wir beste kunden.
> daz moht uns niht gehelfen sus."
> (482.12–23)

> "There is a bird called the pelican: when it has young, it loves them too much: its loyal instincts compel it to pierce its own breast and let its blood flow into the chicks' mouths. Then it dies immediately thereafter. We obtained this bird's blood to see if its loyalty might be therapeutic and rubbed it on the wound as best we could, but it did not help us."

This description ultimately derives from the bestiary rather than from medicinal writings. According to the *Physiologus,* the pelican

> amator est filiorum nimis; si autem genuerit natos et paruuli increuerint, incipiunt percutere parentes suos in faciem; parentes autem colaphizantes eos occident; deinde misericordia moti parentes tribus diebus flent eos, lugentes quos occiderunt; et tercia die mater eorum percutiens costam suam destillat suum sanguinem super eorum corpora mortua (id est pullorum): ipse sanguis suscitat eos de morte.[28]

> excessively loves its young. For if it brings forth young and they start to grow, they begin striking their parents in the face. Striking back, the parents kill them. Then, moved by compassion, the parents weep over them for three days, lamenting those they have killed. On the third day their mother, piercing her side, spills her blood over [the chicks'] dead bodies: the blood itself revives them from death.

[28] *Physiologus latinus versio Y* (1941), 106.

Trevrizent's description lacks the ensuing allegorization of the pelican as a type of Christ, but its derivation from the bestiary is revealed by two turns of phrase: the fact that the pelican loves its young too much, "alze sêre er die minnet" / "amator est filiorum nimis," and the intense motivation of its self-sacrifice, "triwe gelust" / "misericordia moti."

Although representations of the pelican generally seem limited to the bestiary rather than the medical tradition, scholars have often noted the similarities between the pelican and the vulture, specifically the fact that both nurture their young with their blood.[29] And although this similarity may itself have provided Wolfram's cure by analogy, several aspects of pelican lore also invited medical application.[30] The *Dicta Chrysostomi,* a major source for German bestiary adaptations, uses medical terminology to indicate that the resuscitated chicks are "healed" by the flow of blood.[31] Moreover, the most influential version of the *Physiologus,* the B-branch text with additions from Isidore of Seville's *Etymologiae,* describes several varieties of pelican, one living in desert areas and subsisting on venomous reptiles ("alterum in solitudine habitans, et esca eius animalia venenata, hoc est lacerte, serpentes, cocodrilli").[32] An even closer tradition, going back at least as far as St. Jerome and transmitted in medieval encyclopedias, states that the pelican's chicks are killed by a serpent and then revived by the blood of their mother.[33] Either detail would recommend pelican blood as an antidote or allopathic remedy for snake venom.

The fourth set of materia medica employs different parts of the *monoceros,* or unicorn:

> "ein tier heizt monîcirus:
> daz erkennt der meide rein sô grôz
> daz ez slæfet ûf der meide schôz.
> wir gewunn des tieres herzen

[29] See Max Wellmann, *Der Physiologus* (1930), 50; Christoph Gerhardt, "Arznei und Symbol: Bemerkungen zum altdeutschen Geiertraktat" (1981), 123 and 137. On the vulture, see Joachim Stürmer and Gundolf Keil, *Verfasserlexikon,* II.1137–40; and Rainer Möhler, "*Epistula de vulture*" (1990).

[30] The Latin *Cyranides* recommends pelican blood as a cure for epilepsy. *Cyranides,* ed. Louis Delatte (1942), 170.

[31] Friedrich Wilhelm, *Denkmäler deutscher Prosa des 11. und 12. Jahrhunderts* (1914/15; rpt. 1960), II, 38.

[32] *Der "Bestiare Divin" des Guillaume Le Clerc* (1888), (2)41. On Wolfram's familiarity with the B-Is branch, see my "'Signune auf der Linde' and the Turtledove in *Parzival*" (1969).

[33] Pseudo-St. Jerome, Epistola 18, *PL* 30.187. See also Thomas of Cantimpré, *De natura rerum* (V.98), 219; Bartholomaeus Anglicus, *De rerum proprietatibus* (XII.19), 543f.; Vincent of Beauvais, *Speculum naturale* (XVI.127), col. 1226; Albertus Magnus, *De animalibus* XXIII.132 (1916/21), 1506.

über des küneges smerzen.
wir nâmen den karfunkelstein
ûf des selben tieres hirnbein,
Der dâ wehset under sîme horn.
wir bestrichen die wunden vorn,
und besouften den stein drinne gar:
diu wunde was et lüppec var.
daz tet uns mit dem künege wê."
(482.24–483.5)

"There is an animal called the unicorn that acknowledges the purity of maidens by falling asleep in their laps. We obtained that animal's heart to assuage the king's pain. We took the carbuncle on the same animal's forehead where it grows under the horn. We rubbed the edge of the wound and even completely immersed the stone in it: but the wound still seemed poisoned. That was painful to the king, and to us."

This cure also begins with a detail from bestiary lore, the unicorn's capture after falling asleep in the lap of a virgin,[34] again omitting the bestiary allegory and shifting to medical discourse. Here too the Grail society's extrapolation is unusual.[35] Although the specific allusion to the unicorn's heart appears to be unique, the use of animal parts is a major component of ancient and medieval medical practice, represented most prominently for our purposes by Sextus Placitus's *Liber medicinae ex animalibus*, a work transmitted with Pseudo-Apuleius's *Herbarius*, which Wolfram certainly knew. Sextus Placitus prescribes the hearts of several animals (stag, dog, hare, mule, mouse, vulture) for a variety of ailments, although only the latter counteracts venom.[36] Hildegard of Bingen seems to be the first medieval writer to prescribe materia medica from the unicorn—the liver for leprosy, skin to ward off fevers and plague. Use of the unicorn in general as an antidote against poison might be inferred from a passage in her *Physica*, present in the oldest manuscript but not in the printed edition, stating that the animal's heat and pervasive healthiness mitigate pestilence and fevers:[37] "Nam quia idem animal bono calore et magna sanitate perfusum est . . . noxios humores qui pestes et febres homini inferunt mitigat."

With the carbuncle that grows under the unicorn's horn we are on

[34] Guillaume Le Clerc, *Bestiare*, (2)49.
[35] See Jürgen W. Einhorn, *Spiritalis unicornis* (1976), 154–59.
[36] "De vulture" (XXIII.6), in Pseudo-Apuleius, *Herbarius* (1927), 279.
[37] Florence, MS. Laur. Ashb. 1323, fol. 83va. See the *Physica* (VII.5), *PL* 197.1318.

firmer ground.[38] The origin of the motif remains uncertain: the Greek *Kyranides* mention an unnamed stone growing under or on the unicorn's horn, but the twelfth-century Latin translation displaces it to the animal's nose or ears.[39] The oldest manuscripts of Hildegard of Bingen's *Physica* speak of the bone or solid core beneath the unicorn's horn, adding that it is not very precious, "sub cornu enim suo os habet . . . sed tamen non valde pretiosum est."[40] The *Lucidarius* compares its horn with a carbuncle: "daz [hat] nuwen ein horn; daz ist wol vier elen lanc, unde ist schœne als ein karfunkelstein."[41] The closest analogue to Wolfram is Pfaffe Lamprecht's description of the *monoceros*, "daz den carbunkel treget" (5581).[42]

None of these analogues, however, invests the carbuncle with medicinal properties. To be sure, the horn of the unicorn, like that of the stag (whose head or even entire shape the unicorn's resembles),[43] has an extensive history as an antidote to poison.[44] Unfortunately, there is a gap between the earliest references to the alexipharmic use of unicorn horn in Greek antiquity and the explosion of the tradition in the late Middle Ages.[45] Some scholars have suggested that the *dracontis* or stone that grows under the adder's head provided the analogy for the unicorn.[46] But as the

[38] Theodore Ziolkowski, "Der Karfunkelstein" (1961), esp. 306–10.

[39] Fernand de Mély, *Les Lapidaires de l'Antiquité et du Moyen Age*, II (1898), 36 and 71; Delatte, *Textes latins*, 125.

[40] *PL* 197.1318. Emended according to the two oldest manuscripts from ca. 1300, Florence, MS. Laur. Ashb. 1323, fol. 83va, and Herzog August Bibliothek, Wolfenbüttel, Cod. Guelf. 56.2, Aug. 4°, fol. 146^{v}. I am indebted to Melitta Weiss-Amer for providing me with transcriptions.

[41] *Lucidarius*, 13. The Latin source, Honorius of Autun, *PL* 172.124f., does not have the comparison with carbuncle.

[42] Lamprecht, *Alexander*, 317f.

[43] "daz houbet nach eime hirze," *Lucidarius*, 13; Honorius of Autun, *PL* 172.124f., following Pliny, *Naturalis historia* (VIII.76), and Solinus, *Collectanea* (52.39f.). The similarities between the unicorn and the stag provide the basis for the famous episode with "der vremde hirz" in Gottfried's *Tristan.* On the use of stags as antidotes against snakes, see Sextus Placitus, *Liber medicinae ex animalibus*, in Pseudo-Apuleius, *Herbarius* (1927), 236–38; on the bestiary tradition, see Florence McCulloch, *Medieval Latin and French Bestiaries* (1962), 172–74; Nikolaus Henkel, *Studien zum Physiologus im Mittelalter* (1976), 186–87.

[44] Odell Shepard, *The Lore of the Unicorn* (1930), 101–54.

[45] Ibid., 120–23.

[46] Ziolkowski, "Karfunkelstein," 309; Herbert Kolb, "Isidorische 'Etymologien' im *Parzival*" (1970), 127–30. The *dracontis* is described, among others, by Pliny, *Naturalis historia* (XXXVII.10.57) and Solinus, *Collectanea* (30.16), and Isidore, *Etymologiae* (XVI.xiv.7), who places it in the same family as the carbuncle ("De ignitis"). It is identified with the carbuncle in the twelfth-century Old-French *Alphabetical Lapidary*, ed. Paul Studer and Joan Evans, *Anglo-Norman Lapidaries* (1924), 229; in Brunetto Latini's *Li Livres dou Trésor* (1948), 133–34; and the *Peterborough Lapidary* (1933), 85. See Leo J. Henkin, "The Carbuncle in the Adder's Head" (1943).

association is sporadic or late, it seems more logical to inquire whether these properties also inhere in the carbuncle itself. Wolfram's knowledge of lapidaries is likely to have been considerable, judging by two other references to the stone in *Parzival*. One, to the precious stones in Feirefiz's armor, mentions that *karfunkel* is called *antrax* in the Near East (741.13f.), a detail transmitted to medieval science by Isidore of Seville's *Etymologiae* (XVI.xiv.1).[47] The other occurs at the beginning of the thirty-line list of precious stones set in Anfortas's sickbed (791.1–30), which clearly presupposes familiarity with Marbode of Rennes's *De lapidibus*, if not subsequent works as well.[48]

The principal use of carbuncles in medieval lithotherapy seems to have been as amulets and talismans.[49] The difficulty here is that carbuncle is a collective designation that includes garnet and ruby, the latter of which is often treated under hyacinth, so that we have to contend with the migration of properties among red-colored gemstones.[50] According to Albertus Magnus's *De mineralibus* (II.ii.3), the medieval *summa* on minerals,

> [Carbunculus] plus omnium aliorum lapidum virtutes habere dicitur, sicut & superius diximus. Specialis tamen effectus eius est venenum aereum & vaporosum fugare.[51]

> [Carbuncle] is said to have more powers than all other stones, as we have already said [II.i.2]. But its special effect is to disperse poison in air or vapour.

Because of the conflation of red gemstones, the hyacinth, whose most precious variety is the garnet, also a subcategory of carbuncle, provides similar protection against plague and venom:

> In ligaturis autem physicis est usus eius, quod collo suspensus vel digito gestatus, tutum reddit peregrinum & gratum hospitibus, & est contra pestiferas regiones . . . autem hoc specialiter habere dicitur, quod est virtus eius contra toxicum.[52]

[47] See Kolb, "'Etymologien'," 125–27.

[48] The list is traditionally glossed with reference to Marbode, although Arnoldus Saxo's *De virtutibus lapidum* (or, properly speaking, its source) comes closest to the forms used by Wolfram. See Martin, *Kommentar*, 515–18.

[49] See Hermann Fühner, *Lithotherapie: Historische Studien über die medizinische Verwendung der Edelsteine* (1902); John Riddle, "Lithotherapy in the Middle Ages" (1970).

[50] See Albertus Magnus, *Book of Minerals* (1967), 97; Valentin Rose, "Aristoteles *De lapidibus* und Arnoldus Saxo" (1875), 399–401.

[51] In Albertus Magnus, *Opera omnia* (1651), II, 228–29; the translation is by Wyckoff, 77.

[52] Ibid., 232; trans. Wyckoff, 98.

> In *Physical Ligatures* its use is that suspended from the neck or worn on the finger it keeps a traveller safe, and makes him welcome to those who entertain him, and protects him in unhealthy regions . . . it is said to have a special property, and this is its power against poison.

Vincent of Beauvais adds that it provides protection against snakes as well, "tutamen etiam est contra pestilentiam, & contra serpentes atque venena," and in a further elaboration attributed to Aristotle recommends the stone not only for dispersing poison in the air but also for detoxifying wounds by being placed above them: "venenum fumosum tollit, & . . . si est in homine vulnus ponitur supra venenum eius."[53]

The procedure is not too distant from the Grail inhabitants' rubbing the edges of the wound and then inserting the stone into the abscess, a technique that elicits a painful response from Anfortas (483.2–5). Such a treatment is not as bizarre as it might seem at first glance. Because the planets, especially Saturn and the moon, alter the humors in the wound, a fiery red stone such as carbuncle, whose nature is hot and dry,[54] provides—in addition to its detoxifying properties—an allopathic counterbalance to the cold and moisture brought on by their influence. In fact, this treatment is restrained compared with the measures undertaken during Parzival's first visit to the Grail castle in Book VI, when Saturn's influence is so extreme that the frost it precipitates in the wound has to be counteracted by reinserting the spear tip with its burning hot poison (489.24–490.2). A comparison of the two remedies is instructive. The disconcerting scene that Parzival witnesses at Munsalvaesche, with the Grail community's anguished parading of the bloody spear immediately after the surgical intervention, represents a terrifyingly exaggerated version of the earlier, more carefully planned attempt we have been discussing. In the indeterminate period between the insertion of the carbuncle described by Trevrizent and the reinsertion of the spear tip during Parzival's visit, the unmanageable affliction has escalated to a crisis of cosmic proportions under the malevolent influence of Saturn, underlying the Grail inhabitants' frantic behavior as well as revealing the magnitude of Parzival's failure.

The fifth and final stage in the Grail community's attempt to cure Anfortas culminates in a more complicated remedy, using an herb deriving from dragon's blood, dracontea, in conjunction with *des trachen umbevart*:

[53] Vincent of Beauvais, *Speculum naturale* (VIII.76), col. 532.

[54] See the editions of Rose, 354 and 386, and Julius Ruska, *Das Steinbuch des Aristoteles* (1912), 135–36 and 187; Constantinus Africanus, *Opera omnia*, esp. the *Liber de gradibus*, 352, and the *Epistola de incantatione*, 319.

"wir gewunn ein wurz heizt trachontê
(wir hœren von der würze sagen,
swâ ein trache werde erslagen,
si wahse von dem bluote.
der würze ist sô ze muote,
si hât al des luftes art),
ob uns des trachen umbevart
dar zuo möhte iht gefromen,
für der sterne wider komen
unt für des mânen wandeltac,
dar an der wunden smerze lac.
der [würze] edel hôch geslehte
kom uns dâ für niht rehte."
(483.6–18)

"We obtained an herb called dracontea (it is said that wherever a dragon is slain, it grows from the blood. The properties of the herb are those of air) to see if the revolution of the dragon might help in addition, against the return of the planets and the phases of the moon, which caused the pain of the wound. But the high and noble lineage of the herb was of no avail to us."

The first component clearly seems to be the dracontea or draguntea of medieval medical lore. To be sure, the similarities among varieties of the herb (called *aron* as well as *dracontias* in classical medicine, and often confused with each other),[55] and the conflation of dracontea, colubrina, and serpentina in medieval sources,[56] make it difficult to narrow the actual possibilities.[57] Nonetheless, the herb(s) called dracontea have an extended history as a medicine against venom, deriving ultimately from the comparison of the plant's stalk to a snake by Dioscorides (II.195f.), Pliny (XXIV.142), and Isidore of Seville's *Etymologiae* (XVII.ix.35), and en-

[55] See the article "aron" in Pauly-Wissowa, II, 1212–15. Major sources include: Dioscorides, *Arzneimittellehre* II.195–97 (1902), 243–45; Claudius Galenus, *De simplicium medicamentorum temperamentis ac facultatibus*, VI.i.61 (*aron*) and VI.iv.9 (*dracunculus*), in *Opera omnia* (1821/33), XI, 839 and 864–65; Pliny, *Naturalis historia* (XXIV.142–50).

[56] [*Macer Floridus*], *Herbarum varias qui vis cognoscere vires* (1522), fol. qvii^v ("Herbam dragontheam grecorum quam vocat usus / Hec eadem vulgi lingua colubrina vocatur"); *Circa instans* (1939), 112: "Serpentaria et colubrina et draguntea idem est." The association also entered the major thirteenth-century encyclopedias: Bartholomaeus Anglicus, *De rerum proprietatibus* (XVII.50), 831; Vincent of Beauvais, *Speculum naturale* (IX.67), col. 601f.

[57] See Hermann Fischer, *Mittelalterliche Pflanzenkunde* (1929), 260 and 279. W. H. Daems, ed., in *Boec van medicinen in dietsche* (1967), 297, offers a comparable list for *serpentine.*

hanced by the comparison of the root to a dragon's head in Pseudo-Apuleius's *Herbarius.*[58] There is accordingly a talismanic attribution to the herb of the power to ward off snakes,[59] as well as a more "medical" tradition indicating it as an antidote for snakebite.[60] Trevrizent mentions that dracontea grows from the blood of a slain dragon, a detail that can be traced to Pseudo-Apuleius, a basic source of Wolfram's medicinal knowledge: "draconis sanguine nata fertur esse dracontea."[61] Although the assertion that the plant exhibits the properties of air (warm and moist) is not confirmed by standard sources, which usually designate it as warm and dry,[62] Trevrizent may derive the plant's qualities from its origin in blood, which is in fact warm and moist.

If the herb dracontea thus seems appropriate for treating a wound complicated by snake poison, the second component of the cure, "des trachen umbevart," is not immediately obvious. Three different interpretations have been advanced for this crux: the constellation Draco, the ouroboros as a symbol of the alchemical process, and the nodes of the moon (*caput* and *cauda draconis*).[63] The stellar interpretation seems to have had limited astrological significance for interpreting nativities in antiquity.[64] Although hermetic works associating heavenly bodies with herbs occasionally link Sirius (Canis major) or Aquarius with dracontea,[65] none

[58] Pseudo-Apuleius, *Herbarius* (1927), 48: "radix eius ima caput draconis habet."

[59] Dioscorides, *Arzneimittellehre,* II.195; Pliny, *Naturalis historia,* XXIV.148f.; Avicenna, *Liber Canonis,* II.ii. 432 (1582), fol. 142^{r}.; Mesue, *De re medica* II.24 (1544), 104–05.

[60] Pseudo-Apuleius, *Herbarius* (14), 47. Also Pliny, *Naturalis historia,* XXIV.145; [*Macer Floridus*], *Herbarum;* and the passages in Bartholomaeus Anglicus and Vincent of Beauvais cited in note 56.

[61] Pseudo-Apuleius, *Herbarius,* 48. The genesis of the herb is further suggested by some of its synonyms on 47–48: "Pitonion," "Tifonos," and "corcodrillion."

[62] See Galen, *De simplicium,* XI, 839 and 864–65; *Circa instans,* 112; Avicenna, *Liber Canonis,* II.ii.432; and Mesue, *De re medica* II.24, 104–5. Dubé, "Medicine," 187, erroneously asserts that "the element of air assigned to the dragon herb correlates with the information in the *Circa instans.*"

[63] On Draco, see Martin, *Kommentar,* 369. The alchemical claim has been made by Bernhard D. Haage, "Das Ouroboros-Symbol im *Parzival* Wolframs von Eschenbach" (1983), and "Medizinhistorische Aspekte der 'Parzival'-Interpretation" (1986), and more recently in his *Heilkunde,* 154ff. On the nodes of the moon, see Wilhelm Deinert, *Ritter und Kosmos im "Parzival"* (1960), 101–4; and—more knowledgeably—Paul Kunitzsch, "Die Arabica im *Parzival* Wolframs von Eschenbach" (1974), 27–28.

[64] See Hermes Trismegistus, *Neue astrologische Texte des Hermes Trismegistus* (1936), 164 and 174–75.

[65] The association of Sirius and dracontea goes back at least as far as the Hermetic *Tractatus Enoch,* ed. Dellatte, *Cyranides,* 281. The association of Aquarius and dracontea occurs in the "Herbarum singulorum signorum Zodiaci demonstratio," transmitted with Pseudo-Apuleius from the earliest manuscripts to early printed editions. See Hartmut Broszinski, *Kasseler Handschriftenschätze* (1985), 82, and the *Liber de plenitudine* (1528), fol. 37^{v}.

seems related to anything resembling "des trachen umbevart." The alchemical interpretation has no immediate relevance either to the general medicinal context of Wolfram's passage or the motions of the planets and is based principally on a coincidence of vocabulary (the alchemical "dragon") as well as the objection to the nodal theory as uncommon and infrequently documented.[66] Contrary to such objections, the nodes of the moon are a widely recognized phenomenon in Arabic-Latin science and can be placed in a twelfth-century context with a clear bearing on Wolfram's narrative.

Originally a mythic representation of eclipses as a celestial dragon swallowing the sun or moon, the concept eventually became an element of astrological thought, designating the points where the moon's orbit intersects the ecliptic (i.e., where conjunctions or oppositions of the sun and moon cause eclipses) as the "head" and "tail" of the "dragon."[67] Although there are traces of the notion in Greek astrology,[68] the nodes of the moon are most influential in Eastern and Islamic astrology, where they often assume pseudoplanetary functions. Accordingly, they have an established *umbevart* or period of revolution through the zodiac (eighteen years),[69] enter into conjunctions as well as other astrological relationships with the seven planets, and exert an influence on the sublunary sphere. Owing to the translation of Arabic science into Latin under Gerard of Cremona and his school at Toledo,[70] there was a wide variety of Arabic astronomical and astrological treatises available in the West by 1200.[71] In discussing the

[66] Deinert, *Ritter und Kosmos,* 101–02; Dubé, *Medicine,* 209–10; Haage, "Ouroboros-Symbol," 9, and *Heilkunde,* 108–09. I have made a more detailed exposition of the following in "*trachontê* and *des trachen umbevart* (*Parzival* 483)" (1994).

[67] See Auguste Bouché-Leclercq, *L'astrologie grecque* (1899), 121–23; Willy Hartner, "The Pseudoplanetary Nodes of the Moon's Orbit in Hindu and Islamic Iconographies" (1938); Paul Kunitzsch, *Arabische Sternnamen in Europa* (1959), 165–66; Willy Hartner, "al-Djawzahar" (1965), II, 501–02; Kunitzsch, "Arabica," esp. 27–28.

[68] See Tertullian, *Adversus Marcionem* (I.18), CCSL, 1, 459; *Analecta sacra et classica Spicilegio Solesmensi parata,* V.2 (1888), 300–01.

[69] Wolfram's only other use of this word also applies to astronomy, referring to the revolutions of the planets, "der sterne umbevart, der siben plânêten" (518.6f.), a use confirmed by the cognate *umbeloufen* in Cundrie's announcement (782.19). That this is indeed a technical astronomical term is suggested by the Euclidian definition of a sphere in John of Sacrobosco's *Tractatus de sphera,* the standard medieval textbook of astronomy: "'spera ist ain gank einer *úmbverte* ains halben kraizzes . . . die man also lang *umbfúrt,* piz si widerkûmt an die stat irs anvanges'." Konrad von Megenberg, *Die Deutsche Sphaera* (Tübingen, 1980), 6.

[70] See Richard Lemay, "Gerard of Cremona" (1978), XV, 180; Marie-Thérèse d'Alverny, "Translations and Translators" (1982). Gerard of Cremona died in Toledo in 1187 at the age of 73. Most of the Arabic works cited below were translated by him or John of Seville in Toledo; see Lemay, "Gerard," and Lynn Thorndike, "John of Seville" (1959).

[71] For astronomical discussions, see al-Battani (1969), 75–76 and note and 250–51;

following examples, drawn largely from those translations, we should keep in mind that Wolfram clearly alludes to this project by attributing Kyot's sources to heathen writings from Toledo (453.12), an attribution confirmed not only by his use of latinate Arabic planet names in Cundrie's announcement (782)[72] but also by the Grail community's final medical efforts in Book XVI, which also employ contemporary translations of Arabic medicine (see Chapter 8).

Astronomical detail as well as astrological theory suggest how interpreting "des trachen umbevart" as the lunar nodes could explain their use in conjunction with the herb dracontea. The most likely reading would be that the "dragon's revolution" counteracts ("für") the motions of the planets and the phases of the moon (483.12–15). To begin with the most obvious, the movement of the lunar nodes opposes the planets in a literal sense, because their course through the zodiac proceeds in the opposite direction. According to the famous treatise *De dracone* by Petrus Alfonsus, transmitted to western Europe by Walter of Malvern in 1120,[73]

> Inter septem planetas per zodiacum circumeuntes discurrit etiam draco sed contrario motu, quia cum omnium planetarum cursus ab ariete in taurum, a tauro in geminos et sic in cetera feratur, solus draco ab ariete in pisces, a piscibus in aquarium, et sic in cetera ferri perhibetur.

> Among the seven planets revolving through the zodiac, the dragon also moves, but with a contrary motion, because the course of all the planets runs from Aries to Taurus, from Taurus to Gemini, and similarly in the case of the other [signs], but only the dragon is said to move from Aries to Pisces, Pisces to Aquarius, and so on.

Gergis, "De cursu Draconis per Zodiacum" (1936), 229; Petrus Alfonsus, *De dracone* (1943), 87–97. For astrological discussions, see: Dorotheus Sidonius, *Carmen astrologicum* (V.43), ed. David Pingree (Leipzig, 1976), 322; Messahala, "De significatione capitis & Caudae Draconis Lunae," in *Messahalae antiqvissimi ac lavdatissimi inter Arabes Astrologi, Libri tres* (1549), fol. Di^{v}; Alchabitus, "De natura capitis draconis et cauda," in *Alchabitus cum commento noviter impresso* (1512), fols. 12^{v}–13^{r}, and 15^{v}; Albumashar, *De magnis coniunctionibus* (1515), fols. G4^{v}–G7^{v}; John of Spain, "De capite et cauda draconis," in *Isagoga in astronomiam* (cap. 20), in his *Epitome totius astrologiae* (1548), fol. D2^{v}; *Picatrix: The Latin Version of the "Ghāyat al-ḥakīm"* (1986), 95; "De cauda draconis," attributed to Alomar in the *Liber novem judicum in judiciis astrorum* (1509), Aii^{v}–Aiii^{r}.

72 See Kunitzsch, "Planetennamen," 172–73, and "Arabica," 28–29.

73 In José Millás Vallicrosa, "La aportación astronómica de Pedro Alfonso" (1943), 87. See also al-Battani and Gergis, and Bartholomaeus Anglicus, *De natura rerum* (VIII.31), 416: "Sunt autem duae stellae quae non sunt planetae, sed tamen naturam & effectum videntur habere planetarum, scil. caput draconis & cauda, quae moventur cum firmamento, & consequuntur cursum firmamenti."

More important, the nodes of the moon also have an astrological effect that can counteract the influence of the planets. Specifically, the head of the dragon acts to increase planetary influences, the tail to decrease them. The clearest statement is provided by the Latin translation of Pseudo-al-Majrīṭī's *Ghāyat al-ḥakīm* known in the West as the *Picatrix*:[74]

> Et scias quod natura Capitis Draconis est augmentandi; quod si fuerit cum planetis fortunatis augmentantur in suis honoribus et fortitudinibus, et si fuerit cum infortunis augmentantur eorum damna et infortunia. Et similiter Cauda Draconis est de natura diminucionis. Et si fuerit cum planetis fortunis minuit eorum bonum, si vero cum infortunis eorum mala minuit et damnaciones.

> You should know that the nature of the head of the dragon is to cause increase; because if it aspects with lucky planets, their rewards and strengths will be augmented, and if it aspects with unlucky planets, their harm and misfortune will be augmented. Similarly, the tail of the dragon by nature causes diminution; if it aspects lucky planets, it diminishes their good, and if with unlucky ones it decreases their harm and injuries.

Essentially the same information was also provided in earlier Latin translations from Arabic science, such as Alchabitus (al-Qabīṣī) and John of Spain.[75] A likely source for Wolfram is not hard to find: the Latin translation of Alchabitus's text, the most massively transmitted Arabic astrological treatise in the West, was already circulating in Germany during the twelfth century, including Thuringia.[76]

[74] *Picatrix* (1986), 95.

[75] Alchabitus, "De natura capitis draconis et cauda," fols. 12ᵛ–13ʳ:

> Caput draconis est masculinus. Simili[ter] etiam est fortuna et natura eius c[om]posita ex natura Jovis et Veneris: hoc significat regnum et fortunam atque substantiam. Et dixerunt et quidam q[uod] natura eius est augmentatio: qui cum fuerit cum fortuna auget fortunam eorum: et cum fuerit cum malis auget malitiam eorum. et anni fridarie ejus sunt tres.
>
> Cauda vero eius est mala: et natura eius est composita ex natura Saturni et Martis: et significat deiectionem et casum atque paupertatem. Et dixerunt quidam q[uod] natura eius significat diminutionem quoniam cum fuerit cum fortunis diminuit fortunam eorum: et cum fuerit cum malis diminuit malitiam eorum: ideoquo dictum est caput: est fortuna cum est cum fortunis et malum cum malis et cauda mala cum bonis et bona cum malis: et anni eius fridarie ejus sunt duo.

See also John of Spain, "De capite et cauda draconis," fol. D2ᵛ.

[76] Ernst Zinner, *Verzeichnis der astronomischen Handschriften des deutschen Kulturgebiets* (1925), lists under nos. 11–13 three manuscripts dating from the twelfth century: Berlin Staatsbibliothek 2° 307, 29, 35–40, and Pommersfelden Schloßbibliothek 60 no. 3 and

As far as their specific relevance to our particular passage is concerned, the pseudoplanetary nodes of the moon provide a desirable astrological complement to the herbal remedy. Dracontea's efficacy includes its basic function as an antidote to the poison itself, as well as its value as a "hot" allopathic remedy to counter the coldness of the festering wound, a coldness that becomes so severe under the influence of Saturn and the moon that the poisoned spear tip has to be reinserted into the wound (489.22–490.17). *Des trachen umbevart*—more precisely, the tail of the dragon—would thus function, not as an enhancement of the herb itself but as an astrological counterbalance to the celestial situation ("dar zuo" [483.13]), decreasing the influence of an unfortunate planetary aspect or phases of the moon. One might even consider specific functions mentioned by Alchabitus, such as both nodes' counterinfluence on the planets explicitly mentioned as exacerbating the wound in Book IX, Saturn and the moon, the head being inimical to the former, the tail to the latter.[77] More precise astrological determinations would require a knowledge of precise planetary positions, which Wolfram does not provide.

After the failure of this last attempt to combine Latin herbal lore and Arabic astrology, efforts by the Grail society to deal with Anfortas's anguish no longer seek to cure the festering wound, but merely provide lenitives to reduce the pain (484.14), using three well-known pharmaceuticals: the salve nard; theriac, the famous medicinal remedy for snakebite compounded of a wide variety of simples, including viper flesh; and the smoke of aloe wood.[78] The narrator first mentions the latter during Parzival's first visit to the Grail castle (230.11), where it burns in large fireplaces (and in retrospect advertises Anfortas's infirmity); it is still present, as we will see in Chapter 8, during the hero's return in Book XVI, five years later.

---

no. 66, 1–24. Paul Lehmann, *Mittelalterliche Bibliothekskataloge Deutschlands und der Schweiz* (1928), II, 5–6, identifies Pommersfelden 66 as coming from the Collegium Amplonianum in Erfurt, and the location also makes Pommersfelden 60 a likely candidate. According to the catalogue of Amplonius Ratinck, made in 1410–12, the library had Petrus Alfonsus, *De dracone* (p. 25.26), and six copies of Alchabitus (pp. 24.7f., 25.19, 27.19/31/34, 28.6), of which Amplonianus Math. 41 (p. 27.19) is identical with Pommersfelden 60.

[77] *Alchabitus cum commento*, fol. 15^{v}.

[78] Salve using nard occurs as early as Dioscorides, *Arzneimittellehre* (I.7), who also recommends the herb for animal venom. Bernard Silvestris refers to its pleasing ointment in the *Cosmographia* (I.3). On theriac, see Gilbert Watson, *Theriac and Mithridatium* (1966), and Thomas Holste, *Der Theriakkrämer* (1976). On aloe wood, see Heimo Reinitzer, "Zeder und Aloe" (1976), 13–30.

II

Viewed as a whole, the Grail community's efforts to counteract the divine enchantment progress through a graduated series of experiments, each having potential as an antidote for venom. The procedure begins with a daring attempt to circumvent the Adamic origins of poison and human susceptibility to it with a medicinal herb from paradise, treating the fallen Grail king with a prelapsarian antidote. The second remedy undertakes a similar attempt in the realm of classical myth, using the Golden Bough that protected Aeneas in the underworld, in case the heathen's spear has been dipped in the Phlegeton's poisonous fire. Having bracketed, as it were, the mythic extremes of Christian paradise and pagan underworld, the experiments on Anfortas's body proceed up the great chain of being from herbs to animal matter. Here the medication extrapolates from medieval organotherapy to figures in the allegorical bestiary tradition, the pelican and the unicorn, whose redemptive power of *triuwe* and *reine* may also be implied. Within this group of materia medica there is another progression, from animal simples—pelican blood and unicorn heart—to something more complicated, the carbuncle growing under the unicorn's horn, the lithotherapeutic expectations and failure of which are underscored by a double cure, rubbing it on and then inserting it in the wound. The concluding remedy, a final escalation of this process, involves a plant of animal origin (dracontea) as well as a corresponding astrological component (*des trachen umbevart*), in a desperate effort embracing the entire spectrum of medical science from heaven to earth, planets to plants. As with the first attempt by professional physicians to heal Anfortas, the Grail society ultimately discovers that the wound is indeed immedicable. This time, however, writing on the Grail reveals the conditions under which the redeeming question will effect a cure where all medical science has failed (483.20–484.8).

We might pause here to consider some implications of this broad spectrum of remedies, particularly as they have drawn the scorn of historians of medicine as "superstitious."[79] To be sure, the attempt to differentiate science from superstition is a valid historical enterprise, but it does not necessarily do justice to Wolfram's imaginative complexity. For Wolfram's text is not science per se, but a literary representation of science. From this perspective, the list of cures seems to be less a mixture of "superstition" and "science" than a carefully articulated sequence, not only moving up the great chain of being but also progressing historically from prelapsarian to pre-Christian, Christian, and then Arabic-Latin iatromathematical remedies—medical ontogeny recapitulating medical phylogeny.

[79] Haage, "Prolegomena," 112–14; *Heilkunde*, 166–68.

This progression is entirely logical, given the Grail's initial representation as a transcendent plenitude: God's suspension of natural causality through the Grail can be countered only by a correspondingly inclusive spectrum of medicines. The attempted cure is a chronotopically totalizing representation of human medical knowledge across time and space.

Accordingly, the beginning and concluding elements in this series also have particular significance for the narrative's larger concerns: the former because of the presumed origin of poisons (and medicine) after the Fall, which reveals a connection to twelfth-century debates on reconciling religion and science as well as to the utopian project of the Grail society; the latter because of the associations of Arabic knowledge with the Grail messenger Cundrie. Both require a brief elaboration.

The initial cure, obtaining herbs from paradise, derives ultimately from the belief that there was nothing evil before the Fall and that poison and disease are consequences of Adam and Eve's transgression.[80] The biblical sources are Genesis 1.28–31 and 3.18–22, which the exegetical tradition elaborated early in the patristic era.[81] As explained succinctly in the *Glossa ordinaria,*[82]

> Patet quod ante peccatum hominis terra nihil noxium protulit, non herbam venenatam, non arborem sterilem. . . . Spinae anteà erant, sed non vt laborem homini inferrent: cui post peccatum fuerunt ad laborem, & afflictionem; sicut serpentes, & quaecunque noxia, antè innoxia.

> It is evident that before the sin of man the earth produced nothing harmful, no poisonous herb, no sterile tree. . . . Thorns existed before, but not in order to interfere with the work of man, for whom after the Fall they became a cause of labor and affliction; in the same way snakes and whatever things are harmful were harmless before.

Far from being "superstitious," the herb from paradise is central to understanding the larger relationship between the competing discourses of

[80] See, for example, Josef Esser, *Die Schöpfungsgeschichte in der "Altdeutschen Genesis"* (1987), 412–16; Hartmut Freytag, *Kommentar zur frühmittelhochdeutschen "Summa theologiae"* (1970), 69–70 and 126–27; Jean Daniélou, "Terre et paradis chez les pères de l'église" (1954); Gruenter, "Paradisus," 121–44; Frank Egleston Robbins, *The Hexaemeral Literature* (1912), 5 and 70.

[81] For a selection of patristic and medieval sources, see Esser, *Schöpfungsgeschichte,* and Robbins, *Hexaemeral Literature.* On poetic sources, see Prudentius, *Hamartigenia* (216–35, esp. 230f.), CSEL 61.136f.; Dracontius, *De laudibus Dei* (I.292ff.), MGH:AA 14, 38; Alcimus Ecdicius Avitus, *Opera,* MGH:AA 6.2, 210–11.

[82] *Biblia Sacra cum Glossa ordinaria* (1617), I, col. 36 (Gen. 1.28), and I, col. 106 (Gen. 3.18).

salvation history and medicine, even though the connection is seldom drawn in specialized scientific literature. Hildegard of Bingen makes the medical consequences of the Fall clear, as do encyclopedists such as Alexander Neckam:[83] "si non pecasset homo, nullum venenum nocivum esset" (If man had not sinned, there would be no deadly poison).

Moreover, the intersection of salvation history and medicine is a significant feature of the so-called Renaissance of the twelfth century, particularly the attempt to imagine ways in which the new science made available through the recovery of Greco-Arabic materials could be reconciled with theology, helping to raise the human race to a position approximating the one it enjoyed before the Fall. This *opus restaurationis* has been described elsewhere,[84] and we will trace elements of it in Cundrie's announcement of Parzival's redemption in the next chapter. For the moment, we might suggest briefly the more restricted connections between the utopian Grail kingdom and the idea of a quasi paradise imagined for the "new man" in twelfth-century literature.

Unlike Gramision in Bernard Silvestris's *Cosmographia* (II.9) or the *domus naturae* and new Golden Age in Alain de Lille's *Anticlaudianus* (I.55ff. and IX.380ff.), Wolfram's Munsalvaesche is not so much a physical paradise as a society that participates in the potential of paradise. That potential derives from the heavenly renewal of the Grail's power every Good Friday, investing it with the ability to prevent anyone who sees it from dying within the ensuing week or to produce a cornucopian effusion of whatever good things occur on earth (469.15ff.). As we saw in the preceding chapter, this power has both proleptic and analeptic connections with paradise—the Heavenly Kingdom as well as the original Eden, the end and the beginning of salvation history. This double focus helps explain a puzzling detail from the end of Parzival's first evening at Munsalvaesche, when four maidens, attempting to keep the hero awake and thus keep alive the possibility for asking the redeeming question, offer a bedtime snack of "obz der art von pardîs" (244.16). This "fruit of the kind from paradise" reminds us not only of the Grail's heavenly abundance but also of the Adamic temptation of disobedience—in this instance, the warning against prompting the question. Simultaneously, of course, it reflects the quest for antidotes from paradise subsequently narrated in Book IX. Trevrizent calls this "useless effort" (481.27), referring

[83] Alexander Neckam, *De naturis rerum* (1863), 250. See also Hildegard of Bingen, *Causae et curae* (1903), 33; Vincent of Beauvais, *Speculum historiale* I.29 (1624; rpt. 1964), col. 11.; Albertus Magnus, *Summa de creatione* (IV.72.5.9), in *Opera omnia*, XIX, 233.

[84] See M. D. Chenu, *La Théologie au douzième siècle* (1957), 289–308; Winthrop Wetherbee, *Platonism and Poetry in the Twelfth Century* (1972); and Brian Stock, *Myth and Science in the Twelfth Century* (1972).

either to the attempt itself or the inefficacy of remedies brought back to Munsalvaesche, not to mention their failure to stimulate Parzival's curiosity.

The final cure, with its use of dracontea in conjunction with the nodes of the moon, an astrological refinement made available through Arabic science, reminds us that the would-be utopia at Munsalvaesche also includes heathens, especially the Grail messenger Cundrie. The most learned person in the narrative, she has also mastered medicine, "swaz von erzenîe mac geschehn" (579.26), even compounding a salve that helped prevent Anfortas's death (579.28–30)—a powerful affirmation of her ability, given the divine interdiction of a cure. Moreover, as the last-named of those who attempt to heal the Fisher King, Cundrie foreshadows Parzival's redeeming question, which will succeed where all medical remedies have failed.

Indeed, this unlikely pair forms a striking juxtaposition that goes beyond their outward appearance of beauty and ugliness. Of particular significance, given the importance Wolfram attaches to embedding the events of his narrative in salvation history, is the fact that both figures have genealogies extending back to Adam. Parzival's genealogy from Mazadan ("mâc Adam") traces the "wagon-load of sin" through the lineage of chivalric aristocracy, and Cundrie's descent from Adam's daughters traces the same burden in the realm of learning, to which Wolfram devotes an extensive excursus (518.1–519.30).[85] Adam's mastery of the universe is expressed by his familiarity with planets and plants:

er rekant ouch ieslîches art,
dar zuo der sterne umbevart,
der siben plânêten,
waz die krefte hêten:
er rekant ouch aller würze maht,
und waz ieslîcher was geslaht.
(518.5–10)

He also knew the nature of each thing, as well as the revolutions of the seven planets and what powers they had; he also knew the virtues of all herbs and the properties of each.

Whereas the insatiety, or *ungenuht,* underlying Cain's murder of Abel (463.24ff.) provides the model for Parzival's murder and robbery of Ither, the *ungenuht* of Adam's daughters explains Cundrie's appearance:

[85] See Roy Wisbey, "Marvels of the East in the *Wiener Genesis* and in Wolfram's *Parzival*" (1973).

er widerriet in ungenuht.
swâ sîner tohter keiniu truoc,
vil dicke er des gein in gewuoc,
den rât er selten gein in liez,
vil würze er se mîden hiez
die menschen fruht verkêrten
unt sîn geslähte unêrten.
(518.14–20)

He advised them against insatiety. Whenever one of his daughters was carrying a child he often mentioned it to them, never sparing the admonition to avoid herbs that would pervert the human form and disgrace his lineage.

The disobedience of this second commandment leads to a second Fall, the consequences of which are evident generations later in the perverted appearances of Cundrie and Malcreatiure, kinsmen of herbs and the planets, "der würze unt der sterne mâc" (520.3). As a reflection of the harmonious well-being that once linked Cundrie's ancestors to the entire universe, the cures undertaken by the Grail inhabitants begin with a prelapsarian herb from paradise and culminate in a synecdochic totality of "herbs and planets," represented in the combination of dracontea and *des trachen umbevart.* The crisis of succession in the Grail dynasty resulting from Anfortas's disobedience thus has ramifications that recapitulate basic problems of salvation history and extend to the Grail messenger as well as the hero, representatives, respectively, of two diverse social orders—secular learning and chivalric aristocracy.

On a more general level, finally, the attempted treatment of the Fisher King involves several types of genre expectations, whose interaction gives the narrative its characteristic richness. As we saw at the beginning of this chapter, there seems to be a hierarchical opposition between religious and scientific discourses in the divine interdiction of a cure and the Grail society's unsuccessful attempts to heal Anfortas. A simplified form of this opposition frequently occurs in hagiography and miracle literature, where the inability of a magus or doctor to deal with illness is resolved by the intervention of the saint, the natural limitations of the former providing a foil for the divine intermediacy of the latter.[86] Here, of course, the hagiographic polarity has been updated, apparently confirming the superiority of the *deus medicus* over the new Arabic learning as well as Western

[86] See Valerie J. Flint, "The Early Medieval 'Medicus,' the Saint—and the Enchanter" (1989); Peter Assion, "Geistliche und weltliche Heilkunst in Konkurrenz" (1978).

science. At the same time, the conflict has also been transposed from hagiography to romance narrative, with the further implied polarity between clerical and secular modes of discourse. These oppositions will return during the hero's second visit to Munsalvaesche in Book XVI, where a different medical crisis again raises conflicting expectations of the redeeming question, culminating in the foregrounding of chivalric values and the enthronement of a *miles medicus* as Grail king.

CHAPTER SEVEN

From Romance to Revelation: Cundrie's Announcement

Cundrie's announcement of Parzival's redemption and call to the Grail kingship at the end of Book XV is generally acknowledged as one of the supreme moments of Wolfram's narrative. The loathly Grail messenger has previously appeared before Arthur's court in Book VI, condemning the hero for his failure at the Grail castle and thus terminating his first set of adventures. She now arrives to call him to Munsalvaesche after a second set of adventures seems to have culminated in battles with Feirefiz and Gawan, then in his reintegration into Arthurian society.[1] The bipartite structure of failure and success in Hartmann von Aue's *Erec* and *Iwein*, especially the latter's concluding battle with Gawan and prominent messenger role for Lunete, prepares our expectations of Cundrie's second appearance, and these expectations are heightened by the repetition of motifs that identify the approaching messenger well before the loathly damsel finally unveils the visage seen "previously at the Plimizoel" (780.15–17).

The motivic parallels are extensive. As in Book VI, Arthur has again attended mass (307.13, 776.25f.); the Round Tablecloth has been deployed just as we have heard before on the Plimizoel's plain (775.6f.), and the seating follows the same custom (310.5ff., 776.16ff.). The unknown rider approaching this festive scene again wears a French cloak

[1] See Walter Haug, "Die Symbolstruktur des höfischen Epos und ihre Auflösung bei Wolfram von Eschenbach" (1971). Kurt Ruh, *Höfische Epik des deutschen Mittelalters,* II (1980), 136–39, suggests *Iwein* as the model for this portion of the romance. The article by Andree Kahn Blumstein, "The Structure and Function of the Cundrie Episodes in Wolfram's *Parzival*" (1978), adds little; Michael Dallapiazza, "Häßlichkeit und Individualität: Ansätze zu einer Überwindung der Idealität des Schönen in Wolframs von Eschenbach *Parzival*" (1985), places Cundrie's appearance in a larger context.

described in the same manner with identical rhyme (313.7f., 778.17f.) and again commences by addressing King Arthur in French (314.20, 779.11). At the same time, however, several changes draw attention to the different purposes of Cundrie's second visit. She now enters, not on a sickly mule but on a splendid palfrey, her cloak resplendent with golden turtledoves, the heraldic emblem of the Grail. In contrast to his previous warning, the narrator now emphasizes the joyously unfolding day that forms the background for her announcement's sweet tidings, "süezen mære sage" (778.13f.).

Cundrie's greeting to Arthur and Guenevere and the apology for her earlier breach of courtly etiquette in condemning the hero so vehemently seem to be a preliminary formality and are not reported in direct discourse. The eloquent proclamation of her "exalted tidings," "hôhiu mære" (780.30; note the plural), unfolds in a discursively distinct series of three increasingly important messages of ten, twenty, and thirty lines, each marked by a shift from indirect to direct discourse. The first begins with a greeting announcing in general terms the bestowal of God's grace on a hero descended from parents with Arthurian and Grail lineages:

An der selben stunde
ir rede si sus begunde.
"ôwol dich, Gahmuretes suon!
got wil genâde an dir nu tuon.
ich mein den Herzeloyde bar."
(781.1–5)

At once she began her speech thus: "Blessed are you, Gahmuret's son! God intends to manifest his grace in you—I mean the one whom Herzeloyde bore."

The second message, with Parzival now specified as its recipient by the narrator, prepares him for what is to follow by advising both restraint and joy. In accordance with the medieval conception of kingship as an *imago Christi,* Cundrie first bursts into a christological benediction of Parzival's "exalted lot" as a "crown of human salvation," then announces the success of his double quest for *grâl unde wîp* and its implications for his family, conjoining the present moment of his redemption with his immediate task as the redeemer of the Grail king:[2]

[2] Allusion to the king as an *imago Christi* is by no means unusual. See Walther von der Vogelweide 19.5–16. On the larger medieval background, see Ernst Kantorowicz, *The King's Two Bodies* (1957).

zuo Parzivâle sprach si dô
"nu wis kiusche unt dâ bî vrô.
wol dich des hôhen teiles,
du krône menschen heiles!
daz epitafjum ist gelesen:
du solt des grâles hêrre wesen.
Condwîr âmûrs daz wîp dîn
und dîn sun Loherangrîn
sint beidiu mit dir dar benant. . . .
den künec Anfortas nu nert
dîns mundes vrâge, diu im wert
siufzebæren jâmer grôz.
wâ wart an sælde ie dîn genôz?"
(781.11–30)

Then she spoke to Parzival: "now be restrained and yet joyful. Blessed are you for your high lot, you crown of human salvation! The inscription has been read: you shall become lord of the Grail. Condwiramurs, your wife, and your son Lohengrin have both been called there with you. . . . King Anfortas will now be healed by the question from your mouth, which will spare him great moaning and anguish. Where was there ever your equal in blessedness?"

If *Parzival* were what Bakhtin calls a First Line or monologic romance, written in undifferentiated authorial discourse, Cundrie's message could end here, resolving typical plot and family problems and concluding the hero's progression from failure to success in the usual double course of adventures.

But in contrast to the static world of Arthurian romance, the Grail realm has, as our discussion has suggested, a distinctly different organization of space and time, linking its events to a dynamic pattern with cosmological and ultimately eschatological implications. This chronotopically unique dimension, above and beyond the genealogical and familial concerns in the first two sections of Cundrie's message, remains to be addressed. Cundrie's third announcement, now explicitly directed to Parzival, therefore transcends the preceding messages and incorporates his destiny into a higher revelation in the book of nature, which he is invited to perceive in the circling universe above:[3]

[3] On the punctuation and reading of 782.23ff., see p. 185 n.35.

Siben sterne si dô nante (782.1)
heidensch. die namen bekante
der rîche werde Feirafîz,
der vor ir saz swarz unde wîz.
si sprach "nu prüeve, Parzivâl.
der hôhste plânête Zvâl,
und der snelle Almustrî,
Almaret, und der liehte Samsî,
erzeigent sælekeit an dir.
der fünfte heizt Alligafir,
unde der sehste Alkitêr,
und uns der næhste Alkamêr.
ich ensprichez niht ûz eime troum:
die sint des firmamentes zoum,
die enthalden sîne snelheit:
ir kriec gein sîme loufte ie streit.
sorge ist dînhalp nu weise.
swaz der plânêten reise
umblouft, und ir schîn bedecket,
des sint dir zil gestecket
ze reichen und zerwerben.
dîn riwe muoz verderben.
wan ungenuht al eine,
<dane> gît dir niht gemeine;
der grâl und des grâles kraft
verbietent valschlîch geselleschaft.
du hetes junge sorge erzogn:
die hât kumendiu freude an dir betrogn.
du hâst der sêle ruowe erstriten
und des lîbes freude in sorge erbiten."

She then named the seven planets in Arabic. The powerful and noble Feirefiz, who sat there—mixed black and white—before her, recognized the names. She said: "Observe now, Parzival: Zval [Saturn] the highest planet, and the rapid Almustri [Jupiter], Almaret [Mars] and the bright Samsi [sun] show good fortune for you. The fifth is called Alligafir [Venus], and the sixth Alkiter [Mercury], and the closest to us Alkamer [the moon]. I do not speak this in a dream: they are the bridle of the firmament, they restrain its speed; their opposition has always fought against its course. Your care is now an orphan. Whatever the orbits of the planets bound, and their light shines upon, that is set as your goal to achieve and

> attain. Your sorrow must pass away. Only insatiety will not give you membership there; the institution of the Grail forbids companionship with falsity. When young you fostered care; approaching joy has now deprived you of it. You have fought through to peace for the soul and awaited amidst sorrow for the joy of the body.

This third and final statement poses several questions of fundamental importance for understanding the heteroglossic complexity of Wolfram's text: (1) the nature of Cundrie's astronomical information (782.1–16); (2) its significance for Parzival's dominion (782.17–30); (3) its place and significance in the internal chronology of the narrative; and (4) its potential place in twelfth-century debates on imperial power and cultural renovation, especially from the School of Chartres.

I

As is typical for the Grail narrative, the astronomical references on which our understanding of Cundrie's announcement depends seem detailed as well as vague, and have invited a wide variety of responses. The widely accepted reading by Wilhelm Deinert views the passage as alluding to a world-year, a rare but momentous event when the seven planets return to the astrological houses in which they were created, heralding a new era in human history.[4] As attractive as this thesis may seem at first glance, it will not sustain careful scrutiny.[5] In describing planetary motions, Wolfram never refers to astrological houses (Latin *domicilium*; Middle High German *hûs*) but employs a much vaguer term, *zil*, a word that seems only to describe the terminus of circular motion.[6] But Cundrie's announcement does not even have a single reference to a *zil*, let alone to planetary houses or the positions required for denoting a world-year: she merely lists the planets in descending order and describes their motion against the firmament. Paul Kunitzsch is correct in rejecting this and other theories that read into Cundrie's announcement the nonexistent detail of a

[4] Wilhelm Deinert, *Ritter und Kosmos im "Parzival"* (1960), 39–69.

[5] See Paul Kunitzsch, "Die Arabica im *Parzival* Wolframs von Eschenbach" (1974), 26–27.

[6] A description with *zil*, such as "wie lange ieslîcher [stern] umbe gêt, / ê er wider an sîn zil gestêt" (454.13f.), merely describes the return of any heavenly body to any point of origin in a circle. In fact, it is a reasonably close approximation of the Euclidian definition of spherical motion: "ain gank ainer ůmbverte ains halben kraizzes [. . .] di man also lang umbfůrt, piz sie widerkůmt an die stat irs anvanges" (a transit of the circumference of a half-circle that one revolves until it returns to its place of origin). Konrad von Megenberg, *Die Deutsche Sphaera* (1980), 6. See Pliny, *Naturalis historia* II.vi.32, and Macrobius, *Commentarius in "Somnium Scipionis"* I.xiv.25.

real astrological system and in suggesting instead that the passage merely equips Parzival with a "general letter of recommendation."[7]

Letters of recommendation, however, like all genres of fiction, have their own systems of generalities and commonplaces, the particular use of which can sometimes be extremely suggestive. If we examine the astronomical content of the message, there appear to be four types of information:

1. Cundrie lists the planets in descending order according to the "Chaldaic" system, the most common arrangement in pre-Copernican astronomy, naming them in an Arabic intelligible to Feirefiz but sufficiently irregular to suggest Latin intermediaries.[8]

2. Within this scheme, two subgroups of planets are formed by the use of different verbs: those from Saturn to the sun "show good fortune" (782.9) to Parzival; those from Venus to the moon are merely "named" (782.10). This division reflects a common grouping of superior and inferior planets (i.e., those above and below the sun), although "erzeigent sælekeit" could implicitly include all seven planets.[9]

3. Information about the individual planets is provided by a series of descriptive adjectives (782.6–12). Saturn (Zvâl) is "the highest planet"; Jupiter (Almustrî) is "rapid"—a problematic reference to which we will return; the sun (Samsî) is "bright"; Venus (Alligafir), Mercury (Alkitêr), and the moon (Alkamêr) are "the fifth," "the sixth," and "the closest" of the planets, respectively.

4. The catalogue of the planets culminates with a description of their motions (782.14–16). They are the bridle of the firmament, whose overwhelming speed and momentum they contend with in a continual battle but restrain only slightly.[10]

[7] See Kunitzsch, "Arabica," 25–29, for a trenchant criticism, and Johannes Kibelka, "Sternglaube und Willensfreiheit in der deutschen Dichtung des Hochmittelalters" (1965), 96–97.

[8] On the order of the planets, see Georg-Karl Bauer, *Sternkunde und Sterndeutung der Deutschen im 9.–14. Jahrhundert* (1937), 30–31, and Franz Boll, "Hebdomas," in Pauly-Wissowa, VIII, 2561–70; on the Arabic names, Paul Kunitzsch, "Die Planetennamen im *Parzival*" (1969), 172–73, and "Arabica," 28–29.

[9] See Kunitzsch, "Planetennamen," 170. The implied emphasis on the superior planets in a catalogue list is not unfounded. According to Latin and Arabic astrologers, for example, a conjunction of the superior planets signifies *res maximas*; in aspect with the sun it signifies a change of rulership. See Robertus Anglicus's commentary on Sacrobosco's *Sphere* (1949), 163.

[10] The moderating opposition of the firmament and the planets is an idea that goes back to classical antiquity, and one that particularly appealed to Wolfram, judging from his further references to it in *Willehalm* 2.2ff. and 216.9ff. See Pliny, *Naturalis historia* II.vi.33; Isidore of Seville, *Etymologiae* III.35; Bede, *De natura rerum*, *PL* 90, 197; and the

Although this information can be said to reflect general astronomical knowledge, it nonetheless poses two puzzling and ultimately interrelated problems. The first is that it bears no obvious relevance to Parzival's redemption and call to the Grail kingship, except for the brief allusion to his good fortune or "sælekeit." That is: the catalogue cannot even provide a general letter of recommendation, since there is, strictly speaking, no immediately obvious connection between macrocosm and microcosm, between Cundrie's description of the planets and their motions on the one hand and the ensuing description of Parzival's dominion on the other. The second problem is that the reference to Jupiter as rapid, "snel" (782.7), presents an apparent contradiction to the opposing "snelheit" of the firmament (782.15). As we will see, the solution to this second problem also resolves the first—and suggests a strikingly appropriate context for Cundrie's announcement.

"Der snelle Almustrî" has always been a vexing crux in Wolfram scholarship. Along with a similar reference to "der snelle Sâturnus" in Orgeluse's praise of Cidegast (613.21), it seems to provide an embarrassing example of the limitations of Wolfram's scientific knowledge,[11] because Saturn and Jupiter are in fact the "slowest" of the visible planets, that is, they have the longest orbital periods, requiring thirty and twelve years, respectively, to complete their courses through the zodiac. The solutions advanced thus far are not convincing. Wilhelm Deinert argues that "snel" presupposes an extraterrestrial perspective close to the higher and swifter spheres, but this leap of the imagination stumbles over the fact that the vantage point in both references is clearly earthbound.[12] Georg-Karl Bauer advances the conception of *incurtatio* attributed to the Peripatetics in the Middle Ages,[13] according to which the planets have no proper motion and are "dragged along" by the daily rotation of the firmament—a thesis shipwrecked by Wolfram's explicit description of individual planetary motion actively opposing that of the firmament (782.14–16).[14] The most frequent alternative suggests that "snel" must be a meaningless generality, referring to the fact that all celestial motions are rapid.[15] This

---

major twelfth- and thirteenth-century encyclopedias. On German sources, see Deinert, *Ritter und Kosmos*, 46, and Bauer, *Sternkunde*, 26.

[11] The commentaries of Bartsch/Marti, 301, and Martin, 433, avoid the problem presented in 613.21 by paraphrasing the text or avoiding the passage.

[12] Deinert, *Ritter und Kosmos*, 127–28, overlooks the explicit earthly perspective in "wie louft *ob* al den sternen / der snelle Sâturnus" (613.20f.) or "der hôhste plânête Zvâl [Saturn] . . . und *uns der næhste* Alkamêr [Moon]" (782.6–12).

[13] Bauer, *Sternkunde*, 27–29.

[14] See the criticism by Deinert, *Ritter und Kosmos*, 128 n. 1.

[15] See ibid., n. 1; Kunitzsch, "Planetennamen," 170 and "Arabica," 28 n. 70; and Henry Kratz, *Wolfram von Eschenbach's "Parzival"* (1973), 536.

supposition ignores the fact that every other adjective in the series conveys accurate information appropriate to each planet. We should, assuming that Wolfram's catalogue is consistent, be able to account for the specific application of "snel" to Jupiter (and Saturn) as well as the contradictory assumption of the firmament's opposing "snelheit."

A more convincing solution is suggested by the complete model of the medieval universe, which in its simplest terms is reducible to two opposing motions: that of the *primum mobile* or firmament, which completes its revolution from east to west once every twenty-four hours, and that of the planets, which move in their proper courses at varying speeds from west to east. The relationship between these two motions constitutes one of the most famous paradoxes in the history of ancient astronomy, appearing when the two-sphere system began to challenge the one-sphere or vortex system of early Greek philosophy, and leading to the conclusion that "the quickest of the stars is wrongly held to be the slowest, and *vice versa*" (*Laws*, 822A).[16] The most influential formulation is presented in the *Timaeus*, the one text of Plato known to the Middle Ages:

> And because of the motion of the Same, the stars which revolved most quickly appeared to be overtaken by those which moved most slowly, although in truth they overtook them; for, because of their simultaneous progress in two opposite directions, the motion of the Same, which is the swiftest of all motions, caused the body which moves away from it most slowly to appear the nearest. (39AB)[17]

In addition to Chalcidius's translation of Plato's text, the formulation of this paradox was made broadly accessible to the Middle Ages by the *De nuptiis Philologiae et Mercurii* of Martianus Capella, a basic text in the medieval curriculum.[18] During the twelfth and thirteenth centuries, the paradox of heavenly motion became a commonplace.[19]

Perceptive readers will already have realized that the solution both to this paradox and Wolfram's crux depends on whether we separate the motions of the firmament from those of the planets or whether we con-

[16] Plato, *Laws* (1926), II, 115.

[17] Plato, *Timaeus* (1925), 81. For the Latin text, see "*Timaeus*" *a Calcidio translatus commentarioque instructus* (1962), 31.

[18] Martianus asserts (VIII.853) that it makes no difference whether Saturn is the fastest planet and the moon the slowest, or vice versa. See Martianus Capella, *De nuptiis Philologiae et Mercurii* (1978), 449.

[19] In addition to the works cited by Bauer, *Sternkunde*, 27–29, see Roger Bacon, *Quaestiones super undecimum Prime philosophie Aristotelis* (1926), 76–77; Albertus Magnus, *De caelo et mundo* II.3.11, ed. Paul Hossfeld (1971), 165–69; Gottfried of St. Victor, *Fons philosophiae* (1956), 43.

sider their apparent compound motion. If we ignore the diurnal motion of the firmament, the individual planets seem to complete their revolutions in a period of time ranging from thirty or twelve years for Saturn and Jupiter down to twenty-nine days for the moon. According to their proper motions, Saturn will therefore be the slowest, Jupiter the next slowest, and so on, and the moon the fastest of the planets. If, however, we include the motion of the firmament in order to complete the medieval model and account for such minor details as the general course of the heavens from east to west and the alternation of day and night, the relative speeds will be reversed. The daily rotation of the firmament now becomes the fastest celestial motion of all, completing its full rotation in only twenty-four hours. During the same period of time, Saturn (with the slowest proper motion) will have progressed only a fraction of a degree in the opposite direction, whereas the moon (with the fastest proper motion) will have progressed some thirteen degrees. Because the motion of the firmament is dominant, the planets will appear to have been carried along by its overriding momentum. In terms of the resulting compound motion, therefore, Saturn and Jupiter most nearly keep up with the firmament and will be the fastest planets, whereas the moon lags behind the most and will be the slowest.[20]

The first option seems to have been used by Wolfram scholars because it is the simplified form encountered in medieval encyclopedias and enables a translation of apparent planetary speeds from a geocentric to a heliocentric framework. The second option, however, more accurately represents the totality of celestial motions in the medieval model and is a more logical point of departure for sophisticated representations of astronomical phenomena. Dante's cosmos, for example, extends from God through the *primum mobile*, the fastest-moving element of the heavens that "carries everything with it" (*Paradiso* 18.70f.), and thence through the increasingly slower planets to the moon, "the slowest sphere" (*Paradiso* 3.51), down to the stationary earth.[21] Wolfram's cosmos similarly proceeds from a "highest hand" to a firmament whose "snelheit" overcomes the

[20] These two options are neatly summarized with characteristic clarity and precision in the commentary on Aristotle's *De caelo* (II.x) by Thomas Aquinas: "Ita scilicet quod superiores planetae tardius moventur in suis propriis motibus: sed quantum ad motum quo moventur motu primi mobilis, quanto sunt superiores, tanto velociores sunt." *De caelo et mundo* (II.xv), in *Opera omnia* (1889), XXIII, 156. This solution to the paradox of celestial motion was first suggested in the commentary on the *Timaeus* by Proclus (262F). See J. L. E. Dreyer, *A History of Astronomy from Thales to Kepler* (1953), 69–70.

[21] See Giovanni Buti and Renzo Bertagni, *Commento astronomico della "Divina Commedia"* (Florence, 1966), 157–58, and Ideale Capasso, *L'astronomia nella "Divina Commedia"* (Pisa, 1967), 145–46.

restraining motion of the planets, carrying the highest of them, "der snelle Sâturnus" and "der snelle Almustrî," with it at speeds most nearly approximating its own, while the lower planets move unequally (490.6) with increasingly slow compound but increasingly rapid proper motion.

Demonstrating that Wolfram's model of the universe is bipartite and thus both more consistent than has generally been assumed is of course only a preliminary step toward understanding Cundrie's announcement. The Grail messenger, who was identified in Book VI as a student of astronomy (312.25), clearly seems to ask the hero to perceive something about the heavens, "nu prüeve, Parzivâl" (782.5), that is relevant for the ensuing description of his redemption, and we must now attempt to determine what it is.

There are, not surprisingly, many possible relationships between the circling motions of the universe and the ordering principles of human existence, between macrocosm and microcosm, in twelfth- and thirteenth-century thought.[22] Wolfram confronts us with a characteristically gnomic version in Flegetanis's observations of planetary revolutions:

> mit der sternen umbereise vart
> ist <gepruovet> aller menschlîch art.
> (454.15f.)

There seem to be several ways of interpreting this statement.[23] The most likely paraphrase, judging by the cognitive meaning of *prüeven* and the context, which proceeds from Flegetanis's observations of celestial motions to his extrapolation from them of the Grail story (454.9ff.), is that the "course of the heavens provides a model from which principles of

[22] For general studies, see Rudolf Allers, "Microcosmus from Anaximandros to Paracelsus" (1944); Walter Kranz, *Kosmos* (1955); and Marian Kurdzialek, "Der Mensch als Abbild des Kosmos" (1971). In German literature, see Hartmut Freytag, "*Summa Theologiae*, Strophe 9 und 10: Der Mensch als Mikrokosmos" (1974). In the twelfth century, see Philippe Delhaye, *Le "Microcosmus" de Godefroy de St. Victor* (1951), 137–77; Robert Javelet, *Image et resemblance au douzième siècle* (1967), I, 230–32; Marie-Dominique Chenu, *Nature, Man, and Society in the Twelfth Century* (1968), 24–37; Brian Stock, *Myth and Science in the Twelfth Century* (1972), 197–207 and 275–76.

[23] Deinert, *Ritter und Kosmos*, 105–6, makes a convincing argument for *geprüevet* (MSS Ggg, dd) instead of *gepfüfel*, which occurs only in D. His suggestion that *prüeven* has the meaning of "bewirken, beweisen" is adduced in support of his interpretation of limited astrological determinism in *Parzival* but ignores the fact that the basic meaning of the word is "die des nachdenkenden erwägens, prüfens, erkennens, woraus sich weiter die bedeutungen von: beweisen, erweisen, dartun, schildern [. . .] entwickelt haben." Matthias Lexer, *Mittelhochdeutsches Handwörterbuch* (Leipzig, 1869–78), II, 302. The basic meaning seems to belong to a cognitive rather than causal register and thus implies a perceived analogy between the heavens and human nature rather than an influence.

human nature can be discerned." That is, the relationship between the heavens and human affairs is not causal (as in the tradition of Salernitan and Toledan medical texts), but analogical.

Indeed, the belief in analogical relationships between the macrocosm and microcosm is so pervasive in twelfth-century thought that it has been called a cliché.[24] A common formulation states that man alone of all creatures can raise his head to contemplate the stars, employing the laws of the spheres and their motions as a pattern for his own life—a formulation that is not too different in its general outlines from Cundrie's announcement. This generalization is by no means a medieval discovery. The differentiation between man and beast derives from Ovid's *Metamorphoses* (I.84f.),[25] and the application of the celestial order to the ordering of human life has even earlier antecedents. The most ancient and influential occurs in Plato's *Timaeus*, where sight is said to have been granted to humans in order that they might observe the orbits of reason in heaven, make use of them for the revolutions of thought in their own souls, and—by imitating the divine movements that are unerring—bring into order those within them that are astray (47BC).[26]

This analogy follows a correspondence between macrocosm and microcosm presented earlier in the *Timaeus*. After the Demiurge shapes its material to form two circles revolving uniformly around the same axis, the Same or exterior circle revolves with a single and undivided motion from east to west, dominating the Other or inner circle, which revolves in the opposite direction with varying motions resulting from its subdivision into seven unequal circles (36CD). Plato's myth of a cosmic soul that also provides an exemplar for the human soul invited, and received, widespread exegesis. According to the commentary of Chalcidius, the motion of the Same in the soul is reason or intelligence, the Other lesser contrary powers such as anger or cupidity.[27] By the twelfth century, Plato's references to the cosmic soul in *Timaeus* 36CD and the application to the human psyche in 47BC were combined in an analogy between the bipartite motions of both:

> Oculis ergo perpendit homo in superioribus duos motus, scilicet firmamenti et planetarum: alterum rationalem, alterum erraticum. . . . Iterum,

[24] See *The "Cosmographia" of Bernardus Silvestris*, trans. Wetherbee (1973), 56. See also Chenu, *Nature*, 28–29, and Stock, *Myth*, 197–98 and 275–76.

[25] See the many works listed by Theodore Silverstein, "The Fabulous Cosmogony of Bernardus Silvestris" (1948/49), 97 n. 28, and Hartmut Freytag, *Kommentar zur frühmittelhochdeutschen "Summa theologiae"* (1970), 83–85.

[26] *Timaeus*, ed. Waszink, 44. Stock, *Myth*, 201–02, also draws attention to *Asclepius* 6 and 8; Wetherbee, "*Cosmographia*," 158, refers to Macrobius, *Commentarius in "Somnium Scipionis"* II.17, and Chalcidius's *Commentarius* on the *Timaeus* (180).

[27] *Timaeus* (XCV.167), 148.

perpendit in homine duos esse motus, spiritus et carnis; sed motus spiritus rationalis est, motus carnis erraticus. Dedit ergo Deus oculos homini ut, cum perciperet homo duos esse motus in celestibus et similes in se, quemamodum divina ratio facit erraticum motum sequi rationabilem motum firmamenti ita erraticos motus carnis subderet rationabili motui spiritus.[28]

The human eye examines two motions in the heavens, i.e., the firmament and the planets: one rational, the other irrational. Again, it considers there to be two motions in man, spiritual and corporeal; the motion of the spirit is rational, the motion of the flesh erratic. God therefore gave man eyes to perceive two motions in the heavens and two similar ones in himself, so that, just as the divine mind makes the erratic motion of the planets follow the rational motion of the firmament, so too man's spirit of rational motion might subdue the erratic motions of the flesh.

The Platonic analogy between the movements of the heavens and those of the psyche was transmitted to the Middle Ages by a variety of sources in addition to Chalcidius's translation.[29] The most influential of these, Boethius's *De consolatione Philosophiae*, contains several passages. The famous hymn, "O qui perpetua" (Bk. III, met. 9), describes the release of the world-soul throughout the universe as it pursues a course revolving in two circles and, returning to itself, embraces the profound mind and transforms heaven to its own image: "In semet reditura meat mentemque profundam / Circuit et simili conuertit imagine caelum" (16f.). Most commentators assumed the hymn to be a poetic rendition of the *Timaeus*, although the application of the twofold motion of the heavens to that of the human mind in such activities as the subjugation of desire to the will or soul is only one of several interpretations.[30] Commentators are less

[28] Guillaume de Conches, *Glosae super Platonem* (1965), 254. See also the commentary edited by Toni Schmid, "Ein Timaioskommentar in Sigtuna," *Classica et Medievalia* 10 (1948), 249.

[29] Partial statements of the analogy occur in such early seminal sources as Macrobius's *Commentarius in "Somnium Scipionis"* (I.xviif.) and Pseudo-Bede's *De mundi constructione, PL* 90.895. The Platonic tradition has a close counterpart in Aristotelian psychology; see Ernst Stadter, "Die Seele als *minor mundus* und als Regnum" (1968).

[30] See the commentaries of Johannes Scotus Eriugena and Remigius of Auxerre, ed. Hubert Silvestre, "Le Commentaire inédit de Jean Scot Erigène au mètre IX du livre III du *De consolatione Philosophiae* de Boèce" (1952); *Notker des Deutschen Werke* (1933), I, 191–92; Einsiedeln Anonymous and Adalbold of Utrecht, ed. R. B. C. Huygens, "Mittelalterliche Kommentare zum 'O qui perpetua'," *Sacris Erudiri* 6 (1954), 403 and 420–21; Pseudo-Johannes Scotus Eriugena (Erfurt Anonymous), *Saeculi noni auctoris in Boetii "Consolationem Philosophiae" commentarius* (1935), 184–86; Guillaume de Conches, *Des*

hesitant with the more general assertion that Philosophy has formed "totius vitae rationem ad caelestis ordinis exempla" (Bk. I, pr. 4):

> Nota quod vita humana et mores hominum debent formari ad similitudinem cœlestis ordinis. Sicut enim spherae inferiores planetarum obediunt spherae superiori et reguntur motu firmamenti, sic virtus naturae sensibilis debet obedire virtuti rationali et regi ab ipsa.[31]

> Note that human life and the affairs of men should be formed according to the image of celestial order. For just as the spheres of the lower planets obey the superior spheres and are ruled by the motion of the firmament, so the sensible nature should obey the rational nature and be ruled by it.

During the course of the twelfth century, the macro-microcosmic analogy becomes a commonplace in nearly all areas of Latin intellectual discourse, ranging from mythography and classical commentary to the poetic texts loosely associated with the School of Chartres, as well as dictionaries, medical, and encyclopedic texts.[32] In the thirteenth century the topos achieved the status of scientific fact in Sacrobosco's *De sphera*, the basic astronomical text in the university curriculum.[33]

The relevance of this macro-microcosmic topos to Wolfram's narrative seems to have a variety of dimensions. The basic Platonic analogy between world-soul and individual soul often gained a Christian element ultimately derived from St. Augustine's analysis of the Fall in the *De civitate Dei* (Books XIII–XIV), an element that associates the rational motion

---

Commentaires inédits de Guillaume de Conches et de Nicolas Triveth, sur la "Consolation de la Philosophie" de Boèce (1862), 76–77; Pseudo-Thomas Aquinas, in *Opera omnia* (1879), XXXII, 555.

[31] Pseudo-Thomas Aquinas, in *Opera omnia,* XXXII, 452; see also Remigius, *Commentarius in Pseudo-Johannes Scotus Eriugena,* 34–35, and Guillaume de Conches's commentary on Boethius, cited in the *Glosae super Platonem,* 254n.

[32] See Arnulf of Orleans's commentary on Ovid, in Fausto Ghisalberti, "Arnolfo d'Orleans: Un cultore di Ovidio nel secolo XII," Memorie del Reale Istituto Lombardo 24 (Milan, 1932), 181, and the *Glosule super Lucanum* (1958), 432; Bernard Silvestris, *Cosmographia* II.10.15–32 (1978), 141; Alain de Lille, *Anticlaudianus* VII.324–28 (1955), 166; Radulphus de Longo Campo, *In "Anticlaudianum" Alani commentum* (1972), 25–26; Alain de Lille, *De planctu Naturae, PL* 210.443, and the article *mundus* in *Distinctiones, PL* 210.866; Guillaume de Conches, *De philosophia mundi* (1935), 51–52; Hildegard of Bingen, *Causae et curae* (1903), 10; Herrad of Hohenburg, *Hortus deliciarum* (1979), II, 17.

[33] See Johannes de Sacrobosco, *Tractatus de sphera* (1949), 86, and the commentaries of Robertus Anglicus (163), Michael Scotus (303), and Cecco d'Ascoli (377f.).

of the firmament with a turning toward God and the irrational motion of the planets with a turning toward the self.[34] We can observe similarities to this pattern at crucial junctures in Parzival's career. The "irrational" motion accompanies the hero's first set of adventures, beginning with his confusion of knights with God, creatures with their creator, an action that both recapitulates elements of the Fall and begins the pattern of his *tumpheit* in the romance (see Chapter 2). The "rational" motion reasserts its dominion on Good Friday, when Parzival turns his thoughts to his creator for the first time (451.9–12), letting his horse find the path to Fontan la salvatsche and the hermit Trevrizent, and beginning his reordering of the priorities of God and world.

In Cundrie's announcement itself, the bipartite motion of the firmament and the planets, balancing or reconciling two contrary forces, stands as an exemplar for Parzival's achievement. Cundrie begins this climactic part of her revelation by calling the hero's attention to a description of the heavens based on the opposition of the firmament and the planets, which medieval exegetes traditionally extend beyond the opposition of rational and irrational motion to a variety of other antitheses (heavenly and earthly existence, thought and emotion, soul and body). Drawing the analogy from the macrocosm and applying it to Parzival, she concludes with four lines that confirm the reconciliation of similar antitheses in the course of the hero's career:

"du hetes junge sorge erzogn:
die hât kumendiu freude an dir betrogn.
du hâst der sêle ruowe erstriten
und des lîbes freude in sorge erbiten."
(782.27–30)

"When young you fostered care; approaching joy has now deprived you of it. You have fought through to peace for the soul and awaited amid sorrow for the joy of the body."

Although the link between macrocosm and microcosm in the beginning and end of her announcement follows from the implicit commonplace analogy between the world-soul and the human soul, the final emphasis on a biographical and even anagogical process introduces an extended dimension to which we now turn, beginning with Parzival's kingship.

[34] See the extended statement in Konrad von Megenberg, *Deutsche Sphaera*, 20–21.

II

Cundrie's description of the heavens also suggests a new and striking aspect of Parzival's regency. We already know that he is the lawful heir to the Grail (333.30), and the second of Cundrie's three messages has just confirmed his succession in resolving the familial and dynastic concerns of the narrative (781.15–30). But in addition to the Grail territory, he also seems to receive dominion over the sphere below the circling planets, that is, over the entire sublunary world:

> "swaz der plânêten reise
> umblouft, und ir schîn bedecket,
> des sint dir zil gestecket
> ze reichen und zerwerben."
> (782.18–21)

"Whatever the orbits of the planets bound, and their light falls upon, that is set as your goal to achieve and attain."

The difference between the two domains involves more than size: the territory of Munsalvaesche, which he formally receives in Book XVI by divine decree and public acclamation (796.17–21), was already his by birth, whereas this universal earthly kingdom remains a goal of highly symbolic dimensions.

For just as Parzival is not only a specific member of the Grail family but also represents the larger genealogy of man through his descent from the Adamic ancestor Mazadan, the kingdom at Munsalvaesche has an explicit radius of thirty miles *and* a symbolic extension through the Grail's creation of a paradisiacal utopia that simultaneously anticipates the Heavenly Kingdom. Cundrie's insinuation of Parzival's world dominion indirectly reminds us of this extension by simultaneously echoing and fulfilling the prophecy uttered by Sigune when she heard of the hero's first visit to the Grail castle and assumed that he had asked the redeeming question:

> "wol dich der sælden reise!
> wan swaz die lüfte hânt beslagen,
> dar ob muostu hœhe tragen:
> dir dienet zam unde wilt,
> ze rîcheit ist dir wunsch gezilt."
> (252.4–8)

"Hail to you for this blessed journey! For you shall have sovereignty over all the air encompasses: creatures tame and wild shall serve you; supreme majesty is destined for you."

The model for both Cundrie's announcement and Sigune's benediction is God's investiture of Adam with dominion over all creation in Genesis 1.26:

> And he said: Let us make man to our image and likeness: and let him have dominion over the fishes of the sea, and the fowls of the air, and the beasts, and the whole earth, and every creeping creature that moveth upon the earth.

The parallel is anything but fortuitous, given the designation of the Grail as the "perfection of paradise" (235.21), its ability to provide fruit of the kind from paradise (244.16), and its delights that approach those of heaven (238.21–24). This transcendent plenitude of the Grail realm in space and time, geographically including the entire world and typologically and anagogically going backward to man's state of perfection before the Fall and looking ahead to a future state of blessedness, underscores the chronotopic uniqueness of Munsalvaesche in the multiple strands of Wolfram's narrative, its heterochronic and heterotopic difference from conventional Arthurian romances.

In view of this dual nature of Parzival's genealogy and kingdom, it is not surprising that Cundrie also feels constrained to warn him against a consequential transgression:[35]

"wan ungenuht al eine,
<dane> gît dir niht gemeine;
der grâl und des grâles kraft
verbietent valschlîch gesellschaft."
(782.23–26)

"Only insatiety will not give you membership there; the institution of the Grail forbids companionship with falsity."

[35] The difficulties of this passage have been carefully discussed by L. P. Johnson, "'ungenuht al eine' (*Parzival* 782.23)" (1968). My reading follows Johnson's argument against an *apo koinou* construction in 782.25 but emphasizes the biblical ramifications of *ungenuht,* given the early evidence mentioned on 52f. and the close connection of the Grail narrative (as opposed to other narrative strands) to the problem of salvation history. The different uses of the word in the Arthurian and Grail realms comprise a small-scale example of Bakhtin's concept of heteroglossia as opposed to a unified authorial style. See Bumke, *Forschung,* 108–9.

"Ungenuht," or "insatiety," is an uncommon word in Middle High German, usually rhyming with *zuht* or *fruht*, the latter frequently referring to the Fall. Wolfram's principal uses of the latter rhyme concern Adam and his family and occur only in the Grail narrative—not surprisingly, given its extensive use of religious discourse. One of these instances has previously been applied to Parzival and thus has an immediate bearing on the warning that Cundrie now directs to him—Trevrizent's discussion of Cain's murder of Abel during the Good Friday colloquy in Book IX:

"von [Adam and Eve] kom gebürte fruht:
einem riet sîn ungenuht
daz er durch gîteclîchen ruom
sîner anen nam den magetuom."
(463.23–26)

"From Adam and Eve came progeny by birth: insatiety drove one of them by vainglorious greed to take his grandmother's virginity."

The parallel between the beginning of enmity in the family of man, with Cain's greedy murder of Abel, and the beginning of Parzival's knightly career, with the murder and corpse robbing of Ither, soon emerges in the revelation of Parzival's relationship to Ither through their common Adamic ancestor, Mazadan.

This association of *ungenuht* with the beginnings of human disorder after the Fall and the loss of paradise, however, now has a positive counterpart in Cundrie's announcement of Parzival's redemption and call to Munsalvaesche, where the Grail maintains a society explicitly characterized by a *genuht* that anticipates the heavenly kingdom:

wan der grâl was der sælden fruht,
der werlde süeze ein sölh genuht,
er wac vil nâch gelîche
als man saget von himelrîche.
(238.21–24)

For the Grail was the fruit of blessedness, such a satiety of worldly sweetness that it almost equaled what one says of heaven.

Cundrie's announcement thus represents a culmination and resolution of the Adamic motifs that have accompanied Parzival throughout the narrative.

But there is a corresponding element in her genealogy as well, keyed to the other Adamic occurrence of *ungenuht* in the narrative, that contributes to the particular appropriateness of her role as messenger.[36] In condemning Parzival's initial failure during her first appearance in Book VI, she called attention to the antithesis between her ugliness and his beauty, pointedly emphasizing the discrepancy between appearance and moral worth (315.24f.) in characters with genealogies extending back to Adam. Whereas Parzival is descended from Mazadan and is introduced as the handsomest man since the time of Adam (123.17), the hideous Cundrie, along with her aptly named brother Malcreatiure, is descended from the daughters of Adam. Their disobedience recapitulates, as the *fruht/ungenuht* rhyme emphasizes, the transgression of Adam. When they became old enough

daz si berhaft
wurden menneschlîcher fruht,
[Adam] widerriet in ungenuht. . . .
den rât er selten gein in liez,
vil würze er se mîden hiez
die menschen fruht verkêrten
unt sîn geslähte unêrten.
(518.12ff.)

that they were capable of bearing human offspring, he counseled them against insatiety. . . . He warned them repeatedly to avoid many herbs that would deform the human fruit and dishonor his race.

Their subsequent disobedience externalizes the corruption of the Fall in the faces of ensuing generations, destroying the outward appearance that originally reflected man's creation in the image of God. Cundrie's warning to Parzival not to compromise his achievement or his future by *ungenuht* is thus no impersonal message. The exchange between the two children of Adam reminds us that Adam's lineage in general, like Parzival's genealogy in particular, reflects a double aspect as the bearer of both sorrow and joy (465.1f.). For the loathly damsel, it remains the "wagon-load of sin" that forces us to bear the burden of sin (465.5f.); for the handsome hero, it is also the possibility of redemption through human striving and divine grace.

[36] See Deinert, *Ritter und Kosmos,* 60–62, 112–14, and especially Roy Wisbey, "Marvels of the East in the *Wiener Genesis* and in Wolfram's *Parzival*" (1973). Wisbey discusses other interpretations on 37 n. 70.

III

A related, although implicit, component of Cundrie's announcement remains to be considered. If her message transposes this event beyond chivalric narrative to the universal context of the divine plan in space, as reflected by the motions of the planets, it could also be placed in dialogue with the liturgical calendar, which, as we saw in Chapter 5, reflects the divine plan in time. Whereas the retroactive explanation of that plan by the Good Friday colloquy revealed discrepancies between Parzival's actions and the behavior expected of him during his first visit to the Grail castle in Book VI, a similar expansion of focus now illuminates the extent to which his individual destiny accords with the liturgy's celebration of salvation history. At the same time, this background also draws attention to the chronotopic differences between the Arthurian and Grail narratives through their differing relationship to a highly significant feast at the end of Book XV: Pentecost.

This chronology, estimated by nineteenth-century scholars and recently reconfirmed,[37] has to be inferred by correlating a series of time references designed to fix the deadline for Gawan's joust with Gramoflanz. At the Ford Perilous the two knights agree to public combat sixteen days later at Joflanze, which Arthur and his retinue, as mutually desired witnesses, can reach in a week. According to Gramoflanz:

> "von hiute übern ahten tac
> mit grôzer joye er komen mac.
> von hiute am sehzehenden tage
> kum ich durch mîn alte klage
> ûf den plân ze Jôflanze."
> (610.19–23)

> "He can arrive in great pomp in a week from today. On the sixteenth day from today I shall arrive at the field at Joflanze to defend my old accusation."

The position of this reference within a larger chronological framework seems indeterminable at first glance, because the ensuing action is discontinuous. The messenger sent by Gawan to Arthur's court arrives early

[37] F. W. Rührmund, "Chronologische Bestimmung der Begebenheiten in Wolfram's *Parzival*" (1848), 470–72; Carl Jauker, *Über die chronologische Behandlung des Stoffes in den epischen Gedichten Wolframs von Eschenbach* (1882), 8–9, 11, 13; Hermann J. Weigand, "Die epischen Zeitverhältnisse in den Graldichtungen Chrestiens und Wolframs" (1938); rpt. in English in his *Wolfram's "Parzival"* (1969), 61.

one morning (644.21), and the narrator professes not to know how many days the return journey to Schastel Marveile requires (652.23f.).

Once again it is the association of Parzival's Grail adventures with major feasts of the liturgical calendar that provides a fixed point of orientation. Gawan's messenger arrives while Queen Guenevere is reading her psalter in chapel. Her calculation that it has been four and one-half years and six weeks since Parzival left the Plimizoel (646.14–17) can be correlated with Trevrizent's estimate on Good Friday that it has been four and one-half years and three days since Parzival took the spear from his cell (460.22f.). As we saw in Chapter 5, the Queen's reference is made forty days after the hermit's Good Friday calculation, that is, on the Vigil of the Ascension. If Gramoflanz's estimate is correct, it should now take a week, or until the Wednesday before Pentecost, for Arthur and his retinue to arrive at Joflanze.

Inasmuch as the decision to depart is made hastily (651.4) and the messenger promises that Gawan will see Arthur and his retinue in Joflanze before the time set for the combat, "vor der zît" (654.21f.), they must arrive on the scene one day earlier, traveling under attack from Logrois to the River Sabins (661.6ff.), and then continuing unhindered the next morning (667.4ff.) to Joflanze, where Gawan is also expected that day (668.26f.). On the Thursday before Pentecost, the day agreed to by the contestants sixteen days earlier, Gawan rides out for some warm-up exercises and unexpectedly encounters Parzival. The ensuing books focus on Parzival's three inconclusive jousts in as many days: against Gawan that morning, Gramoflanz on Friday, and Feirefiz on Saturday, the Vigil of Pentecost. On the following morning, Pentecost, Cundrie arrives to make the revelations that are the focus of this chapter.

The Grail messenger quite properly begins her announcement with the assurance that God has chosen this particular moment (*nu*) for Parzival's redemption, "got wil genâde an dir nu tuon" (781.4), since a major component of the Pentecostal season celebrates the remission of sins. As contemporary handbooks and sermons observe with unrelenting frequency, the Holy Spirit—whose descent in Acts 2 originates the feast—is the particular vehicle of God's grace: "der heilige geist, daz ist diu gots gnade, iemmer ewic über sin hantgetat."[38] That grace is not limited to the remission of sins but extends to the total regeneration of man:

> die genade und diu wunder die er uns ze disen hochziten getan hat, die enmach dehein mensch wol fuͤr bringen. mit dem heren geist des vaters

[38] Anton E. Schönbach, *Altdeutsche Predigten* (1964), III, 116. The biblical source is John 20.22–23. On the association of Pentecost with the remission of sins in the early church, see Jean Daniélou, *The Bible and the Liturgy* (1956), 324–32.

> und des suns und des heiligen geistes sint die irdischen menschen himelisch worden. alle die witze, allen den wistum, alle die guten list die di menschen habent, die habent si von der gabe und von der lere des heiligen geistes. . . . sein genad und sein gůt verwandelot also gaches an dem sůntær allez unreht, allen ůbeln willen und bechert in zu recht und zu guten werchen.[39]

> No man can satisfactorily relate the grace and the wonders that he has accomplished for us at this feast. With the blessed spirit of the Father and the Son and the Holy Spirit earthly men have become heavenly. All the knowledge, wisdom, and skills that men possess they have from the gift and teaching of the Holy Spirit. Its grace and goodness quickly transform all impropriety and evil will in the sinner and convert him to propriety and good works.

This sudden transformation, as well as the gifts of the Holy Spirit, such as that of healing cited in 1 Corinthians 12.7–10, provide an appropriate context for Parzival's election as the "crown of man's salvation," whose "truthful mouth" is destined to cure the suffering Anfortas (781.24–29).

The astronomical portion of Cundrie's message also reflects the celebration of Pentecost, the liturgy of which is replete with cosmological allusions. The introit to the mass, Wisdom 1.7 ("For the Spirit of the Lord hath filled the whole world"), and several frequently cited antiphons for the Pentecost week, Job 26.13 ("His Spirit hath adorned the heavens"), Psalm 32.6 ("By the word of the Lord, the heavens were established; and all the power of them by the spirit of his mouth"), and especially Psalm 103.30 ("Thou shalt send forth thy spirit, and they shall be created: and thou shalt renew the face of the earth"), extend the theme of man's spiritual regeneration and place it within a universal perspective as the beginning of a "new creation." The identical sermons for Pentecost contained in Honorius of Autun's *Speculum ecclesiae* and Werner of St. Blasien's *Deflorationes patrum*,[40] both favorite sources for Middle High German sermon writers, use these antiphons for illustrating Pentecost typologically as a renovation of the original creation, beginning with the formation of the heavens and their motion ("per Filium firmamentum formatur, per Spiritum sanctum celeri volubilitate rotatur"). Sermons for Pentecost occasionally dilate on the planetary analogy at length, using the seven planets to illustrate the seven gifts of the Holy Spirit[41] or discussing

[39] Schönbach, *Altdeutsche Predigten* (1964), II, 113.

[40] *PL* 172.959 and *PL* 157.983–84. On the relationship between these collections, see Paul Glorieux, "Les *Deflorationes* de Werner de Saint-Blaise" (1951), II, 699–721.

[41] See, for example, Adalbert Jeitteles, *Altdeutsche Predigten aus dem Benediktinerstifte St. Paul in Kärnten* (1878), 110–11.

the motion of the seven planets as a counterbalance to the firmament, exemplifying the providential grace that on this day offsets the severity of judgment.[42]

Given these parallels between Cundrie's announcement and the liturgy of Pentecost (the emphasis on grace; the contrary motion of the firmament and planets, as well as the relationship between macrocosm and microcosm; and the paradisiacal renewal of creation from the heavens to man), it may seem strange that the day is not stated explicitly, but this may be Wolfram's "private joke."[43] The festivities take place, after all, in the company of King Arthur, who is traditionally associated with Pentecost, as Wolfram emphasizes in calling attention to his heteroglot "double fabric" that temporarily weaves together the chronotopically distinct Arthurian and Grail narratives in Book VI:

> Artûs der meienbære man,
> swaz man ie von dem gesprach,
> zeinen pfinxten daz geschach
> odr in des meien bluomenzît.
> (281.16–19)

> Arthur is the man of May, and whatever anyone ever said about him happened at Pentecost or in the flower-time of May.

The disjuncture between static and dynamic worlds, made explicit then by the narrator's juxtaposition of the Arthurian pleasance and the Grail snowfall, reappears now in the implicit intersection of two forms of Pentecost in Book XV: the Arthurian celebration of spring and the Grail's association with the course of redemption history in the cycle of the liturgical calendar. Indeed, the growing consciousness of this different conception of time comprises a major factor in the hero's transition from the Arthurian to the Grail world. With his departure shortly before Pentecost in Book XIV, Parzival acknowledged God's bestowal of joy on the perpetually joyful court, heightened at this moment by the fourfold wedding of Gawan and his relatives and by the ensuing celebrations that seemed to have concluded the Arthurian narrative. The intense and repeated concern with joy, however, contrasts markedly with the still unredeemed sadness that isolates him from that collective:

[42] Isaac of Stella, *PL* 194.1844. See also Alexander Neckam, "De septem donis et septem planetis," in *De naturis rerum* (1863), 41; Alain de Lille, "Sermo de Spiritu Sancto," *PL* 210.221; Jacques de Vitry, "In die sancto Pentecostes," in *Sermones in Epistolas et Evangelia dominicalia totius anni* (1575), 566.

[43] Weigand, *Wolfram's "Parzival,"* 62.

"ich pin trûrens unerlôst.
gelücke müeze freude wern
die endehafter freude gern:
got gebe freude al disen scharn:
ich wil ûz disen freuden varn."
(733.16–20)

"My sadness is unredeemed. May Fortune grant joy to those who desire the completion of joy. May God bestow joy on all this host; I wish to depart from these joys."

The final four lines of Cundrie's announcement, with an unusual display of rhetoric, now provide the explanation of his uniqueness:

"du hetes junge sorge erzogn;
die hât kumendiu freude an dir betrogn.
du hâst der sêle ruowe erstriten
und des lîbes freude in sorge erbiten."
(782.27–30)

"You fostered care when young; approaching joy has now deprived you of it. You have fought through to rest for the soul and awaited amid care for the joy of the flesh."

Parzival's redemption does not occur in a timeless world of joy but only in a providential world of process, where youthful sorrow is led to future bliss; not in Arthur's static realm but in the dynamic universe of the Grail, which reconciles the contraries of God and world, soul and body, submission and endeavor. Parzival concedes that when Cundrie arrived in Book VI to condemn the new member of the Round Table and precipitate his quest for the Grail, it was "not yet time for my salvation"; now, however, he accepts the call to a higher destiny that ends his sadness:

"iedoch het ich niht missetân,
ir het mich zorns etswenne erlân.
done wasez et dennoch niht mîn heil:
nu gebt ir mir sô hôhen teil,
dâ von mîn trûren ende hât."
(783.13–17)

"Yet if I had not done amiss, you would have spared me your anger in the past. But it was not yet time for my salvation: now you give me such an exalted lot that my sorrow comes to an end."

IV

It is less certain whether Cundrie's message also extends beyond Wolfram's narrative, engaging the Grail narrative and the audience, as suggested in Chapter 5, in a dialogue—in this instance, on imperial power and cultural renovation. Some scholars claim to discern parallels between Parzival's dominion at Munsalvaesche and Hohenstaufen images of imperial power.[44] The Proemium to Friedrich II's *Liber Augustalis*, for example, states in a manner reminiscent of Cundrie's that God created the first man as the noblest creature below the orbit of the moon ("a globo circuli lunaris inferius . . . creaturarum dignissimam"), crowning him as king with a diadem of honor and glory ("honoris et gloriae diademate coronato").[45]

This statement, however, represents an innovative conflation of two hitherto distinct moments in biblical history and its medieval reception: the investiture of Adam with dominion over all lesser creatures in Genesis 1.26, and the derivation of human political institutions as a necessary consequence of the Fall by St. Augustine and other writers.[46] Friedrich II's stratagem participates in the complicated dialectic of church-state conflict, outdoing previous clerical derivations of church power from Melchizedek by pushing the origin of secular authority back to Adam (and subsequently being outdone in turn).[47] Wolfram's narrative retains a more conservative differentiation, separating Parzival's precise political dominion at Munsalvaesche, which devolves on him as a result of Anfortas's sin, from Cundrie's announcement of the vague and still unrealized Adamic potential in her paraphrase of Genesis. Given the shifting political relationships between German princes, including Landgrave Hermann, and the competing candidates for emperor in the first decade of the thirteenth century, it is perhaps not surprising that Wolfram should leave the extended political power of the Grail as ambiguous as its location.

However, the mythic dimension of the Grail's power to create a situation reminiscent both of paradise and heaven suggests that a closer context might be contemporary speculation on the renovation of man's condition as a means of restoring him by grace to his natural state of perfection before the Fall.[48] The classic twelfth-century expression of this

[44] Deinert, *Ritter und Kosmos*, 51–69.

[45] *Die "Konstitutionen" Friedrichs II. von Hohenstaufen für sein Königreich Sizilien* (1973), 2.

[46] Cf. Heinrich Fichtenau, *Arenga: Spätantike und Mittelalter im Spiegel von Urkundenformeln* (1957), 149, esp. n. 7.

[47] See Ernst Kantorowicz, *Kaiser Friedrich II.* (1963), I, 236, and II, 107 n. 236. Some clerical theorists even derive secular power from Cain. See Honorius of Autun, *Summa Gloria* (1897), 65.

[48] See M. D. Chenu, "Orientale Lumen," in *La Théologie au douzième siècle* (1957), 289–308, esp. 295.

pattern in Bernard Silvestris's *Cosmographia* is based, not surprisingly, on the now-familiar macro-microcosmic analogy:

> Humanumque genus, quamvis mortale trahatur
> Conditione sua,
> Tale reformandum, quod demigrare supernos
> Possit adusque deos,
> Et dare sub leges quicquid torquente rotatu
> Stellifer axis agit,
> Cognatas sordes innataque crimina certis
> Extenuare modis.
>
> (II.xii.55–62)

> The human race, although it is inhibited by its mortal condition, must yet be so reformed that it may rise to dwell among the heavenly powers, and to subject to its laws whatever the star-bearing sphere impels by its circling, and by all these means redeem the taint of its earthly beginnings and its innate evil.[49]

This promise of renovation, like that of Parzival's redemption, involves overcoming the taint of Adam's transgression by adherence to laws governing human behavior that can be discerned in the heavens above.

We can restrict more suggestive resonances between Cundrie's announcement and twelfth-century Neoplatonism to two writers whose texts reflect concerns often associated with the rise of Arthurian romance,[50] Bernard Silvestris and Alain de Lille. Alain's *Anticlaudianus*, for example, concludes with the creation of a perfect "new man," who defeats the vices in knightly combat and introduces the rule of justice throughout the earthly kingdom (IX.386ff.). Although there has been some controversy over the application of this myth to contemporary politics,[51] Alain's hero seems based on a future realization of the potential of prelapsarian man, "de tali homine procreando qualis futurus esset homo, si in nullo errasset."[52] Wolfram's telescoping of paradisiacal and heavenly elements in his portrayal of the Grail society gains profile against the background of Alain's argument that if Adam had not succumbed to temptation, his

[49] This translation and the paraphrases below are from Winthrop Wetherbee in Bernard Sylvestris, "*Cosmographia*" (1973).

[50] For a survey, see Winthrop Wetherbee, "The Poetry of the Schools and the Rise of Romance," in his *Platonism and Poetry in the Twelfth Century* (1972), 220–41.

[51] See Michael Wilks, "Alan of Lille and the New Man" (1977), and Linda E. Marshall, "The Identity of the 'New Man' in the *Anticlaudianus* of Alan of Lille" (1979).

[52] Alain de Lille, *Anticlaudianus* (1955), 199. See Pierre Duhem, *Le Système du monde* (1915), III, 223.

natural virtues would have sufficed to gain him eternal life.[53] It is probably no coincidence that Alain's version of the macro-microcosmic analogy contains the identical images as Cundrie's announcement and has the firmament subsume the motions of the planets while granting them a positive function in retarding its momentum.[54]

An even better parallel, both to Wolfram's general narrative strategy of reconciling *got unde werlt* and to Cundrie's announcement in particular, is the celebrated speech about the re-creation of man in Bernard's *Cosmographia*, where Noys voices concern that man remain in harmony with the dual principles of existence to which he is inexorably drawn, the desire both to cherish things divine and to have charge of earthly life (II. x.21–25).[55] Man alone of all creatures is capable of raising his head to the stars, employing the laws of the spheres and their unalterable courses as an exemplar for his own course of life,

> Sed, maiestatem mentis testante figura,
> Tollet homo sanctum solus ad astra capud,
> Ut celi leges indeflexosque meatus
> Exemplar vite possit habere sue.
> (II.x.29–32)

Noys therefore determines that the earth will nourish its fruits, the sea its fish, the mountains its flocks, and the wilderness its beasts for him, and proclaims him ruler of creation, that he may subordinate all to himself, reign on earth, and rule the world:

> Terra sibi fruges, pisces sibi nutriat unda,
> Et sibi mons pecudes et sibi silva feras.
> Omnia subiiciat, terras regat, imperet orbi:
> Primatem rebus pontificemque dedi.
> (II.x.47–50)

[53] See the *Tractatus de virtutibus et vitiis et de donis Spiritus Sancti*, ed. Odon Lottin, in his *Psychologie et morale aux XIIe et XIIIe siècles* (Gembloux, 1960), VI, 59, 65–66.

[54] See the definition of *mundus* in the *Distinctiones*, *PL* 210.866, and the description of planetary motion in the *Anticlaudianus* (II.112–14), 76: "Cur celi motu cursus nugetur eodem, / Semper in occasum uergens contra quem planeta / Militet aduerso motu celumque refrenet." The latter text and *Parzival* 782.14–16 share a double set of images: (1) that of the perpetual battle, "contra quem semper militet adverso motu" and "gegen sîme loufte ie streit"; and (2) that of the retarding motion of one motion acting against the other as a bridle, "refrenet" and "zoum." The *strît* of the bipartite model of the universe and the restraining action of one of its motions are commonplace in vernacular texts, but the specific image of the bridle seems limited to the learned Latin tradition, e.g., Remigius of Auxerre, *Commentum in Martianum Capellam* (1962), I, 198; Alain de Lille, *De planctu Naturae*, *PL* 210.449.

[55] Bernard Silvestris, *Cosmographia*, 141.

Inasmuch as Wolfram's narrator explicitly states in Book VI that the scholarly Cundrie knows all languages—including Arabic, French, and Latin—as well as the Liberal Arts (312.20–25), we should not be surprised by the similarities between her announcement and the proclamation of Noys. Bernard's and Wolfram's learned women reflect a contemporary preoccupation with reconciling the antithesis between science and religion, applying Neoplatonic cosmology to a vision of man's restoration to the dominion that was his natural right before the Fall. But if Wolfram transposes the discursive pluralism of the Latin "Renaissance of the twelfth century" into his narrative, his particular transposition also introduces a new and consequential difference.[56] Although Cundrie's announcement avoids controversies over imperial power, it engages in a larger struggle between clerical and lay culture, appropriating contemporary Latin discourses on science and religion for vernacular narrative. Wolfram thus gives renewed emphasis to the decentering process of secularization that profoundly broadened the cultural pluralism of medieval Germany. Indeed, in the next chapter we will see the importance of secular empowerment in a climactic example that brings Parzival's quest to its conclusion: the redeeming question.

[56] On Wolfram's humanism in general, see Max Wehrli, "*diu menscheit hât wilden art*" (1975), II, 189–201.

CHAPTER EIGHT

From Medicine to Miracle: Healing the Fisher King

The final book of Wolfram's narrative is dominated by two controversial speech acts. Although the redeeming question resolves the basic problem of the plot, miraculously effecting Anfortas's cure and the transfer of dominion to Parzival, this singular moment is by no means self-explanatory, as its reception in Trevrizent's "Retraction" amply testifies. Indeed, as the crucial moment of the text, the question and everything about it remain ambiguously heteroglossic, while Trevrizent's ensuing attempt to simplify the event raises further complications that we will pursue in the next chapter. The discussion here begins with the altered situation underlying Parzival's return to the Grail castle at the beginning of Book XVI, proceeding from Anfortas's renewed suffering and the medical response it engenders to the question itself and the miracle that follows.

I

As with Parzival's first trip to Munsalvaesche, the return to the Grail castle in Book XVI involves a change of chronotopes. Most obviously, there is the transition from the Arthurian world to the Grail realm, which the narrator intimates with an allusion to the places of departure and arrival, the distance between which—in keeping with the secret location of Munsalvaesche—remains indeterminate (792.10–15). The Grail realm has heretofore been distinguished from the static springtime landscape of the Arthurian world, and, indeed, its appearance differs substantially from what it was during the last visit. There is a noticeable absence of the elements that imbued it with overtones of a fairy tale or Otherworld in Book V. The apparently straightforward journey involves no extended description:[1] there is no thirty-mile trackless forest with its fallen tree trunks, *jeune bois*, mysterious cedar trees, and lake; no mountainous landscape, precipitous slopes, and wrong paths that marked Parzival's earlier approaches to the Grail. The kingdom is still guarded by Templars, and Cundrie has to restrain Feirefiz from attacking a patrol, but the parties merely espy each other near a lookout, meet on a grassy path, and then ride into the castle together.

The interior of the Grail castle has also lost its mysterious aura. After dismounting on the steps of the palace, the group enters the hall, where according to custom there are again a hundred round carpets with down cushions and long samite quilts (794.11–14). Nothing distinguishes the reception from the ordinary. In contrast to the improvised loan of the queen's coat and the intrusion of the maladroit courtier in Book V, Parzival and Feirefiz receive rich, matching garments and a welcoming drink from gold vessels, then hasten to the room where Anfortas awaits them. We seem to be merely in the castle of a powerful lord.

And although the Grail is brought out after Parzival returns with Condwiramurs a few days later, the narrator makes it clear that the procession, in contrast to its desperate, ad hoc use with the bleeding lance five years before, now serves a function reserved for courtly celebrations (807.14–25). The procession even seems to repeat a familiar ritual (808.12–810.2). The narrator proceeds, in the same order as in Book V, from fireplaces burning *lignum aloe* to the room decorations, from the entrance of twenty-five maidens and Repanse de Schoye to the preparations for serving and the abundance of the Grail. Asides draw attention to the similarities:[2] one now sees "the same" as the audience heard at length before, "ir habt gehôrt ê des genuoc" (808.23–25).

This repetition has a disenchanting, even domesticating effect: the procession reveals nothing paranormal, otherworldly, or even unexpected about the Grail castle. Two rhetorical gestures emphasize the familiar. Engaging in *occupatio*, the narrator refuses to begin a long description of the meal in the interests of brevity, "daz wurde ein alze langez spel: / ich wil der kürze wesen snel" (809.15–24); he concludes by comparing the abundance provided by the Grail with the scarcity at Pelrapeire (809.30–810.2), reducing the differences between the two kingdoms to the most alimentary level, absence versus presence of food. Only the unbaptized Feirefiz finds anything unusual—because he cannot see the Grail providing sustenance.[3] The mysteriousness of the place has been reduced to,

[1] See Marianne Wynn, "Scenery and Chivalrous Journeys" (1961; rpt. 1984), 117–18.

[2] Dagmar Hirschberg, *Untersuchungen zur Erzählstruktur von Wolframs "Parzival"* (1976), 129, calls them "Szenenzitate."

[3] On the parallel between Parzival's first visit to the Grail and the comic heightening

and resides in, the Grail. The otherworldly elements, the unexpected behavior, and disorienting narrative moves that infused the entire Grail realm with a sense of mystery in Book V no longer dominate the scene, distancing Parzival's climactic speech act from the fairy-tale discourse originally behind Chrétien's version of the question. That speech act still resembles the "breaking" of an adventure characteristic of *Märchen*-like episodes in chivalric narrative, but it is even more clearly grounded in other genre expectations, such as the miracle and the saint's life.

This religious component stands in opposition to several secular discourses, especially the aristocratic code of conduct. Anfortas himself forces the issue at the outset of Book XVI, reminding his knights of his chivalric career and their feudal loyalty, threatening to accuse them before the highest Lord at the Last Judgment if they do not release him from his suffering. This appeal to a universal feudal hierarchy is overruled by divine authority, which again inscribes mysterious messages on the edge of the Grail and confirms Trevrizent's information in Book IX (which the narrator also substantiates with a cross-reference):

> si heten kumbers in erlôst,
> wan der trœstenlîche trôst,
> den Trevrizent dort vorne sprach,
> als er am grâle geschriben sach.
> si warten anderstunt des man
> dem al sîn vreude aldâ entran,
> und der helflîchen stunde
> der vrâge von sîm munde.
> (788.13–20)

They would have released him from his suffering, except for the comforting comfort that Trevrizent related above when he saw writing on the Grail. For the second time they await the man whose joy fled previously and the consoling hour of the question from his mouth.

Contrary to Anfortas's attempted coercion of his subjects *sub specie aeternitatis*, the terms of his redemption are related to a particular moment, the "second" coming of the hero and the "consoling hour" of his question. As with Parzival's first visit to the Grail castle, the healing miracle expected of his return is grounded in chronotopically unique ways.

As if to emphasize that the uniqueness of this moment overrides a uni-

of Feirefiz's, see D. H. Green, *The Art of Recognition in Wolfram's "Parzival"* (1982), 256–57.

versal chivalric ethic, the narrator shifts to discourses involving astronomy and medicine. This iatromathematical complex begins with a controversial allusion to planetary motions and their influence. As Parzival, Feirefiz, and Cundrie proceed toward Munsalvaesche, two planets intensify Anfortas's suffering at this particular moment ("nu"):

> nu hete diu wîle des erbiten,
> daz Mars <unde> Jupiter
> wâren komen wider her
> al zornec mit ir loufte
> (sô was er der verkoufte)
> dar si sich von sprunge huoben ê.
> daz tet an sîner wunden wê
> Anfortase, der sô qual,
> magede und rîter hôrten schal
> von sîme geschreie dicke,
> unt die jâmerlîchen blicke
> tet er in mit den ougen kunt.
> er was unhelfeclîche wunt.
> (789.4–16)

> Now the hour of destiny had waited until Mars and Jupiter had returned, angry in their orbits, to that place from whence they had proceeded before: thus he was overwhelmed. That caused such pain in Anfortas's wounds, and he was so in anguish that the maidens and knights constantly heard the sound of his cries, and received piteous glances from his eyes. He was wounded beyond all help.

This passage raises several vexing philological and scientific problems. Manuscript D has "Mars oder Jupiter," Manuscript G has the noncommittal "Mars Jupiter,"[4] and some manuscripts of the d and g classes have "Mars unde Jupiter."[5] The reading "Mars *or* Jupiter" might enable us to single out the former planet, in accordance with its choleric nature, as the "angry" influence on the wound, albeit at the expense of disagreeing with the sentence's plural verbs and pronouns. The reading "Mars *and* Jupiter" would present a plural subject that is syntactically correct but astrologically more complicated, because Jupiter has a sanguine rather than an "angry" influence.

[4] See the facsimile and transcription of Cgm 19 by Gerhard Augst, Otfrid Ehrismann, and Heinz Engels, *Wolfram von Eschenbach: "Parzival," "Titurel," "Tagelieder"* (1970), fol. 67rb.

[5] Such as the thirteenth-century G^{m} (Munich Cgm 61, fol. 123^{v}).

Wilhelm Deinert's study of astronomy in *Parzival* opts for the problematic choice of "Mars oder Jupiter." After asserting that the parallelism between the two Grail episodes requires the presence of Saturn in Book V to be complemented in Book XVI by a single planet, he concludes that the vagueness of a singular subject and plural verbs and pronouns is also necessary to preserve his theory that these astronomical events also reflect the beginning and concluding stages of a world-year.[6] If we prefer instead to adopt the syntactically correct reading of "Mars unde Jupiter," we need first of all to account for an influence of both planets. Inasmuch as this passage introduces a medical discussion, it almost certainly refers to an intense but unspecified moment of astrological influence or "wîle" (789.4),[7] to which Mars and Jupiter have again returned, "wâren komen wider her" (789.6). Although Wolfram is typically ambiguous, the most likely "return" of several planets with an astrological significance involves a conjunction.

Conjunctions of the superior planets usually function in astrological systems as harbingers of momentous changes.[8] One widespread attitude specifies that conjunctions of Mars and Jupiter in particular cause catastrophes and pestilential conditions on earth, a topos traceable from Babylonian astrology to the famous plague treatise of 1348.[9] Jupiter as the superior planet draws forth excess moisture from the terrestrial realm, which Mars then exacerbates and inflames, the result being pestilence and choler, an effect compatible with the "angry course" of the two in 789.5–7. According to Albertus Magnus,

> Coniunctio enim duarum praecipue stellarum, quae sunt Iuppiter et Mars, cum aliis coadiuvantibus faciunt ventos pestilentes, et aeres corruptos, qui subito necant multitudinem hominum et animalium. . . . Iuppiter enim, cum sit calidus et umidus in natura, habet elevare ventos et vapores . . . Mars autem, cum sit intemperate calidus et siccus, ignit vapores elevatos, et ideo incipiunt per aerem multiplicari fulgura et scin-

[6] Wilhelm Deinert, *Ritter und Kosmos im "Parzival"* (1960), 70.

[7] I follow the astrological meaning suggested by Johannes Kibelka, "Sternglaube und Willensfreiheit in der deutschen Dichtung des Hochmittelalters" (1965), 88.

[8] See for example Robertus Anglicus's commentary on the *Sphera* of Johannes de Sacrobosco in Lynn Thorndike, ed., *The "Sphere" of Sacrobosco and Its Commentators* (1949), 163–66. On this subject in general, see Franz Boll, Carl Bezold, Wilhelm Gundel, *Sternglaube und Sterndeutung* (1966), 34.

[9] See Franz X. Kugler, *Sternkunde und Sterndienst in Babel* (Münster, 1907), II.2, 368; Rudolf Sies, ed., *Das "Pariser Pestgutachten" von 1348 in altfranzösischer Fassung* (1977), 28–29.

tillationes et pestiferei vapores et ignes et veneno peracuto inficiunt aerem et ideo inducunt frequenter pestilentias.[10]

For a conjunction of the two particular planets, Jupiter and Mars, with various auxiliary factors, creates pestilential winds and corrupts the air, which quickly kill many men and animals. . . . For Jupiter, being hot and moist by nature, causes winds and vapors to arise . . . while Mars, being inordinately hot and dry, ignites the risen vapors, and lightning and sparks increase, and therefore pestiferous vapors and fires and keen poison corrupt the air, thus frequently occasioning pestilence.

Albertus's source, the pseudo-Aristotelian *Tractatus de causis proprietatum et elementorum quattuor*, translated by Gerard of Cremona in Toledo,[11] derives catastrophic meteorological phenomena more precisely from conjunctions in particular signs of the zodiac.[12]

Of course, this particular system requires a precise knowledge of planetary positions. It is possible to suggest just such positions for Wolfram's apparent conjunction of Mars and Jupiter. As I suggested in Chapter 5, one of the distinguishing features of *Parzival* is the extended network of chronological references, based on major feasts of the liturgical calendar, that link the hero's first visit to the Grail castle and his return five years later. Owing to the occurrence of Easter on the same day in 1203 and 1208, the variability of the liturgical calendar over such a period of time did not obtain, enabling us to posit an imagined internal chronology for the major events in the Grail narrative. If the implicit date for the first visit to the Grail castle in Book V would be the end of September 1203, a time when Saturn dominated the night sky, it is equally tempting to interpret the influence of Mars and Jupiter on Anfortas's wound in Book XVI, which occurs five years later (799.1–3), as a contemporary reference to those planets, which were in fact in conjunction in Cancer in late September and early October 1208.[13] Moreover, an allusion to a contemporary astrological event rapidly becomes unintelligible to later audiences, a process that would also explain the scribal difficulty with "Mars unde Jupiter" in the manuscript transmission of *Parzival.*

[10] Albertus Magnus, *De causis proprietatum elementorum* II.ii.1 (1980), 96.

[11] See Bernard G. Dod, "Aristoteles latinus" (1982), 58 and the table on 79; Richard Lemay, "Gerard of Cremona" (1978), XV, 180; Marie-Thérèse d'Alverny, "Translations and Translators" (1982). Most of the Arabic works cited below were translated by Gerard or John of Seville in Toledo; see Lemay, and Lynn Thorndike, "John of Seville" (1959).

[12] Albertus Magnus, *De causis*, 62.

[13] See William D. Stahlman and Owen Gingerich, *Solar and Planetary Longitudes for Years −2500 to +2000* (1963), 454. Mars and Jupiter respectively are at longitude 138° and 143° on September 27, 1208, and 143° and 144° on October 7, 1208.

Even if one does not wish to accept a chronology based on the time references in *Parzival*, it is important to realize that the Arabic astrological systems most influential in the medieval West consider conjunctions of Mars and Jupiter as originators of pestilential conditions per se, regardless of their precise position in the zodiac. According to Messahala (Māshā' allāh), the two planets create an excess of moisture, then a corruption of the air and choler:

> Coniunctio minor [the third of his four types of conjunction] est coniunctio Iouis & Martis, & hæc significat accidentia, quæ contingunt ex pluuiis & nivibus, & corruptionem æris atque bella.[14]

Albumashar (Abū Maʿshar), the other leading Arabic expert on conjunctions, similarly adduces manifestations of anger in conflict as well as in pestilential "inflammations."[15] Albohazen Haly (Abū al-Ḥasan ʿAlī) adds that the potential epidemic poses a particular threat to the regent: "Quando iungitur Mars cum Jove significat mortem regis per epidemiam."[16]

The normal medical response to this threat would be to change the bad air to good, either by moving the patient or by treating the air. In the latter instance, the constituent elements of pestilential air, foul stench and vaporous humidity, are corrected allopathically by strong aromatics with dry qualities. The relative temperature of the air remains of secondary consideration and is corrected according to the season:

> Si ex ære pestilentie contingant docuit Abohaly patientem ex ære in ærem bonum mutari et de regione in regionem. quod si non valeat mutet habitaculum suum. . . . habitet in domibus altis et rectificet ærem cum aromaticis frigidis vel calidis sicut eius expetit qualitas.[17]
>
> If pestilential contagions from the air are present, Abohaly advises moving the patient from the bad air to good and from one place to another; if that is not effective let him change his place of residence. . . . Let him abide in an elevated residence and rectify the air with cold or hot aromatics as the state of health demands.

[14] In the "Epistola de rebus eclipsium, et de coniunctionibus planetarum," in *Messahalae antiqvissimi ac lavdatissimi inter Arabes Astrologi, Libri tres* (1549), cap. xii, fol. G3^{r-v}; see also Robertus Anglicus's commentary on Johannes de Sacrobosco's *Sphera*, 163.

[15] Albumashar, *De magnis coniunctionibus, annorum revolutionibus ac eorum profectionibus* (1489), fol. E2^{r}.

[16] Albohazen Haly, *Liber in iudiciis astrorum* (1485), fol. 144^{v}.

[17] Mesue, *Vniversa opera* (1479), fol. u^{3}.

The most influential source of this doctrine appears to be the seminal *Canon* of Avicenna (Ibn Sīna), which presents a complete plague treatise in Liber IV, Fen 1, Tractatus 4, describing the foul odor and humidity of pestilential air, the different effects of the seasons, and drugs for drying and sweetening or rectifying the air at various times of the year. The list for winter includes most of those cited by Wolfram, as we will see:

> ex<s>iccetur ær, et fiat boni odoris: et prohibætur eius putredo cum quacunque re sit: et rectificetur cum xyloaloe crudo, et ambra, et thure, et muscho, et costo dulci, et storace . . . et gariophyllis . . . Et de illis quibus ex putredine fit euasio, est administratio theriacæ.[18]

> The air should be dried out and made sweet-smelling, and its corruption should be treated with whatever is appropriate, and it should be rectified with aloe, and ambergris, and frankincense, and musk oil, and costus dulcis, and storax . . . and cloves . . . and to avoid putridity, theriac should be administered.

Translated by Gerard of Cremona, this basic treatise was circulating in the Latin West by the late twelfth century.[19]

In fact, all these medicinal and astrological sources derive principally from translations made in mid-twelfth-century Toledo. The consequences of being able to localize the iatromathematical discourse in Book XVI are far-reaching. It hardly seems coincidental that Toledo is also the city in which Wolfram's Kyot ostensibly finds the astronomical source by Flegetanis "in Arabic" (453.12f.). Whatever we wish to make of Kyot and Flegetanis, Wolfram was clearly familiar with the massive influx of Arabic science into twelfth-century Latin culture; indeed, his narrative constitutes one of the primary documents of its reception. It is even possible that specifying Kyot's writings as coming from Provence (416.25; 827.9) alludes to this region as the earliest area to reflect the dissemination of Toledan translations outside of Spain.[20] Wolfram also seems to have been aware that this material was controversial, emphasizing that Kyot learned the Arabic alphabet without the help of black magic, "ân den list von nigrômanzî" (453.17). We do not have to involve this passage in the extensive literary feud between Wolfram and Gottfried partly invented by German medievalists, as conservative, especially Cistercian, clerics denigrated the Toledan project as necromantic,[21] an attitude popularized by

[18] Avicenna, *Liber Canonis* (1582), fol. 434v.
[19] See Lemay, "Gerard of Cremona," 185.
[20] See d'Alverny, "Translations and Translators," 457–59.
[21] Jaime Ferreiro Alemparte, "La Escuela de nigromancia de Toledo" (1983).

the *Dialogus miraculorum* of Cæsarius of Heisterbach (I.33 and V.4).[22] Wolfram's emphasis that Kyot did not need the "list von nigrômanzî" thus participates in the liberal defense of the new heathen knowledge.

Equally important, interpreting Wolfram's reference to "Mars unde Jupiter" as a conjunction with an inherently pestilential influence on the atmosphere explains why the medical response at the Grail castle does not address the pain of Anfortas's wound. Obviously, the Grail king's suffering is more excruciating than ever before: screams of anguish resound through the halls of the castle, the "hot" qualities of Mars and Jupiter escalating the burning in a wound originally caused by a "hot" poison (481.11). And although Anfortas seems close to death, the pain forces him to open his eyes and see the Grail—which keeps him alive against his will (788.21–29). However, the wound remains incurable because divine intervention continues to render medication ineffectual.

The efforts of the Grail inhabitants are accordingly directed not at the wound itself but at the pestilential atmosphere generated by the influence of Mars and Jupiter and intensified by the stench of the wound:

swenn im diu scharphe sûre nôt
daz strenge ungemach gebôt,
sô wart der luft gesüezet,
der wunden smac gebüezet.
vor im ûfen teppech lac
pigment und zerbenzînen smac,
müzzel unt arômatâ.
durch süezen luft lag ouch dâ
drîakl und amber tiure:
der smac was gehiure.
Swâ man ûfen teppech trat,
cardemôm, jeroffel, muscât,
lac gebrochen undr ir füezen
durh den luft süezen:
sô daz mit triten wart gebert,
sô was dâ sûr smac erwert.
sîn fiwer was lign alôê:
daz hân ich iu gesaget ê.
(789.21–790.8)

Whenever the sharp and bitter anguish inflicted severe discomfort on him, they sweetened the air and lessened the stench of the wound. On

[22] See Karl Sudhoff, "Toledo!" (1930).

> the carpet before him lay spices and aromatic turpentine, musk, and fragrant substances. To sweeten the air there also lay theriac and precious ambergris—their odor was pleasant. Wherever one stepped on the carpet, cardamom, cloves, and nutmeg lay crushed underfoot to sweeten the air. As these were ground by passing feet, the bitter stench was dispersed. His fire was aloe wood—that I've told you before.

Repetition draws our attention to the salient feature of this particular situation. The "perturbatio æris" introduced by Mars and Jupiter, now heightened by the extraordinarily foul, or "sûr," stench (789.21–24, 790.6) of the wound,[23] is countered by aromatic remedies that lie on the floor, releasing their smells either by themselves or after being stepped on, thus "sweetening" the air, a process emphasized four times in eighteen lines (789.23/28/30, 790.4). The smoke of burning lignum aloe, already mentioned during Parzival's first visit to the Grail castle (230.11), completes the list of medicines pouring their odors into the atmosphere.[24] What strikes the modern reader as a rather aromatic form of air pollution is actually contemporary medical practice.[25]

All the remedies mentioned possess the required allopathic qualities for treating pestilence, being aromatics and dry, in addition to the secondary quality of warmth recommended for cold conditions. The former qualities counter the principal characteristics of pestilential air, explicitly replacing its stench, or "sûr smac" (790.6, 789.24), with pleasant smells, or "gehiure smac" (789.30, 789.26), and implicitly drying its excess moisture. Wolfram presents this materia medica in four groups, to which I will add the commentary of the *Circa instans* (*CI*), the standard medieval pharmacopeia from the mid–twelfth century on.[26]

> 1. The first group includes generic pigments and aromatics, the latter representative of "hot" spice drugs in general, and two particular medications, turpentine ("zerbinzînen") and musk oil ("müzzel"). Turpentine, or *terebintina*, as it is called in the *Circa instans*, is hot and dry.[27] Musk oil, or *muscus*, is hot and dry in the second degree, its powerful aroma having the ability to dissolve and absorb even the stench of cesspools (*CI*, 79f.).

[23] Some later medieval medical literature associates foul-smelling wounds with the punishment for sin. See Ingrid Rohland, *Das "Buch von alten Schäden." Teil II: Kommentar und Wörterverzeichnis* (1982), 41–42.

[24] On lignum aloe, see Heimo Reinitzer, "Zeder und Aloe" (1976), 13–30.

[25] "Mutatio aeris propter locum ex fumo fit, dissolutio herbarum, fructuum . . . qui dum ascendit miscetur aeri." Constantinus Africanus, "De pestilentia aeris," in his *Opera reliqua* (1539), 110–11.

[26] Gundolf Keil, "Circa instans" (1978).

[27] Hans Wölfel, ed., *Circa instans* (1939), 115.

2. The second group consists of theriac ("drîakl") and "amber." Theriac, the only compound drug in the list, was previously used in the unsuccessful attempt to treat the wound directly (484.16). It was called upon then as a principal remedy against poisons; it seems to be employed now because of its composition of a large number of aromatic simples.[28] Wolfram's "amber" is *ambra*, or ambergris, which is hot and dry in the second degree (*CI*, 14) as well as highly aromatic, and thus a major element in plague remedies.[29]

3. The third group consists of aromatic spices. Cardamom ("cardemôm"), like all the other simples thus far, is hot and dry in the second degree, with a powerful aromatic effect that lasts for up to ten years (*CI*, 28). "Jeroffel," or cloves, are hot and dry in the second or third degree, with an acutely intense aroma (*CI*, 56). Finally, "muscât," or *nux muscata* (nutmeg), hot and dry in the second degree, has similar beneficial effects (*CI*, 85).

4. The last item mentioned, burning lignum aloe, is hot and dry in the second degree (*CI*, 4); it is sometimes mentioned as a substitute for incense or as a means of cleansing an area made susceptible to infection by smoke and vapors.[30]

Several aspects of these cures and their properties deserve mention. The remedies are consistently aromatic and dry, allopathically replacing the foul-smelling and humid pestilential atmosphere with "sweet," dry air. They also have the secondary quality of warmth recommended for treatment against cold. What this cold might consist of in *Parzival* is not mentioned. One possibility would be the wound itself, which in Books V and IX is described as cold under the influence of the planets, although this seems less likely, given the "hot" nature of Mars and Jupiter. Another possibility would be cold weather per se, whether occasioned by these planets' position in Cancer (a cold and moist water sign) in late September and early October 1208 or, if one resists the internal chronology suggested, more generally by autumn.[31] Whatever the explanation, Wolfram's list reveals an astonishing consistency within the differentiated hier-

[28] See the description in the Latin *Antidotarium Nicolai* in *Eene middelnederlandsche Vertaling van het "Antidotarium Nicolai"* (1917), 145–47.

[29] See Waltraut F. Dubé, "Medieval Medicine in Middle High German Epics" (1981), 121–22, on this passage, and John Riddle, "Pomum ambrae: Amber and Ambergris in Plague Remedies" (1964).

[30] Konrad von Megenberg, *Das Buch der Natur* (1861), 355; Reinitzer, "Zeder und Aloe," 16–17 and 21.

[31] See Chapter 5 and Hermann J. Weigand, "Narrative Time in the Grail Poems of Chrétien de Troyes and Wolfram von Eschenbach," in his *Wolfram's "Parzifal"* (1969), 58–59.

archy of antidote qualities in the Arabic-based system of plague treatises. Finally, although five of the medicinal simples and the compound theriac are in Avicenna's *Canon,* all seven of the former can be found in the Salernitan *Circa instans.* It would seem that Wolfram's scientific knowledge was up-to-date on contemporary pharmacology as well as astrology and epidemiology.

In terms of its function within the work, however, the "new" medicine plays anything but a successful role, as we see from the continuing efforts to help Anfortas by outfitting his sick bed (790.9–791.30). Although the luxurious couch, reminiscent of lovers' beds,[32] reminds us of the origin of his suffering in an illicit love affair, its viper-horn legs and the thirty-line virtuoso—and highly learned[33]—list of precious stones embedded in it reveal what little joy he has as a result. The narrator's summary emphasizes that this lithiatric collection represents a placative aimed at keeping the king alive ("vristen"):

> Etslîcher lêrte hôhen muot:
> ze sælde unt ze erzenîe guot
> was dâ maneges steines sunder art.
> vil kraft man an in innen wart,
> derz versuochen kund mit listen.
> dâ mite si muosen vristen
> Anfortas, der ir herze truoc.
> (792.1–7)

> Some of these [stones] inspired high spirits, and the special property of many a stone was propitious and medicinally efficacious. Anyone with the knowledge to use them found great potency in them. With these they had to keep their beloved Anfortas alive.

This description concludes one of the longest unsuccessful cures in medieval literature, emphasizing again the antithesis between divine wisdom and worldly knowledge implied by the extensive medical descriptions of the narrative.[34] Wolfram now characterizes that antithesis in terms of a hierarchy between "true" help and human help:

[32] Cf. Alwin Schultz, *Das höfische Leben zur Zeit der Minnesinger* (1889; rpt. 1965), 84–89; Joachim Bumke, *Courtly Culture* (1991), 119–20. For a discussion of Middle High German examples, see Reinitzer, "Zeder und Aloe," 4–8.

[33] The list is traditionally glossed with reference to Marbode of Rennes's *Liber lapidum,* although Arnoldus Saxo's *De virtutibus lapidum* (or, properly speaking, its source) comes closest to the forms used by Wolfram.

[34] For a survey of the topos, see Rudolph Arbesmann, "The Concept of 'Christus Medicus' in St. Augustine" (1954).

er was unhelfeclîche wunt:
si mohten im gehelfen niht.
iedoch diu âventiure giht,
im kom diu wâre helfe nuo.
(789.16–19)

He was wounded beyond all help: they were not able to help him. Yet, the adventure affirms that true help was coming to him now.

That relationship will be both confirmed and subverted in the ensuing scene by Parzival's redeeming question and the divine response.

II

Ignoring Anfortas's deceptive warning (795.15), which disobeys the stricture against prompting, Parzival proceeds directly to an emotional inquiry about the Grail, then moves to the task at hand:

alweinde Parzivâl dô sprach
"saget mir wâ der grâl hie lige.
op diu gotes güete an mir gesige,
des wirt wol innen disiu schar."
sîn venje er viel des endes dar
drîstunt zêrn der Trinitât:
er warp daz müese werden rât
des trûrgen mannes herzesêr.
er riht sich ûf und sprach dô mêr
"œheim, waz wirret dier?"
(795.20–29)

In tears, Parzival said, "Tell me where the Grail is lying here. If God's goodness is victorious in me, that will become manifest to this assembly." On his knees there he fell three times in honor of the Trinity: he prayed that it might resolve the sad man's mortal anguish. He stood up and spoke further: "Uncle, what troubles thee?"

Religious elements frame the entire scene. The introduction to the prayer prepares the setting with a conditional sentence anticipating the miracle to follow (intransitively avoiding a direct cause and effect), with a divine origin posited in the *bonitas* of the Holy Spirit, the hero as its agent, and the inhabitants of Munsalvaesche named as its witnesses. Owing to its private nature and the mystery to follow, the prayer is represented in indirect discourse, proceeding from an outward gesture of supplication (a triple genuflection in honor of the Trinity) to the reported content of the prayer itself, again invoking intransitively a power whose ways remain unknown. The narrative following the question then traces the workings of the Trinity's intervention with an extensive description of Anfortas's return to health, ending with praise of the inexhaustible potential of the divine healer (796.16).

The general context for the redeeming question, then, seems to be a type of religious discourse such as the miracle or saint's life. In fact, L. P. Johnson has clearly demonstrated that the ensuing allusion to St. Silvester reveals a particular source for both the allusion itself and the structure of the entire scene: the *Kaiserchronik*.[35] Wolfram conflates two disparate events from that chronicle's legend of St. Silvester, his healing of Constantine (7938–51) and the reanimation of a dead bull at the conclusion of his religious disputation with heathens and Jews (10247–336), appropriating the triple genuflection, prayer, and invocation of Lazarus from the latter and the afflicted king's miraculous return to health from the former episode. Although these elements as well as common stylistic features ground Parzival's action in the genre expectations of a saint's life and a miracle, several changes distance it as well. Because Parzival is a knight rather than a saint, the preparations, prayers, and invocations receive less attention than the miracle itself, and the narrative therefore focuses on the result of the prayer rather than on the miracle-inducing character of the supplicant.

This distancing of Parzival's miracle from a saint's life may also be reflected by a curious textual difficulty. Johnson notes that the allusion calling attention to the *Kaiserchronik* does not refer to St. Silvester's healing of Constantine, the most obvious analogy, but, rather, to the more puzzling one of resuscitating a dead bull at the end of the religious disputation. In spite of my agreement with the argument in general, I find it difficult to believe that Wolfram's allusion to the bull episode should be, so to speak, a narrative stalking horse, "misleadingly" disguising an "elliptical *tertium comparationis*."[36] A shift of focus from the textual aporia and its problem of stylistic coherence to the intertextual relationship between the *Kaiserchronik* and *Parzival* may make equally good sense.

In the *Kaiserchronik* itself, St. Silvester's resuscitation of the dead animal marks the climax of his disputation with heathens and Jews. The principal *Religionsgespräch* in twelfth-century German literature,[37] the debate begins

[35] See Leslie P. Johnson, "Silvester und Anfortas" (1974).

[36] Ibid., 349.

[37] On the genre in general, see Elisabeth Schenkheld, *Die Religionsgespräche der deutschen erzählenden Dichtung bis zum Ausgang des 13. Jahrhunderts* (1930).

with the Trinity and proceeds through the course of salvation history, proving articles of the Christian faith from the Old Testament and culminating in the resuscitation of the bull, at which point (of course) the assembled nonbelievers convert to Christianity. *Parzival* clearly contains a scene modeled on this disputation: the Good Friday colloquy between Trevrizent and Parzival in Book IX. In fact, their discussion begins in the mode of the genre,[38] with Parzival's doubt, or *zwîvel* (464.8), setting the tone for the conversation, which recapitulates the *Kaiserchronik* in tracing the course of salvation history and posing problems designed to "convert" Parzival (467.9). Several passages from the legend, such as the fall of the rebel angels (8794ff. and 9200ff.) and the riddle of the earth's virgin grandmother (9556ff.), seem to have provided the basis for the corresponding passages in Wolfram's text, and a variety of smaller borrowings might be added.[39] These parallels document an implicit but palpable presence of St. Silvester's religious disputation in Book IX of *Parzival*.[40]

Given the intertextual proclivities of Wolfram's narrative, it does not seem fortuitous that the healing of Anfortas in Book XVI again alludes to this same episode of the *Kaiserchronik*. In fact, the two points of intertextual contact provide a measure of the hero's progress. Whereas in Book IX Parzival's alienation from God cast him in a role resembling that of a heathen in a religious disputation, in Book XVI he can now, by analogy to the saint who wins that disputation, precipitate a miracle comparable to St. Silvester's raising of the bull.[41] Of course, Parzival is no saint, and the distinction is important for Wolfram's secular appropriation of the legend. A descendant of Adam, one whose knightly murder of Ither and near-fratricide of Feirefiz remain to be accounted for at the Last Judgment (744.21–24), Parzival can nonetheless be a vehicle for a miracle explicitly compared with Christ's raising of Lazarus and St. Silvester's raising of the bull—a striking assertion of aristocratic religious potential by a chivalric narrative.

And because Wolfram's scene employs the intersecting discourses of saint's life *and* romance to create a secular appropriation of a clerical genre, replacing the traditional saintly *deus medicus* with a chivalric *miles*

[38] Wolfgang Mohr refers to the less obvious parallel in the Faustinius legend, "Parzivals ritterliche Schuld" (1979), 21.

[39] See Reinhold Köhler, "Die Erde als jungfräuliche Mutter Adams" (1862, rpt. 1900), 7–13; Walter Johannes Schröder, *Die Soltane-Erzählung in Wolframs "Parzival"* (1963), 73–74, also calls attention to the parallelism between the two discussions.

[40] Wolfram's use of the *Kaiserchronik* as a model becomes even more obvious in the religious debates in *Willehalm*. See Samuel Singer, *Wolframs "Willehalm"* (1918), 43–45 and 96–97, and Dieter Kartschoke's comments, *Wolfram von Eschenbach, "Willehalm"* (1968), s.v. *Kaiserchronik*.

[41] See Green, *Art of Recognition*, 256.

medicus, the speech act that precipitates the miracle is not the prayer itself, but a different kind of discourse, the long-awaited question.[42] Whereas St. Silvester's threefold genuflection connects his prayers directly to resurrecting the bull, Parzival's question is something different, expressed in addition ("dô mêr") to his preparatory speech, triple genuflection, and prayer:

> er riht sich ûf und sprach dô mêr:
> "œheim, waz wirret dier?"
> (795.28f.)

Clearly differentiated from the genuflection of the prayer by the opposing motion of standing upright, the redeeming question provides the resolution to a different set of narrative expectations, and we must defer our discussion of the long-awaited question by first examining what they are.

As noted, the question seems to belong initially to genre conventions resembling the fairy tale. A divine "enchantment" partially suspends causality in the natural world,[43] so that the wound is aggravated by influences such as the planets and the weather but resists human medical assistance, which God explicitly prevents (481.18). Like the lesser enchantments often found in fairy tales and chivalric narratives, the paranormal situation can be "broken" only by meeting preestablished conditions.[44] According to Trevrizent's reminiscence in Book IX, the unusual situation was revealed through the mysterious script on the Grail:

> "unser venje viel wir für den grâl.
> dar an gesâh wir zeinem mâl

[42] On the question, see Stephen C. Harroff, *Wolfram and His Audience* (1974), 78; L. P. Johnson, "Parzival's Beauty" (1978), 288–89; Volker Mertens, "Parzivals doppelte Probe" (1979); Walter Delabar, *"Erkantiu sippe unt hoch geselleschaft": Studien zur Funktion des Verwandschaftsverbandes in Wolframs von Eschenbach "Parzival"* (1990), 248–60.

[43] Two different forms of enchantment emerge during Parzival's first visit to the Grail castle: the divine punishment inflicted on Anfortas and the human enchantment attached to the sword he presents to Parzival. After breaking on the second blow, the latter can be restored at the Fountain of Lac near Karnant (the principal city of Erec's kingdom) with the help of a charm, or *segen* (253.25, 254.15), that the hero knows or can learn, provided that he has already asked the redeeming question. The disenchanting speech acts at Munsalvaesche and Karnant apparently recapitulate on a small scale a commonly posited hierarchical relationship between Grail and Arthurian worlds: asking the redeeming question is the prerequisite for learning the charm. Moreover, in accordance with the dynamic and static nature of these worlds, there seems to be no clearly predetermined form for the redeeming question, whereas the charm for the sword implies an already known formulation.

[44] See Erich Köhler, "Die Rolle des 'Rechtsgebrauchs' (costume) in den Romanen des Chrétien de Troyes" (1962).

geschriben, dar solde ein rîter komn:
wurd des frâge aldâ vernomn,
sô solde der kumber ende hân:
ez wære kint magt ode man,
daz in der frâge warnet iht,
sone solt diu frâge helfen niht,
wan daz der schade stüende als ê
und herzelîcher tæte wê.
diu schrift sprach, 'habt ir daz vernomn?
iwer warnen mac ze schaden komn.
Frâgt er niht bî der êrsten naht,
sô zergêt sîner frâge maht.
wirt sîn frâge an rehter zît getân,
sô sol erz künecrîche hân,
unt hât der kumber ende
von der hôhsten hende.' "

(483.19–484.6)

"We fell on our knees in prayer before the Grail. At once we saw written on it that a knight would come: if a question were heard from him, our sorrow would come to an end. But if child, maid, or man should prompt him at all about the question, the question would not avail at all, and the wound would remain as before, and be even more painful. The writing said: 'Have you understood? Your prompting can be damaging. If he does not ask the first night, the power of the question vanishes. If his question is posed at the right time, he shall have the kingdom and the suffering will be ended by the hand of the Highest.' "

At the center of this reminiscence is an extended quotation of the Grail script itself. A divine narrator, who is distinct from God and refers to him as the "hôhstiu hant," mediates between the supreme author and human readers by writing on the Grail, albeit not without some degree of browbeating and condescension toward his audience, who must concentrate on an inscription that disappears as soon as it is read (470.28–30)—an unsettling experience for medieval readers used to either puzzling out writing or meditating on it. According to this disembodied metanarrator, the divine enchantment inflicted on Anfortas can be broken under two conditions: that the knight who asks the question not be prompted, and that he ask the question on the first night. Although the insistent repetition of the verb *vrâgen* (483.22/25/26, 484.1/2/3) emphasizes that the knight must ask something, no precise form of the question is given.

It is important to note the clear distancing of the divine author from both the divine narrator and the human one, a basic dialogizing technique for dealing with authoritative language in novelistic discourse.[45] It is especially crucial here, because the question Parzival actually poses in Book XVI differs from the one suggested by the latter narrator and meets none of the conditions stipulated by the former. We saw in Chapter 5 that Trevrizent merely presents his inference of what the question might be and that the question even seems to change during the narrative, part of a shift away from fixed fairy-tale norms to the heteroglossia of novelistic discourse. The two conditions stipulated by the divine narrator are more problematical, although we can differentiate between the stricture against prompting, which Trevrizent relates in indirect discourse, and that concerning the question, which he quotes directly. Prompting in fact seems to contribute to Parzival's failure in Book VI: the Grail retinue's parading of the bloody spear and Anfortas's gift of the sword to Parzival are associated with this forbidden action (232.1–4, 240.6), making ambiguous an already complex situation.[46]

The stipulation that the question be asked the first night in order to be efficacious is more problematical, however, because it is the only part of the divine inscription that Trevrizent quotes in direct discourse. The fact that the hero nonetheless receives a second chance five years later does not require us to posit anything as radical as Gottfried Weber's "Wandel der Gralprämissen" involving a shift from an Augustinian to a Thomistic outlook.[47] Two alternative readings of the text itself seem more plausible.

1. If we accept the first-night limitation in 484.1–2, assuming with other scholars that the ensuing sentence in 484.3–6 merely explains it, then the divine narrator, or Trevrizent in turn, must be fallible, something the latter's "Retraction" might well confirm; or the supreme author changes the expectations of her text. In either case the grounding of the divine message is deferred indefinitely, a conclusion that seems logical in terms of the careful distancing of three narrative personae in this episode—God, the Grail-scriptor, and Trevrizent. The hierarchical structure, which normally creates order, here masks the intentionality of an ultimately inscrutable divine will.[48]

[45] See Gary Saul Morson and Caryl Emerson, *Mikhail Bakhtin: The Creation of a Prosaics* (1990), 314 and 321.

[46] See Hermann J. Weigand, "A Jester at the Grail Castle?" in *Wolfram's "Parzival"* (1952); Christoph Steppich, "'Hinweise geben wird euch schaden': Zu Wolframs *Parzival* 483.24–30" (1990).

[47] See Gottfried Weber, *Parzival: Ringen und Vollendung* (1948), 74–99; and the discussion in Bumke, *Forschung*, 154–56.

[48] One could associate this possibility with Derridean assumptions about language it-

2. It is equally possible to view the two parallel sentences of direct quotation in lines 484.1–6 as stipulating two completely different conditions for the question, the former limiting it to the first night ("Frâgt er niht bî der êrsten naht, / sô zergêt sîner frâge maht"), the second permitting it whenever the time is "right" ("wirt sîn frâge an rehter zît getân, / sô sol erz künecrîche hân"). In this instance, the divine scribe-narrator would brilliantly articulate the deity's potential to foreknow any number of possible contingencies in the realm of human causality. The first such possibility, that of asking the first night, presupposes a type of Arthurian hero in the static world of the folk tale; and it is this unmotivated expectation by the Grail inhabitants that contributes to their strange, almost enchanted behavior during Parzival's first visit to Munsalvaesche in Book VI. The second possibility, that of asking when the time is right, presupposes the changing hero made possible by the narrative's heteroglot discourse. This possibility seems especially appropriate to the chronotopic realm of the Grail. Parzival progresses in the fullness of time to the proper moment or "rehte zît" (484.3) for a second chance, what the narrator now calls the helpful hour, or "helflîche stunde" (788.19), of the question.

In fact, the imagined chronology of 1203–08 posited for the narrative in Chapter 5 suggests a highly appropriate background for this unique moment. Immediately after being invested with dominion over the Grail realm, Parzival proceeds to meet Condwiramurs, whom he has not seen in five years, "diech nie gesach inre fünf jâren" (799.2f.). This is the first and only time computation he makes in the romance, marking the last reference to his longing for the Grail and his wife,[49] and thus revealing—if not a subjective internalization of time—a consciousness of his quest as a process unfolding in time. If this reference is accurate, the Grail question takes place in late September, against the same liturgical background as in Book VI, the liturgical calendar for 1203 and 1208 being identical in both years, owing to the same date for Easter in each year.

Once again the readings for the eighteenth Sunday after Pentecost and Michaelmas provide parallels between the topics in the cycle of the liturgy—entry into the Heavenly City, proper behavior at a feast, whether one should heal on the Sabbath—and the situation in which Parzival finds himself. Now, however, a hero conscious of time can act in harmony with the demands of this redemptive moment, and like a true king and

---

self or with assumptions on deferral as the constitutive maneuver of romance. See Patricia Parker, *Inescapable Romance: Studies in the Poetics of a Mode* (Princeton, 1979).

[49] See James F. Poag, "*Wîp* and *Grâl*: Structure and Meaning in Wolfram's *Parzival*" (1968); Hans Dewald, *Minne und "sgrâles âventiur"* (1975).

christomimetes will heal Anfortas, as a contemporary sermon for the eighteenth Sunday after Pentecost states of Christ's cure in Luke 14, "with his words, without salve, without bandages, without any kind of medicine."[50] With this redemptive moment, Parzival releases Anfortas from the vicious cycle of astrological influence and liturgical prompting between Books VI and XVI, breaking as it were the divine enchantment in which he has been trapped and progressing to the separation of salvation history and secular dynastic history revealed in the stories of Prester John and Lohengrin at the end of the narrative.

Moreover, because Wolfram's Grail world can admit a second chance for a changing hero, it can also admit a different question from the one originally expected. As L. P. Johnson states:

> The question which should have been put in the form "hêrre, wie stêt iwer nôt?" (484.27), if we are to assume that Trevrizent really was formulating the question, now appears as "œheim, waz wirret dier?" (795.29) some five sorrowful years too late. This mutation of the question, if it be such, is most expressive and underlines, indeed almost symbolizes, the passage of time and the changes it has wrought in Parzival. He is able to replace the formal, courtly *hêrre* and *iuwer* with *œheim* and *dier*, showing how he has won through gradually to awareness of his place in his family and uttering at last the sympathy for a fellow-creature which he had not expressed on the first occasion.[51]

No longer a stranger in a strange land, relying on a courtly code of conduct in the face of unique and uncertain expectations, he now knows the victim of his silence as the uncle whose realm he is about to inherit. The form of address may therefore reflect the "*du* of Christian charity,"[52] but its use also expresses something both more specific and more worldly: Parzival's remorseful recognition of his once and future place in the Grail aristocracy. It is an intensely emotional moment of agnatic family history,[53] his own awareness of which has proceeded from the hermit-uncle Trevrizent to this present moment before his regent-uncle Anfortas.

Because the Grail question can be viewed as an act of compassion *and* as a celebration of the basic family structure and dynastic aspirations of high medieval chivalry, it includes both religious and secular elements.

[50] Anton E. Schönbach, *Altdeutsche Predigten* (1886/91, rpt. 1964), I, 134: "mit sinen worten ane salbin, ane binden, ane aller slachte arcteie."

[51] Johnson, "Parzival's Beauty," 288.

[52] Ibid., 289.

[53] See Georges Duby, "The Structure of Kinship and Nobility," in *The Chivalrous Society* (1977), 134–48; and Karl Bertau, "Versuch über Verhaltenssemantik von Verwandten im 'Parzival'," in his *Wolfram von Eschenbach: Neun Versuche* (1983), 190–240.

Indeed, Parzival's redemptive speech act actually consists of two heteroglossic components, the introductory statement and prayer, and the question itself, which are not only differentiated by the opposing motions of genuflecting and standing up but are also grounded in different types of discourse. Whereas the prayer's gesture of submission conveys the impression of supplication for divine assistance, the question's rising gesture of independent action conveys the impression of human striving.[54] Both components of the speech act, prayer to God and concern for a relative, appear to fulfill the complementary demands of grace and merit, God and world, and—on the level of genre—saint's legend and chivalric romance, between which Parzival's quest has been inscribed.

It is not surprising that these forms of discourse intersect at the climactic speech act of the narrative, but it may be more difficult to accept their indeterminacy. It is unclear whether these components stand in a static or dynamic relationship to one another—whether God and world remain in hierarchical harmony, or whether the chivalric world is privileged as the last member of a process of secularization. The former would appeal to clerical utopian nostalgia, the latter to aristocratic dynastic concerns. The polyvalence of the redeeming question would have satisfied rather disparate religious and secular interests in courtly society during the internal and external political conflicts in early-thirteenth-century Germany.

The uncertainty does not end here. Wolfram's narrative also withholds answers on a variety of issues related to the question itself. Anfortas does not answer the inquiry addressed to him at all, since this is a performative speech act rather than a true question. Both the speech act and its formulation as a question mask the relationship—or nonrelationship—between Parzival's actual utterance and the miracle that ensues. The question necessarily precedes, but does not cause or compel, divine intervention. And although the miracle would most appropriately be a response to the preceding prayer for help, the intervening question renders any connection indirect. Immediately following the question and completing its rhyme ("œheim, waz wirret dier?"), but without any reference to the antecedent speech act, the narrative shifts directly to the mysterious workings of the Trinity:

der durch sant Silvestern einen stier
Von tôde lebendec dan hiez gên,
unt der Lazarum bat ûf stên,

[54] On the classical concept of man as characterized by the ability to stand upright and its medieval adaptations, see Hartmut Freytag, *Kommentar zur frühmittelhochdeutschen "Summa Theologiae"* (1970), 32, 46, and 83–85.

der selbe half daz Anfortas
wart gesunt unt wol genas.
swaz der Franzoys heizt flôrî,
der glast kom sînem velle bî.
Parzivâls schœn was nu ein wint,
und Absalôn Dâvîdes kint,
von Ascalûn Vergulaht,
und al den schœne was geslaht,
unt des man Gahmurete jach
dô mann în zogen sach
ze Kanvoleiz sô wünneclîch,
ir decheins schœn was der gelîch,
die Anfortas ûz siechheit truoc.
got noch künste kan genuoc.
(795.30–796.16)

He who through Saint Silvester commanded a bull to rise living from death, and he who bade Lazarus to rise—he helped Anfortas to become well and whole again. What the Frenchman calls "flôrî"—its radiance came to his skin. Parzival's beauty was now nothing, and David's son Absalon, Vergulaht of Ascalun, and all those who inherited beauty, and what was said of Gahmuret, when one saw him enter Kanvoleis so handsomely—none of their beauty was equal to that with which Anfortas emerged from his illness. God still has many skills.

These workings are articulated in two different ways: first in time, as a manifestation of the historical process of redemption; then in space, as a manifestation of the deity's artistry.

In accordance with the ineffable nature of the Trinity, the narrative first traces its intervention into the human realm through a tripartite circumlocution ("he . . . he . . . he") that takes the form of an antonomasia, a trope frequently used in place of proper names to characterize the deity.[55] The same power that raised Lazarus from the tomb and that through St. Silvester brought a bull back to life now resuscitates Anfortas from his living death and restores him to glowing health. In a manner

[55] See Heinrich Lausberg, *Handbuch der literarischen Rhetorik* (1960), I, 580–81, 589–98; Edmond Faral, *Les Arts poétiques du XIIe et du XIIIe siècle* (1962), 53, 68, 90, and the discussions by Matthew of Vendome, *Ars versificatoria* (IV.21), Geoffrey of Vinsauf, *Poetria nova* (949–56), and *Documentum de modo et arte dictandi et versificandi* (11–14). The most detailed definition is Bede's "De schematibus et tropis" (1863), 613.5–17. See also Hartmut Freytag, "'sun, des bewîse dich der / der dich nâch im gebildet hât': Bemerkungen zu Antonomasien in Hartmanns von Aue *Gregorius* und seinen lateinischen und volkssprachigen Bearbeitungen" (1992).

similar to twelfth-century speculation on the Trinitarian progress of history from Gerhoh of Reichersberg to Joachim of Fiore, these three pronominal hypostases of the deity connect events of the New Testament, the patristic era, and the Arthurian age, recuperating the history of the Grail within the larger confines of sacred history.

Moreover, in accordance with twelfth-century emphasis on the deity as the supreme artist (following the reception of Plato's *Timaeus*), the Trinity's action manifests itself to human perception primarily in aesthetic terms, reflected in a threefold emphasis on the beauty, or "schœne" (796.7/10/14), that is finally inscribed on Anfortas's body. Here the process is expressed in one extended sentence that begins and ends with the principals of the scene, Parzival and Anfortas, respectively. Comparisons first with Parzival, then with the biblical example of beauty and with other relatives remind us how the narrator has extolled the hero as the most handsome creation of the *deus artifex.*[56] The divine emanation now deconstructs the human textual tradition established by these references, outdoing everything the narrator has thus far accomplished in describing his hero's appearance by "overwriting" on Anfortas's body a beauty surpassing Parzival's. It then withdraws as imperceptibly as it appeared, leaving the radiance of the Fisher King as its visible residue. The simple concluding sentence, "got noch künste kan genuoc," which finally and explicitly names the divine artist after the fact, succinctly confirms his continuing ("still") potential with the understatement appropriate to a mere human narrator.

The action is brought to a close by the same divine narrator who announced the conditions for resolving the interregnum in Book IX and who now intervenes as a mediator, again through the script on the Grail, confirming with pleasing symmetry the fulfillment of the conditions and the transfer of dominion to Parzival (796.17–21). This ends the narrative sequence of events in the healing of Anfortas, leaving the relationship between the redeeming question and divine intercession still unclear. Precisely what has occurred in the gap surrounding Parzival's speech act and the divine miracle becomes the subject of one of the most puzzling segments of Wolfram's narrative: Trevrizent's "Retraction."

[56] See Johnson, "Parzival's Beauty," and Ingrid Hahn, "Parzivals Schönheit: Zum Problem des Erkennens und Verkennens im *Parzival*" (1975), II, 203–32.

CHAPTER NINE

Inconclusive Speech Acts: Trevrizent's "Retraction"

Parzival's redeeming question and the miraculous cure of Anfortas are followed immediately by several events that seem to promise closure of the narrative. The metanarrator who originally revealed the conditions imposed by God on the adventure at Munsalvaesche now names Parzival as king, his inscription on the Grail cadencing with a final use of the rhyme motif of knowing and naming (*kennen/nennen*) that has accompanied the hero throughout the romance:[1]

> da ergienc dô dehein ander wal,
> wan die diu schrift ame grâl
> hete ze hêrren in benant:
> Parzivâl wart schiere bekant
> ze künige unt ze hêrren dâ.
> (796.17–21)

> There ensued no election other than the script on the Grail naming him as lord. Parzival was quickly acknowledged as king and lord there.

As Parzival's return to Munsalvaesche and accession to rulership only half completes the quest for *grâl unde wîp*,[2] the narrative now shifts to his wife. Parzival's longing for Condwiramurs returns him to the spot where he was entranced by her image in the snow five years before:

[1] See the extended use of *nennen/erkennen* in the first meeting with Sigune (140.6–12), Trevrizent's and Parzival's discussion of the *Gralprämissen* (468.11–14, 472.8–10, 473.5–11), and in Parzival's response to Cundrie's announcement (783.4–10).

[2] See James F. Poag, "*Wîp* and *Grâl*: Structure and Meaning in Wolfram's *Parzival*" (1968).

ze Terre de salvæsche in den walt,
dâ mit der tjoste wart gevalt
Segramors unt dâ der snê
mit bluote sich ir glîcht ê.
(797.7–10)

in the forest at Terre de Salvaesche, where Segremors was felled by the joust and where the snow with blood previously resembled her.

On the way, the hero encounters his uncle Trevrizent, from whom he received spiritual advice on the previous Good Friday, advice that seems to have marked the turning point in his quest. But now the astonished hermit suddenly complicates the narrative with a commentary on the miracle he has not witnessed, praising the mysterious workings of providence and disavowing the advice that led—or so we thought—to Parzival's success.

This, briefly stated, is the context of Trevrizent's "Retraction," which poses unusual difficulties for scholars.[3] Critics have learned to come to terms with Wolfram's "crooked" narrative technique, with his taunting propensity for withholding essential information and then revealing it long after it is needed. Trevrizent's valedictory speech in Book XVI, though, seems to be either hopelessly complicated or hopelessly confused, not agreeing with—and even contradicting—the Good Friday utterances in Book IX to which it refers:

Trevrizent ze Parzivâle sprach
"grœzer wunder selten ie geschach,
sît ir ab got erzürnet hât
daz sîn endelôsiu Trinitât
iwers willen werhaft worden ist.
ich louc durch ableitens list
vome grâl, wiez umb in stüende.
gebt mir wandel für die süende:
ich sol gehôrsam iu nu sîn,
swester sun unt der hêrre mîn.
daz die vertriben geiste
mit der gotes volleiste

[3] For a survey and discussion of the main aspects of the controversy, see Bumke, *Forschung*, 154–56, 168–69, 254–55, and 263–68; Henry Kratz, *Wolfram von Eschenbach's "Parzival"* (1973), 538–40. There have been two recent interpretations, D. H. Green, *The Art of Recognition in Wolfram's "Parzival"* (1982), 337–41, and Bernd Schirok, "'ich louc durch ableitens list': Zu Trevrizents Widerruf und den neutralen Engeln" (1987).

bî dem grâle wæren,
kom iu von mir ze mæren,
unz daz si hulde dâ gebiten.
got ist stæt mit sölhen siten,
er strîtet iemmer wider sie,
die ich iu ze hulden nante hie.
swer sîns lônes iht wil tragn,
der muoz den selben widersagn.
êweclîch sint si verlorn:
die vlust si selbe hânt erkorn.
mich müet et iwer arbeit:
ez was ie ungewonheit,
daz den grâl ze keinen zîten
iemen möhte erstrîten:
ich het iuch gern dâ von genomn.
nu ist ez anders umb iuch komn:
sich hât gehœhet iwer gewin.
nu kêrt an diemuot iwern sin."
(798.1–30)

Trevrizent said to Parzival: "A greater miracle has never happened, for you have forced God by defiance to make his infinite Trinity grant your will. In order to distract you from the Grail, I lied about how things stood with it. Give me penance for my sin: I must now obey you, my nephew and my lord. You were told a story by me that the outcast spirits remained at the Grail with God's permission until they should receive his grace. God is constant in such matters: he forever contends against those whom I here named for you as forgiven. Whoever wishes at all to receive his reward must renounce them. They are eternally lost, a loss they themselves have chosen. I also regret your trials: it was never the custom that anyone could ever win the Grail by fighting—I would gladly have spared you from it. Now things have turned out differently for you: your success is all the loftier. Now turn your thoughts to humility."

A comparison of the corresponding passages from Books XVI and IX reveals four apparent discrepancies. In order of occurrence they are

1. Trevrizent's astonished claim that Parzival has "ab erzürnet" or forced the deity by anger to grant his will (798.2–5) now supersedes a theologically more secure warning that one can wrest nothing from God by defiance: "irn megt im ab erzürnen niht" (463.1).

2. Trevrizent's confession that he prevaricated in order to divert Par-

zival from the Grail (798.6f.) seems to belie the earlier assertion that he could not deceive: "dô sprach aber der guote man / 'ich enbinz niht der dâ triegen kan'" (476.23f.).

3. The hermit states that although he had previously reported that the neutral angels were awaiting God's forgiveness, they are actually damned forever (795.11–22). In fact, he merely said that he did not know whether God forgave or condemned them: "ich enweiz op got ûf si verkôs, / ode ob ers fürbaz verlôs" (471.23f.).

4. He now interprets Parzival's success in straightforward terms as having been won by fighting (798.24–27), whereas his earlier statement on attaining the Grail presupposes that no one can win the Grail unless he is so known in heaven that he is named to it: "jane mac den grâl nieman bejagn, / wan der ze himel ist sô bekant / daz er zem grâle sî benant" (468.12–14).

Two interpretations of these contradictions have dominated Wolfram scholarship. Gottfried Weber postulates that Trevrizent is correct in believing that Parzival has indeed won the Grail by defiant fighting, inferring that the hermit's last statement represents a change in the "Gralprämissen" or conditions for winning the Grail, which in turn reflects the transition from an Augustinian to a Thomistic worldview.[4] Peter Wapnewski argues instead that Parzival has changed, not the conditions for attaining the Grail, which remain constant except for Trevrizent's "Retraction."[5] Inasmuch as that retraction corrects in a contradictory manner what he previously asserted in Book IX, the entire section should be athetized as an unsuccessful later interpolation:

> The Trevrizent of Book IX and the Trevrizent of Book XVI exclude each other. The former encouraged Parzival's quest for the Grail, the latter diverted him from it. Weber sides with the Trevrizent of Book XVI. . . . In order to circumvent the undeniable dilemma, I believe we have to decide for the Trevrizent of Book IX and doubt the expression and validity of the one in Book XVI. Recognition of the internal shakiness of section 798 enabled us to find stylistic and syntactic unevenness. It confirms our doubts about the original genuineness of Trevrizent's speech and supports connecting section 797 directly to 799.

Wapnewski's analysis clarifies many problems of earlier criticism as well as the text itself, but it also allows a different conclusion. Inasmuch as the

[4] Gottfried Weber, *"Parzival": Ringen und Vollendung* (1948), 80ff.

[5] Peter Wapnewski, "Trevrizent: Widerruf und Gralprämissen," in his *Wolframs "Parzival"* (1955), 172–73.

"Retraction" occurs in every complete *Parzival* manuscript and therefore seems authentic, excising it from the text, even as an unsuccessful "later authorial interpolation," remains a confession of interpretative failure.

Before resorting to unprovable genetic suppositions, we might inquire whether the contradictions are intelligible in terms of other narrative considerations. Most obviously, Wapnewski's conclusions derive from a basic but unstated presupposition, namely, that *Parzival* is written in a unified and consistent style, in undifferentiated authorial discourse. This assumption may of course be suited to monoglot romance narratives, where contradictory details and statements can raise issues of authorial consistency. But Wolfram's narrative, as this book has argued, tends toward decentered and pluralistic discourse, heteroglossia rather than monoglossia. In other words, Wolfram does not "write" exclusively in a single "authorial style" but orchestrates a variety of voices, ranging from genres to individual characters, and this variety can include discrepant statements by characters whose views may be partial or limited. In pluralistic discourse, then, the hermit's "Retraction" may still be part of the text precisely because of its contradictions. *Trevrizent's* confusion is, after all, not necessarily *Wolfram's* confusion.

What compels me to make this distinction is that Wolfram's narrator claims repeatedly that he is capable of keeping "straight and true" what may appear to us as "crooked" (805.14f.). In the final books of *Parzival*, for example, this claim seems to be supported by a series of references that underscore the coordination of narrative themes as the plot comes full circle from Parzival's initial failure at the Grail castle to his return five years later. Most frequently, these references use the relatively uncomplicated device of reminding us that we have been told something before: "daz hân ich iu gesaget ê."[6] But the narrator also makes more detailed references to earlier portions of the narrative, and he does so without raising the problem of inconsistencies.

In fact, there are two such references that direct us quite literally to what "Trevrizent said back there" in Book IX (786.4 and 788.15). These are, as we noted in Chapter 1, cross-references to earlier sections of the manuscript text. And one of them relates Parzival's farewell to Arthur's court, accurately quoting one of our crucial passages from Book IX only a few sections before Trevrizent contradicts it in his "Retraction":

> Parzivâl sîn rede alsus huop an.
> en franzoys er zin allen sprach

[6] See 775.6, 790.8, 794.27, 808.23, 809.18, as well as the pointed repetition of the Grail procession (807.16ff.) and the allusions to Parzival's reunion with his wife on the same spot as the *Blutstropfenepisode* (797.4–11, 799.1–11, 802.1–8).

als Trevrizent dort vorne jach,
daz den grâl ze keinen zîten
niemen möht erstrîten,
"wan der von gote ist dar benant."
(786.2–7)

Parzival thus began his speech. In French he told all of them, as Trevrizent said above, that no one could ever win the Grail by fighting, "except one who is called to it by God."

This is a clear and verifiable statement, reporting that Parzival repeats what Trevrizent said "back there" in Book IX:

"jane mac den grâl nieman bejagn,
wan der ze himel ist sô bekant
daz er zem grâle sî benant."
(468.12–14)

"Indeed, no one can win the Grail except that one who is so known in heaven that he is called to it."

In fact, it is an extremely close paraphrase, employing the same vocabulary and syntax, "nieman . . . wan der," and culminating, as the shift from "sî benant" (468.14) to "ist benant" (786.7) suggests, in the transition from indirect discourse to a literal quote.[7] Both statements emphasize the coordination of a series of disparate elements—grace and merit, election and striving, being called to and winning the Grail—in a dialogue of discourses that confirms Cundrie's announcement (782.29f.) and anticipates the desirability of reconciling God and world stated at the romance's conclusion (827.19–24). In contrast to these basic statements on the conditions for attaining the Grail, Trevrizent's "Retraction" places a one-sided emphasis on human volition and action, beginning with Parzival's *aberzürnen* (798.2ff.) and ending with winning the Grail by fighting:[8]

"ez was ie ungewonheit,
daz den grâl ze keinen zîten
iemen möhte erstrîten. . . .
nu ist ez anders umb iuch komn."
(798.24ff.)

[7] On viewing 786.7 as a citation, see Martin, *Kommentar*, 512, and Bartsch/Marti, 160.

[8] See Martin Jones, "Parzival's Fighting and His Election to the Grail" (1975), esp. 52–55 and 68–71.

"It was never the custom that anyone could ever win the Grail by fighting. . . . Now things have turned out differently for you."

To put it bluntly, the narrator of Book XV knows and recalls precisely what the Trevrizent of Book IX said, whereas the Trevrizent of Book XVI either cannot do so or has reached an opinion that stands strikingly alone.

If we cannot rationalize all the inconsistencies in Trevrizent's "Retraction," and I believe that we cannot, we are not compelled to attribute them to Wolfram, who—as these statements suggest—is entirely capable of keeping his narrator's comments in order and distinguishing them from those of his characters. We should rather attribute Trevrizent's inconsistencies to Trevrizent himself, a conclusion that has implications for the question of closure versus open-endedness in Wolfram's discursive practice.

I

An interpretation of Trevrizent's "Retraction" as a fallible assessment of the complex issues involved in Parzival's success might begin with the hermit's confession that he lied (798.6f.). This is a startling admission for a holy man, particularly one who assured the hero in Book IX that he could not deceive him (476.24). The apparent contradiction has been cited as evidence for the inauthenticity of the "Retraction,"[9] but it does not exist. The assertion of truthfulness in Book IX is limited to a response to Parzival's question concerning the deaths of Herzeloyde and Ither:

"sagt mir sunder wankes vâr,
sint disiu mære beidiu wâr?"
dô sprach aber der guote man
"ich enbinz niht der dâ triegen kan."
(476.21–24)

"Tell me without any deceit, are these two reports true?" The good man responded, "I cannot deceive you there."

Unfortunately, Trevrizent's insistence that he actually did lie cannot be substantiated from the text either. One can infer that the hermit suspects he is counseling Lehelin at the beginning of the Good Friday colloquy

[9] Wapnewski, *Wolframs "Parzival,"* 164–65.

(cf. 474.1),[10] and thus would have every reason to discourage a suspected enemy from a quest that could have deadly consequences for him and the Grail society. But such tactics are unnecessary, because Trevrizent can more easily discourage his advisee simply by telling the truth. In fact, he does so by stating the conditions discussed, namely, that no one can win the Grail *unless* he is also called to it by God:

> "ir jeht, ir sent iuch umben grâl:
> ir tumber man, daz muoz ich klagn.
> jane mac den grâl nieman bejagn,
> wan der ze himel ist sô bekant
> daz er zem grâle sî benant.
> des muoz ich vome grâle jehn:
> ich weizz und hânz für wâr gesehn."
> (468.10–16)

"You claim that you long for the Grail: you foolish man, I must deplore this. Indeed, no one can win the Grail except that one who is so known in heaven that he is called to it. This I must report about the Grail: I know it and have seen it to be true."

Once Parzival reveals his identity, Trevrizent does encourage his quest for the Grail (489.1–20),[11] but there is no indication in the rest of Book IX, which encompasses the ensuing two weeks, that the hermit is at all disturbed by anything he has stated earlier.

We are thus left with no explicit evidence for Trevrizent's mendacity but the claim of the "Retraction" itself, which asserts that he lied to discourage Parzival's pursuit of the Grail:

> "ich louc durch ableitens list
> vome grâl, wiez umb in stüende.
> gebt mir wandel für die süende:
> ich sol gehôrsam iu nu sîn,
> swester sun unt der hêrre mîn."
> (798.6–10)

"In order to distract you from the Grail, I lied about how things stood with it. Give me penance for my sin: I must now obey you, my nephew and my lord."

[10] For some discussions, see Bernd Schirok, "Trevrizent und Parzival: Beobachtungen zur Dialogführung und zur Frage der figurativen Komposition" (1976), and Petrus Tax, "Trevrizent: Die Verhüllungstechnik des Erzählers" (1974).

[11] See Wapnewski, *Wolframs "Parzival,"* 156–60.

The assertion is particularly strong (one does not confess a sin without a reason), but it is also vague, because the determination of penance depends on the nature of the sin.[12] This statement, however, can refer either to some unknown lie about the Grail itself, "ich louc vome grâl," or to an even more general lie undertaken to divert Parzival from the Grail, "ich louc durch ableitens list."[13] In either case, a specific untruth is not immediately obvious, and generations of Wolfram scholars have been unable to find anything tangible.[14] The validity of the claim would therefore seem to be subjective,[15] deriving either from Trevrizent's own remorse at having caused Parzival unnecessary travail (798.23/27) or from Trevrizent's own recollection of his statements, which does not seem to be consistent, as the pronouncement on the neutral angels testifies.

This most controversial segment of the "Retraction" has generally been identified as the subject of Trevrizent's lie. The connection is not explicit, and it is difficult to see what a remark of ten lines, embedded in the lengthy discourse on salvation history, could have to do with diverting Parzival from his Grail quest. Several scholars, most recently Bernd Schirok, have argued that Trevrizent, although knowing better, feigns uncertainty about the neutral angels in order not to discourage Parzival:[16]

> What Trevrizent says about the neutral angels is false, but what he wants to tell Parzival with this is correct: in spite of all that has happened, Parzival is not lost; indeed, he can hope for God's grace. If Trevrizent had told the truth in Book IX about the fate of the neutral angels, that would have led Parzival to the wrong conclusion that there was also no longer any hope for him.

Empathetic as the gesture toward therapy may be, it misses the medieval context of the conversation, confessional practice and its relation to theology. In fact, Schirok's supposition even contradicts standard church doctrine, because the angels, as entirely spiritual beings, have no second chance and *therefore* provide a hopeful contrast with men, who as beings of spirit and flesh can fall but still attain salvation:[17]

[12] Schirok's attempt to include the theological discussion of lies, "Trevrizents Widerruf," 68–70, is thus certainly apropos. The problem might be best approached by twelfth-century penetentials, i.e., contemporary pastoral practice, collected in John T. McNeill and Helen M. Gamer, *Medieval Handbooks of Penance* (New York, 1938).

[13] Wapnewski, *Wolframs "Parzival,"* 155–56.

[14] Bumke, *Forschung*, 266.

[15] See David Blamires, *Characterization and Individuality in Wolfram's "Parzival"* (1966), 357.

[16] Schirok, "Trevrizents Widerruf," 67. Similarly Kratz, *Wolfram's "Parzival,"* 405.

[17] Gregory the Great, *Moralia in Iob* (IV.iv.3.4), CCSL 143, 168. The translation is from *Morals on the Book of Job by S. Gregory the Great* (1844), I, 189.

> [Deus] duas uero ad intellegendum se creaturas fecerat, angelicam uidelicet et humanam; utramque uero superbia perculit atque ab statu ingenitae rectitudinis fregit. Sed una tegmen carnis habuit, alia uero nil infirmum de carne gestauit. Angelus namque solummodo spiritus, homo uero est spiritus et caro. Misertus ergo creator ut remideret, illam ad se debuit reducere quam in perpetratione culpae ex infirmitate aliqid constat habuisse; et eo altius debuit apostatam angelum repellere quo cum a persistendi fortitudine corruit, nil infirmum ex carne gestauit.

> [God] made two creations to contemplate Himself, viz. the Angelic and the human, but pride smote both, and dashed them from the erect station of native uprightness. But one had the clothing of the flesh, the other bore no infirmity derived from the flesh. For an angelical being is spirit alone, but man is both spirit and flesh. Therefore when the Creator took compassion to work redemption, it was meet that He should bring back to himself that creature, which, in the commission of sin, plainly had something of infirmity; and it was also meet that the apostate Angel should be driven down to a farther depth, in proportion as he, when he fell from resoluteness in standing fast, carried about him no infirmity of the flesh.

This distinction is popular in didactic literature as well, such as the enormously popular writings of Honorius of Autun, from which it entered Middle High German literature in the *Lucidarius.*[18]

But even if we concede a possible connection between Trevrizent's asserted deception and the neutral angels suggested by Schirok and others, the passage remains problematical. In Book IX Trevrizent stated simply that he did not know whether God forgave or condemned them: "ich enweiz op got ûf si verkôs / ode ob ers fürbaz verlôs" (471.23f.). Now he asserts that whereas he previously claimed they were awaiting God's forgiveness, they were in fact—and still are—irredeemably damned:

> "daz die vertriben geiste
> mit der gotes volleiste
> bî dem grâle wæren,
> kom iu von mir ze mæren,
> unz daz si hulde dâ gebiten.
> got ist stæt mit sölhen siten,

[18] See Pseudo-Isidore, *Differentiae* (II.xv.44), *PL* 83.77; Honorius's *Elucidarius, PL* 172.1114, and "De angelis," *PL* 172.1190; and the *Lucidarius* (1915), 33–34. On the larger context of this problem, see my "The 'Elder' Angel in *Guthlac A*," *Anglia,* 101 (1983), 141–46, esp. 143.

er strîtet iemmer wider sie,
die ich iu ze hulden nante hie."
(798.11–18)

"You were told a story by me that the outcast spirits remained at the Grail with God's permission until they should receive his grace. God is constant in such matters: he forever contends against those whom I here named for you as forgiven."

There is not one contradiction here, but two. The first is one of fact, the actual fate of the neutral angels; the second is one of recollection, between what Trevrizent said then and what he now says he said.

Scholars have focused their attention on the first contradiction, although none of the "sources" for understanding the neutral angels adequately "explains" Wolfram's use of the motif.[19] In this regard, it is important to distinguish between theological and literary discourse on the neutral angels. The theological tradition is both consistent and concise.[20] This is not surprising, for the idea of "neutral" angels is impossible in doctrinal terms, because angelic destiny was already completed at the beginning of creation, when the angels turned either toward or away from God, an event traditionally associated with the separation of light and darkness in Genesis 1.5. Isolated references to neutral angels in apocryphal texts and patristic writings do reflect an attempt to mediate between the either/or polarity of the Christian moral world and the hierarchical Platonic conception of the natural world. But after St. Augustine's vigorous refutation of the middle spirits of the "platonici" in *De civitate Dei*, the doctrinal position on angels consistently reaffirmed the original dichotomy.

Simultaneously, however, the neutral angels flourished on the margins of medieval literature and legend, a more attractive medium for fusing moral and natural middleness from Christian ethics and pagan demonology. The ambiguous nature of these half-fallen creatures is particularly clear in versions of the voyage of St. Brendan, one of the earliest and most important sources of the legend, and a close analogue to the neutral angel sections of Wolfram's *Parzival* and Dante's *Inferno.* Even in the clerical *Navigatio Sancti Brendani* there is a contradictory variety of explanations for the neutral angels' sin with respect to the fall of Lucifer and

[19] See the works listed in Bumke, *Forschung,* 162, 169, and esp. 263–68, and Roy Wisbey, "Marvels of the East in the *Wiener Genesis* and in Wolfram's *Parzival*" (1973). On Dante scholarship, see the *Enciclopedia dantesca,* I (Rome, 1970), 270–71.

[20] See John Freccero, "Dante's 'per se' Angel: The Middle Ground in Nature and Grace" (1962).

his cohorts, agreeing without sinning ("sed non peccando consensimus"), not agreeing to their sins ("sed non peccatis eorum consensimus"), and falling without having sinned or agreed ("sed non peccando aut consentiendo sumus lapsi").[21] The multiplicity appears even in individual texts:[22]

> dô Lucifer der alde
> mit unrehter gewalde
> zû himele werben wolde
> anders dan er solde,
> daz was uns weder lîp noch leit.
> wir wâren engel vil gemeit,
> got hatte wir niht vor ougen,
> wir minneten niht sîn tougen.
> daz ist wol worden an uns schîn:
> wie mohte wir wirs geschaffen sîn?
> wir geniezen ouch des dâmite
> wan wir des hundes site
> zû himele begiengen,
> darumme wir entpfiengen
> diz lant und wurden alle glîche
> gestôzen von dem himelrîche.
> ouch hât uns got der helle irlâzen:
> wir enwolden uns niht ebenmâzen
> zû Luciferes gesellen
> die mit im vielen in die hellen.
> noch hoffe wir vil armen,
> daz got tû über uns sîn irbarmen.
> (1355–76)

When Old Lucifer with unjust force behaved in heaven other than he should have, that neither pleased nor grieved us. We were blessed angels, but we did not concentrate on God and did not love his secrets. That is clear in our case, for how could we have been created worse? We also benefit from having acted like dogs in heaven, for we all received this land and were outcast from heaven. God also spared us from hell: we did not want to elevate ourselves to Lucifer's companions, who fell with him to hell. We miserable creatures still hope that God will have mercy on us.

[21] Ibid., 16–18.

[22] Cited from the Middle German version of ca. 1300, ed. Carl Schröder, *Sanct Brandan: Ein lateinischer und drei deutsche Texte* (1871), 80–81. Other versions are on 119–20 and 186.

This obviously rationalizing composite attempts to account for the "neutral" angels' intermediate position between extremes by attributing to them an aversion from God but indifference to Lucifer's rebellion, a stance that explains their exclusion from both heaven and hell and admits the justness of their punishment but also the hope of redemption.

The composite nature of such analogues, however, should also make us wary of modern attempts to resolve the putative factual contradiction in Trevrizent's statements. Ever since Lachmann, scholars have assumed that the change about the neutral angels between Books IX and XVI (and the raison d'être for the entire "Retraction") stems from Wolfram's discovery of the truth or even from pressure to conform with orthodox opinion.[23] There is, of course, no evidence to support this theory because the clear-cut theological tradition and the ambiguous literary one clearly coexist. If clerical writers about St. Brendan do not impose the former on the latter, why should Wolfram or Trevrizent be compelled to do so?

This brings us, finally, to Trevrizent's second contradiction about the neutral angels, which is often ignored: whereas in Book IX he did not know whether God forgave or condemned them (471.23f.), he now says he claimed they were awaiting God's forgiveness (795.11–22). No matter how many neutral angels are made to dance on the heads of scholarly pins to rescue the hermit's factual consistency, this subjective contradiction about them in his memory cannot be argued away. This does not have to be as angst producing as philologists seem to imagine. Once we differentiate between Wolfram and his characters, there is no need to rescue the latter, since Wolfram may have employed Trevrizent's contradictions to make a narrative point, not about the theological substance of the legend but about the hermit himself. His shifting of gears about the fate of the neutral angels needs to be seen in conjunction with his inconsistent memory, the fact that his statement about what he said does not even coincide with his actual utterances. The hermit's newfound theological certainty about an ambiguous legend and his inability to recall what he had stated earlier should be viewed as reflecting his subjective and potentially erroneous assessment of the situation.[24]

[23] See Karl Lachmann, *Kleinere Schriften* (1876), I, 488; Wapnewski, *Wolframs "Parzival,"* 171, and most recent commentators. On the deficiencies of this assumption, see Bumke, *Forschung*, 169, and Kratz, *Wolfram's "Parzival,"* 404 and 539.

[24] Many commentators have observed that the hermit's initial uncertainty on Good Friday (471.23–25) echoes an earlier statement by Flegetanis (454.21–26). Flegetanis, the fictitious narrative source, and Trevrizent, the fictional narrator, share a similar uncertainty concerning the fate of the unspecified "host" and the neutral angels, an uncertainty that intimates the preliminary nature of their statements about a process that is still incomplete or lies beyond their comprehension. See Bumke, *Forschung*, 267; A. T. Hatto, "'Ine weiz': Diplomatic Ignorance on the Part of Medieval German Poets" (1952), 107; and Schirok, "Trevrizents Widerruf," 59–61.

II

These irreducible discrepancies between Trevrizent's statements in Book IX and his "Retraction" in Book XVI suggest the necessity of differentiating between an author's or narrator's representation and a fictional character's interpretation of events within it. Whether we accept this differentiation depends in large measure on our own—often unstated—interests in the text. Wapnewski's interpretation is devoted to rescuing Wolfram's consistency as an author, and Schirok's focuses on rescuing Trevrizent's credibility as a character. But we do not have to rescue either in a narrative that constructs neither the author nor his characters as centers of authority—a possibility always present in novelistic discourse. Instead, Wolfram uses Trevrizent's "Retraction" to illustrate a larger problem: the limitation of human understanding in reconciling the ways of God to man. Although he can both read scripture, "der wâren buoche mære" (462.12), and interpret Parzival's career, Trevrizent ultimately fails in understanding the relationship between God's plan of salvation and Parzival's quest at the end of the narrative.

In this respect, it is essential to note that Trevrizent's final testament in Book XVI actually consists of *two* statements. The first, beginning with an indefinite introduction, "dô sprach er," dilates in a general way on the mysterious workings of God's providence:

> dô sprach er "got vil tougen hât.
> wer gesaz ie an sînen rât,
> ode wer weiz ende sîner kraft?
> al die engel mit ir gesellesehaft
> bevindentz nimmer an den ort.
> got ist mensch unt sîns vater wort,
> got ist vater unde suon,
> sîn geist mac grôze helfe tuon."
> (797.23–30)

He spoke: "God has many secrets. For who has ever sat at his council, or knows the end of his power? All the angelic host shall never find its limit. God is man and his father's word; God is father and son; his spirit can lend great aid."

The second statement, beginning with the more specific identification of speaker and listener, "Trevrizent ze Parzivâle sprach" (798.1), introduces the actual "Retraction." In keeping with his interpretation, Wapnewski argues that the double introduction is yet another indication of the interpolative nature of the "Retraction."[25] One might consider, however, whether this doubling has a different function. The differentiation of these two incipits suggests that we view them as introducing two types of discourse that may form part of a larger relationship—a general religious truth and an individual interpretation of it directed at a particular recipient—and consider the implications of juxtaposing divine and human discourse, transcendent truth and subjective interpretation.

Scholars who have dealt with section 797.23–30 have usually been content to observe that the passage has a biblical flavor.[26] One line in particular, "wer gesaz ie an sînen rât?" (797.24), has been associated either with Jeremiah 23.18 ("For who hath stood in the counsel of the Lord, and hath seen and heard his word?") or with Romans 11.33–36. In fact, the latter passage closely approximates this one line as well as the context of Trevrizent's entire exclamation:[27]

> 11.33 O the depth of the riches of the wisdom and of the knowledge of God! How incomprehensible are his judgments, and how unsearchable his ways!
>
> 34 For who hath known the mind of the Lord? Or who hath been his counsellor?
>
> 35 Or who hath first given to him, and recompense shall be made him?
>
> 36 For of him, and by him, and in him, are all things: to him be glory for ever. Amen.

Medieval commentaries on Romans 11 bear an even closer resemblance to Trevrizent's paraphrase.[28] Verse 33 is summarized in interlinear glosses as an expression of the many "occulta" or "secreta" of God's providence, which is Trevrizent's "God has many secrets" (797.23). Verse 34 is expanded to exclude even the angels: "ex angelis nullus ei fuit consiliarius." As Trevrizent affirms, "For who has ever sat at his council / or knows the end of his power? / All the angelic host shall never find its limit"

[25] *Wolframs "Parzival,"* 169–71. But see the counterargument of Kratz, *Wolfram's "Parzival,"* 539.

[26] Benedikt Mockenhaupt, *Die Frömmigkeit im "Parzival" Wolframs von Eschenbach* (1942; rpt. 1968), 187.

[27] An identification with Jeremiah is made by the commentaries of Martin, 520, and Bartsch-Marti, 172; Wapnewski, *Wolframs "Parzival,"* 170; with Romans by Anton Sattler, *Die religiösen Anschauungen Wolframs von Eschenbach* (1895), 20; Weber, *Parzival,* 78; Bodo Mergell, "Der Gral in Wolframs *Parzival*" (1951), 70.

[28] The following citations are taken from the *Biblia Sacra cum Glossa ordinaria* (1617), VI, cols. 151–54, and the *Magna glossatura* of Peter Lombard, *PL* 191.1492. For the patristic sources of the individual elements discussed below, see Karl Hermann Schelkle, *Paulus: Lehrer der Väter* (1956), 406–11.

(797.24–27). Verse 35, which seems to be missing, will be discussed with reference to the ensuing "Retraction" in a moment. The doxological conclusion in verse 36 is interpreted on the basis of the three prepositions "of," "by," and "in" (*ex, per, in*) with the singular reflexive pronoun "him" (*ipse*) as an expression of the Trinity:

> *Quoniam* potius *omnia sunt ex ipso* Patre, *ex* quo Filius est; *et per ipsum,* Filium, per quem omnia facta sunt; *et in ipso,* Spiritu sancto, quia sola dilectione creavit et conservit omnia. Ecce Trinitas personarum hic ostenditur, et essentiae unitas.
>
> *For all things are of him,* or rather, of the Father, *from* whom is the Son; *and by him,* the Son, by whom all things are made; *and in him,* the Holy Spirit, because it created and preserves all things by its love alone. Here is shown the Trinity of the persons, but the unity of its being.

Again, as Trevrizent observes, "God is man and his father's word; / God is father and son; / his spirit can lend great aid" (797.28–30).

Trevrizent's entire exclamation in 797.23–30 thus appears to be not only a precise biblical paraphrase but one with a remarkable background in medieval exegesis. The three elements taken from this tradition have a lengthy history. The gloss on verse 33 as "many secrets" cannot be any later than St. Augustine,[29] the exclusion of "all the angels" from knowledge of God's wisdom in verse 34 seems to derive from Augustine and Haymo of Auxerre,[30] and the Trinitarian expansion of verse 36 goes back to the Greek fathers, finding its most seminal versions in texts by St. Ambrose and especially St. Augustine.[31] But all three expansions of the bibli-

[29] See Augustine, *De gratia et libero arbitrio,* cap. 22f., Pseudo-Augustine, *Quaestiones Veteris et Novi Testamenti* 125; Gregory the Great, *Moralia in Iob* XXIX.56; *Glossa ordinaria* VI,153; Abelard, *PL* 178.937; and esp. Hervaeus of Déols, *PL* 181.761f.

[30] The exclusion of all *creatura* goes back at least as far as Origen (*PG* 14.1201f.) and is widespread thereafter (see the sources in Schelkle, *Paulus*). The mention of angels is initially indirect and then explicit: Augustine, *De Genesi ad litteram* II.8; Haymo of Auxerre, *PL* 117.467; *Glossa ordinaria* VI,153; Hervaeus of Déols, *PL* 181.762; Peter Lombard, *PL* 191.1492.

[31] In addition to the works cited in Schelkle, *Paulus,* see Ambrose, *De spiritu sancto* II.9 and *De fide* IV.11; Augustine, *De doctrina christiana* I.5, *De vera religione* lv.113, *Enarrationes in Psalmos* V.3, *De Trinitate* VI.x.12; Gregory the Great, *Moralia in Iob* XXIX.69f.; Pseudo-Ambrose, *PL* 17.512; Pseudo-Augustine, *PL* 42.799f. In commentaries on Romans 11: Cassiodorus, *PL* 70.1329; Sedulius Scotus, *PL* 103.109; Hrabanus Maurus, *PL* 111.1540; Haymo of Auxerre, *PL* 117.468; Bruno the Carthusian, *PL* 153, 99; Hugh of St. Victor, *PL* 175.500; Hervaeus of Déols, *PL* 181.763; *Glossa ordinaria* VI, 153; Peter Lombard, *PL* 191.1492. The Trinitarian expansion of verse 36 not infrequently includes mention of the emanation of the Son as *processio verbi* or "sîns vater wort": Irenaeus, *PG* 7.1121; Origen, *PG* 11.1398; Jerome, *PL* 30.700; Augustine, *PL* 34.172; Haymo of Auxerre, *PL* 117.468; and Peter Lombard, *PL* 191.1494.

cal text begin to be included in commentaries on Romans in the form cited here during the course of the twelfth century. The *Glossa ordinaria* and the *Magna glossatura* of Peter Lombard, the most important school texts for the twelfth century, come closest in wording to the Middle High German passage and are the most likely proximate "sources." Wolfram clearly allows Trevrizent to know Romans 11, and he knows it very well.

Because there appears to be a chronological progression in Wolfram's narrative from Good Friday in Book IX to Pentecost in Book XV, some scholars have postulated that the following Sunday, now the Feast of the Trinity, provides an appropriate liturgical background for the events of Book XVI.[32] Unfortunately, Trinity Sunday was not celebrated in Mainz or Thuringia until the second half of the thirteenth century and became officially recognized by Pope John XXII only in 1334.[33] However, there is also a popular votive mass of the Trinity, attributed to Alcuin, which was celebrated on vacant Sundays between Pentecost and Advent and influenced the development of Trinity Sunday. The feast and the votive mass share an introit derived from Tobias 12.6 ("Blessed be the holy Trinity, and undivided Unity: we will give glory to it because he has showed his mercy to us"), which might be associated with Parzival's invocation of the Trinity before healing Anfortas (795.25ff.).[34] Moreover, the feast and votive mass also share the same Epistle and Gospel readings on occasion. The passage from Romans 11.33–36 that Trevrizent so accurately paraphrases—now the Epistle text for Trinity Sunday—was used early on as one of several readings in the votive mass. The events surrounding Feirefiz's baptism, after which he can see the Grail (which "almost equaled what one says of the kingdom of heaven" [238.23f.]), echoes a Gospel text shared by the votive mass, the octave of Pentecost, and Trinity Sunday (John 3.1–15), which stipulates that no one shall see the kingdom of heaven unless he be born again in baptism.

Given the uncertain development of the liturgy in early thirteenth-century Germany, it will suffice to note that although Trevrizent can read Holy Scripture (462.12), he does not need to consult his Bible, since the

[32] Bumke, *Forschung*, 261, and Mergell, "Der Gral," 70.

[33] On the origins of this feast, see Peter Browe, "Zur Geschichte des Dreifaltigkeitsfestes" (1950), esp. 77–78 for Germany, and the major liturgical handbooks for the twelfth and thirteenth centuries: Rupert of Deutz, *De divinis officiis*, CC:CM 7.395f.; Honorius of Autun, *Gemma animae*, *PL* 172.703; Johannes Beleth, *Explicatio divinorum officiorum*, CC:CM 41A, 111 and 258–60; Sicard of Cremona, *Mitrale*, *PL* 213.385–87; Praepositinus of Cremona, *Tractatus de officiis* (1969), 214–15; Gulielmus Durandus, *Rationale divinorum officiorum* VI.114 (1576), fol. 267^{v}– 268^{v}.

[34] See Walter Howard Frere, *Studies in the Early Roman Liturgy* (London, 1930–35), II, 14, 43, and 63–64, and III, 64 and 68; Paul Pietsch, *Evangely und Epistel Teutsch* (1927), 69; and Karl Stejksal, "Altdeutsches Epistel- und Evangelienbuch III" (1883), 17–18.

Epistle text for the celebration of the "secret council of God's mysteries," or "vil haimlicher rat der gotes tougen,"[35] is obviously very much on his mind when he meets Parzival for the last time in the romance. Along with the preceding verse, "for God hath concluded all in unbelief, that he may have mercy on all," in terms of which it is often interpreted, Romans 11.33–36 provides Wolfram with the perfect expression of Trevrizent's amazement at Parzival's unexpected redemption, again embedding the text in an extensive background associating Parzival's career with the progress of salvation history as it is celebrated during the liturgical year.

The implications of this same text for Trevrizent, however, are rather different. The relationship between his biblical paraphrase and the stance of the "Retraction," unlike that between an Epistle text and a sermon based on it (to take the most analogous situation), is incongruous at the very least. The point of Romans 11.33–36 and its exegetical tradition is clear:[36] God reconciles himself with man in inscrutable ways, and not even angels, let alone the wisest of men, can presume to understand the workings of his providence. The fact that Trevrizent nonetheless immediately proceeds from this encomium of God's mysteries to such an unsatisfactory explanation of them in his "Retraction" is the perfect exemplification of this truth, albeit an ironic one—of which the hermit is not aware.

An attentive audience, however, cannot and should not overlook the disjuncture between the biblical paraphrase and the "Retraction." Indeed, the controversial elements of the "Retraction" contradict not only statements in Book IX but also other elements of the immediately preceding biblical paraphrase. In contrast to his statements on Good Friday, where he stated that one could force nothing from God with angry defiance (463.1), and in contrast to the traditional sense of Romans 11.35 that God's grace is a gift freely given and not compelled by human merit, which Trevrizent's paraphrase rather strikingly omits, we now find the hermit insisting that Parzival has actually forced his success with defiance and has wrested the Grail from the Trinity whose unfathomable workings he has just praised as being inscrutable, even to angels. With these blatant contradictions, not to mention the irreducible confusion over the neutral angels, Wolfram underscores the fact that even the learned Trevrizent has only limited mastery of a complex course of events he has profoundly influenced but is not destined to understand completely.

[35] "Von der drivaltekait," in *Altdeutsche Predigten*, ed. Anton E. Schönbach, III (1891; rpt. 1964), 116.

[36] Augustine's frequent use of "O altitudo" made this text a commonplace reference. See John M. Rist, "Augustine on Free Will and Predestination" (1969), esp. 240–41.

III

Trevrizent's comments do not deny the authority of Scripture, but the disjunction between the biblical exegesis of Romans 11.33–36 and his application of it in the "Retraction" nonetheless problematizes or even defers the intelligibility of that authority. Whether we should read this as a pro- or anticlerical tactic on Wolfram's part, limiting the ability to interpret the Bible to the clergy or denying it altogether, is unclear. But it does seem that the displacement of divine authority and the concomitant deferral of meaning comprise a far-reaching move in terms of Wolfram's narrative, decentering divine discourse and thereby creating space for human heteroglossia.[37]

For Trevrizent is not the only figure in the final episodes who misunderstands the complex course of Parzival's quest by reducing the process to one of its constituent elements. Immediately after Cundrie's announcement emphasizes the double nature of Parzival's success (782.29f.), the hero himself paraphrases Trevrizent's statement of the conditions for winning the Grail, again drawing attention to the interaction of merit and grace, fighting and being called:

> en franzoys er zin allen sprach
> als Trevrizent dort vorne jach,
> daz den grâl ze keinen zîten
> niemen möht erstrîten,
> "wan der von gote ist dar benant."
> (786.3–7)

In French he told all of them, as Trevrizent said above, that no one could ever win the Grail by fighting, "except one who is called to it by God."

The response of the court, however, is a reduction of this dialogue to a single element, being called, to which the narrator wryly attributes the continued isolation of the Grail:[38]

> daz mære kom übr elliu lant:
> kein strît möht in erwerben.
> vil liut liez dô verderben

[37] On the problem of including an authoritative language such as Scripture in novelistic discourse, see Gary Saul Morson and Caryl Emerson, *Mikhail Bakhtin: The Creation of a Prosaics* (1990), 314.

[38] My punctuation. The "daz" in 786.8 can introduce the following statement as well as refer to the preceding one. In the latter case, one would more likely use *diz*—as did the scribe of MS D, whose reading was adopted in Leitzmann's edition.

nâch dem grâle gewerbes list,
dâ von er noch verborgen ist.
(786.8–12)

The story circulated in all lands: no fighting could attain it. Many people then gave up seeking for the Grail, and as a result it still remains hidden.

Ironically, the pacifist Trevrizent imputes Parzival's success to chivalric adventure, whereas the adventurous court denies its efficacy. It would seem, then, that the Grail quest is open to a heteroglot variety of interpretations by observers within the narrative.

Indeed, even the narrator has difficulties maintaining control over that quest in the face of the miraculous events that invade his text. Between the beginning of Book XV and the concluding lines of the narrative, two similar statements even seem to register a shift from his mastery of the narrative to a recognition of its unfinalizability. Assuming the role of the domineering supernarrator familiar from the prologue and subsequent asides, he begins a move toward closure with a new "prologue" to Book XV (734.1–16), assuring the audience that he bears in his mouth the key to the *âventiure*'s conclusion (734.6f.) and promising that Parzival will bring it about, provided his artistry does not fail, "Parzivâl daz wirbet, / ob mîn kunst niht verdirbet" (734.15f.). Minimizing the danger of the impending battle between the hero and Feirefiz, he grounds that artistry in an outcome already worked out in his mind, citing the familiar double motif of the Grail and Condwiramurs as elements that will resolve the encounter:

ich sorge des den ich hân brâht,
wan daz ich trôstes hân gedâht,
in süle des grâles kraft ernern.
in sol ouch diu minne wern.
(737.25–27)

I am concerned for the one I have brought here, except that I have conceived of a solution: the power of the Grail shall save him. Love will also protect him. (My emphasis)

As the battle progresses, however, the narrator seems to lose control of his narrative and be controlled by it instead, first invoking the assistance of the Grail and Condwiramurs that he vaunted as examples of his mastery,

dirre strît müez im erwerben
vors heidens hant ein sterben.
daz wende, tugenthafter grâl:
Condwîr âmûrs diu lieht gemâl.
(740.17–20)

> This battle will win him death by the heathen's hand. Prevent it, noble Grail and fair Condwiramurs!

then—as that fails—imploring Parzival to master the crisis (742.27, 743.14). God himself ultimately terminates the battle between the two half-brothers, forcing the narrator to assume the role of a bystander within a larger narrative, passively bearing witness to the miracle of divine intervention, and ending with a prayer:

ez ist noch ungescheiden,
zurteile stêtz in beiden
vor der hôhsten hende:
daz diu ir sterben wende!
(744.21–24)

> It is still unresolved, since both stand in judgement before the hand of the Highest. May it prevent their death!

As if to emphasize the distinction between human narrative and salvation history in the epilogue, the narrator recalls his comments from the beginning of Book XV, using the identical rhyme and phrasing in the epilogue to admit that his efforts have succeeded because providence also intended the hero's career to be concluded:

sîniu kint, sîn hôch geslehte
hân ich iu benennet rehte,
Parzivâls, den ich hân brâht
dar sîn doch sælde het erdâht.
(827.15–18)

> I have correctly named to you the children, the high lineage of *Parzival, whom I have brought to the place which, nonetheless, providence had conceived for him.* (My emphasis)

A variety of possibilities lurk behind the intrusive "doch," or "nonetheless." One is certainly the implication that the human narrator and divine providence have cadenced in spite of the gap that separates them. The narrator, like Trevrizent, is unable to anticipate the workings of divine providence, although he can, by consent of that higher power, function in harmony with it.

Trevrizent's "Retraction," the court's misunderstanding of the Grail quest, and finally the narrator's impotence vis-à-vis the divine author would seem illogical in terms of a unified and undifferentiated authorial style that imbues its characters with omniscient uniformity. Unfortunately, we cannot delete the narrator any more than we can delete the court or Trevrizent's "Retraction." Novelistic discourse needs to be measured not in terms of a unifying consistency—the hobgoblin of philological minds—but in terms that include the potential of characters to change and even contradict themselves, to express the messiness and unfinalizability of human existence. These "inconsistencies," in other words, draw attention to the fact that Trevrizent, the court, and even the narrator are part of a process of striving for wisdom and redemption in which all human beings participate but ultimately never control.

With these decentering gestures of closure, Wolfram's narrative, to borrow one of Bakhtin's favorite metaphors, seems to leave a "Ptolemaic" world of unitary, authorial discourse behind. Of course, I do not think that *Parzival* attains the "Galilean" world of completely decentered discourse that Bakhtin's metaphor reserves for novels in a narrower modern sense, nor am I sure that it is, to narrow the metaphor, even entirely "Copernican." But searching for some additional detail about the neutral angels to rescue Trevrizent's consistency, like adding epicycles to the geocentric model of the universe in order to "save the appearances," may ultimately be less fruitful than simply changing our own perspective and preconceptions of "medieval" versus "modern" narrative. We miss a major difference between *Parzival* and other Middle High German romance narratives—and many as yet undiscovered similarities—by not acknowledging its extensive realization of the pluralistic potential inherent in novelistic discourse. Wolfram's text speaks to us not in a single voice, but in a diapason of voices. Not the least of its achievements is the discursive multiplicity that intimates the vigor of an emerging secular culture, and confirms the medievalness of our own modernity.

Works Cited

PRIMARY SOURCES

Alain de Lille. *Anticlaudianus*. Ed. Robert Bossuat. Textes philosophiques du Moyen Age 1. Paris, 1955.

Albertus Magnus. *De animalibus*. Ed. Hermann Stadler. Beiträge zur Geschichte der Philosophie des Mittelalters, 15–16. Münster, 1916–21.

——. *Book of Minerals*. Trans. Dorothy Wyckoff. Oxford, 1967.

——. *De caelo et mundo*. Ed. Paul Hossfeld. Münster, 1971.

——. *De natura loci, De causis proprietatum elementorum, De generatione et corruptione*. Ed. Paul Hossfeld. Münster, 1980.

——. *Opera omnia*. Ed. Petrus Iammy. 21 vols. Lyon, 1651.

Albohazen Haly [Abū al-Ḥasan ʿAli]. *Liber in iudiciis astrorum*. Venice, 1485.

Albumashar [Abū Maʿshar]. *De magnis coniunctionibus*. Venice, 1515.

——. *De magnis coniunctionibus, annorum revolutionibus ac eorum profectionibus*. Venice, 1489.

Alchabitus [al-Qabīṣī]. *Alchabitus cum commento noviter impresso*. Venice, 1512.

Alexander Neckam. *De naturis rerum*. Ed. Thomas Wright. Rolls Series 34. London, 1863.

Alexandri Magni Iter ad Paradisum. Ed. Julius Zacher. Königsberg, 1859.

Alomar. "De cauda draconis." In *Liber novem judicum in judiciis astrorum*. Venice, 1509.

Analecta sacra et classica Spicilegio Solesmensi parata. Ed. Jean Baptiste Pitra. 8 vols. Paris, 1876–91.

Anglo-Norman Lapidaries. Ed. Paul Studer and Joan Evans. Paris, 1924.

Antidotarium Nicolai. Eene middelnederlandsche Vertaling van het Antidotarium Nicolai. Ed. Wouter S. van den Berg. Leiden, 1917.

Pseudo-Apuleius. *Herbarius*. In *Antonii Musae De herba vettonica liber, Pseudoapulei Herbarius, Anonymi De taxone liber, Sexti Placiti Liber medicinae ex animalibus etc.* Ed. Ernst Howald and Henry E. Sigerist. Corpus medicorum latinorum 4. Leipzig, 1927.

Aquinas, Thomas. *Opera omnia*. Ed. Stanislaus Fretté and Paul Maré. 34 vols. Paris, 1874–89.

Pseudo-Aristotle. *Das Steinbuch des Aristoteles.* Ed. Julius Ruska. Heidelberg, 1912.

Arnulf of Orleans. *Glosule super Lucanum.* Ed. Berthe M. Marti. Papers and Monographs of the American Academy in Rome 18. Rome, 1958.

Augustine, Saint. *De trinitate libri XV.* Ed. W. J. Mountain. 2 vols. CCSL 50–50a. Turnholt, 1968.

Avicenna [Ibn Sīna]. *Avicennae Liber Canonis.* Venice, 1582.

Bacon, Roger. *Quaestiones super undecimum Prime philosophie Aristotelis.* Ed. Robert Steele. Oxford, 1926.

Bartholomaeus Anglicus. *De rerum proprietatibus.* 1601. Rpt., Frankfurt am Main, 1964.

al-Battani. *Opus astronomicum.* Ed. Carlo Alfonso Nallino. 2 vols. 1903. Rpt., Frankfurt am Main, 1969.

Bede. "De schematibus et tropis." In *Rhetores latini minores,* ed. Karl Halm. Leipzig, 1863.

——. *De temporibus liber.* In *Bedae Opera de temporibus,* ed. Charles W. Jones. Medieval Academy of America Publications 41. Cambridge, Mass., 1943.

Bernard Silvestris. *Cosmographia.* Ed. Peter Dronke. Leiden, 1978.

——. *The "Cosmographia" of Bernardus Silvestris.* Trans. Winthrop Wetherbee. New York, 1973.

Berthold of Regensburg. *Predigten.* Ed. Franz Pfeiffer. 2 vols. 1862–80. Rpt., Berlin, 1965.

Biblia Sacra cum Glossa ordinaria. 6 vols. Douai, 1617.

Boec van medicinen in dietsche: Een middelnederlandse compilatie van medisch-farmaceutische literatuur. Ed. W. H. Daems. Janus Supplement 7. Leiden, 1967.

Boethius, Anicius Manlius Severinus. *Philosophiae consolatio.* Ed. Ludwig Bieler. CSEL 94. Turnholt, 1957.

Brunetto Latini. *Li Livres dou Trésor.* Ed. Francis J. Carmody. University of California Publications in Modern Philology 22. Berkeley, 1948.

Chrétien de Troyes. *Christian von Troyes sämtliche erhaltene Werke.* Ed. Wendelin Förster and Alfons Hilka. 5 vols. Halle, 1884–1932.

Circa instans. Ed. Hans Wölfel. *Das Arzneidrogenbuch "Circa instans" in einer Fassung des XIII. Jahrhunderts aus der Universitätsbibliothek Erlangen.* Med. diss., Berlin, 1939.

Constantinus Africanus. *Constantini Africani Opera omnia.* Basel, 1536.

——. *Opera reliqua.* Basel, 1539.

Corpus christianorum: Continuatio medievalis. Turnholt, 1964–.

Corpus christianorum: Series latina. Turnholt, 1954–.

Corpus scriptorum ecclesiasticorum latinorum. Vienna, 1866–.

Cyranides. In *Textes latins et vieux français relatifs aux Cyranides,* ed. Louis Delatte. Bibliothèque de la Faculté de Philosophie et Lettres de l'Université de Liège 93. Liège, 1942.

Diemer, Josef, ed. *Deutsche Gedichte des elften und zwölften Jahrhunderts.* 1849. Rpt., Darmstadt, 1968.

Dioscorides. *Arzneimittellehre.* Trans. Julius Berendes. Stuttgart, 1902.

Durandus, Gulielmus. *Rationale divinorum officiorum.* Venice, 1568.

Eilhart von Oberge. *Tristrant.* Ed. Hadumod Bussmann. ATB 70. Tübingen, 1969.

——. *Tristrant.* Ed. Franz Lichtenstein. QF 19. Straßburg, 1877.
Eneas: Roman du XIIe siècle. Ed. Jacques J. Salverda de Grave. 2 vols. Paris, 1925–29.
Ibn Ezra, Abraham ben Meīr. *El libro de los fundamentos de las tablas astronómicas.* Ed. José Millás Vallicrosa. Madrid, 1947.
Faral, Edmond, ed. *Les Arts poétiques du XIIe et du XIIIe siècle.* 1923. Rpt., Paris, 1962.
Friedrich II. *Die "Konstitutionen" Friedrichs II. von Hohenstaufen für sein Königreich Sizilien.* Ed. and trans. Hermann Conrad, Thea von der Lieck-Buyken, and Wolfgang Wagner. Cologne, 1973.
Galenus, Claudius. *Opera omnia.* Trans. Carolus Gottlob Kühn. 20 vols. Leipzig, 1821–33.
Gergis. "De cursu Draconis per Zodiacum." In *Liber de astronomiae disciplinae peritia,* ed. Mstislav Sangin. *Catalogus codicum astrologorum graecorum* 12. Brussels, 1936.
Gottfried of St. Victor. *Fons philosophiae.* Ed. Pierre Michaud-Quantin. Namur, 1956.
Gottfried of Viterbo. *Pantheon.* In *Rerum Germanicarum scriptores* I, ed. Johannes Pistorius. Ratisbone, 1726.
Gottfried von Straßurg. *Tristan.* Ed. Peter Ganz. 2 vols. Deutsche Klassiker des Mittelalters 4. Wiesbaden, 1978.
——. *Tristan und Isold.* Ed. Friedrich Ranke. 9th ed. Zurich, 1964.
Graffunder, Paul, ed. "Daniels Traumdeutungen: Ein mittelalterliches Traumbuch in deutschen Versen." *ZfdA* 48 (1906–07), 507–31.
Gregory the Great, Saint. *S. Gregorii Magni Moralia in Iob.* Ed. Marcus Adriaen. 3 vols. CSEL 143. Turnholt, 1979–85.
——. *Morals on the Book of Job by S. Gregory the Great.* Oxford, 1844.
Guillaume de Conches. *Des Commentaires inédits de Guillaume de Conches et de Nicolas Triveth, sur la "Consolation de la Philosophie" de Boèce.* Ed. Charles Jourdain. Notices et extraits des manuscrits de la Bibliothèque Imperiale 20.2. Paris, 1862.
——. *Dialogus de substantiis physicis.* 1567. Rpt., Frankfurt am Main, 1967.
——. *Glosae super Platonem.* Ed. Edouard Jeauneau. Textes philosophiques du Moyen Age 13. Paris, 1965.
——. *De philosophia mundi. Un brano inedito della "Philosophia" di Guglielmo di Conches.* Ed. Carmelo Ottaviano. Naples, 1935.
Guillaume Le Clerc. *Der "Bestiare Divin" des Guillaume Le Clerc.* Ed. Max Friedrich Mann. Französische Studien 6.2. Heilbronn, 1888.
Hartmann von Aue. *Der arme Heinrich.* Ed. Hermann Paul. 13th ed. rev. Ludwig Wolff. ATB 3. Tübingen, 1966.
——. *Erec.* Ed. Albert Leitzmann. 3d ed. rev. Ludwig Wolff. ATB 39. Tübingen, 1963.
——. *Gregorius.* Ed. Hermann Paul. 11th ed. rev. Ludwig Wolff. ATB 2. Tübingen, 1966.
——. *Iwein.* Ed. G. F. Benecke and Karl Lachmann. 6th ed. rev. Ludwig Wolff. Berlin, 1962.
Heinrich von Veldeke. *Heinrich von Veldeke.* Ed. Ludwig Ettmüller. Dichtungen des deutschen Mittelalters 8. Leipzig, 1852.
——. *Henric van Veldeken: "Eneide" I: Einleitung, Text.* Ed. Gabriele Schieb and Theodor Frings. DTM 58. Berlin, 1964.

Heldris de Cornuälle. *Le Roman de Silence.* Ed. Lewis Thorpe. Cambridge, 1972.
Hermann of Carinthia. *De essentiis: A Critical Edition with Translation and Commentary.* Ed. Charles Burnett. Studien und Texte zur Geistesgeschichte des Mittelalters 15. Leiden, 1982.
Hermes Trismegistus. *Neue astrologische Texte des Hermes Trismegistus.* Ed. Wilhelm Gundel. Abhandlungen der Bayerischen Akademie der Wissenschaften. Philosophisch-historische Abteilung. NF 12. Munich, 1936.
Herrad of Hohenburg. *Hortus deliciarum.* Ed. Rosalie Green et al. Studies of the Warburg Institute 36. 2 vols. London, 1979.
Hildegard of Bingen. *Causae et curae.* Ed. Paul Kaiser. Leipzig, 1903.
Honorius of Autun. *Imago mundi.* Ed. Valerie Flint. *AHDLMA* 49 (1982), 7–153.
——. *Summa gloria.* MGH: Libelli de lite 3. Hannover, 1897.
Isidore of Seville. *Etymologiae.* Ed. W. M. Lindsay. 1911. Rpt., Oxford, 1962.
Jacques de Vitry. *Sermones in Epistolas et Evangelia dominicalia totius anni.* Antwerp, 1575.
Jeitteles, Adalbert, ed. *Altdeutsche Predigten aus dem Benediktinerstifte St. Paul in Kärnten.* Innsbrück, 1878.
Johannes de Sacrobosco [John of Holywood]. *The "Sphere" of Sacrobosco and Its Commentators.* Ed. Lynn Thorndike. Chicago, 1949.
——. *Tractatus de sphera.* In *The "Sphere" of Sacrobosco and Its Commentators,* ed. Lynn Thorndike. Chicago, 1949.
Johannes Scotus Eriugena. *Annotationes in Marcianum.* Ed. Cora Lutz. Medieval Academy of America Publications 34. Cambridge, Mass., 1939.
Johannes Scotus Eriugena and Remigius of Auxerre. "Le Commentaire inédit de Jean Scot Erigène au mètre IX du livre III du *De consolatione Philosophiae* de Boèce." Ed. Hubert Silvestre. *Revue d'histoire ecclésiastique* 47 (1952), 58–64.
Pseudo-Johannes Scotus Eriugena [Erfurt Anonymous]. *Saeculi noni auctoris in Boetii "Consolationem Philosophiae" commentarius.* Ed. E. T. Silk. Papers and Monographs of the American Academy in Rome 9. Rome, 1935.
John of Salisbury. *Metalogicon.* Ed. Clement C. I. Webb. Oxford, 1929.
John of Spain. *Epitome totius astrologiae.* Nuremberg, 1548.
Die "Kaiserchronik" eines Regensburger Geistlichen. Ed. Eduard Schröder. MGH: Deutsche Chroniken 1. 1892. Rpt., Berlin, 1964.
Konrad von Megenberg. *Das Buch der Natur.* Ed. Franz Pfeiffer. Stuttgart, 1861.
——. *Die Deutsche Sphaera.* Ed. Francis Brévart. ATB 90. Tübingen, 1980.
Lamprecht. *Alexander.* Ed. Karl Kinzel. Germanistische Handbibliothek 6. Halle, 1884.
Leyser, Hermann, ed. *Deutsche Predigten des XIII. und XIV. Jahrhunderts.* Bibliothek der gesammten deutschen National-Literatur 11.2. Quedlinburg, 1838.
Liber de plenitudine. Paris, 1528.
Lucidarius. Ed. Felix Heidlauf. DTM 28. Berlin, 1915.
Lucretius. *De rerum natura.* Ed. Cyril Bailey. 2d ed. Oxford, 1963.
[*Macer Floridus.*] *Herbarum varias qui vis cognoscere vires.* Grenoble, 1522.
Macrobius. *Commentarius in "Somnium Scipionis."* Ed. James Willis. Leipzig, 1970.
Malvenda, Thomas. *De Paradiso voluptatis.* Rome, 1605.

Map, Walter. *De nugis curialium.* Ed. and trans. M. R. James, rev. C. N. L. Brooke and R. A. B. Mynors. Oxford, 1983.

Martianus Capella. *De nuptiis Philologiae et Mercurii.* Ed. Adolf Dick. Rev. Jean Preaux. Stuttgart, 1978.

Mély, Fernand de, ed. *Les Lapidaires de l'Antiquité et du Moyen Age.* 3 vols. Paris, 1896–1902.

Messahala [Māshā' allāh]. *Messahalae antiqvissimi ac lavdatissimi inter Arabes Astrologi, Libri tres.* Nuremberg, 1549.

Mesue [Yūḥannā n. Māsawayh]. *De re medica.* Paris, 1544.

——. *Vniversa opera.* Venice, 1479.

Le Mystère d'Adam. An Anglo-Norman Drama of the Twelfth Century. Ed. Paul Studer. 1918. Rpt., Manchester, 1962.

Notker. *Notker des Deutschen Werke I: Boethius De consolatione Philosophiae.* Ed. E. H. Sehrt and Taylor Starck. 3 vols. ATB 32. Halle, 1933–34.

Patrologia Latina. Patrologiae cursus completus, sive Biblioteca universalis, Series Latina. Ed. J.-P. Migne. 221 vols. Paris, 1844–64.

Peterborough Lapidary. Ed. Joan Evans and Mary S. Serjeantson. *English Medieval Lapidaries.* Early English Text Society, o.s. 190. Oxford, 1933.

Petrus Alfonsus. *De dracone.* In José Millás Vallicrosa, "La aportación astronómica de Pedro Alfonso." *Sefarad* 3 (1943), 87–97.

Physiologus latinus versio Y. Ed. Francis J. Carmody. University of California Publications in Classical Philology 12.7. Berkeley, 1941.

Picatrix: The Latin Version of the "Ghāyat al-ḥakīm." Ed. David Pingree. Studies of the Warburg Institute 39. London, 1986.

Plato. *Laws.* Trans. R. G. Bury. Loeb Classical Library. 2 vols. London, 1926.

——. *Timaeus.* Trans. R. G. Bury. Loeb Classical Library. London, 1925.

——. *"Timaeus" a Calcidio translatus commentarioque instructus.* Corpus Platonicum medii aevi 4. Ed. J. H. Waszink. London, 1962.

Pliny. *Naturalis historia.* Ed. Ludwig Ian and Carl Mayhoff. 1906. Rpt., Stuttgart, 1967.

Praepositinus of Cremona. *Tractatus de officiis.* Ed. James A. Corbett. Notre Dame, Ind., 1969.

Radulphus de Longo Campo. *In "Anticlaudianum" Alani commentum.* Ed. Jan Sulowski. Warsaw, 1972.

Remigius of Auxerre. *Commentum in Martianum Capellam.* Ed. Cora E. Lutz. 2 vols. Leiden, 1962–65.

Roger Frugardi of Salerno. *Chirurgia.* Ed. Karl Sudhoff. *Beiträge zur Geschichte der Chirurgie im Mittelalter.* Studien zur Geschichte der Medizin 11–12. Leipzig, 1918.

Salimbene of Parma. *Cronica Fratris Salimbene de Adam Ordinis Minorum.* Ed. Oswald Holder-Egger. MGH: SS. 32. Hannover, 1905–13.

Sanct Brandan: Ein lateinischer und drei deutsche Texte. Ed. Carl Schröder. Erlangen, 1871.

Schönbach, Anton E., ed. *Altdeutsche Predigten.* 3 vols. 1886–91. Rpt., Darmstadt, 1964.

Sies, Rudolf, ed. *Das "Pariser Pestgutachten" von 1348 in altfranzösischer Fassung.* WMF 7. Pattensen, 1977.

Silk, E. T., ed. *Saeculi noni auctoris in Boetii "Consolationem Philosophiae" commentarius.* Papers and Monographs of the American Academy in Rome 9. Rome, 1935.

Solinus. *Collectanea rerum memorabilium.* Ed. Theodor Mommsen. Berlin, 1864.

Somniale Danielis: An Edition of a Medieval Latin Dream Interpretation Handbook. Ed. Lawrence T. Martin. Europäische Hochschulschriften: Lateinische Sprache und Literatur 10. Frankfurt am Main, 1981.

Speculum ecclesiae, altdeutsch. Ed. Johannes Kelle. Munich, 1858.

Stejksal, Karl, ed. "Altdeutsches Epistel- und Evangelienbuch III." *ZfdPh* 15 (1883), 10–48.

Storms, Godfrid, ed. *Anglo-Saxon Magic.* The Hague, 1948.

Thomas of Cantimpré. *Liber de natura rerum.* Ed. Helmut Boese. Berlin, 1973.

Thomasin von Zirclaria. *Der wälsche gast.* Ed. Heinrich Rückert. 1852. Rpt., Berlin, 1965.

Vincent of Beauvais. *Speculum naturale.* 1624. Rpt., Graz, 1964.

Vita Heinrici IV. imperatoris. Ed. Georg Heinrich Pertz. MGH: Scriptores rerum Germanicarum 58. Hannover, 1855.

Wackernagel, Wilhelm, ed. *Altdeutsche Predigten und Gebete aus Handschriften.* Basel, 1876.

Walther von der Vogelweide. *Gedichte.* Ed. Karl Lachmann, rev. Carl von Kraus and Hugo Kuhn. 13th ed. Berlin, 1965.

"Weingartner Predigten." Ed. Anton E. Schönbach. *ZfdA* 28 (1884), 1–20.

Wiener Genesis. Die frühmittelhochdeutsche "Wiener Genesis." Ed. Kathryn Smits. PSQ 59. Berlin, 1972.

Wilhelm, Friedrich, ed. *Denkmäler deutscher Prosa des 11. und 12. Jahrhunderts.* 2 vols. 1914–18. Rpt., Munich, 1960.

Wirnt von Grafenberg. *Wigalois der Ritter mit dem Rade.* Ed. J. M. N. Kapteyn. Rheinische Beiträge und Hülfsbücher zur germanischen Philologie 9. Bonn, 1926.

Wolfram von Eschenbach. *Wolfram von Eschenbach.* Ed. Karl Lachmann. 6th rev. ed. Eduard Hartl. 1926. Rpt., Berlin, 1965.

——. *Wolfram von Eschenbach.* Ed. Albert Leitzmann. 5 vols. ATB 12–16. Rev. ed. Tübingen, 1961–65.

——. *Wolfram von Eschenbach: "Parzival," "Titurel," "Tagelieder": Cgm 19 der Bayerischen Staatsbibliothek München.* Ed. Gerhard Augst, Otfrid Ehrismann, and Heinz Engels. Stuttgart, 1970.

——. *Wolframs von Eschenbach "Parzival" und "Titurel."* 4th rev. ed. Karl Bartsch and Marta Marti. Deutsche Klassiker des Mittelalters 9–11. Leipzig, 1927–1932.

SECONDARY LITERATURE

Ackerman, Robert W. "The Knighting Ceremonies in the Middle English Romances." *Speculum* 19 (1944), 285–313.

Alemparte, Jaime Ferreiro. "La Escuela de nigromancia de Toledo." *Anuario de estudios medievales* 13 (1983), 205–68.

Allers, Rudolf. "Microcosmus from Anaximandros to Paracelsus." *Traditio* 2 (1944), 319–407.

Altman, Charles. "Two Types of Opposition and the Structure of Latin Saints' Lives." *MH* 6 (1975), 1–11.

d'Alverny, Marie-Thérèse. "Translations and Translators." In *Renaissance and Renewal in the Twelfth Century*, ed. Robert L. Benson and Giles Constable, 421–62. Cambridge, Mass., 1982.

Arbesmann, Rudolph. "The Concept of 'Christus Medicus' in St. Augustine." *Traditio* 10 (1954), 1–28.

Assion, Peter. "Geistliche und weltliche Heilkunst in Konkurrenz." In *Bayerisches Jahrbuch für Volkskunde 1976/77*, 7–23. Volkach, 1978.

Bakhtin, Mikhail. *The Dialogic Imagination: Four Essays.* Trans. Caryl Emerson and Michael Holquist. Ed. Michael Holquist. Austin, Texas, 1981.

——. *Problems of Dostoevsky's Poetics.* Ed. and trans. Caryl Emerson. Theory and History of Literature 8. Minneapolis, 1984.

——. *Rabelais and His World.* Trans. Hélène Iswolsky. Cambridge, Mass., 1968.

——. *Speech Genres and Other Late Essays.* Trans. Vern W. McGee. Ed. Caryl Emerson and Michael Holquist. Austin, Texas, 1986.

Bartsch, Karl. "Die Eigennamen in Wolframs *Parzival* und *Titurel.*" *Germanistische Studien* 2 (1875), 114–59.

Bauer, Georg-Karl. *Sternkunde und Sterndeutung der Deutschen im 9.–14. Jahrhundert.* Berlin, 1937.

Bauer, Gerhard. "Parzival und die Minne." *Euphorion* 57 (1963), 67–96.

Bayer, Hans. "'guotiu wîp, hânt die sin' (*Parz.* 827.25): Wolfram von Eschenbach und der thüringische Landgrafenhof." *Euphorion* 74 (1980), 55–76.

Bertau, Karl. "Versuch über den späten Chrestien und die Anfänge Wolframs." In Ganz/Schröder, *Probleme mittelhochdeutscher Erzählformen*, 73–106. Rpt. in his *Wolfram von Eschenbach: Neun Versuche*, 24–59.

——. *Wolfram von Eschenbach: Neun Versuche über Subjektivität und Ursprünglichkeit in der Geschichte.* Munich, 1983.

Bischoff, Bernhard. *Mittelalterliche Studien: Ausgewählte Aufsätze zur Schriftkunde und Literaturgeschichte.* 3 vols. Stuttgart, 1966–69.

——. "The Study of Foreign Languages in the Middle Ages." *Speculum* 36 (1961), 209–24.

Blamires, David. *Characterization and Individuality in Wolfram's "Parzival."* Cambridge, 1966.

Blank, Walter. "Die positive Utopie des Grals." In *Sprache—Literatur—Kultur: Studien zu ihrer Geschichte im deutschen Süden und Westen. Wolfgang Kleiber zu seinem 60. Geburtstag gewidmet*, ed. Albrecht Greule and Uwe Ruberg, 337–53. Stuttgart, 1989.

——. "Der Zauberer Clinschor in Wolframs *Parzival.*" In Gärtner/Heinzle, *Studien zu Wolfram von Eschenbach*, 321–32.

Blumstein, Andree Kahn. "The Structure and Function of the Cundrie Episodes in Wolfram's *Parzival.*" *GQ* 51 (1978), 160–69.

Boll, Franz, Carl Bezold, and Wilhelm Gundel. *Sternglaube und Sterndeutung: Die Geschichte und das Wesen der Astrologie.* 5th ed. Darmstadt, 1966.

Bouché-Leclercq, Auguste. *L'Astrologie grecque.* Paris, 1899.

Brackert, Helmut. *Rudolf von Ems: Dichtung und Geschichte.* Heidelberg, 1968.

Brall, Helmut. "'diz vliegende bîspel': Zu Programmatik und kommunikativer Funktion des *Parzival*prologes." *Euphorion* 77 (1983), 1–39.

——. "Familie und Hofgesellschaft in Wolframs *Parzival.*" In Kaiser/Müller, *Höfische Literatur,* 541–82.

——. *Gralsuche und Adelsheil: Studien zu Wolframs "Parzival."* Heidelberg, 1983.

Brinkmann, Hennig. "Der Prolog im Mittelalter als literarische Erscheinung." *WW* 14 (1964), 236–41. Rpt. in his *Studien zur Geschichte der deutschen Sprache und Literatur,* 2: 79–105. Düsseldorf, 1966.

Broich, Ulrich, and Manfred Pfister. *Intertextualität.* Tübingen, 1985.

Broszinski, Harmut. *Kasseler Handschriftenschätze.* Kassel, 1985.

Browe, Peter. *Beiträge zur Sexualethik des Mittelalters.* Breslau, 1932.

——. "Zur Geschichte des Dreifaltigkeitsfests." *Archiv für Liturgiewissenschaft* 1 (1950), 65–81.

——. *Die Verehrung der Eucharistie im Mittelalter.* 1933. Rpt., Rome, 1967.

Brownlee, Kevin, and Marina Scordilis Brownlee, eds. *Romance: Generic Transformations from Chrétien de Troyes to Cervantes.* Hanover, 1985.

Brunel, Clovis. "Les Hanches du Roi Pêcheur (Chrétien de Troyes, *Perceval* 3513)." *Romania* 81 (1960), 37–41.

Brunner, Horst. "*Artus der wise höfsche man*: Zur immanenten Historizität der Ritterwelt im *Parzival* Wolframs von Eschenbach." In *Germanistik in Erlangen: Hundert Jahre nach der Gründung des Deutschen Seminars,* ed. Dietmar Peschel, 61–73. Erlangen, 1983.

——. "'Von Munsalvaesche wart gesant / der den der swane brahte': Überlegungen zur Gestaltung des Schlusses von Wolframs *Parzival.*" *GRM* 41 (1991), 369–84.

Buettner, Bonnie. "Gawan in Wolfram's Parzival." Ph.D. diss., Cornell University, 1984.

——. "The Good Friday Scene in Chrétien de Troyes' *Perceval.*" *Traditio* 36 (1980), 415–26.

Bumke, Joachim. *Courtly Culture: Literature and Society in the High Middle Ages.* Trans. Thomas Dunlap. Berkeley, 1991.

——. "Höfische Kultur: Versuch einer kritischen Bestandsaufnahme." *PBB* 114 (1992), 414–92.

——. *Mäzene im Mittelalter: Die Gönner und Auftraggeber der höfischen Literatur in Deutschland, 1150–1300.* Munich, 1979.

——. "Parzival und Feirefiz—Priester Johannes—Loherangrin: Der offene Schluß des *Parzival* von Wolfram von Eschenbach." *DVJS* 65 (1991), 236–64.

——. "Parzivals 'Schwertleite'." In *Taylor Starck Festschrift,* ed. Werner Betz, Evelyn S. Coleman, and Kenneth Northcott, 235–45. London, 1964.

——. *Studien zum Ritterbegriff im 12. und 13. Jahrhundert.* Beihefte zu Euphorion 1. Heidelberg, 1964.

——. "Die Utopie des Grals: Eine Gesellschaft ohne Liebe?" In *Literarische Utopie-Entwürfe,* ed. Hiltrud Gnüg, 70–79. Frankfurt am Main, 1982.

——. *Wolfram von Eschenbach.* SM 36. 6th ed. Stuttgart, 1991.

——. *Die Wolfram von Eschenbach Forschung seit 1945: Bericht und Bibliographie.* Munich, 1970.

——. *Wolframs "Willehalm": Studien zur Epenstruktur und zum Heiligkeitsbegriff der ausgehenden Blütezeit.* Heidelberg, 1959.

Burns, E. Jane. "Quest and Questioning in the *Conte du graal.*" *RPh* 41 (1988), 251–66.

Busby, Keith, *Gauvain in Old French Literature.* Amsterdam, 1980.
Carruthers, Mary. *The Book of Memory: A Study of Memory in Medieval Culture.* Cambridge, 1990.
Chenu, Marie-Dominique. *Nature, Man, and Society in the Twelfth Century.* Trans. Jerome Taylor and Lester K. Little. Chicago, 1968.
——. *La Théologie au douzième siècle.* Paris, 1957.
Clanchy, M. T. *From Memory to Written Record: England, 1066–1307.* 2d ed. Oxford, 1993.
Classen, Albrecht. "Keie in Wolframs von Eschenbach *Parzival*: 'Agent provocateur' oder Angeber?" *JEGP* 87 (1988), 382–405.
Colby, Alice. *The Portrait in Twelfth-Century French Literature: An Example of the Stylistic Originality of Chrétien de Troyes.* Geneva, 1965.
Cormeau, Christoph. *"Wigalois" und "Diu Crône": Zwei Kapitel zur Gattungsgeschichte des nachklassischen Aventiureromans.* MTU 57. Munich, 1977.
Crane, Susan. *Insular Romance: Politics, Faith, and Culture in Anglo-Norman and Middle English Literature.* Berkeley, 1986.
Curschmann, Michael. "Das Abenteuer des Erzählens: Über den Erzähler in Wolframs *Parzival.*" *DVJS* 45 (1971), 627–67.
——. "Hören—Lesen—Sehen: Buch und Schriftlichkeit im Selbstverständnis der volkssprachlichen literarischen Kultur Deutschlands um 1200." *PBB* (Tübingen) 106 (1984), 218–57.
Curtius, Ernst Robert. *European Literature and the Latin Middle Ages.* Trans. Willard Trask. New York, 1963.
Dallapiazza, Michael. "Häßlichkeit und Individualität: Ansätze zu einer Überwindung der Idealität des Schönen in Wolframs von Eschenbach *Parzival.*" *DVJS* 59 (1985), 400–421.
Daniélou, Jean. *The Bible and the Liturgy.* University of Notre Dame Liturgical Studies 3. Notre Dame, Ind., 1956.
——. "Terre et paradis chez les pères de l'église." *Eranos-Jahrbuch* 22 (1954), 433–72.
Deinert, Wilhelm. *Ritter und Kosmos im "Parzival": Eine Untersuchung der Sternkunde Wolframs von Eschenbach.* MTU 2. Munich, 1960.
Delabar, Walter. *"Erkantiu sippe unt hoch geselleschaft": Studien zur Funktion des Verwandschaftsverbandes in Wolframs von Eschenbach "Parzival."* GAG 518. Göppingen, 1990.
Delhaye, Philippe. *Le "Microcosmus" de Godefroy de St. Victor: Etude théologique.* Lille, 1951.
Dewald, Hans. *Minne und "sgrâles âventiur": Äußerungen der Subjektivität und ihre sprachliche Vergegenwärtigung in Wolframs "Parzival."* GAG 158. Göppingen, 1975.
Dod, Bernard G. "Aristoteles latinus." In *The Cambridge History of Later Medieval Philosophy, 1100–1600,* ed. Norman Kretzmann, Anthony Kenny, and Jan Pinborg, 45–79. Cambridge, 1982.
Dreyer, J. L. E. *A History of Astronomy from Thales to Kepler.* Rev. ed. New York, 1953.
Dubé, Waltraut F. "Medieval Medicine in Middle High German Epics." Ph.D. diss., Indiana University, 1981.
Duby, Georges. *The Chivalrous Society.* Trans. Cynthia Postan. Berkeley, 1977.

——. *The Knight, the Lady, and the Priest.* Trans. Barbara Bray. New York, 1983.
Duhem, Pierre. *Le Système du monde: Histoire des doctrines cosmologiques de Platon à Copernic.* 10 vols. Paris, 1913–65.
Eggers, Hans. "*Non cognovi litteraturam* (zu *Parzival* 115.27)." In *Festgabe für Ulrich Pretzel.* Berlin, 1963. Rpt. in Rupp, *Wolfram von Eschenbach,* 533–48.
Ehrismann, Gustav. "Duzen und Ihrzen im Mittelalter." *Zeitschrift für deutsche Wortforschung* 5 (1903/04), 127–220.
Einhorn, Jürgen W. *Spiritalis unicornis: Das Einhorn als Bedeutungsträger in Literatur und Kunst des Mittelalters.* MMS 13. Munich, 1976.
Elliott, Alison Goddard. *Roads to Paradise: Reading the Lives of the Early Saints.* Hanover, 1987.
Elliott, Dyan. *Spiritual Marriage: Sexual Abstinence in Medieval Wedlock.* Princeton, 1993.
Esser, Josef. *Die Schöpfungsgeschichte in der "Altdeutschen Genesis."* GAG 455. Göppingen, 1987.
Fichtenau, Heinrich. *Arenga: Spätantike und Mittelalter im Spiegel von Urkundenformeln.* Graz, 1957.
Fischer, Hermann. *Mittelalterliche Pflanzenkunde.* Munich, 1929.
Fleckenstein, Josef, ed. *Curialitas: Studien zu Grundfragen der höfisch-ritterlichen Kultur.* Göttingen, 1990.
——. "Miles und clericus am Königs- und Fürstenhof. Bemerkungen zu den Voraussetzungen, zur Entstehung und zur Trägerschaft der höfisch-ritterlichen Kultur." In Fleckenstein, *Curialitas,* 302–25.
Flint, Valerie J. "The Early Medieval 'Medicus,' the Saint—and the Enchanter." *Social History of Medicine* 2 (1989), 127–45.
Flori, Jean. "Pour une histoire de la chevalerie: L'adoubement dans les romans de Chrétien de Troyes." *Romania* 100 (1979), 21–53.
Fourquet, Jean. *Wolfram d'Eschenbach et le "Conte del Graal": Les divergences de la tradition du "Conte del Graal" de Chrétien et leur importance pour l'explication du texte du "Parzival."* Publications de la Faculté des Lettres et Sciences Humaines de Paris-Sorbonne. Série Etudes et méthodes 17. Paris, 1966.
Franz, Adolf. *Die Messe im deutschen Mittelalter.* Freiburg im Breisgau, 1902.
Freccero, John. "Dante's 'per se' Angel: The Middle Ground in Nature and Grace." *Studi danteschi* 39 (1962), 5–38.
Frere, Walter Howard. *Studies in the Early Roman Liturgy.* 3 vols. London, 1930–35.
Freytag, Hartmut. *Kommentar zur frühmittelhochdeutschen "Summa theologiae."* Medium Aevum 19. Munich, 1970.
——. "*Summa Theologiae,* Strophe 9 und 10: Der Mensch als Mikrokosmos." *Studien zur frühmittelhochdeutschen Literatur.* Ed. L. P. Johnson, H. H. Steinhoff, and R. A. Wisbey, 74–82. Berlin, 1974.
——. "'sun, des bewîse dich der / der dich nâch im gebildet hât': Bemerkungen zu Antonomasien in Hartmanns von Aue *Gregorius* und seinen lateinischen und volkssprachigen Bearbeitungen." In *Latein und Volkssprache im deutschen Mittelalter, 1100–1500,* ed. Nikolaus Henkel and Nigel Palmer, 142–57. Tübingen, 1992.
Fühner, Hermann. *Lithotherapie: Historische Studien über die medizinische Verwendung der Edelsteine.* Med. diss., Straßburg, 1902.

Ganshof, François L. "Qu'est-ce que la chevalerie?" *Revue générale belge* 27 (Nov. 1947), 77–86.
Ganz, Peter. "*curialis/hövesch.*" In Kaiser/Müller, *Höfische Literatur,* 39–55.
Ganz, Peter F., and Werner Schröder, eds. *Probleme mittelhochdeutscher Erzählformen.* Berlin, 1972.
Gärtner, Kurt, and Joachim Heinzle, eds. *Studien zu Wolfram von Eschenbach. Festschrift für Werner Schröder zum 75. Geburtstag.* Tübingen, 1989.
Geil, Gerhild. *Gottfried und Wolfram als literarische Antipoden: Zur Genese eines literaturgeschichtlichen Topos.* Cologne, 1973.
Gerhardt, Christoph. "Arznei und Symbol: Bemerkungen zum altdeutschen Geiertraktat mit einem Ausblick auf das Pelikanexempel." *Natura loquax.* Ed. Wolfgang Harms and Heimo Reinitzer. Mikrokosmos 7. Frankfurt am Main, 1981. 109–82.
Ghisalberti, Fausto. "Arnolfo d'Orleans: Un cultore di Ovidio nel secolo XII." Memorie del Reale Istituto Lombardo 24 (1932), 157–234.
Ginzberg, Louis. *The Legends of the Jews.* 7 vols. Philadelphia, 1906–38.
Ginzburg, Carlo. *The Cheese and the Worms: The Cosmos of a Sixteenth-Century Miller.* Trans. John and Anne Tedeschi. New York, 1982.
Glorieux, Paul. "Les *Deflorationes* de Werner de Saint-Blaise." In *Mélanges Joseph de Ghellinek,* 699–721. Gembloux, 1951.
Gnädinger, Louise. "Rois Peschiere/Anfortas: Der Fischerkönig in Chrestiens und Wolframs Graldichtung." In *Orbis mediaevalis: Mélanges de langue et de littérature médiévale offerts à Reto Raduolf Bezzola,* ed. Georges Güntert, Marc-René Jung, and Kurt Ringger, 127–48. Bern, 1978.
Godzich, Wlad, and Jeffrey Kittay. *The Emergence of Prose: An Essay in Prosaics.* Minneapolis, 1987.
Graf, Arturo. *Miti, leggende e superstizioni del medio evo.* 2 vols. Turin, 1892–93.
Gransden, Antonia. *Historical Writing in England, ca. 550 to ca. 1307.* Ithaca, 1974.
Grape-Albers, Heide. *Spätantike Bilder aus der Welt des Arztes: Medizinische Bilderhandschriften der Spätantike und ihre mittelalterliche Überlieferung.* Wiesbaden, 1977.
Green, Dennis H. *The Art of Recognition in Wolfram's "Parzival."* Cambridge, 1982.
——. "Dichtete Wolfram von Eschenbach am Schreibtisch?" In Green/Johnson, *Approaches to Wolfram,* 265–71.
——. "Homicide and *Parzival.*" In Green/Johnson, *Approaches to Wolfram,* 11–82.
——. "Parzival's Departure—Folktale and Romance." *FMS* 14 (1980), 352–409.
Green, Dennis H., and L. P. Johnson. *Approaches to Wolfram von Eschenbach.* Mikrokosmos 5. Bern, 1978.
Greenfield, John. "The 'Tageliet' in Wolfram's *Parzival.*" *Neophilologus* 71 (1987), 154–57.
Grimm, Reinhold. *Paradisus coelestis, Paradisus terrestris: Zur Auslegungsgeschichte des Paradieses im Abendland bis um 1200.* Medium Aevum 33. Munich, 1977.
Groos, Arthur. "Astronomy and Medicine in Book XVI of Wolfram's *Parzival.*" *Sudhoffs Archiv* 76 (1992), 74–86.

——. "Cundrie's Announcement (*Parzival* 782)." *PBB* 113 (1991), 384–414.
——. "Dialogic Transformations: The Grail Hero Wins a Wife." In Wisbey/Jones, *Chrétien de Troyes and the German Middle Ages,* 257–76.
——. "Parzival's *swertleite.*" *GR* 50 (1975), 245–59.
——. "Perceval and Parzival Discover Knighthood." In *Magister Regis: Studies in Honor of Robert Earl Kaske,* ed. Arthur Groos, 117–37. New York, 1986.
——. "'Sigune auf der Linde' and the Turtledove in *Parzival.*" *JEGP* 67 (1968), 631–46.
——. "Time Reference and the Liturgical Calendar in Wolfram's *Parzival.*" *DVJS* 49 (1975), 43–65.
——. "*trachontê* and *des trachen umbevart* (Parzival 483)." *Trivium* 28 (1993), 23–37.
——. "Treating the Fisher King (*Parzival,* Book IX)." In *German Narrative Literature of the Twelfth and Thirteenth Centuries: Studies Presented to Roy Wisbey on His Sixty-fifth Birthday,* ed. Volker Honemann, Martin H. Jones, Adrian Stevens, and David Wells, 275–304. Tübingen, 1994.
——. "Trevrizent's Retraction: Interpolation or Narrative Strategy?" *DVJS* 55 (1981), 44–63.
——. "Wolfram von Eschenbach's 'Bow Metaphor' and the Narrative Technique of *Parzival.*" *MLN* 87 (1972), 391–408.
——. "Wolfram's Lament for Herzeloyde (*Parzival* 128.23ff.)." *MLN* 89 (1974), 359–66.
——. "Wolframs Schlangenliste (*Parzival* 481) und Pseudo-Apuleius." In *Licht der Natur: Medizin in Fachliteratur und Dichtung. Festschrift für Gundolf Keil zum 60. Geburtstag,* ed. Josef Domes, Werner E. Gerabek, Bernhard D. Haage, Christoph Weisser, and Volker Zimmermann, 129–48. GAG 585. Göppingen, 1994.
Grotefend, Herbert. *Zeitrechnung des deutschen Mittelalters und der Neuzeit.* 3 vols. Hannover, 1891–98.
Gruenter, Rainer. "Der paradisus der *Wiener Genesis.*" *Euphorion* 49 (1955), 121–44.
Grundmann, Herbert. "Dichtete Wolfram von Eschenbach am Schreibtisch?" *AKG* 49 (1967), 391–405.
Haage, Bernhard D. "Medizinhistorische Aspekte der *Parzival* - Interpretation." *Zusammenhänge, Einflüsse, Wirkungen: Kongreßakten zum ersten Symposium des Mediävistenverbandes in Tübingen, 1984,* ed. Jörg O. Fichte et al., 130–44. Berlin and New York, 1986.
——. "Das Ouroboros-Symbol im *Parzival* Wolframs von Eschenbach." *WMM* 1 (1983), 5–22.
——. "Prolegomena zu Anfortas' Leiden im *Parzival.*" *WMM* 3 (1985), 101–26.
——. *Studien zur Heilkunde im "Parzival" Wolframs von Eschenbach.* GAG 565. Göppingen, 1992.
Haas, Alois. *Parzivals "tumpheit" bei Wolfram von Eschenbach.* PSQ 21. Berlin, 1964.
Hagen, Paul. "Untersuchungen über Kyot." *ZfdA* 45 (1901), 187–217.
Hahn, Ingrid. "Parzivals Schönheit: Zum Problem des Erkennens und Verkennens im *Parzival.*" In *Verbum et signum: Beiträge zur mediävistischen Bedeutungsforschung,* 2 vols., ed. Hans Fromm, Wolfgang Harms, and Uwe Ruberg, 2, 203–32. Munich, 1975.

Haidu, Peter. *Aesthetic Distance in Chrétien de Troyes: Irony and Comedy in "Cligès" and "Perceval."* Geneva, 1968.
Hanning, Robert W. *The Individual in Twelfth-Century Romance.* New Haven, 1977.
——. *The Vision of History in Early Britain: From Gildas to Geoffrey of Monmouth.* New York, 1966.
Hänsch, Irene. "*Parzivâl. der nam ist rehte enmitten durch*: Zum Problem von Namen und Identität in Wolframs *Parzival.*" *Euphorion* 76 (1982), 260–74.
Harms, Wolfgang. *Homo viator in bivio: Studien zur Bildlichkeit des Weges.* Medium Aevum 21. Munich, 1970.
——. *Der Kampf mit dem Freund oder Verwandten in der deutschen Literatur bis um 1300.* Medium Aevum 1. Munich, 1963.
Harroff, Stephen C. *Wolfram and His Audience.* GAG 120. Göppingen, 1974.
Hartner, Willy. "al-Djawzahar." *Encyclopaedia of Islam.* 2, 501–02. Leiden, 1965.
——. "The Pseudoplanetary Nodes of the Moon's Orbit in Hindu and Islamic Iconographies." *Ars islamica* 5.2 (1938), 113–54.
Harvey, E. Ruth. *The Inward Wits: Psychological Theory in the Middle Ages and the Renaissance.* London, 1975.
Haseloff, Arthur. *Eine thüringisch-sächsische Malerschule des dreizehnten Jahrhunderts.* Studien zur deutschen Kunstgeschichte 9. Straßburg, 1897.
Hatto, A. T. "'Ine weiz': Diplomatic Ignorance on the Part of Medieval German Poets." *German Studies Presented to L. A. Willoughby,* 98–107. Oxford, 1952.
Haug, Walter. "Hat Wolfram von Eschenbach Chrétiens *Conte du Graal* kongenial ergänzt?" In *Arturus Rex II: Acta conventus Lovaniensis 1987,* ed. Willy Van Hoecke, Gilbert Tournoy, and Werner Verbeke, 236–58. Louvain, 1991.
——. *Literaturtheorie im deutschen Mittelalter: Von den Anfängen bis zum Ende des 13. Jahrhunderts.* Darmstadt, 1985.
——. "*Parzival* ohne Illusionen." *DVJS* 64 (1990), 199–217.
——. *Strukturen als Schlüssel zur Welt: Kleinere Schriften zur Erzählliteratur des Mittelalters.* Tübingen, 1989.
——. "Die Symbolstruktur des höfischen Epos und ihre Auflösung bei Wolfram von Eschenbach." *DVJS* 45 (1971), 668–705. Rpt. in *Strukturen,* 483–512.
Haupt, Jürgen. *Der Truchseß Keie im Artusroman: Untersuchungen zur Gesellschaftsstruktur im höfischen Roman.* PSQ 57. Berlin, 1971.
Heinzle, Joachim. "Stein und Banner. Zu Wolframs *Willehalm* 16.10–19." *Textkritik und Interpretation: Festschrift für Karl Konrad Polheim zum 60. Geburtstag,* ed. Heimo Reinitzer, 69–84. Bern, 1987.
——. *Stellenkommentar zu Wolframs "Titurel."* Hermaea: Germanistische Forschungen 30. Tübingen, 1972.
Henkel, Nikolaus. *Studien zum Physiologus im Mittelalter.* Hermaea: Germanistische Forschungen 38. Tübingen, 1976.
Henkin, Leo J. "The Carbuncle in the Adder's Head." *MLN* 58 (1943), 34–39.
Hennig, Ursula. "Die Gurnemanzlehren und die unterlassene Frage Parzivals." *PBB* (Tübingen) 97 (1975), 312–32.
Henzen, Walter. "Das IX. Buch des *Parzival*: Überlegungen zum Aufbau." In *Erbe der Vergangenheit: Festgabe für Karl Helm,* 189–217. Tübingen, 1951. Rpt. in Rupp, *Wolfram von Eschenbach,* 125–57.
——. "Zur Vorprägung der Demut im *Parzival* durch Chrestien." *PBB* (Tübingen) 80 (1958), 422–43.

Hilgers, Heribert A. "Versuch über deutsche Cisiojani." *Poesie und Gebrauchsliteratur im deutschen Mittelalter*, ed. Volker Honemann et al., 127–63. Tübingen, 1979.

Hirschberg, Dagmar. *Untersuchungen zur Erzählstruktur von Wolframs "Parzival."* GAG 139. Göppingen, 1976.

Hoffmann, Harmut. *Gottesfriede und Treuga Dei.* Schriften der Monumenta Germaniae Historica 20. Stuttgart, 1964.

Hoggan, David G. "Le Péché de Perceval: Pour l'authenticité de l'épisode de l'ermite dans le *Conte du graal* de Chrétien de Troyes." *Romania* 93 (1972), 50–76 and 244–75.

Holste, Thomas. *Der Theriakkrämer. Ein Beitrag zur Frühgeschichte der Arzneimittelwerbung.* WMF 5. Pattensen, 1976.

Holtorf, Arne. "Cisiojanus." *Verfasserlexikon* I (1978), 1285–89.

Huby, Michel. "Wolframs Bearbeitungstechnik in *Parzival* (Buch III)." *Wolfram-Studien* 3 (1975), 40–51.

Huygens, R. B. C., ed. "Mittelalterliche Kommentare zum 'O qui perpetua'." *Sacris Erudiri* 6 (1954), 372–427.

Iwand, Käthe. *Die Schlüsse der mittelhochdeutschen Epen.* Germanische Studien 16. Berlin, 1922.

Jaeger, C. Stephen. *The Origins of Courtliness: Civilizing Trends and the Formation of Courtly Ideals, 939–1210.* Philadelphia, 1985.

Jaritz, Gerhard. "Zur materiellen Kultur des Hofes um 1200." In Kaiser/Müller, *Höfische Literatur*, 19–37.

Jauker, Carl. *Über die chronologische Behandlung des Stoffes in den epischen Gedichten Wolframs von Eschenbach, im "Erec" und "Iwein" Hartmanns von Aue und im "Tristan" Gottfrieds von Straßburg.* Separatabdruck aus dem 4. Jahresberichte der k.k. Staatsoberrealschule in Graz. Graz, 1882.

Javelet, Robert. *Image et resemblance au douzième siècle.* 2 vols. Paris, 1967.

Johnson, Leslie P. "Dramatische Ironie in Wolframs *Parzival.*" In Ganz/Schröder, *Probleme mittelhochdeutscher Erzählformen*, 133–52.

——. "Lähelin and the Grail Horses." *Modern Language Review* 63 (1968), 612–17.

——. "Parzival's Beauty." In Green/Johnson, *Approaches to Wolfram*, 273–91.

——. "Silvester und Anfortas." In *Studien zur frühmittelhochdeutschen Literatur*, ed. L. P. Johnson, H.-H. Steinhoff, and R. A. Wisbey, 344–57. Berlin, 1974.

——. "'ungenuht al eine' (*Parzival* 782.23)." In *Probleme mittelalterlicher Überlieferung und Textkritik*, ed. Peter F. Ganz and Werner Schröder, 49–66. Berlin, 1968.

Johnson, Sidney M. "Herzeloyde and the Grail." *Neophilologus* 52 (1968), 148–56.

——. "Parzival and Gawan: Their Conflict of Duties." *Wolfram-Studien* 1 (1970), 98–116.

Jones, Martin. "Formen der Liebeserklärung im höfischen Roman bis um 1300." In *Liebe in der deutschen Literatur des Mittelalters*, ed. Jeffrey Ashcroft, Dietrich Huschenbett, William Henry Jackson, 36–49. Tübingen, 1987.

——. "Parzival's Fighting and His Election to the Grail." *Wolfram-Studien* 3 (1975), 52–71.

Jones, Martin, and Roy Wisbey, eds. *Chrétien de Troyes and the German Middle Ages.* Cambridge, 1993.
Kaiser, Gert, and Jan-Dirk Müller, eds. *Höfische Literatur, Hofgesellschaft, höfische Lebensformen um 1200.* Studia humaniora 6. Düsseldorf, 1986.
Kampers, Franz. *Mittelalterliche Sagen vom Paradiese und vom Holze des Kreuzes Christi.* Köln, 1897.
Kantorowicz, Ernst. *Kaiser Friedrich II.* 2 vols. 1931–36, rpt. Düsseldorf and Munich, 1963.
——. *The King's Two Bodies: A Study in Medieval Political Theology.* Princeton, 1957.
Kartschoke, Dieter. *Wolfram von Eschenbach, "Willehalm."* Berlin, 1968.
Keil, Gundolf. "Circa instans." *Verfasserlexikon* I (1978), 1282–85.
Kellermann, Wilhelm. *Aufbaustil und Weltbild Chrestiens von Troyes im Percevalroman.* Zeitschrift für romanische Philologie, Beiheft 88. Halle, 1936.
Kern, Peter. *Die Artusromane des Pleier: Untersuchungen über den Zusammenhang von Dichtung und literarischer Situation.* PSQ 100. Berlin, 1981.
Kibelka, Johannes. "Sternglaube und Willensfreiheit in der deutschen Dichtung des Hochmittelalters." *WW* 15 (1965), 85–98.
Kieckhefer, Richard. *Magic in the Middle Ages.* Cambridge, 1989.
Kleiber, Wolfgang. "Dialektale Bestandteile in Wolframs Wortschatz. Beiträge zur Erschließung des historischen fränkischen Winzerlexikons." In Gärtner/ Heinzle, *Studien zu Wolfram von Eschenbach,* 51–66.
Klibansky, Raymond, Erwin Panofsky, and Fritz Saxl. *Saturn and Melancholy: Studies in the History of Natural Philosophy, Religion, and Art.* London, 1964.
Köhler, Erich. "Die Rolle des 'Rechtsgebrauchs' (costume) in den Romanen des Chrétien de Troyes." In his *Trobadorlyrik und höfischer Roman,* 205–33. Berlin, 1962.
Köhler, Reinhold. "Die Erde als jungfräuliche Mutter Adams." *Germania* 7 (1862), 476–80. Rpt. in his *Kleinere Schriften,* 1, 7–13. Berlin, 1900.
Köhn, Rolf. "'Militia curialis.' Die Kritik am geistlichen Hofdienst bei Peter von Blois und in der lateinischen Literatur des 9.–12. Jahrhunderts." *Miscellanea Mediaevalia* 12.1 (1979), 227–57.
Kolb, Herbert. "Chanson-de-geste-Stil im *Parzival.*" *Wolfram-Studien* 3 (1975), 189–216.
——. "Isidorische 'Etymologien' im *Parzival.*" *Wolfram-Studien* 1 (1970), 117–35.
——. "*Schola humilitatis:* Ein Beitrag zur Interpretation der Gralerzählung Wolframs von Eschenbach." *PBB* (Tübingen) 78 (1956), 65–115.
Kranz, Walter. *Kosmos.* Archiv für Begriffsgeschichte 2. Bonn, 1955.
Kratz, Henry. *Wolfram von Eschenbach's "Parzival": An Attempt at a Total Interpretation.* Bern, 1973.
Krüger, Sabine. "'Verhöflichter Krieger' und *miles illitteratus.*" In Fleckenstein, *Curialitas,* 326–49.
Kuhn, Hugo. "*Parzival:* Ein Versuch über Mythos, Glaube und Dichtung im Mittelalter." In his *Dichtung und Welt im Mittelalter,* 151–80 and 271–77. Stuttgart, 1959.
Kully, Rolf Max. "Cisiojanus. Studien zur mnemonischen Literatur anhand des spätmittelalterlichen Kalendergedichts." *Schweizerisches Archiv für Volkskunde* 70 (1974), 93–123.

Kunitzsch, Paul. "Die Arabica im *Parzival* Wolframs von Eschenbach." *Wolfram-Studien* 2 (1974), 9–35.
——. *Arabische Sternnamen in Europa*. Wiesbaden, 1959.
——. "Die Planetennamen im *Parzival*." *ZfdS* 25 (1969), 169–74.
Kurdzialek, Marian. "Der Mensch als Abbild des Kosmos." *Miscellanea Mediaevalia* 8 (1971), 35–75.
Lachmann, Karl. *Kleinere Schriften*. 2 vols. Berlin, 1876.
Lausberg, Heinrich. *Handbuch der literarischen Rhetorik*. 2 vols. Munich, 1960.
Lee, Anthony van der. *Zum literarischen Motiv der Vatersuche*. Verhandelingen der Koninklijke Nederlandse Akademie van Wetenschappen, Afd. Letterkunde, NS 63.3. Amsterdam, 1957.
Lehmann, Paul. *Mittelalterliche Bibliothekskataloge Deutschlands und der Schweiz, II: Bistum Mainz, Erfurt*. Munich, 1928.
Lemay, Richard. "Gerard of Cremona." In *Dictionary of Scientific Biography*, XV, 173–192. New York, 1978.
Lessiak, Primus. "Gicht: Ein Beitrag zur Kunde deutscher Krankheitsnamen." *ZfdA* 53 (1914), 101–82.
Lewis, Gertrud Jaron. "Die unheilige Herzeloyde. Ein ikonoklastischer Versuch." *JEGP* 74 (1975), 465–85.
Lindberg, David C. "Alhazen's Theory of Vision and Its Reception in the West." *Isis* 58 (1967), 321–41.
Lofmark, Carl. "Der höfische Dichter als Übersetzer." In Ganz/Schröder, *Probleme mittelhochdeutscher Erzählformen*, 40–62.
——. "Wolfram's Source References in *Parzival*." *MLR* 67 (1972), 820–44.
——. "Zur Interpretation der Kyotstellen im *Parzival*." *Wolfram-Studien* 4 (1977), 33–70.
Lottin, Odon. *Psychologie et morale aux XIIe et XIIIe siècles*. 6 vols. Louvain, 1942–60.
Lubac, Henri de. *Exégèse médiévale: Les quatre sens de l'Ecriture*. 4 vols. Paris, 1959–64.
McCulloch, Florence. *Medieval Latin and French Bestiaries*. Rev. ed. University of North Carolina Studies in Romance Languages and Literatures 33. Chapel Hill, 1962.
McFarland, Timothy. "Clinschor. Wolfram's Adaptation of the *Conte du Graal*: The Schastel Marveile Episode." In Jones/Wisbey, *Chrétien de Troyes and the German Middle Ages*, 277—94. Cambridge, 1993.
Maddox, Donald. *The Arthurian Romances of Chrétien de Troyes: Once and Future Fictions*. Cambridge Studies in Medieval Literature 12. Cambridge, 1991.
Marshall, Linda E. "The Identity of the 'New Man' in the *Anticlaudianus* of Alan of Lille." *Viator* 10 (1979), 77–94.
Martin, Ernst. *Wolframs von Eschenbach "Parzival" und "Titurel." II: Kommentar*. Germanistische Handbibliothek 9.2. 1903. Rpt., Darmstadt, 1976.
Massmann, Ernst Heinrich. *Schwertleite und Ritterschlag*. Ph.D. diss., Hamburg, 1932.
Mausbach, Joseph. *Die Ethik des heiligen Augustinus*. 2 vols. Freiburg im Breisgau, 1909.
Mennung, Albert. *Der "Bel Inconnu" des Renaut de Beaujeu in seinem Verhältnis zum "Lybeaus Disconus," "Carduino" und "Wigalois."* Halle, 1890.

Mergell, Bodo. "Der Gral in Wolframs *Parzival*." *PBB* (Halle) 73 (1951), 1–94; 74 (1952), 77–159.

Mersmann, Walter. *Der Besitzwechsel und seine Bedeutung in den Dichtungen Wolframs von Eschenbach und Gottfrieds von Straßburg.* Medium Aevum 22. Munich, 1971.

Mertens, Volker. "Parzivals doppelte Probe." *ZfdA* 108 (1979), 323–39.

Millás Vallicrosa, José. "La Aportación astronómica de Pedro Alfonso." *Sefarad* 3 (1943), 65–105.

Minnis, A. J. *Medieval Theory of Authorship.* 2d ed. Philadelphia, 1988.

Mockenhaupt, Benedikt. *Die Frömmigkeit im "Parzival" Wolframs von Eschenbach.* 1942. Rpt., Darmstadt, 1968.

Möhler, Rainer. *"Epistula de vulture": Untersuchungen zu einer organotherapeutischen Drogenmonographie des Frühmittelalters.* WMF 45. Pattensen, 1990.

Mohr, Wolfgang. "König Artus und die Tafelrunde: Politische Hintergründe in Chrétiens *Perceval* und Wolframs *Parzival*." In his *Wolfram Aufsätze*, 170–222.

——. "Parzival und die Ritter. Von einfacher Form zum Ritterepos." *Fabula* 1 (1958), 201–13. Rpt. in his *Wolfram Aufsätze*, 1–13.

——. "Parzival und Gawan." *Euphorion* 52 (1958), 1–22. Rpt. in his *Wolfram Aufsätze*, 62–93.

——. "Parzivals ritterliche Schuld." *WW* 2 (1952), 148–60. Rpt. in *Der arthurische Roman*, ed. Kurt Wais, WdF 157, 332–54, Darmstadt, 1970, and in his *Wolfram Aufsätze*, 14–36.

——. "Spiegelungen des Tagelieds." In *Mediaevalia litteraria: Festschrift für Helmut de Boor zum 80. Geburtstag*, ed. Ursula Hennig and Herbert Kolb, 287–304. Munich, 1971.

——. "Die *vrouwe* Walthers von der Vogelweide." *ZfdPh* 86 (1967), 1–10.

——. *Wolfram von Eschenbach: Aufsätze.* GAG 275. Göppingen, 1979.

Morson, Gary Saul. "For the Time Being: Sideshadowing, Criticism, and the Russian Countertradition." In *After Poststructuralism: Interdisciplinarity and Literary Theory*, ed. Nancy Easterlin and Barbara Riebling, 203–33. Evanston, Ill., 1993.

Morson, Gary Saul, and Caryl Emerson. *Mikhail Bakhtin: Creation of a Prosaics.* Stanford, 1990.

Morvay, Karin, and Dagmar Grube. *Bibliographie der deutschen Predigt des Mittelalters: Veröffentlichte Predigten.* MTU 47. Munich, 1974.

Murdoch, Brian. *The Fall of Man in the Early Middle High German Biblical Epic.* GAG 58. Göppingen, 1972.

Nellmann, Eberhard. "Wolfram und Kyot als *vindære wilder mære.* Überlegungen zu *Tristan* 4619–88 und *Parzival* 453.1–17." *ZfdA* 117 (1988), 31–67.

——. *Wolframs Erzähltechnik: Untersuchungen zur Funktion des Erzählers.* Wiesbaden, 1973.

Northcott, Kenneth J. "Seeing and Partly Seeing: Parzival's Encounter with the Grail." In *Spectrum Medii Aevi: Essays in Early German Literature in Honor of George Fenwick Jones*, ed. William C. McDonald, 409–28. GAG 362. Göppingen, 1983.

Ochs, Ingrid. *Wolframs "Willehalm"-Eingang im Lichte der frühmittelhochdeutschen geistlichen Dichtung.* Medium Aevum 14. Munich, 1968.

Ohly, Friedrich. "Ein Admonter Liebesgruß." *ZfdA* 87 (1956/57), 13–23.
——. "Die Suche in Dichtungen des Mittelalters." *ZfdA* 94 (1965), 171–84.
——. "Wolframs Gebet an den heiligen Geist im Eingang des *Willehalm.*" *ZfdA* 91 (1961/62), 1–37. Rpt. in Rupp, *Wolfram von Eschenbach*, 455–518.
Owen, D. D. R. "The Development of the Perceval Story." *Romania* 80 (1959), 473–92.
Panzer, Friedrich. *Vom mittelalterlichen Zitieren.* Sitzungsberichte der Heidelberger Akademie der Wissenschaften. Phil.-hist. Klasse 36.2. Heidelberg, 1950.
Patterson, Lee. *Negotiating the Past: The Historical Understanding of Medieval Literature.* Madison, 1987.
Patze, Hans. "Die Bildung der landesherrlichen Residenzen im Reich während des 14. Jahrhunderts." In *Stadt und Stadtherr im 14. Jahrhundert: Entwicklungen und Funktionen*, ed. Wilhelm Rausch. Beiträge zur Geschichte der Städte Mitteleuropas 2, 1–54. Linz, 1972.
——. *Die Entstehung der Landesherrschaft in Thüringen.* Mitteldeutsche Forschungen 22. Cologne, 1962.
Patze, Hans, and Walter Schlesinger. *Geschichte Thüringens II.1: Hohes und spätes Mittelalter.* Cologne, 1974.
Perlina, Nina. "Funny Things Are Happening on the Way to the Bakhtin Forum." Kennan Institute Paper 231. Washington, D.C., 1989.
Peschel-Rentsch, Dietmar. "Wolframs Autor: Beobachtungen zur Entstehung der Autor-Figur an drei beispielhaften Szenen aus Wolframs *Parzival.*" *DVJS* 64 (1990), 26–44.
Peters, Ursula. *Fürstenhof und höfische Dichtung: Der Hof Hermanns von Thüringen als literarisches Zentrum.* Konstanz, 1981.
Pickens, Rupert T. *The Welsh Knight: Paradoxicality in Chrétien's "Conte del Graal."* French Forum Monographs 6. Lexington, Ky., 1977.
Pietsch, Paul. *Evangely und Epistel Teutsch: Die gedruckten hochdeutschen Perikopenbücher, 1473–1523.* Göttingen, 1927.
Pietzner, Fritz. *Schwertleite und Ritterschlag.* Ph.D. diss., Heidelberg, 1934.
Poag, James F. "Heinrich von Veldeke's *minne*; Wolfram von Eschenbach's *liebe* and *triuwe.*" *JEGP* 61 (1962), 721–35.
——. "*Diu verholnen mære umben grâl.*" *Wolfram-Studien* 2 (1974), 72–83.
——. "*Wîp* and *Grâl*: Structure and Meaning in Wolfram's *Parzival.*" *JEGP* 67 (1968), 204–11.
Ragotzky, Hedda. *Studien zur Wolfram-Rezeption. Die Entstehung und Verwandlung der Wolfram-Rolle in der deutschen Literatur des dreizehnten Jahrhunderts.* Studien zur Poetik und Geschichte der Literatur 20. Stuttgart, 1971.
Ranke, Ernst. *Das kirchliche Perikopensystem aus den älteren Urkunden der römischen Liturgie dargelegt.* Berlin, 1847.
Reinitzer, Heimo. "Zeder und Aloe." *AKG* 58 (1976), 2–34.
Riddle, John. "Lithotherapy in the Middle Ages." *Pharmacy in History* 12 (1970), 39–50. Rpt. in his *Quid pro Quo.*
——. "Pomum ambrae: Amber and Ambergris in Plague Remedies." *Sudhoffs Archiv* 48 (1964), 111–22. Rpt. in his *Quid pro Quo.*
——. *Quid pro Quo: Studies in the History of Drugs.* Brookfield, Vt., 1992.
Rist, John M. "Augustine on Free Will and Predestination." *Journal of Theological Studies* 20 (1969), 420–27. Rpt. in *Augustine: A Collection of Critical Essays*, ed. R. A. Markus, 218–252. Garden City, N.Y., 1972.

Robbins, Frank Egleston. *The Hexaemeral Literature: A Study of the Greek and Latin Commentaries on Genesis.* Ph.D. diss., Chicago, 1912.

Rohland, Ingrid. *Das "Buch von alten Schäden." Teil II: Kommentar und Wörterverzeichnis.* WMF 23. Pattensen, 1982.

Rose, Valentin. "Aristoteles *De lapidibus* und Arnoldus Saxo." *ZfdA* 18 (1875), 321–455.

Rosskopf, Rudolf. *Der Traum Herzeloydes und der Rote Ritter.* GAG 89. Göppingen, 1972.

Ruberg, Uwe. *Beredtes Schweigen in lehrhafter und erzählender deutscher Literatur des Mittelalters.* MMS 32. Munich, 1978.

Ruh, Kurt. *Höfische Epik des deutschen Mittelalters I: Von den Anfängen bis zu Hartmann von Aue.* Grundlagen der Germanistik 7. Berlin, 1967.

——. *Höfische Epik des deutschen Mittelalters II.* Grundlagen der Germanistik 25. Berlin, 1980.

——. "Wolfram von Eschenbach heute." *Wolfram-Studien* 3 (1975), 9–19.

Ruh, Kurt, et al., eds. *Die deutsche Literatur des Mittelalters: Verfasserlexikon.* 2d ed. Berlin, 1978–.

Ruhe, Ernstpeter. *De amasio ad amasiam: Zur Gattungsgeschichte des mittelalterlichen Liebesbriefes.* Beiträge zur romanischen Philologie des Mittelalters 10. Munich, 1975.

Rührmund, F. W. "Chronologische Bestimmung der Begebenheiten in Wolframs *Parzival.*" *ZfdA* 6 (1848), 465–78.

Rupp, Heinz. "Die Funktion des Wortes *tump* im *Parzival* Wolframs von Eschenbach." *GRM* 38 (1957), 97–106.

——, ed. *Wolfram von Eschenbach.* WdF 57. Darmstadt, 1966.

Rutledge, Amelia A. "Perceval's Sin: Critical Perspectives." *Œuvres et Critiques* 5 (1980/81), 53–60.

Salzer, Anselm. *Die Bilder und Beiworte Mariens in der deutschen Literatur und lateinischen Hymnenpoesie des Mittelalters.* 1886–94. Rpt., Darmstadt, 1967.

San-Marte [Albert Schulz]. *Parcival. Rittergedicht von Wolfram von Eschenbach.* 2d. ed. Leipzig, 1858.

——. "Über die Eigennamen im *Parzival* des Wolfram von Eschenbach." *Germania* 2 (1857), 385–409.

Sargent-Baur, Barbara Nelson. "Promotion to Knighthood in the Romances of Chrétien de Troyes." *RPh* 37 (1983/84), 393–408.

Sattler, Anton. *Die religiösen Anschauungen Wolframs von Eschenbach.* Graz, 1895.

Sauer, Margret. *Parzival auf der Suche nach der verlorenen Zeit.* GAG 323. Göppingen, 1981.

Sayce, Olive. "Prolog, Epilog und das Problem des Erzählers." In Ganz/Schröder, *Probleme mittelhochdeutscher Erzählformen*, 63–72.

Schelkle, Karl Hermann. *Paulus: Lehrer der Väter: Die altkirchliche Auslegung von Römer 1–11.* Düsseldorf, 1956.

Schenkheld, Elisabeth. *Die Religionsgespräche der deutschen erzählenden Dichtung bis zum Ausgang des 13. Jahrhunderts.* Ph.D. diss., Marburg, 1930.

Schieb, Gabriele. *Henric van Veldeken (Heinrich von Veldeke).* SM 42. Stuttgart, 1965.

Schirok, Bernd. "'ich louc durch ableitens list': Zu Trevrizents Widerruf und den neutralen Engeln," *ZfdPh* 106 (1987), 46–72.

——. *Parzivalrezeption im Mittelalter.* Erträge der Forschung 174. Darmstadt, 1982.

——. "*Die senewe ist ein bîspel:* Zu Wolframs Bogengleichnis." *ZfdA* 115 (1986), 21–36.

——. "Trevrizent und Parzival: Beobachtungen zur Dialogführung und zur Frage der figurativen Komposition." *ABäG* 10 (1976), 43–71.

Schmid, Elisabeth. *Familiengeschichten und Heilsmythologie: Verwandtschaftsstrukturen in den französischen und deutschen Gralromanen des 12. und 13. Jahrhunderts.* Zeitschrift für romanische Philologie, Beiheft 211. Tübingen, 1986.

Schmidt-Wiegand, Ruth. *Studien zur historischen Rechtswortgeographie. Der Strohwisch als Bann- und Verbotszeichen: Bezeichnungen und Funktionen.* MMS 18. Munich, 1978.

Schnell, Rüdiger. "Literarische Beziehungen zwischen Hartmanns *Erec* und Wolframs *Parzival.*" *PBB* (Tübingen) 95 (1973), 301–32.

Schofield, William Henry. *Studies on the "Libeaus Desconus."* Harvard Studies and Notes in Philology and Literature 4. Boston, 1895.

Schreiner, Klaus. "'Hof' (*curia*) und 'höfische Lebensführung' (*vita curialis*) als Herausforderung an die christliche Theologie und Frömmigkeit." In Kaiser/Müller, *Höfische Literatur,* 67–138.

Schröder, Eduard. "Parzival und Gregorius." *ZfdA* 53 (1912), 398–400.

Schröder, Walter Johannes. *Die Soltane-Erzählung in Wolframs "Parzival."* Heidelberg, 1963.

Schröder, Werner. *Die Namen im "Parzival" und im "Titurel" Wolframs von Eschenbach.* Berlin, 1982.

——. "Parzivals Schwerter." *ZfdA* 100 (1971), 111–32.

——. "Zur Chronologie der drei großen mittelhochdeutschen Epiker." *DVJS* 31 (1957), 264–302.

Schubert, Paul. "Die Reichshofämter und ihre Inhaber bis um die Wende des 12. Jahrhunderts." *Mitteilungen des Instituts für Österreichische Geschichtsforschung* 34 (1913), 427–501.

Schultz, Alwin. *Das höfische Leben zur Zeit der Minnesinger.* 2 vols. 1889. Rpt., Osnabrück, 1965.

Schumacher, Marlis. *Die Auffassung der Ehe in den Dichtungen Wolframs von Eschenbach.* Heidelberg, 1967.

Schweikle, Günther. "*stiure* und *lêre.* Zum *Parzival* Wolframs von Eschenbach." *ZfdA* 106 (1977), 183–99.

Schwietering, Julius. "Natur und *art.*" *ZfdA* 91 (1961/62), 108–37.

Segre, Cesare. "What Bakhtin Left Unsaid." In Brownlee/Brownlee, *Romance,* 23–46.

Seiffert, Leslie. "The Terms of Kindred, or Kindred on Good and Bad Terms: Parzival's Vulgar Slaying of His Father's *neve* Ither." *Forum for Modern Language Studies* 26 (1990), 160–84.

Shepard, Odell. *The Lore of the Unicorn.* London, 1930.

Silverstein, Theodore. "The Fabulous Cosmogony of Bernardus Silvestris." *MP* 46 (1948/49), 92–116.

Singer, Samuel. *Wolframs "Willehalm."* Bern, 1918.

Smits, Kathryn. "Einige Beobachtungen zu gemeinsamen Motiven in Hartmanns *Erec* und Wolframs *Parzival.*" In *Festschrift for E. W. Herd,* ed. August

Obermayer. Otago German Studies 1, 251–62. Dunedin, New Zealand, 1980.
Southern, R. W. *The Making of the Middle Ages.* New Haven, 1953.
Spiegel, Gabrielle. "Genealogy: Form and Function in Medieval Historical Narrative." *History and Theory* 22 (1983), 43–53.
Stadter, Ernst. "Die Seele als *minor mundus* und als *regnum.*" *Miscellanea Mediaevalia* 5 (1968), 56–72.
Stahlman, William D., and Owen Gingerich. *Solar and Planetary Longitudes for Years −2500 to +2000 by Ten-Day Intervals.* Madison, Wisc., 1963.
Stallybrass, Peter, and Allon White. *The Politics and Poetics of Transgression.* Ithaca, 1986.
Steiner, George. *After Babel: Aspects of Language and Translation.* Oxford, 1975.
Steinhoff, Hans-Hugo. *Die Darstellung gleichzeitiger Geschehnisse im mittelhochdeutschen Epos.* Medium Aevum 4. Munich, 1964.
Steppich, Christoph. "'Hinweise geben wird euch schaden': Zu Wolframs *Parzival* 483.24–30." *ZfdA* 119 (1990), 259–89.
Stevens, Adrian. "Heteroglossia and Clerical Narrative: On Wolfram's Adaptation of Chrétien." In Jones/Wisbey, *Chrétien de Troyes,* 241–55.
Stock, Brian. *Myth and Science in the Twelfth Century: A Study of Bernard Silvester.* Princeton, 1972.
Suard, François. "Place et signification de l'épisode Blanchefleur dans le *Conte du graal* de Chrétien de Troyes." In *Mélanges de langue et de littérature médiévale offerts à Pierre Le Gentil,* 803–10. Paris, 1973.
Sudhoff, Karl. "Toledo!" *Sudhoffs Archiv* 23 (1930), 1–6.
Tax, Petrus. "*Felix culpa* und *lapsit exillis*: Wolframs *Parzival* und die Liturgie." *MLN* 80 (1965), 454–69.
——. "Gahmuret zwischen Äneas und Parzival: Zur Struktur der Vorgeschichte von Wolframs *Parzival.*" *ZfdPh* 92 (1973), 24–37.
——. "The Grail Kingdom and Parzival's First Visit: Intrigue, Minne, Despair." In *Medieval and Renaissance Studies. Proceedings of the Southeastern Institute of Medieval and Renaissance Studies* 7, ed. Siegfried Wenzel, 20–37. Chapel Hill, 1978.
——. "Trevrizent: Die Verhüllungstechnik des Erzählers." In *Studien zur deutschen Literatur und Sprache des Mittelalters: Festschrift für Hugo Moser zum 65. Geburtstag,* ed. Werner Besch et al., 119–34. Berlin, 1974.
Thorndike, Lynn. "John of Seville." *Speculum* 34 (1959), 20–38.
Treis, Karl. *Die Formalitäten des Ritterschlags in der altfranzösischen Epik.* Ph.D. diss., Berlin, 1887.
Uhlig, Claus. *Hofkritik im England des Mittelalters und der Renaissance: Studien zu einem Gemeinplatz der europäischen Moralistik.* QF, n.s. 56. Berlin, 1973.
Van Cleve, Thomas Curtis. *The Emperor Frederick II of Hohenstaufen.* Oxford, 1972.
Vorderstemann, Jürgen. *Die Fremdwörter im "Willehalm" Wolframs von Eschenbach.* GAG 127. Göppingen, 1974.
Wapnewski, Peter. *Wolframs "Parzival": Studien zur Religiosität und Form.* Heidelberg, 1955.
Watson, Gilbert. *Theriac and Mithridatium: A Study in Therapeutics.* London, 1966.
Weber, Gerd Wolfgang. "Irreligiosität und Heldenzeitalter: Zum Mythen-

charakter der altisländischen Literatur." *Speculum norroenum: Norse Studies in Memory of Gabriel Turville-Petre,* ed. Ursula Dronke, 474–505. Odense, 1981.

Weber, Gottfried. *"Parzival": Ringen und Vollendung. Eine dichtungs- und religionsgeschichtliche Untersuchung.* Oberursel, 1948.

Wehrli, Max. *Formen mittelalterlicher Erzählung.* Zürich and Freiburg im Breisgau, 1969.

——. "*diu menscheit hât wilden art.*" In *Verbum et signum: Beiträge zur mediävistischen Bedeutungsforschung,* ed. Hans Fromm, Wolfgang Harms, and Uwe Ruberg. 2 vols., 2, 189–201. Munich, 1975.

Weigand, Hermann J. "Die epischen Zeitverhältnisse in den Graldichtungen Chrestiens und Wolframs." *PMLA* 53 (1938), 917–50. Rpt. in English as "Narrative Time in the Grail Poems of Chrétien de Troyes and Wolfram von Eschenbach," in his *Wolfram's "Parzival,"* 18–74.

——. "A Jester at the Grail Castle in Wolfram's *Parzival*?" *PMLA* 67 (1952), 485–510. Rpt. in his *Wolfram's Parzival,* 75–119.

——. *Wolfram's "Parzival": Five Essays with an Introduction.* Ed. Ursula Hoffmann. Ithaca and London, 1969.

Weinhold, Karl. *Über die deutsche Jahrtheilung.* Rede zur Feier des Geburtstages Sr. Majestät des Königs Frederik's VII. Kiel, 1862.

Wellmann, Max. *Der Physiologus: Eine religionsgeschichtlich-naturwissenschaftliche Untersuchung. Philologus* Supplementband 22.1. Leipzig, 1930.

Wesle, Carl. "Zu Wolframs *Parzival.*" *PBB* 72 (1950), 1–38.

West, G. D. *An Index of Proper Names in French Arthurian Verse Romances, 1150–1300.* Toronto, 1969.

Wetherbee, Winthrop. *Platonism and Poetry in the Twelfth Century: The Literary Influence of the School of Chartres.* Princeton, 1972.

White, Lynn. *Medieval Technology and Social Change.* Oxford, 1964.

Wiessner, Edmund, and Harald Burger. "Die höfische Blütezeit." In *Deutsche Wortgeschichte,* ed. Friedrich Maurer and Heinz Rupp. 3d ed., 187–253. Berlin, 1974.

van Wijk, Walter Emil. *Le Nombre d'or: Etude de chronologie technique suivie du texte de la "Massa Compoti" d'Alexandre de Villedieu.* The Hague, 1936.

Wilks, Michael. "Alan of Lille and the New Man." In *Renaissance and Renewal in Christian History,* ed. Derek Baker. Studies in Church History 14, 137–57. Oxford, 1977.

Wisbey, Roy. "Marvels of the East in the *Wiener Genesis* and in Wolfram's *Parzival.*" In *Essays in German and Dutch Literature,* ed. W. D. Robson-Scott. Publications of the Institute of Germanic Studies 15, 1–41. London, 1973.

Wisbey, Roy, and Martin Jones, eds. *Chrétien de Troyes and the German Middle Ages.* London, 1993.

Wolf, Alois. "Literarhistorische Aspekte von Parzivals Schweigen." In *Zeiten und Formen in Sprache und Dichtung. Festschrift für Fritz Tschirch,* ed. Karl-Heinz Schirmer and Bernhard Sowinski, 74–95. Cologne, 1972.

——. "*Ein mære wil ich niuwen, daz saget von grôzen triuwen*: Vom höfischen Roman Chrétiens zum Meditationsgeflecht der Dichtung Wolframs." *Literaturwissenschaftliches Jahrbuch der Görres-Gesellschaft* 26 (1985), 9–73.

Wolff, Ludwig. "Die höfisch-ritterliche Welt und der Gral in Wolframs *Parzival.*"

PBB (Tübingen) 77 (1955), 254–78. Rpt. in his *Kleinere Schriften zur altdeutschen Philologie*, ed. Werner Schröder, 195–216. Berlin, 1967.

Wynn, Marianne. "Parzival and Gawan—Hero and Counterpart." *PBB* (Tübingen) 84 (1962), 142–72. Rpt. in her *Wolfram's "Parzival,"* 160–95.

——. "Scenery and Chivalrous Journeys in Wolfram's *Parzival*." *Speculum* 36 (1961), 393–423. Rpt. in her *Wolfram's "Parzival,"* 84–133.

——. *Wolfram's "Parzival": On the Genesis of Its Poetry*. Mikrokosmus 9. Frankfurt am Main, 1984.

Wyss, Ulrich. "Parzivals Sohn: Zur strukturalen Lektüre des Lohengrin-Mythos." *Wolfram-Studien* 5 (1979), 96–115.

Zarncke, Friedrich. *Der Priester Johannes*. Abhandlungen der Königlichen Sächsischen Gesellschaft der Wissenschaften 7.8 (1879), 827–1030; and 8.1 (1883), 1–186.

Zinner, Ernst. *Verzeichnis der astronomischen Handschriften des deutschen Kulturgebiets*. Munich, 1925.

Ziolkowski, Theodore. "Der Karfunkelstein." *Euphorion* 55 (1961), 297–326.

Zutt, Herta. "Parzivals Kämpfe." In *Festgabe für Friedrich Maurer*, ed. Werner Besch, Siegfried Grosse, and Heinz Rupp, 178–98. Düsseldorf, 1968.

Index